PIERCING THE FUTURE

PROPHECY AND THE NEW MILLENNIUM

TERRY JAMES   TIM LAHAYE   JACK VAN IMPE
JOHN WALVOORD   ZOLA LEVITT   ARNO FROESE
CHUCK MISSLER   DAVE BREESE   PHIL ARMS
ED HINDSON   THOMAS ICE   DAVE BENOIT
ANGLE PETERS   LARRY SPARGIMINO
DAVID A. LEWIS   TOM CLOUD   MICHAEL HILE
DAYMOND R. DUCK   PHILLIP GOODMAN

Piercing the Future: Prophecy and the New Millennium
Terry James

Print Edition
Copyright © 2018 by Terry James (as revised)

CKN Christian Publishing
An Imprint of Wolfpack Publishing
6032 Wheat Penny Avenue
Las Vegas, NV 89122

christiankindlenews.com

All rights reserved. No part of this book may be reproduced by any means without the prior written consent of the publisher, other than brief quotes for reviews.

Characters, places and incidents are used fictitiously, and any resemblance to actual persons, living or dead, business establishments, events, or locales is entirely coincidental.

Paperback ISBN 978-1-64119-403-7
eBook ISBN 978-1-64119-402-0

CONTENTS

Author Note v
Acknowledgments vii
Introduction xiii

Part I
FORETELLING THE FATE OF THE NATIONS
1. The Peace Predicament 3
2. Eurosphere - Reshaping the World 25
3. Part 1: Russian Roulette 66
4. Part 2: Russia and Friends 74
5. Asia's Armageddon Army 84
6. What About America? 141
7. Judgment at Jerusalem 177

Part II
GAZING INTO YOUR FUTURE
8. Your Future and Your Money 197
9. Your Future and Technology 220
10. Your Future Living Conditions 241
11. Your Future and Religion 286
12. Why I Believe the Bible Teaches Rapture Before Tribulation 306
13. Prophecy - Fulfillment, Not Fear 325

Part III
PROBING YOUR PLANET'S PROPHETIC FUTURE
14. Believers Bow Before the Bema 337
15. Babylon — Rebuilding a Debacle 373
16. Forewarning the Future Fuhrer 390
17. Forecasting Earth's Furious Finish 419
18. Peering Into the Millennium 460
19. World Without End 492

Conclusion	509
Endnotes	526
A Look At: Are You Rapture Ready?	535
About Terry James	537

Scripture verses in the introduction, conclusion and chapters 1, 2, 3, 4, 5, 6, 8, 13, 14, 15, 16, 18 or that are marked by KJV are from the King James Version of the Bible.

Scripture verses in chapter 17 are from the New King James Version (NKJV) of the Bible. Copyright © 1979, 1980, 1982 by Thomas Nelson, Inc.

Scripture verses in chapters 7, 11 are from the New American Standard Version (NASB) of the Bible. Copyright © 1960, 1962, 1962, 1968, 1971, 1972, 1973, 1975, 1977 by The Lockman Foundation.

Scripture verses in chapters 9, 10, 12 are from the New International Version (NIV) of the Bible. Copyright © 1973, 1978, 1984 by the International Bible Society.

ACKNOWLEDGMENTS

Piercing the Future: Prophecy in the New Millennium is a book that is truly a labor of love. Every aspect, every facet of this volume was written, assembled, edited and published through much intensive work analyzing the issues and events of our time, always striving to maintain absolute integrity with regard to the handling of God's Word. Most of all, we give honor and glory to our Lord Jesus Christ and His love in allowing God's children a preview of things to come (Isaiah 45:11).

To each of my wonderful friends who have so generously given a part of their time to produce the cutting-edge essay/chapters, my deepest gratitude. It does not escape my notice that all of the authors have given sacrificially the part of their dynamic energies that might otherwise be applied to accomplishing work on their own tremendously important projects.

To my dear family-close friend and associate Angie Peters, whose many attributes and contributions mean more to me than I am capable of expressing, my deepest love and thanks. To her husband, Kurt, and children, Nick and Lindsey, my love and my thanks for allowing me into their lives in a sometimes work-intrusive way. To our very special girl and newest member of the Peters family, Erin Leah, my most particular love on behalf of the James family and both sets of grandparents.

My greatest love to Margaret, Nathan and Terry for all they mean to me.

These late months of 1999 have brought both sadness and joy. Sadness because two of my longest and dearest friends, Mrs. Thelma Sutton and John Leslie, will no longer be there to call upon for prayers and support. Joy because I know where they are, that they are alive and ecstatically happy beyond our ability to understand this side of heaven, and because I know I will see them and be with them again. This volume is dedicated to their memory and to my reunion with them in mind.

Thanks especially to my mother, Kathleen James-Basse and to her husband, S. E., "Sonny," for their love and much helpfulness in so many ways.

To those who read *Piercing the Future,* thank you for pausing to consider these deep matters of eternal consequence. Contemplate carefully their individual and collective significance. "The testimony of Jesus is the spirit of prophecy" (Revelation 19:10).

PIERCING THE FUTURE

INTRODUCTION

BY WILLIAM T. JAMES

Futuremania

People of planet earth have looked nervously toward the millennium's dawning horizon. More than mere curiosity fuels the increasing fascination with what the year 2000 and beyond might bring.

Psychologists, psychiatrists, and sociologists insist that this has been the norm for every turn-of-the-millennium generation. Never before, however, have earth dwellers been assisted in generating hysteria and paranoia about the future by media that seem totally driven by profit motives. The results of powerful interactions between this generation and the propaganda machines which stir and whip the millennium maelstrom is truly phenomenal and unique to our time.

Nostradamas, Edgar Casey, Jeane Dixon, L. Ron Hubbard, and other seers have become icons of soothsaying as mankind desires to pierce the future. Many programs aired by *The Learning Channel, Discovery, Arts & Entertainment* and others continue to put forward the so-called prophecies of these ancient and modern oracles.

Television viewers and moviegoers are force-fed quasi- prophetic gobbledygook by false prophets whose accuracy rates are at best dismal. At the same time, very little attention and air time are given to the true prophets of the Bible, whose accuracy rates are in every case 100 percent. Those prophets who did not meet that criterion of 100 percent accuracy were stoned to death as false prophets.

Media of both the news and entertainment varieties continue to whip up futuristic frenzy in their grab for larger shares of nightly viewers. Programs and movies with the words "Armageddon" and "Apocalypse" used prominently in their titles are coming at this generation from every angle. Most all of those angles are erroneous. Nonetheless, even the secular world obviously senses something unusual is in the air — and for that matter, in the earth and in space — at the close of one millennium and the beginning of another.

Piquing our interest is a deluge of reports of UFO sightings and abductions, along with fearful reports of ozone-layer depletions and tremendous storms spawned by El Nino and La Nina, accounts of terrible earthquakes and troubled speculations about future earthquakes and great volcanic explosions. While global warming is said to be enveloping planet earth, comets, meteors and asteroids are said to be threats that could strike at any time.

Euphoric Optimism

Great optimistic predictions that project man will make life on earth a utopian paradise through brilliant innovations and technological breakthroughs is the other side of the futuremania coin. Humanism long ago replaced God in man's plan to create heaven on earth within the evolutionists' paradigm. The many global movements point to the day in these optimists' futuristic thinking when mankind's collective effort will solve all problems and produce prosperity for all of earth's inhabitants.

God's Word, however, holds the only truth about the future. Each of the authors who has contributed to this book explores that truth in a broad, general sense as well as in a defined, specific sense.

Israel and the nations in prophecy are aligning precisely as foretold in God's Holy Word. Geophysical and astrophysical signs predicted for the Apocalypse are already coming into view. Ecumenism and heresy point to the coming apostasy. The Apostle Paul's "perilous times" seem to be already upon us. Many signals validate the fact that prophecies given by God through the prophets of the Old and New Testaments are the only prophecies that can be trusted.

God alone sees down the corridors of time and into eternity. We who have participated in presenting this volume hope that it will leave the reader with the confidence that he or she will better understand God's plan for his or her life. Also, we hope in some way to help convince the reader that Jesus Christ alone holds in His omnipotent, omniscient hands the ultimate destiny of all things created.

Signals of Things to Come

God is as active in the affairs of men today as He has always been. He is not an existential deity who once set the world in motion, then moved on to leave this planet spinning alone in the cold, dark void of space. God, in His great love for man whom He created in His own image, has pierced the future with His Word. Believers not only can know the very beginning of their human routes, but their ultimate destiny as well. God has given us many signals to look for to determine where we stand on His prophetic time line.

Our generation is passing through a time literally overflowing with signs of prophetic significance; so many, in fact, that unless we are acutely spiritually attuned to what is happening all around us, we are in danger of becoming desensitized to the portentous issues and events flooding our daily lives.

Nations of Prophecy

Amazing issues and events of prophetic importance continue to stir the Middle East boiling pot. Turbulence surrounding Israel already makes that nation a "burdensome stone" and a "cup of trembling" as prophesied in Zechariah 12. Geopolitical heat increases hourly, turned up by the global powers that be in order to force Israeli Prime Minister Ehud Barak and others of that nation's leadership to give in to Palestinian Liberation Authority (PLA) demands that Israel give up land so that the so-called peace process can move forward.

God's prophetic Word deals with Israel and with Jerusalem as with no other nation or city on earth. Thus, the accuracy of Biblical prophecy can be denied only by those who foolishly will not accept truth. Their understanding is darkened because they refuse to acknowledge that God alone can provide truth about what will happen in the future.

God's prophetic Word foretold that Israel's people would be scattered into the world and would be persecuted by the world, but then miraculously regathered and reborn as a nation in a single day. These things, of course, have all happened within relatively recent history. Even more astounding things are occurring at present.

The ire of practically the whole world, including that of the current U.S. presidential administration, seems turned upon the tiny state of Israel. Hostile Islamic forces threaten on three sides while Israel is being bullied toward the prophesied pseudo-peace covenant of Daniel 9:27.

At the same time, the nation prospers, much to the chagrin of her enemies and former friends. Just as God foretold, Israel, through industrious application of genius, continues to lead the world in many innovations involving science, technology, medicine, etc. Indeed, the accuracy of God's prophetic Word is in full view for anyone who cares to examine the history of Israel, its present status, and the future course which the geopolitical dynamics of our times are forcing that nation to take. Thankfully, we can know because of the faithfulness of God's prophetic truth that Israel has a glorious destiny as the head of all nations under the reign of the King of kings, Jesus Christ.

Meanwhile, pressure is building, particularly from one

very important prophetic player. We are witnessing at this exciting time in human history the formation of the colossus-state whose absolute dictator will lead all nations of the world into the Middle East for mankind's last war termed "Armageddon." This reviving of the ancient Roman Empire exactly as predicted by Daniel the prophet is yet another astonishing proof that God alone can accurately tell us about things to come.

The European Union

New Europe, with at least a partial implementation of the Maastricht Treaty and the euro, brings the world ever closer to the ten-kings power sphere of Revelation 17:12-13. That antichrist consortium - first seen by Nebuchadnezzar in Daniel 2 as the ten toes of iron and miry clay so identified by Daniel the prophet - looks to be forming at this present hour.

Again, God's perfectly accurate prophecy is dramatically distinguished from the false prophets and their false prophecies through this singular evolving power sphere. This development in our day is stunning-enough proof that we serve the true God of heaven. Considered, however, alongside the developments in Israel and all of the other nations mentioned prophetically, the emergence of the European superstate overwhelmingly verifies that Biblical prophecy is in the process of fulfillment; that is, the stage is quickly being set and the actors moved into their places for fulfillment of the last act of the great drama called human history.

Historians, political thinkers, and strategists have over the years acknowledged that the European drive throughout the ages has been to reunite into roughly the configuration that was the old Roman Empire. Most of these "authorities" have admitted - usually reluctantly - that because of the diversity of languages and cultures so deeply ingrained and because of sovereignties' autonomy and desire for monetary independence, such reunification was impossible.

Napoleon tried reunification. Hitler tried it, and others have at least philosophically thought to try it. God's prophetic Word, on the other hand, predicted in very specific terms that not only was reunification of much of ancient Rome possible, but that it will at the end of the age be the matrix out of which will grow antichrist's one-world government.

Suddenly, in this generation, the feet of the metallic monster which the great King Nebuchadnezzar saw in his dream vision appears ready to begin stamping the residue of the lesser nations the beast-state will eventually tread underfoot. Sadly, even the United States is destined to succumb to this seemingly unstoppable ogre.

Recent events in the Balkans transfixed the attention of true prophecy observers. The fledgling, final-world-empire beast continues to demand its own way under the guise of the international community. Powerful military arms have emerged, provided primarily by the United States. At the same time, a number of heads are developing that seemingly direct its movements - i.e., a New World Order brain-trust stemming from the G-7, whose platform they proclaim is one of peacekeeping.

Like the rider of the white horse in Revelation 6, they come claiming peace and yet through that peace they have destroyed many, as will antichrist, as prophesied in Daniel 11:21-24.

The very fact that the United Nations and NATO (primarily the European Union and the United States) want to end ethnic cleansing is another infallible proof that God alone knows the end from the beginning. Jesus, in the Olivet Discourse, said in answer to His disciples' question, "What shall be the sign of thy coming, and of the end of the age?" that, "Nation shall rise against nation and kingdom against kingdom." The word for "nation" here is the Greek word *ethnos*. Consider how many times in the past year we have heard the word "ethnic" or "ethnic cleansing" in news accounts of Serbian atrocities against the Albanian Kosovars.

This, of course, is not to excuse Slobodan Milosovic's cruel treatment of those people. Rather, it is to point out that the prophetic tide of events is sweeping this generation toward the tragic tribulation hour. By these events, we know that the Apocalypse and Armageddon cannot be far off.

World Wars I and II began in that region of the world that we best know as Yugoslavia. However, it takes no stretch of the imagination at all to understand how easily the conflict currently taking place in that part of Europe can be swiftly transferred to the very heart of the prophesied battlefield for mankind's final war.

The European Union - with the blessings of the current U.S. presidential administration - recently issued the Israeli government an ultimatum with regard to the time line for giving the Palestinians the territory they desire, thus to guarantee Yasser Arafat's Palestinian state.

April 4, 2000, is the date Israel must agree to in the matter of Palestinian statehood.

The Kosovo-Palestinian connection now becomes unmistakably clear. The United Nations, NATO, the European Union and, tragically, the United States of America, have issued a warning to the Israeli leadership. To refuse to give in to international community demands that the Palestinian Authority be given land and statehood might bring New World Order discipline like in the case of the Balkans. Israel might, the New World Order policemen strongly imply, be considered guilty of ethnic genocide, as was Slobodan Milosovic's regime, if that nation does not comply.

Once again, reuniting Europe is almost certainly the reviving Old Roman Empire - i.e., the fourth and last great kingdom prophesied by Daniel the prophet. This is yet one more major piece of mounting evidence that God's prophetic Word is 100 percent accurate in every detail.

This is important because in this change-of-the-millennium era, the believer in God and His Holy Word can cut with great discernment through the fearmongering and the euphoric hyperbole of the futuremania of these crucial times. To know that God alone foretells things yet future with unerring accuracy provides a sound basis for understanding that the Scriptures contain God-given truths by which the Almighty intends for people to conduct their lives.

Mankind's rejection of Jesus Christ, by whom and for whom all things were made, will one day bring judgment that will put an end to the rebellion. We continue with an examination of the nations of prophecy in opposition to the Creator of the universe.

Russia and the Magog Alliances

The "evil empire," it is suggested by media pundits, never really existed in the first place. They proclaim at the same time *ad nauseam* that the Cold War is dead. Russia's influence in the region north of Israel and in regions encircling that small country nonetheless remains profound.

Ezekiel 38 and 39 forecast that a leader called Gog out of the land of Rosh (the ancient name for present-day Russia) will think "an evil thought" and lead Russia and a coalition force called Magog over the mountains of Israel with intentions of taking "great spoil."

Reports coming out of that region, particularly out of Russia herself, indicate that those historically militant people are near the depths of depression, both economically and emotionally.

Boris Yeltsin, then Russia's president, overturned government at the highest levels several times during 1998 and 1999 looking for leadership to bring that nation out of its economic morass. Yeltsin's actions were little more than a shell game in an attempt to offer the Russian people hope that a new leadership might somehow find the magical bean that would blossom into prosperity.

Russia's deep despair opens the way for an "evil thought" in the mind of a leader or leaders who either want to get a stronger grip on control or who believe they can take control of power in Russia by a bold move such as mounting a massive attack to gain riches and warm-water ports, thus to alleviate Russia's desperate economic plight.

The strange coalition that has been formed between Russia and the pan-Islamic entities led for the most part by despots might well become the Magog force actuated by the "evil thought" of Ezekiel 38 and 39. Certainly, Russian generals are hungry for renewed power, and troops under them are hungry for food and power. As has been the case since the fall of the Soviet Union, officers, their troops and their families continue to suffer as much as Russia's general population. Russian Navy, Army and Air Force personnel receive pay only sporadically and always in far lesser amounts than in the glory days when the Soviet war machine was one of the most powerful on earth.

That war machine is still awesome. However, it is less controlled and therefore more dangerous. Nuclear stockpiles are reportedly being cannibalized and sold to terrorists within the region and around the world. The Russian bear is indeed a more formidable beast because it lacks many of the controls and safeguards of the pre-Gorbachev days.

The Russian governmental leaders have tried to appear as responsible global citizens by entering into quasi-memberships in the G-8, NATO, and other geopolitical organizations. But meanwhile, they have formed back-alley alliances with radical Islamic groups which count among their brethren the most dangerous of terrorist organizations on the planet today.

With more than 80 suitcase-type nuclear bombs missing from Russia's arsenal, concern over the possibility of American cities being vaporized by terrorist acts cannot be overstated. Adding to the volatile mix that portends future troubles, Russia continues to assert herself through bullying tactics at every opportunity; for example, Russian troop intervention following the supposed NATO forces' victory in the Balkans during 1999.

God's Word, of course, foretells with 100-percent accuracy and in great detail the future of mankind. The city of Damascus, for example, will apparently be reduced to rubble in one gigantic catastrophe that will leave it uninhabitable. Contemplating Israel's unofficial "Samson option" - that if it looks like the nation will be defeated, Israel will unleash the whole of its nuclear arsenal, thus perishing along with all of its Middle Eastern enemies - the prophecy of Isaiah 17:1, which states that Damascus "shall be a ruinous heap," could take place at any time.

China

The kings of the east force prophesied to march across the dried-up Euphrates River (Revelation 16:12) remains perhaps the most enigmatic part of prophecy scheduled to occur just before Christ's second coming to earth. However, God's Word says in Daniel 12 that a book dealing with end-time matters will be opened near the end of the age, implying that people alive at that time will receive increased understanding about many eschatological matters. Certainly, it appears that ongoing developments in China and the Orient in general are now coming into prophetic focus.

Some scholars believe that the 200-million-strong

army prophesied in Revelation will be comprised of the demonic beings loosed from the bottomless pit. These beings, they believe, will then inflict their horror upon not only the humans doing battle in the Armageddon conflict, but also upon those throughout the world who do not know Christ. However, I believe it is not far-fetched to consider whether these hordes unleashed from the pit might enter in and possess the army of 200 million soldiers who march across the supernaturally dried-up or perhaps technologically dried-up Euphrates River.

In that regard, it is wise to consider the fact that girl babies continue to be aborted by the millions in China as part of China's one-child policy. Millions of other baby girls are murdered immediately following birth because Chinese families want boy children to serve as agricultural and industrial workers once they are old enough to do so. This infanticide portends a time when young men who have no women will most likely eagerly embrace a military existence that promises spoils of war which will include, of course, women from the lands they intend to conquer. The many nefarious maneuverings in which present-day Chinese leadership engages - for instance, getting heavily involved in the American political process through illegal campaign contributions to those whom they wish to extract favors - makes it clear that Chinese communist leadership intends to make that nation the dominant superpower of the world. Chinese hegemony over most of the Asian Orient nations - even intimidating powerful economic countries like Japan and others - make the gargantuan Chinese dragon a candidate for use by that old serpent, the devil, from now through Armageddon.

China's recent saber-rattling, threatening Taiwan and others of her neighbors while America seems to be hedging on security pacts signed with the Taiwanese government, might well be foreshadowing troubling things to come. The Communist Chinese continue to sell and give military-applicable technology stolen from the west to diabolist nations such as North Korea. Experts concede now that China and perhaps even North Korea, Iraq, and others most likely possess ever- increasing ballistic missile delivery capabilities. With Pakistan and India at each other's throats, each trying to outdo the other in the race to produce usable nuclear weaponry, and with China acting as an agitating irritant in the vast Asian region, the world faces a greatly troubled future.

China looks very much to be the king of the kings of the east in the making. Unquestionably, the stage is being set for the fulfillment of prophecy as outlined in the Armageddon scenario. Can it be mere coincidence that this power sphere is developing at the same time Israel is back in the land and is a cup of trembling to the whole world? That Gog is on the Magog trail toward the mountains of Israel? That Europe is about to become the revived Roman Empire?

While we watch our daily headlines and minute-by-minute reports from nations around the world, the voracity of God's Word about planet earth's future becomes more compelling. That God alone can pierce the future and give understanding to His own is validated by history's unfolding in our time.

Today's Knowledge Explosion Prophesied

"...many shall run to and fro, and knowledge shall be increased" (Daniel 12:4). Daniel the prophet again spoke to our generation in terms so relevant that His prophecies for our day cannot be missed by anyone who earnestly seeks discernment. With knowledge said to be doubling every 18 months, and with technology, particularly as concerns military application, more than seven years advanced beyond that which we are told about, wondrous yet frightening things lurk just ahead. Be assured, however, and comforted by the fact that God is not surprised by these elements. Daniel prophesied things that he for the most part did not himself understand. Yet he prophesied them, trusting that God would use the forewarnings to perfect advantage.

Daniel's faith in his Lord was well justified. Here we are in the dawning stages of the 21st century, and these prophecies so nebulous to the prophet are crystal clear at this exciting time in human history.

Some scholars interpret Daniel's words to mean that understanding of prophetic matters is scheduled to burst upon those spiritually attuned to the Scriptures. This interpretation of Daniel's prophecy is no doubt correct. Others believe that Daniel's prophecy on knowledge indicates an explosion of human understanding of the geophysical and astrophysical realms. Undoubtedly, both views of Daniel 12:4 are correct.

We have been looking closely at a number of prophetic matters that have become more and more manifest in just the past few years and decades. As we have said, the stage is being set at a rapid pace for the hour of Apocalypse.

Human knowledge, at the same time, has exploded exponentially and continues to do so at every level of human endeavor. Science cuts at the frontiers of every discipline, bringing us new wonders to consider on an hourly basis. The very fact that we are learning of these advances on an hourly basis is proof God's Word foretold accurately: "knowledge shall be increased." The information age itself gives instantaneous affirmation that God is piercing the future through His written Word for all who will believe.

God obviously wanted His people of the end-time generation to know that a super increase in knowledge will mark their era in order to alert them to the lateness of the hour in which they live. This alert was, however, meant to be more than merely a signal or a signpost of the extremity of the age. God no doubt gave the prophecy to Daniel in order to forewarn of the dangers the expansion in knowledge will bring. We see the Lord's warning more clearly defined in Revelation 13. This ominous prophecy He gave to John, another of His prophets whom, like Daniel, He called "beloved."

Revelation 13, "...and he causeth all, both small and great, rich and poor, free and enslaved, to receive a mark in their right hand, or in their foreheads, And that no man might buy or sell, except he that had the mark, or the name of the beast, or the number of his name. Here is wisdom. Let him that hath understanding count the number of the beast; for it is the number of a man; and his number is six hundred three-score and six" (Revelation 13:16-18).

Computers, which the prophets Daniel and John could not begin to fathom, but which the God of heaven knows all about, are wonderful instruments that sometimes can perform near miracles. Our work in these books would be greatly slowed and hampered without these machines. The rate at which computers are accelerating knowledge at every level is almost incomprehensible. There is nothing intrinsically evil about this brilliant human invention.

The Internet, too, is absolutely stupefying in its applications and future possibilities. Revelation 13:16-18 tells us, however, in very stark prophetic terms, where these products of the human mind will ultimately take us. Like the discovery of nuclear energy, the discovery of computer power will finally bring horrific consequences to mankind. Products of the human mind apart from God's holy, loving discipline always bring horrific consequences.

Antichrist will use technology of every sort to force human beings to worship him and his father, Satan. The computer, in whatever advanced form it will have evolved to by the time antichrist and his dictatorship take power, will inflict pseudo godlike electronic bondage upon its victims.

Today's astounding computer advancements increasingly imbue man with the notion that he is God-like. However, though man has great, God-given genius which he employs to create many wondrous things, he falls far short of godhood: 1) there first must be matter with which to build that God himself created from nothingness; and 2) human endeavor without God to govern brings destruction.

Therefore, man, as he runs to and fro in his frantic

drive to mold and shape - to create - his own future, only mires himself more deeply in Lucifer's seductive, pride-filled quagmire that promises self-salvation through humanistic progress. The promise is utopian perfection; the reality is eternal perdition.

The harder man struggles to build heaven on earth, the deeper in bondage he finds himself. He is, in fact, in the process of producing the technology that antichrist will use to enslave him within the most tyrannical regime imaginable.

The Genesis 11 Babel account tells us that it is mankind's consuming passion to humanistically control the future in a god-like fashion. Nothing more confirms this than the control technologies presently under development.

Technological Groundwork for a Foreboding Future Time

There is great cause for optimism because the Scriptures marvelously tell of a coming time when Jesus Christ will return to put an end to fallen man's madness and create a Garden-of- Eden-like millennial paradise. However, at the same time we must recognize that before Jesus comes back, earth and its inhabitants will suffer greatly for unrepentant rebellion. People will endure a miserable existence under the regime of the world's last and most terrible dictator. Do we see any evidence that antichrist's regime of horror might already be interjecting itself in the world today?

Developments are under way in America, Canada and

Britain that present staggering possibilities in thinking about coming control technologies.

The television program *Discovery* recently examined those developing technologies. The narrator for the program said regarding biometrics: "The characteristics that are unique to us, our fingerprints, our eyes, our voices, even our body odors are going to be used as biological proof of our identity" (*Discovery*, June 8, 1999).

An expert on biometrics interviewed during the program said, "Biometrics is the measurement of the human body or human function. The way I sign my autograph, or my handprint, or my height. They are all biometric indicators. And perhaps my [foremost] biometric is a fingerprint used for criminal evidence."

The narrator then stated, "Fairfax County, Virginia, is one of the first jurisdictions in the country to implement the biometric databases that comply with FBI initiatives for a national criminal database." Another guest said, "The FBI initiative will require all 50 states in the United States to transmit fingerprints electronically. Currently we have file cabinets filled with photographs, file cabinets filled with fingerprint cards. And that will all be digitized so that when we are searching on a person, we can get that instantly."

The narrator reported, "A series of digital photographs is matched against electronic fingerprint records from 12 regional jurisdictions and provides police with 100 percent positive identification in under two minutes."

All of this, of course, is for the good of the society the police establishment is assigned to protect, according to yet another person interviewed on the program. "This is just the tip of the iceberg. We can no longer afford, as law enforcement agencies, to be islands of information. This new technology will allow us to go across borders, across agencies. We will eventually be able to go totally paperless. And this will be something that the officers will actually be able to access from the cruisers."

The narrator of the program questioned with anonymous tone, "Few can argue with biometrical identification of the criminal population. But what happens when one day we are catalogued in biometrical databases?"

Another man said, "The future biometric system is going to know you more intimately than your mother does."

The narrator concluded, "Our body parts become our passwords in the fusion of the machine with the human."

An authority interviewed throughout the program cut to the heart of the coming technology and its potential for control. "What the biometrics industry will do is systematically pick off captive markets until there is nobody left. Those people who refuse to be biometrically identified in fact [will] become targets of surveillance because they are marginalized."

This is precisely how antichrist and his super-sophisticated, electronic/biometric control system will bring all under his despotic thumb. He will "cause all to receive a mark... or be killed" (Revelation 13:16-18).

The program examined in depth the surveillance camera program already established in Britain. More than 100,000 street-corner cameras, many with infrared night vision capabilities, now watch 24 hours a day in the more troublesome areas of certain communities. Already many abuses of such surveillance have caused citizens personal pain as a result of loss of privacy. The same technology is being implemented in Canada, according to the program's narrator. Additionally, there is talk of such a system for America in the not-too-distant future.

The expert interviewed on these matters for the program said, "It means we have created the most extraordinary network of surveillance systems, all compatible, all able to absolutely determine what we are doing at any moment of the day. All these technologies integrate and because they are all fallible, it means that innocent people will routinely be persecuted" (*Discovery*, June 8, 1999).

All of this, combined with tremendous breakthroughs in DNA identification procedures, will undoubtedly give antichrist and his associates the means of absolute control over most of the population of the world. The American military, for example, is already collecting gene information on everyone who enters service. Few regulations govern the collection of such information and even private endeavors such as insurance companies are into collecting the data. All 50 states are in the process of collecting DNA with the thought of establishing databases that will no doubt eventually be merged into a national system.

The expert interviewed by *Discovery* warned: "DNA is likely to be the final nail in the privacy coffin. If the state starts demanding our DNA blueprint, it's going to be the spark which ignites the privacy movement. That alone will be a spark which creates the conflict between the state and the citizen. I know that that's going to happen because the state is going to constantly push so that everything, everybody is perfectly identifiable in every facet of their lives. That's the future. That's the nightmare."

How far along, in actuality, has this all-consuming drive for controlling every individual on earth come? Yet another authority tells us, "Most of us are not aware of the fact that the intelligence-gathering organizations of the free world have put together a system called Eschalon, which is capable of intercepting all the world's communications at any time. That's ALL the world's communications - be it police, taxi cab, telephone, television, radio, cell phone, e-mail, laptops. All the world's communications are susceptible to interception by the system called Eschalon. And that's a very, very scary thing" (*Discovery*, June 8, 1999).

Since coincidence, it has been said, is not in God's vocabulary, He must have had a special purpose in putting His angel- delivered message to Daniel, "...knowledge shall be increased...." in such close proximity to the powerful commandment, "...seal the book, even to the time of the end" (12:4).

Our generation has witnessed as no other generation a fantastic explosion of knowledge and that knowledge's overwhelmingly obvious relationship to prophecy's unfolding. That is, this generation is witnessing the prophecy's dual meanings: 1) Humankind's knowledge database is doubling every 18 months; and 2) We can, I believe, determine beyond any reasonable doubt that the technology produced by that increased understanding is almost certainly the technology that will lead to the enslaving antichrist control system of Revelation 13. Thus, we witness a great increase in human knowledge and a great increase in the understanding of prophecy.

You Can Know Your Future

The God who created you has not left you suspended in space on a planet whirling toward some unknown destiny. Fulfilled prophecy is proof that He is a hands-on Creator who loves His creation.

Even in His wrath, His love shines through. His judgments are measured and perfectly designed to call those who will turn from wickedness out from among the incorrigibly rebellious.

The book of Revelation clearly demonstrates God's supreme love for mankind, even through human history's most terrible hour when His judgment must deal righteously with sin. He will at that time employ great supernatural ways to convince those who will believe to come out from among the rebels. Read carefully God's foretelling of those times. Consider the reading of Revelation while praying that your spiritual eyes will be open to the truth of those prophecies. Ask God to give you understanding that those prophecies, though wrapped in symbolic language in some instances, are meant to be taken as absolutely literal. The symbolic language represents actual events that are far more dramatic and intense - far more profoundly traumatic - than their awesome representative depictions.

The book of Revelation is the terminus point of all other Scriptures of the preceding 65 books. God pierces the future from the very beginning with the promise that the seed (Christ, the Redeemer) of the woman (Eve) will crush the head of the serpent (Satan). Read Genesis 3:15. What an exciting prospect! God has let us in on knowledge of what will happen in the future from the very beginning of His Holy Word! By reading and meditating upon His written Word from Genesis to Revelation, we can understand our past, our present, and our future!

Indeed, the Revelation itself is not, as many say, a book too difficult to be understood, merely symbolism and allegory or representative of history that already has been accomplished. Revelation is not called the book of mystery. God titled it "the Revelation," that is, "the unveiling" of Jesus Christ in all of His glory. That 66th book of the Bible is to be understood - as is all of God's Word - in terms of His Son, Jesus, who is the Living Word (John 1:1).

Jesus told us: "...I am the way, the truth, and the life; no man cometh unto the Father, but by Me" (John 14:6). The Lord also said, "For God so loved the world, that He gave His only begotten Son, that whosoever believeth in Him should not perish, but have everlasting life" (John 3:16). Jesus went on to say, "He that believeth on Him is not condemned; but he that believeth not is condemned already" (John 3:18).

All of the good we do in this life means nothing in terms of the salvation of our souls. No amount of good work we do for church, community, society, neighbors, family, or anything or anyone else will make us righteous in God's holy eyes. Only true acceptance of and belief in Jesus Christ and His sacrificial death on the cross at

Calvary almost 2,000 years ago and belief that God has raised Him from the dead will satisfy God's righteousness in the matter of man's lost condition. Salvation is freely given to all who believe. Salvation is God's grace gift to mankind through Jesus Christ, the Lamb who takes away the sins of the world (John 1:29).

God's Word tells us, "For by grace are ye saved through faith; and that not of yourselves, it is the gift of God - Not of works, lest any man should boast" (Ephesians 2:8-9).

Pray a simple prayer of faith, believing that Jesus Christ died for your sins. Ask the Lord to come into your life and change it for His sake. God's Holy Spirit will instantaneously indwell you and begin transforming your life to all your heavenly Father wants you to become. While you read, study and meditate upon God's Word, the Bible, and pray for enlightenment, your spiritual vision will become increasingly acute. The Creator of all the universe will help you in piercing the future with His prophetic Word.

PART I
FORETELLING THE FATE OF THE NATIONS

1

THE PEACE PREDICAMENT

BY ZOLA LEVITT

The prophet Daniel must have stopped writing at the point where the angel declared to him, "By peace shall he [the antichrist] destroy many" (8:25). It would give any of us pause to imagine that a peacemaker would kill people with his overtures of peace.

But life in the 1990's has proved to make Daniel seem very up-to-date indeed. He is like a political commentator on the Middle East, and he finds peace, that soothing and reassuring term, can indeed be responsible for wholesale destruction.

Peace is being used to transfer land from the Chosen People to sojourners and pagans. Peace is being used to make the government of Israel seem intractable and unwilling to deal reasonably with her neighbors. And, peace is being used to fearsomely arm the Middle East for a ferocious upcoming war, which may well prove to be the War of Armageddon.

End-times prophecy, sometimes not appreciated, deals

almost 100 percent with Israel. While the world at large faces many calamities, they all seem in association with Israel and the mad policies of those who wish to dominate her at the very end. A knowledge of Bible prophecy shows exactly why we find ourselves in this "peace predicament" (rather than a true "peace process"). The prophecies cover the dispersion of the Jews and the miraculous regathering, and they go on to detail Israel's recent history. It is truly very difficult to understand Scripture and not relate it to current events in the Holy Land.

Despite all the pressure on that small democracy, Israel is prospering, also in accordance with Scriptural prophecy. It is an important nation, and one which now vies with even the Western European cultures in terms of its productivity and the lifestyle of its people. Truly, it is an oncoming 21st century nation.

Since 1948, when the nation was almost stillborn due to Arab attacks immediately after its Declaration of Independence, Israel has continually advanced. In the 1950's, it took in wholesale immigration and began serious cultivation of its land and resources. In the 1960's, it coped with the Arabs and their latest posture - that the so-called Palestinians have been in the land forever contesting with the Jews for its ownership. (An entire history and culture were fabricated for the Western media to write about and celebrate, but no such culture ever really existed in Israel.) In the 1970's, the enemies of Israel tried oil boycotts, and these influenced the Western media to think of Israel as causing terrible economic hardships throughout the world. The press turned against the country it formerly respected. In the 1980's, the incursion into Lebanon and the Intifada - the "war" of stone-throwing against Israeli police — turned world attention to making some kind of peace in the Promised Land. And the 1990's have seen the Madrid Conference, the Oslo Accords, and so forth - all vain attempts to undermine the Jewish nation of Israel and create another Arab dictatorship, this time in the land.

With all that said, the future would look bleak if it were not for the Biblical scenario. Prophetically, there is still suffering and war to come, but in the end, the calamities will bring King Messiah back to His land, and a true peace will reign in the Holy Land and in the entire earth. We are suffering birth pangs, but God will ultimately deliver the kingdom!

I am indebted to Todd Baker, theologian with Zola Levitt Ministries, for many of the Scriptural observations below about the role of Israel, and particularly Jerusalem, in prophecy.

THE BURDENSOME STONE

JERUSALEM IS the city of divine destiny. Its name in Hebrew means "city of peace," but, ironically, it has only known war, tumult, and bloodshed for over 2,700 years. Jerusalem has been razed, ransacked, and rebuilt over 30 times throughout her tragic and war-torn history, yet it continues to stand and is unique above and beyond any other major city of the world in the past, the present, or the future.

This city was chosen by the God of Israel forever to be a place where His name would be known and sanctified.

"I have chosen Jerusalem, that My name might be there ... that My name might be there forever .... In this house [the temple of God], and in Jerusalem, which I have chosen ... I will put my name forever" (2 Chronicles 6:6; 7:16; 33:7).

The eternal city in God's eyes is not Rome, but Jerusalem, where He will place His Son on a restored throne of David as King over the earth at His glorious return. This is His eternal decree in Psalm 2:6-8, which shall be accomplished in the future in spite of the fierce international resistance by the nations of the world now and especially at the time of the end.

That Jerusalem is important to God is underscored by the fact that it is mentioned by name in Scripture over 800 times. It is the only city in history that God commands all to pray for its peace on a continual basis (Psalm 122:6). Jerusalem was called "the city of the great King" by the Messiah Jesus (Matthew 5:35) who came humbly riding on a donkey to offer redemption and the Messianic kingdom, only to be rejected and crucified by the city's leaders a few days later.

We should be cognizant of the fact that the people fining the Mount of Olives in that Palm Sunday parade might have numbered in the thousands. They shouted "Hosannah!" or "Hosheanu!" in Hebrew, which means "save us," and they evidently all believed. But the leadership, who already had a profitable religion in place, did not want a Messiah. This rejection prompted Jesus to lament over Jerusalem's forlorn and tragic fate that would come 40 years later when the Romans laid siege to the city. The burning of the temple and the crashing of a great city to the ground seemed to be because Jerusalem rejected the King when He came (Luke 19:41-44). Jerusalem occupied a central place in the heart of the Messiah then - and still does now. He cried for Jerusalem, and still weeps for her lost condition today.

Indeed, God has placed Jerusalem and Israel at the center of the world and all of the nations. Thus says the Lord God, "This is Jerusalem; I have set her at the center of the nations, with lands around her" (Ezekiel 5:5). Any map of the world or globe amazingly verifies that the tiny nation of Israel and its Jewish capital lie dead center in the world's land mass. How appropriate that as God has made Jerusalem the center of the world geographically, He made it the center theologically and prophetically.

Theologically, He made it the center of world history with the death and resurrection of Christ and the beginning point for Christianity. Prophetically, God will it make it the center of future end-time events. The latter really started with the recapture of Jerusalem by the Jews during the Six-Day War in May 1967.

Since the recapture, Jerusalem has become the epicenter of international tension in geopolitical affairs just as the prophet Zechariah predicted it would be (12:1-3). With the series of so- called peace accords like the Madrid, Oslo, and Wye accords between Israel and the Palestinian Authority, control of Jerusalem has become the center of controversy between the Jews and their Arab enemies.

The acts of terrorism against Jews have significantly

increased more than any other time since Israel has made these peace accords. David Bar-Illan, executive editor of *The Jerusalem Post* and senior advisor to former Prime Minister Benjamin Netanyahu, observed in 1995:

> *Since the signing of the Oslo agreement, 150 Israelis have been killed by terrorists, 98 of them since Yasser Arafat took over in Gaza and Jericho. This is a much larger figure than in any similar period since the establishment of the state.*

Of course, those who are in the know Biblically and have a basic understanding of the Middle East situation today know that groups like the PA are using the peace process as a ruse, a diplomatic disguise to eventually regain control of Jerusalem from Jewish hands and displace the nation of Israel as well. Arafat admitted as much back in 1994 as he told his Arab audiences from the Middle East to South Africa that the efforts of the Jihad to regain Jerusalem as the Palestinian capital must continue under the cover of peace.

He even compared the Oslo agreement to Mohammed's treaty with the Koriesh tribe. Mohammed made a false treaty of coexistence with this tribe with the intention of breaking it once his forces were stronger than the Koriesh. When this goal was achieved two years later, Mohammed and his militant followers ambushed the Koriesh tribe and slaughtered most of them. We must suspect that the real Arafat is more like his ancestor Mohammed than a true Nobel Peace Prize winner. Like Mohammed, Arafat is using peace as a pretense for war. Later on, once he thinks Israel has let her guard down to his overtures for peace, he will attack.

The woeful words of Isaiah certainly apply to these calculated and clever hypocrites who clamor and harangue at Israel for "peace in the Middle East" without the Prince of Peace:

"Woe unto them who call evil good, and good evil; who put darkness for light, and light for darkness; who put bitter for sweet, and sweet for bitter! ... There is no peace saith my God to the wicked" (Isaiah 5:20; 57:21).

Arafat has made it a point to declare that he and the PA will not stop until Jerusalem is theirs. It is possible that the recent ousting of Benjamin Netanyahu is related to the PA posturing since the Prime Minister did not give in to the intense pressure of giving up more land for peace and affirmed that Jerusalem is non-negotiable. Now, the recently elected Ehud Barak is already talking about negotiating away the Golan Heights to the dictator of Syria, Hafez Assad.

Netanyahu's reluctance to hand any more land over to the Palestinians so disturbed the Clinton administration that Jim Carville, Clinton's campaign strategist, was sent over to help the liberal opposition party defeat Netanyahu in the recent May elections of 1999. Syria's hatred for Israel is legendary. One such horrible story gives a vivid description of how a Syrian soldier took a bound Israeli prisoner and publicly chewed him to death to bloodthirsty cheers of the crowd looking on. Hatred for Israel is fanatically instilled in Syrian school children at an early age.

How can one obtain peace with governments that

support, harbor, and solicit terrorists and their organizations?

"It Is Written"

FROM A PROPHETIC POINT OF VIEW, the peace process for Israel is nothing but a preparatory stepping stone for the predicted final peace covenant of Daniel 9:27 when Israel will be forced to make peace with her enemies as it is brokered by the antichrist. The city of Jerusalem will figure prominently in this future seven-year treaty that will commence Daniel's 70th week (Daniel 9:27). This future covenant could very well involve the rebuilding of the Temple and the reinstitution of animal sacrifices in that Temple. At the present time, any attempts to rebuild the Temple (like the one in 1991 when the group called The Temple Mount Faithful attempted to lay the cornerstone on the Temple Mount in Jerusalem) would immediately inspire the Arab world to all-out war with Israel.

Some event or series of events will trigger the need for this ability to have the power to work between the Arabs and the Jews. Perhaps Israeli concessions on surrendering land for peace will also include the Palestinians having their capital in Jerusalem along with Israel - the first country in the world that could have two capitals. Whatever the exact scenario for the final peace treaty that will take place - the feverish attempts to bring peace in the Middle East by the international community - the situation will apparently culminate in the infamous "peace" covenant of Daniel 9:27.

The Bible has foretold the hollow cries of peace that are heard all around us today concerning Israel and her Arab enemies. This situation is evidently a prelude to destruction that will indeed come upon an unbelieving, Christ-rejecting world during the horrific events of the great tribulation period. The Apostle Paul points out in 1 Thessalonians 5:3: "For when they say, 'Peace and safety!' then sudden destruction comes upon them as labor pains upon a pregnant woman." The Bush and Clinton administrations' ideas for peace in Israel simply do not and will not work, no matter how hard the Israel-bashing media continually blame the Jews for failure of peace now. One simple reason Israel cannot make real peace with the Arabs is because the Arab countries are dictatorships. They will not tolerate any democracy in that region, particularly one operated by the Jews. One cannot, of course, deal with a dictator with confidence, since he could be replaced at any moment, and a new dictator may not wish to keep the terms of a previous agreement.

A second reason peace is difficult is the Arab world's united hatred for Israel and subsequent desire to see her eradication, no matter what it takes. The only thing Israel has gained from these peace treaties with their neighboring enemies so far is more pressure from the United States to give away more of their homeland for peace, giving the Arab world the idea that they can eradicate Israel through "peace" instead of war, since every time Israel gestures for peace it does so through costly acts of giving up land.

Dividing the land of Israel and the city of Jerusalem is a thing abhorrent to God and will be one of His chief reasons for gathering the nations at Armageddon where He will personally deal with them very harshly. God declares in Joel 3:2:

> I will gather all nations and bring them down to the Valley of Jehoshaphat; And I will enter into judgment with them there on account of My people, My heritage Israel, whom they have scattered among the nations; They have also divided up My land.

Note that in Joel 3:1, the time frame for this prophetic event is after the Lord has brought back the Jews from worldwide dispersion. This brings us to another important series of events in Bible prophecy concerning the end-times - namely, the scattering and regathering of the Jews to the Promised Land. God's prophetic Word foretold that Israel would be scattered to all the nations of the world and persecuted wherever they went. It was fully 3,500 years ago that God spoke through Moses and foretold that the Jews would be dispersed throughout the world for their disobedience (see Deuteronomy 28:64-68; Leviticus 26:33-34).

These dire prophecies were fulfilled with the destruction of Jerusalem and the Temple by the Romans in 70 A.D. One of the horrible consequences of the Roman defeat was the removal of the Jews from the land and their scattering to the Gentile nations of the world. This was not made complete until some 65 years later (135 A.D.) when the Roman Emperor Hadrian crushed the last

Jewish revolt and drove the remaining Jews out of the land. He razed Jerusalem with plowshares and thus literally fulfilled the prophecy of Micah 3:12, made over 750 years earlier. Yet, in spite of the Jews' worldwide dispersion, God said He would preserve their ethnic and national identity wherever they were scattered. "For surely I will command and will sift the house of Israel among all nations, as grain is sifted in a sieve. Yet not the smallest grain shall fall to the ground" (Amos 9:9). During this long period, Israel would be without the privilege of Temple, priest, sacrifice or Davidic king. "For the children of Israel shall abide many days without king or prince, without sacrifice, or sacred pillar, without ephod or teraphim" (Hosea 3:4).

Many of the prophecies about the Jews' dispersion also include, in the same sentence or verse, prophecies about their restoration to their land in "the last days" (Deuteronomy 30:1-10; Isaiah 11:11-12; Ezekiel 20:33-34, 36, 37; Jeremiah 12:1415; 32:37-38; Amos 9:14-15). A particularly revealing prophecy about the restoration of Israel in the last days is the one cited above in Jeremiah 12:14-15. In that passage, it is expressly stated that after the Jews return to the land of Israel, the Lord will Himself "return" to have compassion on them (see also the Authorized Version of Deuteronomy 30:3). "Then it shall be, after I have plucked them out, that I will return and have compassion on them and bring them back everyone to his heritage and everyone to his land" (Jeremiah 12:14-15). The sequence and the sign here are extremely important in our day - especially with the national rebirth of Israel in May of 1948. Note when

God begins to bring the Jews back from the nations of the world (to "pluck them out"), He will return and gather all the Jews to the Land of Promise. Thus, the return of the Jews to their land in this century is a conspicuous sign that the return of the Messiah is at hand.

What began to happen with Israel in May 1948 is indisputably the greatest fulfillment of Bible prophecy since the first coming of Christ and is a clear signal to our generation that the end of the present age with Christ's return is very near. The preservation of the Jewish people and their return to their ancient homeland after being scattered in small groups throughout the world for almost 2,000 years is nothing short of miraculous. In fact, one could argue for the Bible being divine rather than human in origin from this fulfilled prophecy alone. Truly, the Jews are the eternal people of God and are promised in Jeremiah 31:35-37 that the Lord will protect and preserve them as His chosen people for all time. For just as the sun, moon, and stars are permanent features of the created universe that God made, so too has He promised that Israel will be His forever people on an unconditional basis.

> Thus says the Lord who gives the sun for a light by day, the ordinances of the moon and the stars for a light by night ... If those ordinances depart from before Me, says the Lord, then the seed of Israel shall also cease from being a nation before Me forever. Thus says the Lord: If heaven above can be measured, and the foundations of the earth searched out beneath, I will also cast off all the

seed of Israel for all that they have done (Jeremiah 31:35-37).

This great promise, which will endure for eternity, and the fact Israel is a nation against all odds should open one's eyes that the Bible is truly the Word of God and the Jewish people a people of divine destiny. To still assert otherwise in the face of facts, to hold, say, to Replacement Theology and claim that the church has replaced Israel, is to deny the undeniable. The indestructibility of the Jew is historical proof of God's faithfulness to preserve them, and that's all there is to that.

But just as God chose the Jewish people for His plan and purpose of the ages, which included the recording of His Word to man and the coming of the Redeemer to save the world, Satan also chose them as well for purposes of destruction and annihilation. If the devil could successfully exterminate the Jewish people after all, he would make God's promises made to the chosen people through the Covenants (i.e., the Abrahamic, Davidic, and New Covenants) irrelevant. The Bible would become the relic book of an extinct people if somehow God's enemy could be rid of His Chosen Ones. Hence, the only reasonable explanation for the phenomenon of anti-Semitism is found in the supernatural hatred of the Jews by the adversary, which is a further reflection of the devil's rebellion and hatred for God Himself. Those who are averse to the Jews or the nation of Israel - be they so-called Christians, Muslims, politicians, or media pundits - are, in a very real way, siding with the enemy of God.

The shootings at a Jewish children's daycare center in a

suburb of Los Angeles should be no surprise to astute students of Bible prophecy. The Lord predicted the rise of anti-Semitism as well as persecution of Christians to be signs of the approaching end. Jesus said, "You will be hated of all nations for My name's sake" (Matthew 24:9). Hatred for Jews is a worldwide phenomenon that apparently is even seething under the surface of America - a country that values freedom and religious tolerance. America could very well become a "goat" nation during the tribulation period, or, as some hold, it has become that way before the tribulation even begins.

When the King returns at the end of the great tribulation to judge the "sheep and goat nations" before "the throne of His glory," Matthew 25:31-46 teaches that the basis of this judgment of the Gentile nations will be how they treated Christ's brethren - the Jews. This judgment will be prior to the start of the millennium and will concern Gentile nations only. The Jews cannot be in it because they are not to be "reckoned among the nations" (Numbers 23:9). During the tribulation period, the "sheep" nations will be those who treat the Jewish people (the 144,000 and other Jewish believers) kindly by feeding, clothing, and visiting them in prison. Their reward for showing this evidence of saving faith will be their entrance into the millennial kingdom of Christ on earth.

The "goat" nations will be those who will mistreat the Jews by way of indifference, neglect, and an utter unwillingness to help them during their plight. The King will punish them with banishment from His kingdom and cast them into bondage with the devil. If there is any doubt of what God thinks about people who hate the Jews, the future judgment of the goat nations who are evidently anti-Semitic makes it quite clear that He will not tolerate it.

Even now, as we draw closer to the ominous events of the great tribulation, nations are unwittingly positioning themselves by how they view Israel. If America's foreign policy ever becomes decidedly anti-Israel and detrimental to the Jews' right to exist as a nation with Jerusalem as its capital, then judgment from God is sure to come as night inexorably follows day. The stipulations of the "everlasting covenant" God made with Abraham and his descendants in Genesis 12:1-3 are still in force. Any nation or person who has in effect "cursed" God's Chosen People will be cursed by God in the end. History bears witness to this sobering truth.

The graveyard of nations is filled with those who tried to harm and destroy the Jews (like ancient Egypt, Babylon, Assyria, Medo-Persia, the Roman Empire, etc.) and the price they have paid is extinction! With the United States, perhaps the freest and fairest nation of history, we still have a dichotomy over religious belief in general. American born-again believers tend to be outstandingly supportive of Israel and tirelessly take up its causes. But the more liberal "Christians," and finally the large portion of American unbelievers, feel quite the other way about Israel. In the end, the rapture will divide this country so that what remains will truly be a nation of unbelievers who care nothing about Israel or its destiny. Those who have blessed Israel will literally be gone, and those who cursed Israel will be in charge. Thus, the Abrahamic covenant will be undoubtedly violated by what remains of America.

Despite the enemies of Israel outnumbering the Israeli armed forces 80 to 1, the Jewish nation has successfully defended itself against four major assaults instigated by the Arabs. In the last 50 years since the Jews returned to the land, they have been able to transform what was once a malarial wasteland of swamps and deserts into a burgeoning and thriving agricultural success. It is noteworthy that the Ottoman Empire and various Arabs and Bedouins, who controlled Israel before the modern Jewish state, were unable to successfully cultivate the land.

The prophet Ezekiel foresaw this great agricultural transformation of the Promised Land after it had been barren and desolate for a long time (Ezekiel 36). This change would occur at the same time the Lord would bring back the Jewish people to the Land He gave them. The renewal of the Land to almost Eden-like conditions as prophesied in Ezekiel is a significant sign of the end-times. Barren Israel has somehow become a major exporter of fruits and vegetables to Europe and much of the rest of the world.

The Signs of the Times

JUST AS JESUS CHRIST gave signs that He was the Messiah and the Son of God when He came to Israel the first time, so that His generation could "discern the signs of the times" (Matthew 16:3), so now is the rebirth of the nation of Israel a sure prophetic sign that He is coming again soon. No other Christian generation until now has witnessed the mass return of the Jews to the land of Israel, and the rebuilding and repossession of their capital city, Jerusalem. Both indeed are clear "signs of the times" that soon, perhaps very soon, the Lord is going to return to redeem Israel again with compassion and mercy.

In this revealing light, Psalm 102:13-16 stands on the verge of fulfillment: "For when the Lord shall build up Zion; He shall appear in His glory" (Psalm 102:16). But like the myopic Pharisees in the days of Christ's first coming, there are those in the churches and seminaries who deny, deprecate, and diminish the singular importance of the fact that modern Israel is, without question, an astounding fulfillment of Bible prophecy and a sign that Jesus is going to return soon.

Some theologians who claim an expertise in knowing Scripture can't or won't see the obvious correlation between Bible prophecy and the miraculous rebirth of the nation of Israel in 1948 - even when they have been taught that it is one of the last great signs to be fulfilled before the return of Christ. They know what the Bible says about the regathering of the Jews into the Promised Land and then, having witnessed this magnificent end-time event, still incomprehensibly refuse to admit as much. Perhaps there is an aversion for what is Jewish, disguised with theological window dressing, or a jealousy that Israel is now fast becoming the object of God's attention again as the Church Age winds down.

Whatever the motive, this much is sure: What Jesus

said to the religious leaders of His day in their failure to discern the obvious signs pointing to Him as the Messiah in their midst is sadly true of many leaders in Christendom today.

"When it is evening you say, 'It will be fair weather, for the sky is red,' and in the morning, 'It will be foul weather today, for the sky is red and threatening.' Hypocrites! You know how to discern the face of the sky, but you cannot discern the signs of the times" (Matthew 16:2-4).

Like the Pharisees, they can read the natural signs of the clouds, wind, and the sky but are bereft of spiritual discernment to understand the great sign of restored Israel in our time.

Currently in the geopolitical arena, the general consensus of the international community is largely against Israel and pro-Palestinian. A recent UN declaration made by its secretary-general stated that the great majority of member states of the United Nations believed Israel was responsible "directly or indirectly" for acts of provocation that undermine goodwill and spark hostilities and that the only chance for peace in that region is a "land for peace" solution.

"O, Jerusalem..."

THE MAJOR BONE of contention between the Jews and the rest of the world is the future status of Jerusalem. As we look at Bible prophecy and current events, we know that the city of Jerusalem will be the center object of international focus. This is where all these "peace talks" are eventually leading. Questions about Jerusalem are myriad: Who will control the city? To whom does the city belong? Will it be the capital city of Israel? Will it be the capital of Palestine? Will it be divided? Who has the final say about the city - Israel, the PA, the Arabs, or a UN-mandated international coalition? Already Jerusalem is becoming a thorny problem among world leaders and politicians.

Jerusalem is gradually becoming the burdensome stone that Zechariah 12:3 predicts this city of divine destiny will be. Jerusalem will become a cup of strong wine so that the nations of the world will become so intoxicated by it they will send the armies of the world against the city to control, divide, and rule over it, which will lead the world on a collision course with the Defender of Israel - the Messiah at the battle of Armageddon.

There in that great valley of the same name will be gathered all the armies of the antichrist and the nations of the world to try for the last time to exterminate the Jewish presence from the earth. The simple reason Satan and the Gentile nations of the world hate Israel and want Jerusalem taken out of Jewish hands is because they oppose God's plan for Messiah to rule there over the world (see Psalm 2). They want it for themselves. But the long history of Gentile dominance, hostility, and the mad preoccupation for total control over Jerusalem will be the very thing that will cut them down to pieces in the end. Opposition against Israel and the Jewish ownership of it by most of the Gentile world today is really a hatred and rebellion against the God of Israel and the King Messiah who is destined to reign there for a thousand years. The enemies of Israel are plotting through pseudo-peace maneuvers, secret arming programs, and other furtive strategies to no avail. At Armageddon, when these same infernal entities marshal all their military forces against this tiny nation, God will respond to them with derision as He sends His Son back. With one spoken word from His mouth, Christ will destroy these demon-led armies and their last desperate anti-Semitic act.

"He who sits in the heavens shall laugh; the Lord shall have them in derision. Then He shall speak to them in His wrath, and distress them in His deep displeasure: Yet I have set My King [Jesus] on My holy hill of Zion [Jerusalem] ... You shall break them with a rod of iron; You shall dash them in pieces like a potter's vessel" (Psalm 2:4-6).

Israel and the Future

To look at events in Israel from a worldly standpoint, the future looks bleak. A recent change of government has a more appeasing Prime Minister, Ehud Barak, in place of Benjamin Netanyahu, and a seemingly more accommodating Israeli attitude toward the Palestinian Authority. Most recently, a "safe passage" was created for the Palestinians to move freely from Gaza to the West Bank. The Israelis approved and will monitor this safe passage.

But even that name, "safe passage," is propagandistic.

Palestinians were never unsafe moving around in Israel. Even if they had to present identity cards at borders, in no case were they anything but safe in one of the world's safest countries. The ones who seem to need safe passage through the Promised Land are the Jews who are occasionally blown up by terrorists, stabbed by passersby on streets or shot at from passing cars. The so-called Palestinian people are not merely "safe," but they enjoy the most advanced life style of Arabs anywhere in the Middle East. Their life span, their medical care, their schools, their water, and almost everything else they use in Israel is superior to that of any Arab country, even the wealthy emirates.

But, as the above chapter indicates, the Arabs are made to seem like an underdog, and the Israelis like some brutal controlling force in Israel. If we had only a worldly perspective to go on, one could easily predict that the Arabs will, piece by piece, take the Holy Land away from the Jews and, in the end, attack and kill them (or that a possible nuclear defense of Israel would be undertaken by the Jews, and the killing would be worse than imagined). But we have the Biblical perspective, and it's entirely different. In some ways, one fully understands the conflict in Israel because it more logically brings on the end-times and the return of the King.

Our chapter has' been devoted almost entirely to the Scriptural outcomes of Israel's future, but suffice it to say that in the end, this will be the happiest, most prosperous, most peaceful land the world has known since the Garden of Eden. Israel will yet take her place at the head of the nations as the most respected spiritual and political center on the face of the earth. The labor pains we are undergoing are difficult, but delivery will present a beautiful "child" - the kingdom of God on earth, and the first truly righteous government in world history.

Until that time, pray with the Apostle John, "Amen. Even so, come, Lord Jesus" (Revelation 22:20).

2

EUROSPHERE - RESHAPING THE WORLD

BY ARNO FROESE

When I received the invitation to write this chapter, the word "reshaping" in particular stuck in my mind for several weeks. In this chapter, we will take some new steps toward "rethinking" our understanding of the "reshaping of the world" as well as the continuous development of this process and its final fulfillment.

Our basis of interpreting the prophetic Word is the indisputable fact that prophecy was given by God to man through the Holy Spirit. Men of God wrote it down and passed it on to us. We can be absolutely certain that the prophetic Word will be fulfilled in its finest detail. Those of us who have dealt with this fascinating, but often confusing subject of eschatology have frequently discovered that certain aspects of the fulfillment of Bible prophecy have not turned out the way we anticipated.

Gog and Magog Invasion

. . .

I, for one, believed that when Communism was marching forward to conquer in the '50's, '60's, '70's and beyond, the great invasion of the Northern Confederacy would take place upon Israel any day.

Libya

With Colonel Muammar Abu Minyra al-Quadhafi's rise to power on September 1, 1969, we saw Libya falling in line with the Soviet Union.

Ethiopia

The next country was Ethiopia, prominently mentioned in Ezekiel 38:5. She fell into the camp of the Soviet-aligned nations when Haile Selassie was deposed on September 13, 1974.

Iran

Ethiopia was followed by Iran, the Biblical country of Persia. The separation from the pro-western bloc took place on January 31, 1979, with the arrival of religious leader, Ayatollah Ruhollah Kaomeini, when he returned to Iran from his exile in France. Although this country did not become Communist, they did separate themselves from the Western Alliance; subsequently, their leaning towards the Soviet Union became obvious.

Germany

ANOTHER COUNTRY IDENTIFIED in the great invasion of Israel is "Gomer." Many scholars agree that this is at least part of Germany. As a child, I recall hearing the song, "We are staying in our Gomer land."

These four countries: "Persia, Ethiopia, Libya, and Gomer" (Ezekiel 38:5-6) made prophecy look easy. When analyzing political developments, we realized that one country after another had favorably aligned themselves with the nation known as "Gog" in the land of Magog. Geographically located in the uttermost north, everything seemed to be in the right order.

With the fall of the Soviet Union, however, things began to look differently. "Gomer" became part of West Germany. Libya is in the process of being welcomed back into the family of nations, and Ethiopia has become partially democratic. Today, Iran is desperately seeking friendship and economic relationship with whomever they can.

Having said this, one may ask, "Do you now think that there will be a northern invasion upon the land of Israel?" I can only base my answer on what the Bible says; that answer would be a definite YES. The invasion upon the land of Israel, as described in Ezekiel 38 and 39, has not taken place yet, therefore it is a prophecy that will be fulfilled in the future.

We must consider the fact that political realities can change overnight. One day, the world will experience a sudden, unexpected invasion of the land of Israel by the Northern Confederacy under the leadership of Gog with their allies; this is exactly the way the Bible predicted.

Although this summary of the Gog/Magog event has no direct relationship to the subject of this chapter, I feel compelled to point out that this particular circumstance shows that we must not look at the world to see if we can detect similarities to the prophetic Scripture, establishing as a result an interpretation limited to our timing. Instead, we should understand the Word of God. In so doing, we will receive increased wisdom about what is happening in the world. We don't understand the Word of God through the world, however, we can understand the world through the Word of God. James C. Morris, in his book, *Keys To Bible Prophecy*, fittingly writes: We do not gain an understanding of the Bible from external information, we gain an understanding of external information from the Bible (page 99).

Rethinking

In our "rethinking" process, we must understand that as

far as Bible prophecy is concerned, all people fall into three categories: Gentiles, Jews, and Christians.

Christians are those who, by their own free will, have recognized their corrupt nature, realized their lost condition, and come in humility to Jesus, asking forgiveness of their sins. As a result, such people become born-again of the Spirit of God and belong to a very unique group of people called the church.

First Peter 2:9 describes these people with the following words, "ye are a chosen generation, a royal priesthood, a holy nation, a peculiar people; that ye should shew forth the praises of him who hath called you out of darkness into his marvelous light." If you are born again, then you have become a citizen of a "holy nation." Your life is now totally dedicated to that nation. You unconditionally serve the nation's leader, the Lord Jesus Christ. You do everything in your strength to be a good citizen because your desire is to please your Lord, who has purchased you with His own precious blood and pardoned you from the coming judgment to be executed upon all who sin against God.

Christians

WHILE YOU ARE NOW a citizen of this "holy nation," you are simultaneously a citizen of another nation. Usually, that citizenship is of the country where you were born, or to which you obtained citizenship through the process of naturalization. It is important to understand that this other citizenship is earthly, worldly, and of little, if any, significance. For example, your citizenship in Canada, France, the United States, or China is absolutely useless in heaven. While your earthly citizenship is temporal, your heavenly citizenship is eternal.

The sad mistake many citizens of the "holy nation" commit is confusing their earthly citizenship with their heavenly one. They are constantly tossed to and fro in this conflict between nationality and serving the Lord. Many well-meaning Christian leaders try very hard to unite these two citizenships, but in vain. The Bible does not confirm this unity. Why? Because no one can serve two masters!

It is impossible to serve both God and country. This statement may offend some because many of us have been brought up on the slogan, "God and country" but that's where the confusion begins. Let me clarify this: I am 100 percent for God, and I am 100 percent for my country; however, I can never be "for God and country."

We must learn to differentiate between these two important positions: 1) our heavenly citizenship, with all of its spiritual responsibilities and duties, and 2) our earthly citizenship, which is directed toward our earthly government. When we put this in its proper perspective, Romans 13 falls into place.

The Scripture addressing this matter is very plain, yet we easily become confused if we don't separate these two issues.

Scripture says, "Let every soul be subject unto the higher powers. For there is no power but of God: the powers that be are ordained of God. Whosoever therefore resisteth the power, resisteth the ordinance of God: and they that resist shall receive to themselves damnation" (Romans 13:1-2). The Word of God does not give us a choice. It does not say, if the "power or government is based on God's principle" or "if it agrees with our interpretation of Scripture." It simply says, "There is no power but of God." I can almost hear some readers saying, "Wait a minute, you surely don't mean we are to be subject to socialists, Communists, Nazis, or dictators?" The answer is that Scripture means exactly what it says; otherwise, it would clearly state "only the government which the majority of the people support, accept, and want to serve."

JESUS ENDORSED ROMAN Rule

IF YOU HAVE a problem subjecting yourself to authorities, let me give you one example from the Lord Jesus Himself. By telling the people "to render unto Caesar the things which are Caesar's," He was endorsing the dictatorial, occupational government of Rome. Not only that, but Jesus also says, "pay your taxes."

Study the Apostles and you will find that none opposed the government. They knew that if they resisted, in actuality they would be resisting the ordinance of God. God is not fighting a battle between good and evil. He already sent His Son, the Lord Jesus Christ, who died on Calvary's Cross for our sins, defeating the powers of darkness once and for all; Jesus is Victor, here and now. He does not have to fight toward the victory. You and I are partakers of this victory and must subject ourselves to the government which God ordains.

This simple matter of learning the difference between our eternal, heavenly citizenship and our temporary, earthly citizenship is of utmost importance. Once we grasp that, we can understand the words many have stumbled over, "shall there be evil in a city, and the LORD hath not done it?" (Amos 3:6).

It doesn't matter how much we love our nation, it is still ruled by Satan, the god of this world. He rules the nations with one desire: to be the "real" supreme ruler of the universe. I must emphasize that God is still in control. Even though the nations are ruled by the enemy, Satan can only go as far as God allows. God is the ultimate authority in establishing and deposing governments. The devil has no authority other than that given him by God.

Thus, we understand why the Bible instructs Christians, citizens of the "holy nation," to obey whatever government God permits for a certain nation.

All Nations Equal

The fundamental principles of God-ordained government are found in all systems. No nation on the face of the earth rewards adulterers and murderers or encourages stealing and lying. The assumption that one country is "more Biblical" in its principles than others is actually nothing more than wishful thinking.

. . .

Nationalism

When I became a Christian in 1967, I remember looking at the Bible, particularly Biblical prophecy, from a nationalistic perspective. Dr. Wim Malgo, founder of Midnight Call Ministry, corrected me and said, "Take that little silly flag away from your eyes so you can see the Word of God clearly." That was a great lesson to me. From that point on, I looked at the prophetic Word from a heavenly perspective, and things fell into place. The moment we rise above our temporary earthly citizenship, we begin to see God's Word from an eternal perspective. We will not be swayed by the cunning devices of Satan; whose aim is to deceive and lead astray.

To reinforce this truth, let's look at one of the greatest Christians, the Apostle Paul. He had every reason to be proud of his heritage. He writes, "Circumcised the eighth day, of the stock of Israel, of the tribe of Benjamin, a Hebrew of the Hebrews; as touching the law, a Pharisee" (Philippians 3:5). He was of the stock of Israel, the only nation chosen by God, of the tribe of Benjamin, and the first one integrated into the royal tribe of Judah. He was a true Hebrew, the custodians of God's law to the world. I don't think any of us can even come close to being as "qualified" as the Apostle Paul. He had all the reason in the world to be proud of his heritage, his nation, his family, and his religion. But what does he say? "I do count them but dung" (verse 8). This statement makes it very clear: If you are still proud of your nation and your earthly citizenship, take the advice of Paul so you will not be misguided by the darkness of nationalism, resulting in the inability to recognize God's plan for the world

Jews

THE JEWS DO NOT BELONG to this exclusive, special nation due to their free will. Rather, their citizenship is the result of God's ordinance. He chose them. "For thou art a holy people unto the LORD thy God, and the LORD hath chosen thee to be a peculiar people unto himself, above all the nations that are upon the earth" (Deuteronomy 14:2). The Word makes it clear that they are a "holy people." However, unlike Christians, Israel has a geographic, physical, political, and economic promise. They are to be "above all nations." Christians are not.

God gave us His ordinances through Israel. The Bible is a Jewish book, written by Jewish people who have been destined to be "above all the nations that are upon the earth." Note the words "upon the earth." This is not a heavenly promise.

Gentiles

ALL OTHERS outside the church who are not Jews are commonly referred to as Gentiles. Based on Scripture, there is no difference between the various groups or races. God reveals what He thinks about the nations of the world in Psalm 2:1-2, "Why do the heathen rage, and the people imagine a vain thing? The kings of the earth set themselves, and the rulers take counsel together, against the LORD, and against his anointed." How does the Lord react? "He that sitteth in the heavens shall laugh" (verse 4). In case you thought your nation was an exception, read Isaiah 40:17, "All nations before him are as nothing; and they are counted to him less than nothing, and vanity."

To the Christians from among the Gentiles, the Apostle Paul has this to say, "That at that time ye were without Christ, being aliens from the commonwealth of Israel, and strangers from the covenants of promise, having no hope, and without God in the world" (Ephesians 2:12). These few words suffice to show the total hopelessness of anyone outside of Christ: no promise, no hope.

Proclamation of Prophecy

We need to realize that the Word of God is creative. On the first page of our Bible we read, "And God said, Let there be light: and there was light" (Genesis 1:3). Later, John writes about this creating Word when he says, "In the beginning was the Word, and the Word was with God, and the Word was God. The same was in the beginning with God. All things were made by him; and without him was not anything made that was made" (John 1:1-3). When God speaks through His Word, via His chosen prophets, we may as well consider it done. Regardless of our understanding or ignorance; agreement or disagreement, the Word of God stands eternally.

Birth in Bethlehem

An example can be found in Micah 5:2, where we read, "But thou, Bethlehem Ephratah, though thou be little among the thousands of Judah, yet out of thee shall he come forth unto me that is to be ruler in Israel; whose goings forth have been from of old, from everlasting." This prophecy was made over 700 years before the birth of Christ. It seems that nothing happened during those many years until the time came for the visible fulfillment. Then, with great joy, we read the angelic proclamation, "And, lo, the angel of the Lord came upon them, and the glory of the Lord shone round about them: and they were sore afraid. And the angel said unto them, Fear not: for, behold, I bring you good tidings of great joy, which shall be to all people. For unto you is born this day in the city of David a Saviour, which is Christ the Lord. And this shall be a sign unto you; Ye shall find the babe wrapped in swaddling clothes, lying in a manger. And suddenly there was with the angel a multitude of the heavenly host praising God, and saying, Glory to God in the highest and on earth peace, good will toward men" (Luke 2:9-14).

In order for this fulfillment to have taken place, the whole world had to be involved, "in those days, that there went out a decree from Caesar Augustus, that all the world should be taxed" (Luke 2:1). Today, it's called "taking a census." Surely, the citizens of the Roman Empire must have murmured and complained about this terrible inconvenience to go back to the town or city of their birth to be registered. They didn't have computers, faxes, telephones, or "Next Day Express" mail service. They had to go in person back to their place of birth in order to be counted. Rome apparently wanted to know how strong she was.

The real reason, however, behind this population census was the fulfillment of prophecy. Verse 4 reveals, "And Joseph also went up from Galilee, out of the city of Nazareth, into Judaea, unto the city of David, which is called Bethlehem; (because he was of the house and lineage of David)" (Luke 2). Think about it. A prophecy over 700 years old identifying that the Messiah would be born in Bethlehem. This could not be fulfilled if Jesus were born in Nazareth.

The Bible reports the finest details about this event, "To be taxed with Mary his espoused wife, being great with child. And so it was, that, while they were there, the days were accomplished that she should be delivered. And she brought forth her firstborn son, and wrapped him in swaddling clothes, and laid him in a manger; because there was no room for them in the inn" (Luke 2:5-7). Note the words, "while they were there." Where? In Bethlehem! This was fulfillment of Bible prophecy in its time.

While part of Micah's prophecy about Jesus being born in Bethlehem was fulfilled, something was - and still is - missing today, "out of thee (Bethlehem) shall come forth unto me that is to be ruler in Israel." Jesus had not become the ruler of Israel. As a matter of fact, the people rejected Him from being ruler in Israel. When they were presented with the choice of Jesus, the King of the Jews, they plainly stated, "We have no king but Caesar." So, in simple words, that prophecy "to be ruler in Israel" has not been fulfilled, but it will be fulfilled in the future.

There is another unfulfilled prophecy regarding the birth of Jesus. The angelic host proclaimed, "good tidings of great joy, which shall be to all people ... Glory to God in the highest, and on earth peace, good will toward men" (Luke 2:10,14). This good news, the "tidings of great joy" continues to be presented for almost 2,000 years to all people in the world. But "on earth peace" has not yet been fulfilled. The Lord Jesus Himself made this prophecy, "ye shall hear of wars and rumors of wars ... nation shall rise against nation, and kingdom against kingdom" (Matthew 24:6-7). "Peace on earth" has yet to come. At His first coming as the babe in Bethlehem, He became the Lamb of God, dying on Calvary's cross for the sin of all men. But at His second coming, He will be "ruler in Israel" and only then will "peace on earth" become a reality.

Final Fulfillment

I was happy to read that Terry James, General Editor, designated "Reshaping the World" as the title of this chapter. That is extremely important, because you can only reshape something which already exists. During the remainder of this chapter, I want to discuss this issue. Therefore, come with me on a journey to the Roman

Empire. Please keep in mind that the Roman Empire does not need to be reborn or resurrected, only reshaped.

ROMAN EMPIRE: **Past, Present and Future**

QUITE FREQUENTLY, I hear and read Bible scholars talking about the building of the antichrist empire. They predict that when enough unity is created in the European Union, it will become the strongest power structure on earth. The antichrist will then take over the reins, and from that point will globally rule the nations. Such analysis is only partially true. Why? Because when examining the prophetic Word and the subsequent developments from such a point of view, we are led to a conclusion that everything lies in the future. Please understand: The future cannot happen until the present is prepared. Jesus could not come and be born in Bethlehem because His mother was still living in Nazareth. The great Caesar Augustus had to give the order to all his subjects to return to the place of birth, so Jesus could be born in Bethlehem.

Too often, we ignore the fact that we are in the midst of Bible prophecy fulfillment. Europe is not only going to lead the world, but it has led for the last 2,000 years, and will continue to do so until the climax when the epitome of evil is revealed, the son of perdition, the antichrist.

When we assume that the development in Europe is thoroughly evil, demonic, and of anti-Christian character, we naturally think that our nation, or all other groups of people and countries, will not be under the jurisdiction of the antichrist. That is exactly what the great deceiver wants us to believe.

I have yet to meet people from other nations who do not indulge in pointing out the errors of others.

All Have Sinned

This should not surprise us because all people, without exception, are evil by nature - lost, corrupt, self-centered, egotistic - just as our first parents were. Listen to Adam's defense when God put him and Eve on the spot: "Hast thou eaten of the tree, whereof I commanded thee that thou shouldest not eat?" (Genesis 3:11). What was Adam's reply? "The woman whom thou gavest to be with me, she gave me of the tree and I did eat" (verse 12). In today's language, "It really wasn't my fault; the woman is the one to blame. After all, you are the one who gave her to me." How did Eve react when God asked her to justify her transgression? "What is this that thou hast done? The woman said, The serpent beguiled me, and I did eat." Same response, "It's not my fault, Lord, the serpent made me do it."

Do you hear the philosophy of modern gospel preachers who base their proclamation on the deceitful philosophy of psychology? Some proclaim that there are no sinners - people just went wrong somewhere along the line, perhaps due to a dysfunctional family, a bad experience in their early life, etc. Blame gets passed to everybody and everything and the person is not led to confess, "I have sinned, I am guilty, please forgive me, Lord."

Perpetual Existence of Empires

Babylon, Medo-Persia, Greece, and Rome may not exist today as political entities, but the influence of each of these powers is found in all nations of the world, even today. Each nation is simply a continuation of one of those four empires. The entire Western world is clearly built upon the principles of Roman-Greek civilization. Within that civilization, we find Medo-Persian and Babylonian characteristics as well. While each one of the four empires were geographically centered in a certain area in the Middle East (as seen from the West), their influence, more or less, continued to remain upon all the nations of the world.

There is no question about European nations being influenced by the Romans, Greeks, Medo-Persians, and Babylonians. Neither can we deny that this is equally applicable to new countries such as the United States, for example. The U.S.A. is closely related to the Roman Empire. Roman philosophy, culture, and law are the foundation of virtually all Western civilized nations until this very day. For example:

The emperor Justinian's monumental compilation of the Digests, the Institutes, and the Revised Code, completed in A.D. 534, has served as the foundation of Western law ever since (*National Geographic*, August 1997, p.68, Taken from *Saddam's Mystery Babylon*, p.31).

THE ASSUMPTION that the founding fathers of the United States coined the Constitution based on their own wisdom is a step in the wrong direction, and not supported by history.

The ideal of written law as a shield - to protect individuals against one another and against the awesome power of the state - was a concept the Romans took from the Greeks. But it was Rome that put this abstract notion into daily practice, and the practice is today honored around the world (*National Geographic*, August 1997, pp.63-64, *Saddam's Mystery Babylon*, p.30).

While European countries were influenced by heritage, tradition, culture, language, and millennia of experience, the American system had to be newly established. They could not gather from tradition, culture, heritage, or experience, thus, leading the founding fathers to lean heavily upon the existing Roman laws:

The Roman process of making laws also had a deep influence on the American system. During the era of the Roman Republic (509 to 49 B.C.), lawmaking was a bicameral activity. Legislation was first passed by the comitia, the assembly of the citizens, then approved by the representative of the upper class, the senate, and issued in the name of the senate and the people of Rome. Centuries later, when the American founding fathers launched their bold experiment in democratic government, they took republican Rome as their model. Our laws, too, must go through two legislative bodies. The House of Representatives is our assembly of citizens, and, like its counterpart in ancient Rome, the U.S. Senate was originally designed as a chamber for the elite (it was not until the 17th Amendment, in 1913, that ordinary people were allowed to vote for their senators) (*National Geographic*, August 1997, p.70, *Saddam's Mystery Babylon*, pp.31-32).

The assumption that only Europe is the manifestation of the coming Anti-Christian Empire totally ignores the historical fact that even relatively new countries are also built upon the foundation of Roman law and civilization. Colonial continents such as Africa, America, and Australia were established on the foundation of Roman principles, as we have just read.

But Asia, too, could not function in modern society unless it utilized the Roman philosophical principles of law, business practices, and even languages.

This leads us to say that the Roman Empire, as prophesied in the Bible, has continued to exist for over 2,000 years.

Now, we should understand that the coming European power structure, which will be ruled by the antichrist, is no more or less evil than any nation since the beginning of the Roman Empire. The Roman system never ceased to exist; it never died. There is no need for a so-called resurrection of the Roman Empire, the only need is for reshaping of that empire.

. . .

TERRY JAMES

The First Superpower

We will now take a look at prophecies made more than 2,500 years ago about the Gentile world empires.

Although we hear much about superpowers in the media, the Bible recognizes only four: Babylon, Medo-Persia, Greece, and Rome. Any other power, nation, or group of people can be reckoned as part of one of those four empires. Rome has been leading the world for over 2,000 years and is still in charge today.

When I say "Rome," I do not mean the city alone, or the limited geographical area in history when the Romans ruled the world. We will notice in our further study that the Roman system will incorporate the entire world.

Two-Thousand-Year History

The most fundamental description of the Gentile world is found in Daniel 2. Most of us are familiar with the image Nebuchadnezzar saw in a dream. The Jewish prophet Daniel told Nebuchadnezzar of his dream:

> This image's head was of fine gold, his breast and his arms of silver, his belly and his thighs of brass, His legs of iron, his feet part of iron and part of clay. Thou sawest till that a stone was cut out without hands, which smote the image upon his feet that were of iron and clay and brake them to pieces. Then was the iron, the clay, the

brass, the silver, and the gold, broken to pieces together, and became like the chaff of the summer threshing floors; and the wind carried them away, that no place was found for them: and the stone that smote the image became a great mountain, and filled the whole earth (Daniel 2:32-35).

After reading these verses, notice that the leading role is played by the fourth kingdom. When Daniel interpreted the dream for King Nebuchadnezzar, he told him, "Thou art this head of gold" (verse 38). That is the first kingdom. Daniel used just 24 words to describe the next two kingdoms, "And after thee shall arise another kingdom inferior to thee, and another third kingdom of brass, which shall bear rule over all the earth" (verse 39).

When he came to the fourth kingdom, he revealed some amazing details, "And the fourth kingdom shall be strong as iron: forasmuch as iron breaketh in pieces and subdueth all things: and as iron that breaketh all these, shall it break in pieces and bruise" (verse 40). We all know that Rome's political and military machine was irresistible. When Rome decided to take on an enemy, she made absolutely sure the enemy would be crushed. The next step after winning the victory was to implement Roman law, which usually resulted in Roman liberty, Roman justice, and Roman prosperity. Rome made sure that the conquered people became unified with Rome.

Within the broad sweep of uniformity, Roman administration at the local level was flexible, tolerant, and open.

When Rome conquered a new province, the defeated general and his army were carted away in chains; almost everyone else came out ahead. The local elite were given positions in the Roman hierarchy. Local businesses gained the benefit of Roman roads, water systems, the laws of commerce and the courts. Roman soldiers guarded the town against pirates and marauders. And within a fairly short period, many of the provincial residents would be made cives Romani - citizens of Rome - with all the commensurate rights and duties (*National Geographic*, July 1997, p.30, *Saddam's Mystery Babylon*, E29).

Positive Destruction?

Quite often, we are misled by the words "breaketh in pieces," "subdueth all things," "breaketh all these," "shall it break in pieces and bruise." This sounds like total destruction, but that was not the case, as we just read.

Unfortunately, most of our understanding of history, including Roman, is based on Hollywood movies which show Roman soldiers brutally oppressing the conquered enemies and turning the whole nation into slaves. In most cases, oppression did not happen, but prosperity did. No nation has ever achieved any measurable greatness when it has enslaved its people.

Many mighty buildings and remnants of great projects testify to the glory of Rome. In order to raise such remarkable structures throughout the Roman world, craftsmen were needed, as well as engineers, architects, and surveyors. Likewise, schools and colleges had to be established. It is also noteworthy that archaeologists tell us that various Roman building systems were distinguished by different countries. In other words, it is evident that when Rome conquered a country, they utilized the available technology, including intellectuals, craftsmen, architects, and engineers to build Roman infrastructures throughout Europe. Correctly, *National Geographic* reports, "Almost everyone came out ahead."

When we read these facts in Scripture, our ultimate authority we are challenged to rethink the negative connotation of the words "breaketh," "subdueth," "bruise," etc. I mentioned the fact that some of our Roman history lessons originate in Hollywood. The Hollywood rendition would often show Roman soldiers brutally whipping the opposition into submission and destroying their civilization and culture to establish Roman authority; however, we have already proven by historic documentation that such was not always the case. The majority of people Rome conquered gladly became subjects of Rome. Many strived to become Roman citizens.

What then do the words, "breaketh," "subdueth," and "bruise" really mean? I want to present evidence that this has a positive connotation.

Let's look at the following example: When European settlers came to the American continent, did they not break to pieces, subdue all things, and bruise, even kill, those who were in the way? My daughter-in-law, Debby, born in Brazil and educated in Uruguay, states that virtually all Uruguayan Indians were killed to make room for the Spanish settlers. They destroyed in order to make new. In other words, the traditional laws, customs, and cultures of the native people had to make room for a new system. For America, the new system included freedom, justice, liberty, and pursuit of happiness for all, which, as we already mentioned, is based on Roman principles. So, we must ask, is the establishment of the United States an evil thing? Is it destructive? You be the judge.

The overwhelming majority of Americans are proud and happy to be ruled by a democratic system. Many Americans openly express the idea that the whole world should be like America. How was this "freedom" made possible? Precisely by the implementation of these negative words, "breaking in pieces, subduing all things, and bruising." In other words, the settlers destroyed the old; abolished it, outlawed it, and created something new.

Commercial Success

Such principles are the cornerstone of commercial success as well. Factories that utilize old, outdated equipment cannot compete with new ones. If they are unwilling to change, they may be forced to close. Only the new, the modern, the energetic have a chance to survive and take full advantage of our times.

Many of us remember how the Chairman of Chrysler Corporation, Lee Iaccoco, promoted his vision of a new Chrysler Corporation. In television commercials, he showed how the old factories were blown up, new ones were built. Today, this company is a great success story. They produced such excellent products that they became the first American auto manufacturer to be integrated into a truly global company - Mercedes Benz.

Religious Freedom

ONE OF THE basic principles of Roman law was religious freedom. This, incidentally, is what the American founding fathers realized, and adopted those very principles of religious freedom for the new country. Religious, as well as political freedom, was the key to Rome's success.

Let's look at a Biblical example. When the Apostle Paul was arrested, we read the following in Acts 22:25, "as they bound him with thongs, Paul said unto the centurion that stood by, Is it lawful for you to scourge a man that is a Roman, and uncondemned?" Here we clearly see the principle of "innocent until proven guilty," implemented in Biblical time. Paul made proper use of his Roman citizenship.

The chief captain, who was not born a Roman citizen, testifies, "With a great sum obtained I this freedom" (verse 28). He apparently paid a great price to become a Roman citizen. By this statement, we can prove that the greatest asset at that time was to be a citizen of Rome. Paul said, "I was free born" (verse 28).

Religious freedom was quite evident throughout the Roman Empire. Synagogues built during Roman times can be found throughout all of Europe and the Middle East. When on his missionary journeys to Syria, Turkey,

Greece, and Rome, the Apostle Paul always went to the synagogue first. In order to build such a building, one must have an assembly of Jews. It stands to reason that you can't assemble a group of people if you don't have religious freedom. In order to build a synagogue, the Jews had to buy land, have it surveyed, hire an architect, engineers, and a contractor. The next step was to establish a financial system so this undertaking could be financed. The fact that so many remnants of ancient synagogues are discovered throughout the old Roman Empire proves that religious freedom was in fact a reality.

When a certain centurion was concerned about the sickness of his servant, he sought help from Jesus. The people around him testified about this centurion, "he loveth our nation, and he hath built us a synagogue" (Luke 7:5).

Further proof of the close relationship between the Romans and the Jews in Israel is found in Acts 10:1-2, "There was a certain man in Caesarea called Cornelius, a centurion of the band called the Italian band, A devout man, and one that feared God with all his house, which gave much alms to the people, and prayed to God always." This centurion who came directly from Italy was part of the system that "breaketh in pieces and subdueth all things" in the land of Israel. Roman law prevailed, but religious freedom was granted. This man became the first Gentile to be converted to living faith in the Lord Jesus Christ. I find no evidence in the Scripture that he was relieved of his position or punished in any way, shape, or form because of his new-found faith.

This short study should suffice to show that the

fundamental principles of human rights, democratic practices of government, free enterprise, and religious freedom were part of the Roman system. Just as it was 2,000 years ago, the same Roman system is being fought for today. Particularly with the fall of the Soviet Union, Roman democracy, with all its other beneficial implications, is now marching forward to conquer the world, and "breaketh in pieces and subdueth all things."

Israel, the Center

We all know that Israel is the center of the world and God's primary concern. He chose for Himself a people for His name, brought forth His Son in the flesh Who sacrificed Himself on Calvary's cross to redeem mankind from sin. He is the One Who not only died, arose, and ascended into heaven, but will come again and establish the real peace on earth.

It is significant to realize that during the Babylonian, Greek, Persian, and Roman Empires, Israel was part of all four, while Europe only was part of the fourth one, the Roman. This fourth and final empire, however, also incorporates the three previous ones. Therefore, we may expect that the Middle East, including Iraq, Turkey, Syria, Israel, Jordan, Egypt, and the Mediterranean countries, will either be admitted into the European Union or will form a secondary union closely related to the EU.

. . .

TERRY JAMES

Iron and Clay

CONTRARY TO THE three previous kingdoms, however, the fourth one consists of a mixture. The Bible says, "iron and clay." It is not difficult to identify the iron; it is the Roman system which established its presence throughout the then-known world. But we have a problem here because another component is added; "part of clay." Thus the question: who or what is represented by the clay?

This material is not clearly identified in Scripture and opinions differ among scholars. My interpretation is simply based on the fact that there are four superpowers and the fourth becomes the fifth, incorporating an element that really doesn't belong to the Gentile power structures, and that is the Jews.

The Eugen Schlachter translation of Daniel 2:43 reads, "You have seen the iron mixed with clay, means that the people will mix by marriage but will not hold to each other, just as iron cannot be mixed with clay." And the New JPS translation from the Hebrew reads, "You saw iron mixed with common clay; that means: they shall intermingle with the offspring of man but shall not hold together just as iron does not mix with clay." Who are "they" who intermarry with the seed of man? I think the logical answer here is that they are the Jewish people.

As far as the Gentiles are concerned, intermingling was not an issue. The new countries, particularly the United States, consist of about 87% Europeans. They represent every nation from that continent. Particularly the mixture of Europeans has been successful. Americans have established an independent identity by dividing themselves from their European roots. They have intermarried, and successfully - thus, they cannot be the people who "mix by marriage but will not hold to each other." But the Jews are different. Although they, too, have mixed with the Gentiles, particularly in this century, they have not lost their identity. A Jew will always be a Jew; he is different by the ordinance of God.

Israel to be Separate

When Balaam, the heathen prophet, was supposed to curse Israel on behalf of Balak, he says about Israel, "the people shall dwell alone, and not be reckoned among the nations" (Numbers 23:9). You can count and enumerate and classify every nation, whether capitalist or communist, nationalist or socialist, monarchy or dictatorship. From God's point of view, they all are Gentiles - they belong to the iron empire - but there is only one different, and that is Israel, the Jewish people.

Deuteronomy 7:6 has this to say, "For thou art a holy people unto the LORD thy God: the LORD thy God hath chosen thee to be a special people unto himself, above all people that are upon the face of the earth."

None of us Gentiles has such a promise. Whether we are Europeans, Asians, or Africans, we belong to the iron empire. The Jews, however, have this unique calling and promise of God to be separate, to be different, and to be superior, "to make thee high above all nations which he hath made, in praise, and in name, and in honour" (Deuteronomy 26:19).

It is also significant that Israel was commanded to worship God by building an altar without using a tool of iron, "And there shalt thou build an altar unto the LORD thy God, an altar of stones: thou shalt not lift up any iron tool upon them" (Deuteronomy 27:5). We must remember that Israel did not choose herself, God chose this people, based on His eternal resolutions.

As a matter of fact, Israel did not like being the "chosen" nation. When Samuel was judge in Israel, the "elders of Israel gathered themselves together and said make us a king to judge us like all the nations" (1 Samuel 8:4-5). After Samuel warned them about their error, they nevertheless said, "Nay; but we will have a king over us; That we also may be like all the nations" (1 Samuel 8:19-20). Not only did Israel desire to be like the heathens, but they rejected their own king and chose the Roman king who occupied their land, "Pilate saith unto them, Shall I crucify your King? The chief priests answered, We have no king but Caesar" (John 19:15).

The Jews have mingled with all the nations of the world, but they have not lost their identity. Why not? Because the clay cannot mix with iron!

In Isaiah 64:8, we hear the people confess, "But now, O LORD, thou art our father; we are the clay, and thou our potter; and we all are the work of thy hand." Further, in Jeremiah 18:6 we read, "O house of Israel, cannot I do with you as this potter? saith the LORD. Behold, as the clay is in the potter's hand, so are ye in mine hand, O house of Israel."

Israel's Modem Identity Crisis

WHILE THE JEWS kept their identity for 2,000 years in the Diaspora, today, many concerned Israelis are voicing alarm that the Jewish identity may disappear in the next century.

It seems as if desperate Israel wants to be part of the nations. Jewish literature clearly reveals Israel's identity crisis and, therewith, the Jews in the world. Not only do Jews intermarry at an all-time high level, but the population in general vehemently opposes even the suggestion that they are somehow different from all the nations of the world.

Therefore, I must conclude that when Israel will be accepted in the European Union, it will constitute the covenant with the antichrist. The European Roman System of free enterprise, democracy, and freedom of religion is now sweeping the entire world. The one who will take credit for the unifying of the new One World Order, causing people to live in peace and prosperity one with another, is not too far off. To conclude, let me quote some of the literature I have recently obtained while at the European Parliament in Brussels, Belgium.

One of the stumbling stones in interpretation of the book of Daniel and Revelation 17 is the identity of the "ten horns" in Daniel 7:7 and the "ten horns" of Revelation 17:12, identified as "ten kings."

The first visible picture of unity of Europe caused

students of eschatology and scholars to be alert. In March 1957, the European Atomic Energy Commission (EAEC, better known as Eurotom) and the European Economic Community (EEC), established treaties generally known as "the Treaties of Rome." The office for official publications of the European Community answers the question, "How does the European Unity work?" with the following excerpts:

THE IDEA of Europe is an old one - it even takes its name from a character in Greek mythology. The will to create institutions leading to 'an ever-closer union among the peoples of Europe,' however, arose out of the ashes of the Second World War.

THE WASTEFULNESS OF WAR, resulting in immeasurable suffering and destruction, forced the European nations to do everything in their power to unite. The article continues:

THE PRECURSOR of today's European Union was the European Coal and Steel Community (ECSC), which was set up in 1952. Unlike these other organizations, its six founder members — Belgium, the Federal Republic of Germany, France, Italy, Luxembourg and the Netherlands — quite consciously sought to sow the seeds of greater European integration: pooling their production of coal and steel (products which then had great strategic importance) under a common organization was perceived as the best guarantee of a lasting peace in Europe.

WE MUST TAKE note that the goal of this unity is prosperity and peace. Here is how this publication explains the basis for the European Union:

THE TREATY ON EUROPEAN UNION, generally called the Maastricht Treaty, gives a single legal framework to the three European Communities (ECSC, Euratom, EEC), the origins of which go back to the 1950's.

OF THESE THREE COMMUNITIES, the European Economic Community has always occupied a special place: it has increasingly accompanied its purely economic objective - the achievement of a large common market - with complementary sectorial policies such as social and environmental policies or the development of disadvantaged regions. In order to take account of this diversification of Community tasks, the Maastricht Treaty decided to formally rename the EEC: in future, it would be known simply as the European Community.

DIVERSITY SUCCESS

DIVERSITY BECAME the key word during the continuous

development of the Union, now called the European Union. Contrary to the new countries such as America, Brazil, South Africa, Australia, Mexico, Argentina, Canada, etc., where new citizens had to separate themselves from their homeland, tradition, culture, and language, based on the doctrine of Babel, the European Union emphasizes diversity. Thus, each group of people can retain their individuality and specialize in the development of their national treasures for the benefit of the Union.

This point is extremely important to understand. When the United States, for example, reached her climax during the time when a large bulk of its population consisted of immigrants, representing an amazing diversity of people with cultural differences, traditions and languages. But they all were united under one flag, one nationality, speaking one language. In the meantime, this has proven to be of great disadvantage, particularly for English-speaking nations. Today, the customer is king. It is therefore difficult to sell an American product to France, for example, using the English language. Europe, however, has the advantage of over 40 different languages, permitting each to develop their own unique characteristics, proven for millennia. The world is diverse, and Europe is the most diverse continent, thus, she has the best chances to succeed.

SINGLE VOICE, Not Single Language

. . .

ANOTHER PUBLICATION, issued by the European Parliament, *titled* The Amsterdam Treaty and the European Parliament, *introduces the reader with these words:*

"The people of Europe want a European Union which is more democratic, more transparent and closer to their concerns. They feel that the Union should not only speak with a single voice on the international stage and coordinate economic and social policies in order to boost employment but should also be able to influence their everyday lives." The codecision procedure, involving the European Parliament and the Council of Ministers, is intended to meet this expectation. Through the codecision procedure, Parliament and the Council are also preparing together the future of the European Union.

Once the Treaty of Amsterdam, which will considerably expand the scope of this procedure, has been ratified, Parliament and the Council will have to work together in important areas such as social policy, combating fraud and the introduction of a genuine European citizenship.

We note, "A single voice on the international stage and the introduction of genuine European citizenship."

Presently, several proposals are being presented on regulating European citizenship, as represented by one passport in their respective languages.

Special resolutions were made on November 19, 1997, in the European Parliament:

- it considered that the revision of the treaty constituted genuine progress in certain important areas but did not go far enough in others;

- it welcomed the decisions taken with particular reference to employment, social rights, freedom, security and justice for the benefit of the people of Europe;
- it deplored the fact that a number of decisions were still dependent on unanimous agreement among Member States.

We Want More Europe

During my attendance at a lecture for visitors at the European Parliament in Brussels, Belgium, August 1998, we were clearly told that the progress "did not go far enough." In other words, we need more Europe and less independent national sovereignty. At this point, decisions must be made unanimous to reach agreements between member states. Obviously, that will have to be changed so other nations can be accepted as members.

Turkey, a member of NATO, has unsuccessfully tried to become a member of the European Union because Greece, a bitter enemy of Turkey, denied access for the country to join the Union. The larger the group of nations grows, the more difficult it will be to accept new members, thus, "Unanimous agreement among member states" will have to be changed in the future.

After being lectured for several hours and reading volumes of material on the development of the European Union, one message became crystal clear: European nations must unite to solidify their position as world leaders. This reminds us of Revelation 17:13, "These have one mind, and shall give their power and strength unto the beast."

Ten Toes, Ten Kings, Ten Horns

During the early development of the European Community, scholars saw ten European nations arise, which would be ruled by antichrist. Under his leadership, this union would subdue the world. In the meantime, however, there are not ten, but fifteen-member nations, with many more to be added in the near future. Therefore, we must rethink our understanding of these prophecies regarding the ten toes and the ten kings. They do not constitute ten European nations.

We have already looked at the four Gentile superpowers and emphasized that the fourth one is special, or as we read in Daniel 7, it's called "diverse" in verses 7, 19 and 23. Before the Roman Empire, a democratic system did not exist, thus, the last one is definitely different from all the others. Especially when we read chapter 7 of Daniel, we note that the previous three are clearly identified: the lion is Babylon, the bear is Medo-Persia, and the leopard is Greece. Yet, there is no animal found that could appropriately symbolize the fourth and last empire. It simply says that it is "diverse from all the beasts that were before it."

Daniel 2 clearly says that this rulership shall "bear rule

over all the earth." Revelation 13, which describes the antichrist and the false prophets, says, "and all the world wondered after the beast" (verse 3) with the end result that "all that dwell upon the earth shall worship him" (verse 8). I think this enables us to see that the Bible is not talking about ten European nations, but a truly global world.

The Global World Today

Realistically speaking, from political, economic, financial and military aspects, it is impossible for a certain group of people to literally and physically take over the world. Why? Because the world is already one. From my office in West Columbia, I can access virtually any news media in the world instantaneously through the Internet.

I can invest in futures in Australia; buy stocks in a chemical company in Israel or buy and sell U.S. Saving Bonds using the Internet without leaving my office.

The reshaping of the world is now in full progress and is much further advanced than we may want to admit. A recent article in the local newspaper revealed that for every five American jobs created, four were created by foreign companies.

Europe Leads

. . .

PIERCING THE FUTURE

AT THIS POINT IN TIME, Europe is the most powerful economic entity on earth. Democracy and free enterprise originated in Europe. Europe has the largest number of exports in the world, the greatest cash reserve. European employees enjoy a much higher income than their cousins in the United States with significantly greater benefits. For example, German citizens enjoy a minimum six-week compulsory vacation compared to only two weeks typically offered to workers in the United States.

We must add that this is only the beginning. While Americans are willing to work excessively hard for less money, they have built an amazing economic power structure. But the question we must ask is, "How long can this go on?" The old saying will come true sooner or later, "You can fool some people for some time, but you cannot fool all people all of the time."

Americans will get tired of working hard on the average 47 1/2 hours, while their European cousins, earning about 50% more, work only 35 hours a week.

Since the fall of the Berlin Wall, Europeans have experienced an economic downturn. However, we must not overlook the fact that during that time, a brand new state-of-the-art industrial infrastructure is being created and the chance to compete will be even more difficult. While the cost to accept additional Eastern European nations into the European Union may seem overwhelmingly high at the moment, the payoffs in the long run will be astronomical.

Presently, the average hourly cost for a production worker in the United States stands at $17.20. Except for the United Kingdom, Ireland, Spain, and Portugal, who are below this rate, the rest of Europe have a substantially higher scale, with Germany leading at $31.88 for one production hour. Today, protesting voices are being heard in Europe about several million jobs that have been exported to the United States because of "cheap labor." This was unthinkable only 25 years ago!

This development should not surprise students of eschatology because the fourth empire, Rome, and all that is associated with it, must lead the world just as it did when Jesus was born. The people of the prince, who destroyed the Jewish Temple on Mount Moriah in Jerusalem, will be in charge of world politics, economy, finances, military, and religion at the second coming of Jesus.

The reshaping of Europe and the world is in full swing today and nothing will stand in the way for the prophetic Word to be fulfilled.

In closing, let me quote another publication titled, *Europe On The Move*, a European-commissioned publication completed in April 1996:

THE DEMOCRATIC FORM of government bequeathed to us by the Greeks was to become a cornerstone of European civilization. With their written law, the Romans endowed Europe with the rules which order our relations with each other. In the 16th and 17th centuries, the likes of Copernicus, Galileo, Kepler, Descartes, Huygens and Newton paved the way for modern science. Before the advent of nationalism, 'European careers' were quite normal. Craftsmen plied their trade all over the continent, learning as they went from one country to the next, without worrying about borders. Erasmus, who was born in Rotterdam 500 years ago, studied in Paris, obtained a doctorate in Turin and taught in Cambridge for more than a decade. He died in Basle. Despite the many languages and regional dialects, the knowledge of philosophers and scientists spread everywhere, contributing to the cross fertilization of ideas. Artists from all countries met to exchange ideas. The peoples of Europe have always been linked by a shared culture.

DEMOCRACY IS MARCHING ON; so is free enterprise, resulting in more freedom, more prosperity, more material advantages, and more knowledge than ever before. This is exactly in line with the prophecies found in Revelation 18:3:

> For all nations have drunk of the wine of the wrath of her fornication, and the kings of the earth have committed fornication with her, and the merchants of the earth are waxed rich through the abundance of her delicacies.

3

PART 1: RUSSIAN ROULETTE

BY DAVID BENOIT

The Hibernating Bear and Her Crafty Cubs

When you read the newspapers, it is easy to fall into the trap of believing that the Russian bear is dead, or that her powers are diminished because of her limited movement. Some may tell you that she is financially strapped and unable to aggressively launch an all-out attack. What we are seeing in Russia is not a sickly, helpless bear. What we are seeing is a hibernating bear.

Before a bear goes into hibernation, it will conquer and devour as much food as it can before its winter rest. During the cold war, Russia, through Communistic doctrine, went about conquering and consuming, and she was storing up for her winter nap. Let's take a look at the correlation between the Russian bear and the hibernating bear.

In preparation for hibernation, a bear will store up

food. Bears, however, are not perfect hibernators. Unlike smaller animals, a bear will awaken during the hibernation period. There are several reasons bears will awaken:

1. They will awaken if they did not store up enough body fat. Russia had a feast time during the cold war. Now she is satisfied for a time.

2. They will awaken if it warms up during the winter and food becomes available. As things start to heat up in the Middle East, this bear will interpret this time as spring and will start to eye Israel as an easy meal.

3. Mothers who give birth to cubs during this time may not hibernate at all. This mother bear is resting, but she is about to perform a freak of nature. Usually a bear will only give birth to 1-3 cubs. The Russian bear will give birth to five cubs. The five nations that will join Russia are as follows:

1. Persia   Modern Iran
2. Ethiopia   Black African nations (South Africa)
3. Libya   Arabic African nations (North Africa)
4. Gomer   East Germany
5. Togarmah   Southern Russian and Cossacks
                 or perhaps Turkey

4. Bears can be awakened by noises in the woods. The sounds of war and rumors will reach the ears of this bear. She will awaken and will wander in her post hibernation stupor.

It is quite amazing to me that every time America challenges a country in the Middle East, Russia tells us to back off. Even when NATO went into the Balkans, you could hear the rumbling in Russia.

5. A bear that awakens from hibernation will look weak because it has lost some body fat during the seven months of dormancy. But, do not be fooled into believing this bear is weak. A weak bear has been known to chase down elk and break the neck of that elk. That is some kind of power!

History tells us that Hitler was once lured into believing that Russia could be overtaken. To think that the Russian bear was limited in its resources for war was a grave mistake that would prove to be disastrous to Hitler's campaign. The newspapers would have us to believe that Russia is weak, poor, and compliant. The media would have you believe that Russia is collapsing right before our eyes. We send billions of dollars to Russia to help save their economy. Humanitarian aid is sent to Russia by Americans every year. I have personally been in Moscow and fed hungry people and passed out Bibles, but I am not buying it for one minute that Russia is a feeble country who has lost her desire to conquer.

Ezekiel 38:4-6 gives us a look at this bear and the power that she will have as she comes down on Israel:

> And I will turn thee back, and put hooks into thy jaws, and I will bring thee forth, and all thine army, horses and horsemen., all of them clothed with all sorts of armor, even a great company with bucklers and shields, all of them handling swords: Persia, Ethiopia, and Libya with them; all of them with shield and helmet; Gomer, and all

his bands; the house of Togarmah of the north quarters, and all his bands: and many people with thee.

Therefore, son of man, prophesy and say unto Gog, thus saith the Lord GOD; In that day when my people of Israel dwelleth safely, shalt thou not know it?

How Do We Know it is the Russian Bear That Attacks Israel?

THE BOOK of Ezekiel tells us that the enemy will come from the north down on Israel:

> 38:15 — And thou shalt come from thy place out of the north parts, thou, and many people with thee, all of them riding upon horses, a great company, and a mighty army.
>
> 39:2 — And I will turn thee back, and leave but the sixth part of thee, and will cause thee to come up from the north parts and will bring thee upon the mountains of Israel.

A quick look at a world map will show you that Russia is directly north of Israel.

Why Does the Bear Attack Israel?

. . .

Dr. Harold Willmington gives three good reasons for Russia to come down on Israel:

1. To cash in on the riches of Palestine (Ezekiel 38:11, 12).
2. To control the Middle East. Ancient conquerors have always known that he who would control Europe, Asia, and Africa must first control the Middle East bridge which leads to these three continents.
3. To challenge the authority of the antichrist (Daniel 11:4044) *(Willmington's Guide to the Bible,* p. 221).

What Will Be the Results of This Attack?

This battle will be an incredible battle, and one that Israel will win. Let's read what the Bible has to say about this war:

1. There will be a killer earthquake.

Ezekiel 38:19,20 - For in my jealousy and in the fire of my wrath have I spoken, Surely in that day there shall be a great shaking in the land of Israel; So that the fishes of the sea, and the fowls of the heaven, and the beasts of the field, and all creeping things that creep upon the earth, and all the men that are upon the face of the earth, shall shake at my presence, and the mountains shall be thrown down, and the steep places shall fall, and every wall shall fall to the ground.

2. The troops will turn on themselves.

Ezekiel 38:21 - And I will call for a sword against him throughout all my mountains, saith the Lord GOD: every man's sword shall be against his brother.

3. The armies will be plagued.

Ezekiel 38:22 - And I will plead against him with pestilence and with blood; and I will rain upon him, and upon his bands, and upon the many people that are with him, an overflowing rain, and great hailstones, fire, and brimstone.

4. God will destroy many troops by raining hailstones on them.

Ezekiel 38:22 - And I will plead against him with pestilence and with blood; and I will rain upon him, and upon his bands, and upon the many people that are with him, an overflowing rain, and great hailstones, fire, and brimstone.

5. God will send fire down on them.

Ezekiel 39:6 - And I will send a fire on Magog, and among them that dwell carelessly in the isles: and they shall know that I am the LORD.

THE DEVASTATION **of this war will destroy communism forever:**

1. 83% of the troops will be killed.

Ezekiel 39:1,2 - Therefore, thou son of man, prophesy against Gog, and say, Thus saith the Lord GOD; Behold, I am against thee, O Gog, the chief prince of Meshech and Tubal: And I will turn thee back and leave but the sixth part of thee, and will cause thee to come up from the north parts, and will bring thee upon the mountains of Israel.

2. It will take seven months to bury all the dead.

Ezekiel 39:11-15 - And it shall come to pass in that day, that I will give unto Gog a place there of graves in Israel, the valley of the passengers on the east of the sea: and it shall stop the noses of the passengers: and there shall they bury Gog and all his multitude: and they shall call it the valley of Hamongog.

And seven months shall the house of Israel be burying of them, that they may cleanse the land.

Yea, all the people of the land shall bury them; and it shall be to them a renown the day that I shall be glorified, saith the Lord GOD.

And they shall sever out men of continual employment, passing through the land to bury with the passengers those that remain upon the face of the earth, to cleanse it: after the end of seven months shall they search.

And the passengers that pass through the land, when any seeth a man's bone, then shall he set up a sign by it, till the buriers have buried it in the valley of Hamongog.

3. It will take seven years to destroy all the weapons.

Ezekiel 39:9,10 - And they that dwell in the cities of Israel shall go forth, and shall set on fire and burn the weapons, both the shields and the bucklers, the bows and the arrows, and the hand staves, and the spears, and they shall burn them with fire seven years: so that they shall take no wood out of the field, neither cut down any out of the forests; for they shall burn the weapons with fire: and they shall spoil those that spoiled them, and rob those that robbed them, saith the Lord GOD.

For the last few years we have seen the Russian bear hibernating. When she wakes up, she will be hungry. She will cast her eyes on Israel and she will try to take the spoil. There will be only one thing that this atheistic country does not consider and that is a divine intervention by an almighty God.

God will show no mercy to this bear and her cubs.

4

PART 2: RUSSIA AND FRIENDS

BY WILLIAM T. JAMES

Russia is in turmoil perhaps even beyond that of its pre-Revolutionary days during the first part of the 20th century. Like the Bolshevik rumblings, the growlings of the Russian military and the groanings of the Russian people are beginning to elicit serious concerns from the international community today.

Recent political struggles within Russia's ruling circles reflect the chaos rampant throughout the nation itself. My belief is that only God's staying hand has kept the bear at bay through a quasi-democratic effort in the aftermath of the Soviet Union's dissolution. Only God Himself knows what will happen now that Boris Yeltsin has resigned.

Certainly, Russia continues to be a powder keg whose fuse is lit. The explosion is coming, and God's Word says it is coming thusly:

> Be thou prepared, and prepare for thyself, thou, and all

thy company that are assembled unto thee, and be thou a guard unto them. After many days thou shalt be visited; in the latter years thou shalt come into the land that is brought back from the sword, and is gathered out of many peoples, against the mountains of Israel, which have been always waste; but it is brought forth out of the nations, and they shall dwell safely, all of them. Thou shalt ascend and come like a storm; thou shalt be like a cloud to cover the land, thou, and all thy hordes, and many peoples with thee. Thus saith the Lord God: It shall also come to pass that at the same time shall things come into thy mind, and thou shall think an evil thought; And thou shalt say, I will go up to the land of unwalled villages; I will go to those who are at rest, who dwell safely, all of them dwelling without walls, and having neither bars nor gates, To take a spoil, and to take a prey (Ezekiel 38:7-12a).

Gog in the Making

RUSSIA'S TURMOIL forced Boris Yeltsin to juggle that nation's leadership. He fired Victor Chernomyrdin, Yevgeny Primakov and Sergei Stepashin, who vowed to fight the tremendous poverty in Russia and to deal severely with crime and criminals while implementing economic reforms. Yeltsin then replaced Stepashin with Vladimir Putin, who, as prime minister, likewise vowed to perform economic wizardry.

The shake-ups continue today. The moves seem meant to rev up the Russian economy. No one, however, including Vladimir Putin — who has since been appointed Russia's president — seems to know from where the economic infusion will come.

The Ezekiel 38 scenario seems to indicate that economic considerations are the primary stimuli that convince the leader of the invasion force to go and "take a great spoil." Certainly, democratic free-market reforms have not worked for Russia to this point. Seventy-four-plus years of soul-shattering Communist rule all but denuded a number of generations of their will and productive ambition. It will likely require a jump-start of spectacular proportions for Russia's economy to stir to life in the foreseeable future.

"Taking spoil" from a neighbor would be much more in the Cossack history and tradition of the region called, in ancient Biblical terms, Magog. Apparently, this fact of history is not lost on the last-days Russian leader called Gog who will convince these to do what they historically have done best, plunder and ransack their enemies.

Stepashin apparently agreed with Gog's assessment, if his words upon being confirmed are to be believed. Stepashin said:

> .... history shows that poverty and economic fall create very favorable conditions for the advent to power of criminal structures. This scenario is the worst for Russia ever. It is extremely dangerous and highly probable (*CNN Headline News,* May 19, 1999).

OTHER CONSIDERATIONS

RUSSIA CONTINUES to build militarily despite the fact that the nation is in deep economic depression. While their leadership talks of the desire for peace and reform to a freer enterprise system, they arm for warfare against undisclosed enemies. They claim in the post-Cold War era that they have turned their ICBM missiles to the oceans of the world away from former targeted cities within the United States. Yet by all accounts it would take no more than three minutes to retarget those cities.

Perhaps most troubling of all is recent discoveries of underground subways beneath the city of Moscow. Also, Bill Gertz, a journalist with the *Washington Times* and author of the number-one best-seller non-fiction book *Betrayal*, says his investigation shows the Russians:

> ....are continuing to build a multi-billion dollar, in ruble equivalent, underground command facility in the Urals Mountains ... [no one is] actually sure why they're doing this. But the fact of the matter is it's a sign that the Russians feel it important enough to invest money enough to protect their leaders from nuclear attack. There are a couple of suggestions. One is that it is a command structure. This is a very large area ... an underground city about the size of the area inside the Washington D.C. Beltway ... its construction has been going on for years.

Here is almost a bankrupt state, Russia, investing billions of dollars ... you've got to ask the question 'why?' They are obviously anticipating that in the future they might have to fight a nuclear war (*Point of View, USA Radio Network,* May, 1999).

Marlin Maddoux, as part of his interview with Bill Gertz, read an excerpt from Maddoux's book:

> There are suggestions that nuclear missiles may be secretly deployed at this site as part of what has been called The Dead-Hand Doomsday System, a nuclear command program designed to fire nuclear missiles automatically in the aftermath of a first strike on Russia (*Point of View, USA Radio Network,* May, 1999).

All of the talk about dismantling ICBM weapons is just that, "talk," at least as far as Russia is concerned. While it is true that America continues to destroy its nuclear arsenal in compliance with Strategic Arms Limitations Talk agreements, Russia continues to construct and deploy weapons capable of reaping total devastation anywhere on earth.

Again, Bill Gertz spoke to the facts regarding Russia's nuclear arms build-up in relationship to the billions of dollars given them by the International Monetary Fund (IMF) which, of course, is mostly funded by the United States. Speaking about America's agreeing to release these funds to Russia, Gertz said:

> You have a situation where the American administration adopted a program that they call the Cooperative Threat

Reduction. They titled it as something that is good for American national security. But in reality, it's one of those programs [that's] the foreign policy equivalent of throwing money at a problem. The program hasn't been focused. The Russians didn't really want the money. They are not that interested in dismantling their weapons. But what it did do with this program is to free up other money that the Russians have so that they can go ahead and develop a new nuclear missile.

They have a new second-generation mobile missile. They are the only country in the world that has deployed a mobile intercontinental ballistic missile. Why is that a concern? Because we saw during the Persian Gulf War, when we tried to find Iraqi short- range missiles it was almost impossible to track down these mobile missiles. They can be driven, they can be hidden ... if you have a missile that can travel intercontinental range that can also be driven around everywhere, it poses a real threat. It can be stolen. It can be driven away. It can be driven out of the country. [This second-generation] is called the SS-27 (*Point of View, USA Radio Network*, May, 1999).

Russia's alliances of late portend trouble for the future. Before his dismissal, Primakov made many trips to leaders of nations surrounding Russia and reportedly cemented pacts calling for at the very least mutual cooperation in like-regional interests. In doing so, many animosities have apparently been forgotten so that common purpose can be pursued. We must wonder if that common purpose might at some point include oil and mineral riches to Russia's south and the spoils of Israel in particular.

Several concerns involving Russia occupy the thinking of a number of geopolitical observers at this moment in history. Some of these include:

LAUNCH CONTROLS

EXPERTS in nuclear weaponry and delivery systems have expressed concern that former Soviet ICBM launch controls have degraded to a dangerous point. This in conjunction with Russia's early warning system failures cause alarm for those who study such things. Human error and miscalculation round out the scope of the problem.

The world came perilously close to a nuclear Armageddon on January 25, 1995, when Russian President Boris Yeltsin learned that Russian early-warning systems had picked up signals indicating a possible ICBM launch toward Russian territory. He had four minutes to decide whether to begin a retaliatory response.

When the rocket's boosters fell back to earth, Russian early- warning systems indicated the possibility that the representations on the screens were possibly multiple re-entry warheads. As the moment of decision for Yeltsin swiftly approached, he was informed at the last second that the launch in question was a meteorological rocket fired from Norway to gather information about the Aurora Borealis. It was later learned that Moscow had been notified in advance of the Norwegian launch, but no one thought to pass word onto senior military officials.

Reportedly, such near-mishaps have also plagued America's early-warning systems of late.

Future Technological Fears

MANY EXPERTS FEARED that the year 2000 computer problems might cause accidental launches or inadvertent early warning signals that launches had occurred. Thankfully, that did not happen. The millennium bug that some said could cause massive disruptions throughout the world was particularly troubling to those who feared computer chip components might fail when the clock rolled over at midnight, December 31, 1999.

Particularly troubling was the knowledge that Russia's satellite computer ICBM linkages were far from being Y2K compliant. Even the normally highly secretive Russians agreed to exchange on-the-spot observers with United States counterparts as the midnight hour approached.

The Chinese nuclear launch facilities lagged even farther behind the Russians in Y2K compliance. Much of the Chinese technologies — as we now know — have been stolen by or purchased by our supposed Chinese trading partners. Because America's launch capabilities required intensive work in order to prevent Y2K problems, we can know that the Chinese faced the same problems. The Chinese, however, have not been willing to admit they possess purchased or stolen ICBM launch technologies, much less were they willing to allow American observers in their launch facilities in order to avert possible problems as the year 2000 roll-over occurred. I believe many prayers were answered.

Russian - Chinese Weapons Technology Transfers

Chinese war-making capabilities have been greatly enhanced on the conventional level as well. Russia has been primarily responsible for upgrading China's conventional war machine.

Chief among the technologies from the Russians is the SU27 Flanker fighter plane which is the equivalent to America's F-16 Falcon. It is estimated that they are producing 2,000 per year.

Additionally, China is rapidly building its navy and ICBM forces using technology - as stated before - from American manufacturers such as Boeing, McDonnell Douglas and other major multinational corporations.

The Chinese are apparently now able to test nuclear weapons - the weapons which they have also stolen or purchased - by using only computer simulation technologies given them by spies operating with the Alamogordo, New Mexico, top-secret laboratories.

Chinese Transfer of War Technologies

. . .

To further exacerbate the growing threat of global war, the Communist Chinese continue to give, for certain militarily beneficial exchange, computer and missile technologies stolen from the West to diabolist regimes in the East.

Both Iran and Iraq are feared to be the beneficiaries of such technology transfers. Apparently, it is just a matter of time before either of these two tyrant-led nations will be capable of striking not only their neighbors within the region but America's heartland as well.

Truly Gog is in the making. While Ezekiel 38 and 39 can be seen coming into focus just on the horizon, so that red dragon, China, is clearly developing as a potential candidate for the rising sun king of the East force of Revelation 9:14-18 and Revelation 16:12.

5
ASIA'S ARMAGEDDON ARMY

BY J. MICHAEL HILE

One morning after returning from an early church service in a small town in the heart of America, the railroad crossbars went down, and the bell loudly clanged its familiar warning. As the long train slowly moved northward, the names printed on the sides of the boxcars were noticeably different from the companies and manufacturers that had been a familiar sight on America's railroads for almost half a century. The boxcars were all labeled with names of Chinese companies.

Most of the Chinese acronyms were unfamiliar; however, the name "COSCO" kept showing up on many of the boxcars. COSCO stands for the Chinese Overseas Shipping Company. While waiting at the railroad crossing on this sunny July 4th, some 200-plus years after the Declaration of Independence was signed, I pondered the many changes that have taken place in the United States in recent years. How long would we continue to enjoy the freedoms that have been passed down to us by the founding fathers of this nation? How long would God's hand of protection be upon us despite the rapid moral and spiritual decline that has engulfed our country? How long, O Lord, before You intervene in the affairs of mankind and set up your eternal kingdom? How long, O Lord?

While attending a Bible college in the late 1950's in southern Arkansas, my sister studied under an economics teacher, an old professor who, cognizant of the future, told his class one of the things they should fear was Red China. Today, that "sleeping giant" has awakened from centuries of dormancy to begin its rise to world prominence as anticipated by many students of Bible prophecy.

The Kings of the East Head West

THE BOOK of Revelation speaks of an "end-time" gathering of kings from the East that will join other armies in the valley of Megiddo in order to take control of the land given to Abraham, Isaac, Jacob and their descendants. Although China's name is not specifically mentioned in the Bible, this large country located east of the Euphrates is uniquely qualified as a candidate for the final battle of the age that is sometimes called "the battle of Armageddon."

> And the sixth angel poured out his vial upon the great river Euphrates; and the water thereof was dried up, that the way of the kings of the east might be prepared. And I

saw three unclean spirits like frogs come out of the mouth of the dragon, and out of the mouth of the beast, and out of the mouth of the false prophet. For they are the spirits of devils, working miracles, which go forth unto the kings of the earth and of the whole world, to gather them to the battle of that great day of God Almighty. Behold, I come as a thief. Blessed is he that watcheth, and keepeth his garments, lest he walk naked, and they see his shame. And he gathered them together into a place called in the Hebrew tongue Armageddon (Revelation 16:12-16).

THE BATTLE of Armageddon

ALTHOUGH MANY IN the world consider the word "Armageddon" synonymous with any major war that appears on the horizon, "Armageddon" is the ultimate final battle between good and evil that will be fought by the King of kings and Lord of lords at the close of this dispensation. The armies of the world, who have been deceived by the dragon, the beast, and the false prophet, will be marshaled into action by a hoard of demonic spirits who have destructive designs for planet earth he events leading up to the climax of Armageddon described in chapter 16 of Revelation are detailed in chapter 9, where the kings of the East destroy a large portion of the earth's population as they traverse westward across the Euphrates River en route to the Promised Land.

And the sixth angel sounded, and I heard a voice from the four horns of the golden altar which is before God, saying to the sixth angel which had the trumpet, loose the four angels which are bound in the great river Euphrates. And the four angels were loosed, which were prepared for an hour, and a day, and a month, and a year, for to slay the third part of men. And the number of the army of the horsemen were two hundred thousand, and I heard the number of them. And thus I saw the horses in the vision, and them that sat on them, having breastplates of fire, and of jacinth, and brimstone: and the heads of the horses were as the heads of lions; and out of their mouths issued fire and smoke and brimstone. By these three was the third part of men killed, by the fire, and by the smoke, and by the brimstone, which issued out of their mouths. For their power is in their mouth, and in their tails: for their tails were like unto serpents, and had heads, and with them they do hurt. And the rest of the men which were not killed by these plagues yet repented not of the works of their hands, that they should not worship devils, and idols of gold, and silver, and brass, and stone, and of wood: which neither can see, nor hear, nor walk: Neither repented they of their murders, nor of their sorceries, nor of their fornication nor of their thefts (Revelation 9:13-21).

THE SATANIC FACTOR

. . .

THE ARMY of 200 million horsemen is marshaled into action by four demonic angels bound at the Euphrates River. They are commissioned to kill a third of the earth's population. The fourth seal which unleashes the pale horse in Revelation 6:8 has already killed one-fourth of the human race with sword, hunger, death, and the beasts of the earth. With less than three-fourths of the earth's population remaining when the 200-million-man army begins its carnage, an additional third of the people on earth are killed, thus reducing the population of the earth by one-half.

The world's population crossed the six-billion mark during the latter half of 1999. Using that figure as a benchmark and discounting the effect of future wars and famines, there will be at least three-billion people killed prior to the final battle that takes place in Israel at the close of the great tribulation. This will include one-and-one-half billion deaths worldwide after the fourth seal is opened and an additional one-and-one-half billion, primarily in Asia, after the sixth angel sounds his trumpet.

Mobilizing the Largest Army on Earth

WHETHER THE 200-MILLION-MAN army is a human army that is demonically influenced or an army that is entirely demonic in nature is not altogether clear from the text. The fire, smoke, and brimstone is an apt description of modern warfare involving gunpowder and explosives, however, the strange-looking horses may be demonic in nature like the locusts described in the preceding verses of chapter nine. Since the kings of the east are destined to bring their armies across the Euphrates, the large army is probably comprised of humans rather than of demons riding horses.

In 1965, an article in *Time* magazine stated that China was able to field an army of 200 million men. China had an estimated population of 1.2 billion in 1998 and projects 1.8 billion by the year 2020. Since several kings of the east are involved in the march toward Israel, fielding a 200-million- man army is in the realm of possibility. The logistics of quickly moving an army this size across the Euphrates River and into the Mideast is formidable due to the large amount of food and water necessary. This army, however, is energized by the demons loosed from the Euphrates and it will be capable of superhuman endurance.

If the 200-million-man army is a hoard of demons, one wonders why these demons will have lost their ability to function as free spirits, as opposed to being confined to a cavalry-based army.

On the other hand, the earth during this time will experience a bombardment of demonic forces from the bottomless pit (center of earth) that has never been witnessed before. Understanding the true nature of the 200-million-man army may not be possible from our perspective. It is possible the apocalyptic riders will be both human and demonic in nature since Satan will be exerting his influence on the armies of the world in a way that this world has never seen before.

. . .

The Euphrates River to **Be Dried Up**

Perhaps the most conspicuous force gathered at the battle of God Almighty (Armageddon) is these kings of the east who miraculously cross the Euphrates River which will be dried up through drought or possibly because of a series of dams that have been constructed in recent years.

Prior to the 20th century and the invention of airplanes, rockets, and other forms of modern warfare, an invasion of the Middle East from nations east of the Euphrates, as described in the book of Revelation, would be expected to be primarily ground forces with a large contingent of horsemen. With the advent of new weapon systems, including advanced fighter jets, intercontinental ballistic missiles (ICBMs) and other strategic weapons following World War II, the scenario describing the large armies that are to cross the Euphrates seems to be primitive by today's standards of combat.

We need to remember, however, that a large portion of the earth's population will have been exterminated toward the latter stages of the great tribulation. Many of the weapons of mass destruction will already have been used or rendered useless by a warfare technology called electromagnetic pulsing or deemed inappropriate for accomplishing strategic goals in the land of Israel. Whatever the reason, the kings of the east seem to follow a more primitive mode of warfare involving large numbers of soldiers rather than the high-tech weapons in abundance today that could quickly decimate a large army. The ability of the kings of the east to cross the Euphrates and enter the Holy Land without being quickly wiped out indicates that more conventional weapons will be used rather than today's strategic nuclear weapons.

WHO ARE the Kings of the East?

IT IS NOT YET evident from our vantage point which nations will make up "the kings of the east." Until the 200 million warriors actually cross the Euphrates, we can only speculate as to who they will be. Traditionally, China has been the major candidate mentioned among Bible scholars. "Kings of the east," however, implies a confederacy of several nations that unites to accomplish a diabolical plan. Since the Euphrates River will be dried up to prepare the way for the kings of the east, we must obviously include only those nations that are east of the Euphrates.

The Euphrates, which is the longest river in western Asia, is 1,700 miles in length. It begins its journey in the mountains of eastern Turkey around the 40th parallel, crosses eastern Syria, and flows southeastward through Iraq where it joins the Tigris River. The two rivers merge in a swamp to form the Shatt-el- Arab, which empties into the Persian Gulf at the 30th parallel.

The land between the Euphrates and Tigris supported an early center of civilization called Mesopotamia. The kingdoms of Assyria to the north and Babylon to the south, described in the Old Testament, are the progenitors of modern-day Syria and Iraq. When the Assyrian and Babylonian armies invaded Israel between 722 and 586 BC, they followed the Euphrates River northwest and then cut back southwest across modern- day Syria and Lebanon to enter the land of Israel.

This route assured an adequate water supply and prevented certain death in the Syrian Desert to the south, which is located in today's Jordan and Saudi Arabia. If the kings of the east follow a similar route when they hasten to their appointment with destiny in the valley of Megiddo, they will cross the Euphrates around the 35th parallel before heading southwest toward the Promised Land.

If we assume that the invading armies from the east (Revelation 16:12) cross the Euphrates at the same location (35th parallel) that was followed by the ancient armies of Assyria and Babylon, we can extend an imaginary line eastward to see which nations might comprise "the kings of the east." An imaginary line crossing the Euphrates in Syria and going east would pass through Iraq (ancient Babylon), Iran (ancient Persia), Afghanistan, Pakistan, India and China. The same imaginary line extended eastward from Jerusalem (32nd parallel) would pass through the same countries.

The westward march of the large army from the east would of necessity incorporate or decimate all the nations that it would pass through. Nations from Southeast Asia that might join Asia's Armageddon army include Nepal, Bhutan, Pakistan, Burma, Thailand, Laos, Cambodia, Malaysia, and North and South Vietnam. Japan, known as "the land of the rising sun," and Taiwan are both east of China and would qualify as "kings of the east" or "kings of the sunrise," however, their involvement will likely be limited due to a lack of direct access to the Asian mainland. Since the "kings of the east" implies nations directly east of the Euphrates, the primary candidates for this designation, based upon today's national boundaries, would be Iran, Afghanistan, Pakistan, India, and China.

China's Rise to Power

Up until the latter half of the 20th century, China remained a primitive country for the most part, with minimal progress in its economic and manufacturing base. The limited influx of modern technology into China from 1949 to 1973 restricted economic growth and expansion that was commonplace in the United States and Europe. That has all changed in the last decade. The label "Made in China" has recently replaced "Made in Japan" and "Made in Taiwan" on many of the goods purchased in America and throughout the world. In his bestselling book, *Megatrends Asia,* John Naisbitt states:

> What is happening in Asia is by far the most important development in the world today. Nothing else comes close - not only for Asians but for the entire planet. The modernization of Asia will forever reshape the world as we move toward the next millennium ... Until the 1990's everything revolved around the West. The West set the rules. Japan abided by these rules during its economic emergence. But now Asians - the rest of Asia - are

creating their own rules and will soon determine the game as well.

In the 1990's, Asia came of age ... Asia will become the dominant region of the world: economically, politically and culturally. We are bn the threshold of the Asian Renaissance ... the principal emphasis is on China, Hong Kong, India, Indonesia, Japan, South Korea, Malaysia, the Philippines, Singapore, Taiwan, Thailand and Vietnam. That is where the main dynamic of growth and change is located ... The global axis of influence has shifted from West to East. Asia was once the center of the world, and now the center is again returning to Asia (*Megatrends Asia, Eight Asian Megatrends that are reshaping our world,* John Naisbitt, Simon & Schuster, 1996, pp. 10, 12, 16).

CHINA: **The Last Superpower**

THE RAPID RISE of China to world prominence is likely to have major implications for world peace during the Twenty- first Century. Nearly 200 years ago, Napoleon Bonaparte, French military leader and emperor of France (1804-15), stated: "When China awakens, the world will tremble." The sleeping giant awoke during the final decade of the 20th century as the Bush and Clinton administrations allowed the Chinese spy network to infiltrate many of the military and defense installations and steal the nation's top military secrets. *The Cox Report* published in May of 1999 detailed much of the espionage engaged in by the Chinese.

During the years following World War II, the United States helped rebuild Japan's economy. Devastation caused by the atomic bombs that were dropped on Hiroshima and Nagasaki prompted Japan to neglect the rebuilding of its military in order to pursue a purely commercial course involving the manufacture of goods and services. For many years, the words "Made in Japan" were associated with cheap, inferior products. Japan quickly reversed its course and jumped into the manufacture of electronics and automobiles and became a world leader in high- tech goods and services. Brands such as Toshiba, Nissan and Toyota are commonplace in today's economy.

The words "Made in Japan" were soon joined by "Made in Taiwan" and more recently "Made in China" as inexpensive products from the Far East flooded the marketplace and whetted the appetites of the industrialized nations in the West. In recent years, China's mass production of goods and services with cheap labor has attracted the attention of foreign investors and businesses from both the United States and Europe.

China's ready access to American technology and top military secrets has opened a Pandora's box that will accelerate an arms buildup of both nuclear and conventional weapons among the enemies of "the free world." Many observers, this writer included, believe that the irresponsible and insane actions of the power brokers and politicians in Washington will likely come back to haunt the United States and perhaps the whole world in the foreseeable future.

RUSSIA - CHINA: The New World Superpower

ON JANUARY 4, the 1999 annual forecast and Global Intelligence Update from STRATFOR.COM titled *"A New and Dangerous World"* projected that "Russia and China will be moving into a closer, primarily anti-American alliance in 1999 ... The Post-Cold War world quietly ended in 1998. A new era will emerge in 1999 ... We should not think of the period 1989-1998 as an era. It was an interregnum, a pause between two eras ... 1999 is the first of many years of increasing tension and conflict involving not only minor players, but also the world's great powers. It is the beginning of what will prove to be a tense first decade in the 21st century."

Russia and China's new strategic alliance is designed to neutralize the effect of the United States in the economic and geopolitical spheres. How they plan to accomplish that goal has ominous implications since neither Russia nor China can compete economically with the United States. Colonel Stanislav Lunev, the highest-ranking military officer ever to defect to the U.S., in an article titled *"Russia-China, the New World Superpower"* written for NEWSMAX.COM, states:

> Seminal change has taken place in the balance of world power, and scant notice has been paid to this dramatic

shift. Russia and China, for decades hostile enemies, are moving ever closer to forming a political and military alliance to challenge the United States and the West .... The military ties between Russia and China began to develop in 1992. These were, and still are, characterized by active military sharing on the highest levels, with ongoing cooperation in the development and production of the most modern weapons systems .... The West should be alarmed by such an alliance. The two countries together would combine the largest conventional army, the Chinese army, with the largest atomic arsenal, the Russian nuclear stockpile. Again, this menacing shift of power, which will likely be realized in the next few months, will have dramatic consequences for our civilization that cannot be overestimated.

At a meeting on June 9, 1999, between Russian Prime Minister Sergei Stepashin and Chinese delegation-head Zhang Wannian, deputy chief of the Central Military Commission of the CCP Mr. Stepashin made it absolutely clear that: "Building close ties with China is one of Russia's top foreign-policy priorities and that the two nations desire a strong strategic partnership." According to Lunev:

Both nations have already introduced compatible weapons systems. By integrating the weapons systems of the Russian Armed Forces and the Chinese People's Liberation Army, the two countries are rapidly becoming a superpower. More-over, cooperation between Russia and Red China is expanding in the area of intelligence, which is laying the foundation for a climate of mutual trust in Russian-Chinese relations, including guarantees of each other's mutual security. Thus, all the necessary preconditions for the strategic alliance between the Russian Federation and Communist China are in place. And this alliance could threaten the United States and the West much sooner than anyone thinks.

Russia, China, NATO and the New World Order

The Kosovo crisis in the Spring of 1999, initiated by NATO (North Atlantic Treaty Organization), under the direction of President Bill Clinton and Prime Minister Tony Blair of Great Britain, greatly increased tensions between the United States, Russia, and China. This first-time use of NATO as an offensive force rather than for defensive purposes set a new precedent that some believe may be used to provide the military muscle necessary to set up and enforce the new world order (now called "global governance"). This abuse of power marked the first time that NATO forces had invaded a sovereign nation, Yugoslavia. The United Nations (UN) was not consulted by the leaders of NATO since it is certain that both Russia and China would have vetoed the invasion had the UN become involved in the decision-making process.

The invasion of the province of Kosovo in Yugoslavia provided cover for the Clinton administration scandals and helped set the stage for future military excursions by NATO. This act of military aggression may be part of a larger plan to use NATO to enforce global peacekeeping operations. Peacekeeping troops sent to the island of Timor in Indonesia during the latter part of 1999 serve as another example of the movement towards an international peacekeeping force.

One of Clinton's global strategists, Strobe Talbott, Deputy Secretary of State, before joining the administration, wrote in an essay titled *"The Birth of the Global Nation"* which appeared in *TIME* magazine that he is looking forward to government run by "one global authority." "Here is one optimist's reason for believing unity will prevail... within the next hundred years ... nationhood as we know it will be obsolete; all states will recognize a single, global authority," Talbott remarked in the July 20, 1992, issue. He continued, "All countries are basically social arrangements, accommodations to changing circumstances. No matter how permanent and even sacred they may seem at any one time, in fact they are all artificial and temporary."

Talbott's allusion to a 100-year goal for setting up a world government is a smoke screen to disguise the real intentions of the globalists, who are looking at a shorter time span, perhaps a few months or years, to put their plan in place. The linkage between a global government and Christ's return is contained in Daniel's vision of the great image, and an amazing future glimpse of God's displeasure with the nations of the world is revealed in the book of Psalms.

And the fourth kingdom (Final Gentile World Empire)

shall be strong as iron: forasmuch as iron breaketh in pieces and subdueth all things: and as iron that breaketh all these, shall it break in pieces and bruise ... And in the days of these kings shall the God of heaven set up a kingdom, which shall never be destroyed (Daniel 2:40, 41).

> Why do the heathen (nations) rage, and the people imagine a vain thing? The kings of the earth set themselves, and the rulers take counsel together, against the Lord, and against his anointed, saying let us break their bands asunder, and cast away their cords from us. He that sitteth in the heavens shall laugh: the Lord shall have them in derision. Then shall he speak unto them in his wrath and vex them in his sore displeasure ... Thou shalt break them with a rod of iron; thou shalt dash them in pieces like a potter's vessel (Psalm 2:1-9).

The coming world government system, which is already in an advanced stage of development, will seek to stifle religious freedom and expression and outlaw the teachings contained in the Bible. As Psalm 2 alludes, the nations of the world will directly oppose God, the Word of God, and those who follow God. This soon-coming global government, which may be only months or years away, should be a wake-up call to all believers, since the events of the great tribulation and the return of Christ are directly linked to implementation of a world government system.

Russia and China **Accelerate Relationship**

. . .

As a result of NATO's military involvement in Kosovo, Russia and China accelerated their movement toward a strategic partnership. In June of 1999, the Secretary of Russia's Security Council and Federal Security Service Director Vladimir Putin (now acting-president) met with the Deputy Chairman of the Central Military Council of the People's Republic of China, Zhang Wannian, in the Kremlin. Putin was quoted as saying, "In the light of the rapidly changing situation in the world, relations between Russia and China have assumed strategic nature."

The STRATFOR.COM third-quarter forecast on June 27, 1999, stated that the Russia-China alliance was:

> ... the most important global trend today. It is well under way and is also intensifying ... The purpose of the alliance is twofold. First, it is to create a counterweight to the United States that would force the U.S. to take Russia and China seriously. The second purpose would be to provide a focal point for secondary states looking for a safe haven from American power, which would, in turn, enhance the power of the Sino-Russian bloc ... We therefore expect that the Third Quarter of 1999 will bring Russia and China to the brink, if not over the edge, of a formal alliance whose goal will be to contain American power and provide a counterbalance to American geopolitical power ... The Post-Cold War is over. We are now deep into the transition to a new era.

TERRY JAMES

Russia and China Hold Joint Naval Exercises

On September 24, 1999, the ITAR-Tass news agency reported that Russian and Chinese warships would take part in first- ever joint maneuvers in early October. "The Russian Pacific Fleet destroyer Burny and missile cruiser Varyag will visit the port of Shanghai on Oct. 2-6 to mark China's 50th anniversary and the 50th anniversary of Russian-Chinese diplomatic relations, said Russian Navy spokesman Igor Dygalo."

During the visit, the two Russian vessels were to hold joint exercises with ships from China's Eastern Fleet. "It was to be the first joint maneuver between the two fleets," ITAR-Tass said "...Russian-Chinese relations have been warming steadily since the early 1990's, following decades of tension. China is a top client for Russia's ailing military industrial complex, purchasing billions worth of jets, missiles and submarines."

Where is the United States in Bible Prophecy?

What does the current strategic position of the United States in world affairs have to do with Russia, China, Israel, Europe, and the end-time prophetic scenario? If we are close to the fulfillment of end-time events described in the books of Daniel and Revelation, students of Bible prophecy and current events should be asking probing questions such as: Where is the United States in Bible prophecy? Why does the United States not appear to have a major part in the end time prophecies? After all, the U.S. was, up until recent years, the strongest military nation to ever exist on the face of the earth.

To the chagrin of some, the United States will probably not be a prominent player in the end-time events described in the Bible. Although America is today the strongest nation in the world economically, the United States will more than likely be neutralized economically and/or militarily so that she will not be a major factor in future prophetic events that take place in Europe, Asia and the Mideast.

Whether removal of the United States from its position of economic and military authority takes place gradually or, God forbid, through a preemptive strike by Russia's nuclear arsenal remains to be seen. The United States has been unilaterally disarming under the Clinton administration. On the other hand, Russia has been steadily building its war machine for decades and has surpassed the United States in military strength, especially in the area of nuclear weapons. Conventional weapons will not be a major factor in a nuclear war.

America Disarms While Russia and China Prepare for War

In a provocative book published by NEWSMAX.COM, Christopher Ruddy states:

> The only thing that makes Russia a great power is its nuclear weapons. One pundit has described Russia as 'Bangladesh with nukes.' In fact, Russia has more nuclear weapons than every other country in the world combined, over 30,000. [The United States only has approximately 10,000 such weapons.] .... To put it briefly, the West has been disarming, while the Russians and Chinese have been building their militaries rapidly - especially their strategic forces, or 'superweapons'...

Although it has been largely unreported by the national media, President Clinton has overseen the destruction of nearly two-thirds of America's nuclear weapons stockpile. He has removed America's "launch on warning" policy and has replaced it with one that says America will retaliate only after it has been attacked. This policy from the Clinton administration means that American cities and military targets must first be destroyed before America retaliates. To the contrary, Russia's President Boris Yeltsin, on December 17, 1997, issued a 37-page policy statement reneging on previous pledges not to use nuclear weapons first.

Clinton has proposed removing computer circuitry from land-based missiles so that they could not be launched in an emergency. He has also proposed making it much more difficult for our submarines to launch their weapons and has suggested welding shut the missile hatches on our submarines. The American people need to wake up, get informed, and get involved in the political process, especially at the national level, if our republic is to survive. Sir Winston Churchill once said, "If you don't look the facts in the face, they have a way of stabbing you in the back." If America does not have a strong-enough military to defend its vital interests, our entire way of life and western civilization as we know it is in jeopardy!

THE SINO-RUSSIAN ALLIANCE: **Threat to World Peace**

AFTER DECADES of peace and economic prosperity, the American people have been lulled to sleep and think war with Russia and China is now impossible. Unfortunately, leadership of Russia and China do not think that way. Russia and China have murdered tens of millions of their own citizens and have tens of thousands of strategic and tactical nuclear weapons pointed at the United States. Never before has the strategic balance been so favorable to Russia and China. Recent activities in these countries indicate that they are at the least contemplating nuclear blackmail of the United States. These ominous developments include:

- An enormous military build-up which includes expansion of their arsenal of strategic nuclear weapons and an introduction of new biological and nuclear weapons with first- strike capability.
- A huge expansion of their navies (while the U.S. mothballs over half of its ships).
- A new form of brinkmanship, where Russia and China regularly probe America's defenses.

- Large new civil-defense programs, including enormous fallout shelters in Russia (One new underground city is larger than Washington, DC).
- While Russia and China have been preparing for war, the Clinton administration has cut the U.S. military to the bone, leaving America more vulnerable to foreign attack than at any time since the Cold War.
- Clinton has slashed troop levels in the U.S. Army, Navy and Marines by 30-40 percent. Most remaining battle troops are now deployed overseas, in the Middle East, Bosnia, South America and elsewhere.
- The U.S. arsenal of cruise missiles has dropped to a dangerously low number with less than 100 left. The few remaining missiles are being quickly discarded through senseless engagements in Kosovo, Iraq, and the Middle East, and the Clinton administration is not building any more.
- Clinton has slashed defense spending from 28 percent of the federal budget in 1988 to 17 percent in 1999.
- The Navy has decommissioned almost half of its ships, down from 600 in 1991 to 336, which is the lowest level since 1938.
- The critical balance of nuclear weapons is now heavily in Russia's favor. Many of our remaining nuclear weapons are vulnerable to attack, since the strategic bombers that carry

the nuclear warheads, located in the United
States, are in the Middle East and Europe.

THE UNITED STATES has practically no civil defense system to protect its citizens from a biological, chemical or nuclear attack, and there is no anti-ballistic missile system to protect against incoming missiles. Former Secretary of Defense, Casper Weinberger states in his book *The Next War*, "...the United States has embarked on a massive disarmament. Since 1985, the military budgets have declined 35 percent. Spending on research and development has been slashed by 57 percent, and procurement of newly produced weapons by a whopping 71 percent." Never before has the United States been so vulnerable to attack by the worst mass murderers in human history, and never before has an American leader so jeopardized America's ability to defend herself.

THE GREATEST THREAT to Freedom

THE GREATEST THREAT to America and modern civilization is not a stock market crash, an international banking crisis, or some other unexpected disruption of the global economy. The greatest danger to America is a preemptive nuclear strike from Russia. This danger is not imaginary, as some would like to believe. Unlike Russia, the United

States does not have an anti-ballistic missile defense or an active national civil defense plan.

Anatoliy Golitsyn, a high-ranking KGB defector who predicted the collapse of the Soviet Union several years before it happened, alleged in his 1984 book *New Lies for Old* that the coming Soviet collapse will be orchestrated by the KGB in order to disarm the West. Gen. Jan Sejna, a Czech defector, made a similar claim in 1982 in his book, *We Will Bury You*. Both Golitsyn and Sejna described a long-range Soviet plan that involved a grand deception, unprecedented in scope. According to Sejna, "One of the basic problems with the West is its frequent failure to recognize the existence of any Soviet 'grand design' at all. Those rejecting this concept unwittingly serve Soviet efforts."

In 1984, Golitsyn predicted a Russian military alliance with China that will be formed toward the end of the "final phase" of the long-range strategy. Golitsyn's book suggested that the end of the "final phase" would roughly coincide with the year 1999. He believed the West would disarm after the Communist collapse, and Russia would form a military partnership with China while both countries continue their buildup in military power. Golitsyn's predictions have been remarkably accurate.

According to J.R. Nyquist, a *WorldNetDaily* contributing editor and author of *Origins of the Fourth World War*, nuclear war has two basic objectives. "The first objective is the elimination of the enemy's strategic weapons. The second objective is the preservation of friendly nuclear strength in order to blackmail the surviving countries. A country that successfully destroys all opposing nuclear weapons (while retaining a large nuclear reserve) can dictate the shape of the future."

In Russian strategy, a nuclear war would not simply be an exchange of nuclear strikes, but many countries would be invaded and occupied in the process. These countries wouldn't dare resist with conventional forces without risking annihilation by Russia's reserves of nuclear and biological weapons. The successful side in a nuclear exchange would be able to translate the slaughter and destruction into their design for a New World Order.

If the United States' nuclear arsenal were ever destroyed, Russia and China would gain control of the whole earth. Therefore, members of the Russian military staff have their eyes fixed on America's nuclear missiles. That is what they care most about and what they worry most about. Without our nuclear deterrent, we would be "sitting ducks." America's nuclear weapons protect western civilization from annihilation and conquest by the barbaric, Communist leaders of Russia and China.

According to CIA analyst Peter Vincent Pry, "Soviet military textbooks written in the 1960's, 1970's, and 1980's generally endorsed the view that nuclear war could be won, and that victory was likely to go to the side that struck first." Russia has been making many provocative statements in recent months concerning their use of force against the Western nations, specifically the United States. During November 1999, Gen. Valery Manilov, deputy chief of the Russian General Staff, said, "When aggression cannot be stopped by conventional weapons, when it poses a threat to the very existence of Russia and its people, then Russia has the right to use all its potential in defense of its sovereignty, including its nuclear potential."

The Russian generals are taught that war involves preparations in three areas;

1. Preparationof the armed forces;
2. Preparationof the national economy;
3. Preparationof the population.

Again, quoting Nyquist:

Preparation is 90 percent of the game. The leaders of a successful nuclear offensive must plan for the survival of their own people. They must lay the groundwork for post-war economic recovery. Without such preparations the war becomes an exercise in suicide. Therefore, if Russia's leaders have decided on war, their preparations must give them away .... For example, the Americans see Russia mobilizing forces in 1999 (authentic information), but American analysts are nonetheless tricked into concluding that the mobilization is to deal with a terrorist threat in the North Caucasus (erroneous conclusion). They will not notice that a deployment exceeding 100,000 troops is out of proportion to the 5,000 lightly armed guerrillas that are led by one of the GRU's own agents (in this case, Shamil Basayev). As the operation proceeds, the Chief Directorate of Strategic Camouflage will continue to generate diversions and feints.

PIERCING THE FUTURE

AMERICA'S WILLINGNESS TO ignore and write off warning signs that are increasingly prevalent is a reflection of the arrogance and naivete present among many of the politicians who live in the Washington beltway. "Men are so simple, and so much creatures of circumstance," wrote Machiavelli in *The Prince*, "that the deceiver will always find someone ready to be deceived."

Nyquist lists ten indicators of Russian military preparations for nuclear war:

1. Significant troop mobilizations in response to a fabricated crisis;
2. An increase in missile tests, to assure the readiness and accuracy of the Strategic Rocket Forces;
3. An increase in prohibited underground nuclear tests;
4. An increase in war exercises of all service branches;
5. Significant troop mobilizations in satellite or allied countries, especially China, North Korea, Iraq, or Serbia;
6. Any attempt to create a unified nuclear command;
7. Efforts to extend the range of fighter-bomber formations by upgrading them with extra fuel tanks and in-flight refueling capability;
8. An increase in high-level meetings between government and military leaders;
9. Misleading official statements about the military readiness of the armed forces;

10. The sudden distribution of a new generation of conventional weapons to the armed forces.

EVERY INDICATOR in the above list has been reported and verified by the Russian or Western press, except for item 6, the creation of a unified Russian nuclear command; however, its creation was reported last January and then supposedly dropped. Nyquist lists ten key economic indicators of Russian war preparations:

1. The unusual stockpiling of nonferrous and rare metals;
2. Significant cutbacks in petroleum exports for increased military consumption and/or stockpiling;
3. Large government purchases of gold;
4. A large increase in food imports (above normal domestic consumption);
5. Large imports of agricultural machinery;
6. The creation of hardened underground sites for the relocation of war factories;
7. The sudden closing of heavy industrial plants or key scientific centers involved in aerospace research;
8. An increase in shipping assets operating along the Volga and Caspian waterways;
9. A sharp increase in rail traffic in the Ural Mountains and Far East regions; and
10. A sudden rise in domestic energy consumption.

Except for item 8, all of the above indicators have been reported in the Russian or Western press. The third area of war preparation described in Russian military writings involves preparation of the population. The four areas listed in Russian military texts include:

1. Warning the population in advance of attack;
2. Evacuating areas which lack blast or fallout shelters;
3. Construction of emergency shelters;
4. Proper instruction of the population on protective measures against weapons of mass destruction.

Psychological preparation of the population is very important in preparing for war. According to *Soviet Military Strategy*, "The political preparation of the morale of the people is of decisive importance ... since the use of weapons of mass destruction in war imposes exceptionally high and unprecedented demands on the political morale of the population." The population must be conditioned to have a strong "love of the Motherland." To accomplish this, the Russian leadership must effectively paint America as a vicious and warmongering country.

NATO's attack on Kosovo and Yugoslavia in the spring of 1999, which included the Chinese embassy, was used by Russian and Chinese propagandists to generate hatred toward the western nations and America in particular. Quoting from the text of *Soviet Military Strategy*, "Hatred of the enemy should arouse the desire to destroy the armed forces and military-industrial potential of the aggressor and achieve complete victory in a just war." In order to psychologically prepare the Russian public for war, the Kremlin must:

1. Convince the Russian people that America is out to destroy them;
2. Show that Western capitalists have been looting the Russian economy;
3. Say that the United States has designs on Russia's neighbors, or on Russian resources;
4. Say that the United States is preparing to build new weapons - in violation of treaty obligations - that will make America invincible to attack;
5. Suggest that corrupt Russian officials and capitalist "oligarches" are agents of the CIA;
6. Work behind the scenes to provoke a regional crisis that makes the United States appear in the role of aggressor;
7. Repeatedly expose the public to official statements that nuclear war is close at hand;
8. Increase the number of civil defense drills;
9. Require the population to organize itself into voluntary civil defense units; and
10. Initiate a new program of education on methods of defense from nuclear weapons and fallout radiation.

According to Nyquist, all of the above indicators have been reported in open press reports except for item 9. A special Kremlin meeting chaired last summer by former Prime Minister Stepashin focused on civil defense and the creation of an improved program for the people. Detailed reports about specific policy changes or programs were not given. In the event a nuclear war is close at hand, perhaps only a few hours away, additional danger signals will become evident. Nyquist lists 10 indicators that suggest a nuclear attack is probably imminent, with any three simultaneous occurrences being a "red flag" of warning.

1. A rash of high level-assassinations within the United States and other Western countries;
2. A sudden outbreak of an unknown and virulent disease which quickly kills or debilitates thousands of people in a matter of hours;
3. Unexplained underwater nuclear explosions in the North Atlantic, Norwegian Sea, North Pacific or Arctic;
4. Reports or rumors of an attempted military coup against the president of the United States;
5. A collapse of the power grid throughout most of North America;
6. Failure of the phone system in the United States and Canada;
7. Motor vehicles with computerized ignition systems failing to start up;
8. Widespread terrorism, mayhem in the cities, rioting, looting, fires and general unrest caused

by "unknown forces" (regardless of who is blamed);
9. The Russian population is moved into fallout and blast shelters; and
10. Russia evacuates many small towns and rural districts.

Ultimately, the fate of America and the freedom of the world rest in God's hands. God has preserved this nation for over 200 years; however, many evil forces are working overtime to destroy the spiritual and moral foundations of this country that were based upon the teachings in the Bible. Isaiah received a vision from the Lord concerning Judah and Jerusalem that should also be a wake-up call to our generation: "If ye be willing and obedient, ye shall eat the good of the land: But if ye refuse and rebel, ye shall be devoured with the sword: for the mouth of the Lord hath spoken it" (Isaiah 1:19,20).

Lessons from the Past

THE UNITED STATES in recent years has invited Chinese and Russian military leaders to inspect military facilities in our country that are classified and off-limits to average American citizens. What madness! The Washington bureaucrats are more interested in appeasing our enemies than in protecting the vital interests and security of this nation. Good judgment and common sense have been abandoned in the interest of pursuing a global government agenda that is believed will bring peace to the world.

During the days of Hezekiah, King of Judah, prior to the Babylonian captivity that began in 606 BC, the king decided to open his country to foreign inspection in the hopes of achieving peace and appeasing his enemies.

> At that time Merodachbaladan, the son of Baladan, king of Babylon, sent letters and a present to Hezekiah: for he had heard that he had been sick, and was recovered. And Hezekiah was glad of them, and shewed them the house of his precious things, the silver, and the gold, and the spices, and the precious ointment, and all the house of his armor, and all that was found in his treasures: there was nothing in his house, nor in all his dominion, that Hezekiah shewed them not.

Then came Isaiah the prophet unto king Hezekiah, and said unto him, What said these men? And from whence came they unto thee? And Hezekiah said, They are come from a far country unto me, even from Babylon. Then said he, What have they seen in thine house? And Hezekiah answered, All that is in mine house have they seen: there is nothing among my treasures that I have not shewed them.

Then said Isaiah to Hezekiah, Hear the word of the Lord of hosts: Behold, the days come, that all that is in thine house, and that which thy fathers have laid up in store until this day, shall be carried to Babylon: nothing shall be left, saith the Lord. And of thy sons that shall issue from thee, which thou shalt beget, shall they take away; and they shall be eunuchs in the palace of the king of Babylon (Isaiah 39: 1-7).

In 586 BC, exactly 100 years after Hezekiah's death, Isaiah's prophecy was literally fulfilled when King Nebuchadnezzar completed his third invasion of Judah, destroyed Jerusalem and took the national treasures and many of the Jews captive to Babylon. The fatal breach of national security by King Hezekiah is being copied by the United States as we open our borders, military bases, defense industries and other national treasures to inspection by those who have vowed to destroy us.

Welcoming adversarial nations into our midst is a "recipe for disaster," and signing treaties with foreign nations who break them when it is convenient is bad foreign policy. We should realize from past experience that treaties bind the righteous rather than the wicked and give license to those who have evil intentions. The Psalmist accurately reveals the heart of those who seek a military advantage, "The words of his mouth were smoother than butter, but war was in his heart: his words were softer than oil, yet were they drawn swords" (55:21).

How many weeks, months, or years remain before God says, "Enough is enough?!" "For, lo, the wicked bend their bow, they make ready their arrow upon the string, that they may privily shoot at the upright in heart. If the foundations be destroyed, what can the righteous do?" (Psalm 11:2, 3)

Daniel explains why God allowed Judah to be taken captive by the Babylonians:

As it is written in the law of Moses, all this evil is come

upon us: yet made we not our prayer before the Lord our God, that we might turn from our iniquities, and understand thy truth. Therefore hath the Lord watched upon the evil and brought it upon us: for the Lord our God is righteous in all his works which he doeth: for we obeyed not his voice (9:13, 14).

The leadership of our country needs to take Isaiah's warning seriously and reverse the policies that are destroying the moral foundations on which our nation was founded. If not, God will allow our enemies to destroy us as he did with Judah. We should guard diligently the national heritage that has been passed down to us from the founding patriarchs of our nation. If not, we will reap the fruits of our negligence.

The Final Battle: How Do We Get There From Here?

At some point in the future, the world-power structure will shift back to Europe, Asia and the Mideast. If the return of Christ for His Bride is near, what events must transpire for us to move from the current state of world affairs to the end-time conditions depicted in Revelation 16 where the kings of the east mobilize for the final battle of God Almighty (Armageddon)? The kings of the east show up at the end of the great tribulation which is a 3½-year period that begins when the seven-year covenant in Daniel 9:27 is broken (Matthew 24:15). How do we get there from here?

Although there is nothing prophetically significant in the Bible concerning the new millennium we are entering, many prophetic scenarios are developing simultaneously throughout the world that deserve the close attention of serious Bible students. Some of the most interesting parallel, prophetic passages in the New Testament are found in Matthew 24, Mark 13, and Luke 21. Jesus' description of events leading up to His return, sometimes called the Olivet Discourse, depicts an atmosphere that is increasingly hostile to Christians. Luke tells us that there will be "wars and commotions" and "nation shall rise against nation, and kingdom against kingdom" (Luke 21:9-10).

Are the international conflicts currently taking place around the world setting the stage for the period of "wars and rumors of wars" that will precede Christ's return? During recent months, several hot spots around the world have threatened global peace. Conflicts in 1999 alone include NATO's intrusion into Kosovo in Yugoslavia, India and Pakistan's squabble over the province of Kashmir in Northern India, the United States and Iraq, Iran and Afghanistan, North Korea and South Korea, China and Taiwan, the island of Timor in Indonesia, and the ongoing Mideast conflict between Israel and the Palestine Liberation Organization (PLO), also called the Palestinian Authority (PA). Many of these nations have nuclear weapons or will soon have them.

The pseudo "peace and security" agreements (1 Thessalonians 5:3) taking place in the Mideast and other parts of the world today will prove fatal, according to the prophetic Word. Daniel the prophet was informed by a heavenly messenger more than 2,500 years ago that at the time of the end, many would run to and fro and knowledge would increase (12:4). He was also told that the wicked would prosper but not understand "the big picture" spiritually; however, the wise would understand what was taking place (12:10).

We are entering one of the most challenging times in world history as Daniel's prophecies unfold before our very eyes and set the stage for the end-time players. At the end of the great tribulation, the kings of the east appear to have the military advantage as they cross the Euphrates River en route to "the battle of that great day of God Almighty" with the King of kings and Lord of lords.

By assuming that China, symbolized by the dragon, will be one of the kings of the east, as described in Revelation 16:12, we can begin to make some projections based upon our current understanding of the prophetic Scriptures and world events as they exist today. If we are living in "the time of the end" as described by Daniel the prophet, what should we expect to happen in order to move from the strategic alignment of nations present today to the alignment present during the latter days of the great tribulation?

THE REVIVED ROMAN EMPIRE

THE FOCUS of economic and military power during the last half of the 20th century has been centered around the United States and Russia. The center of power during the last seven years (Daniel's 70th week) before Christ returns will be a ten- nation confederacy headquartered in Europe and controlled by the "man of sin," commonly referred to as the antichrist. Before the revived Roman Empire, as pictured by the ten toes in Daniel 2 and the ten horns in Revelation chapters 13 and 17, can become the final world kingdom of the Gentiles, economic and military superiority must be relinquished by the United States and Russia.

In the case of the United States, its economic output has increased at a phenomenal rate, but its military strength has decreased dramatically during the final decade of the millennium as she unilaterally disarms in favor of social programs and implementation of a one-world government system. On the other hand, Russia's civilian economy has fallen apart while its military economy has been growing at an alarming rate. The United States has for the most part dominated the world militarily since World War I. U.S. military might reached a peak during the Reagan years of the 80's but has decreased rapidly during the 90's under the Clinton administration. The unilateral disarming of the United States at a time while Russia and China have been rapidly building their stockpile of nuclear and conventional weapons may have ominous prophetic implications.

Although it is perhaps safer and less controversial to relegate all prophetic events to the distant past or the distant future, the times in which we are living invite a fresh approach to interpret the prophetic Scriptures. The Pharisees and Sadducees were rebuked harshly by Jesus for not paying attention to the times in which they were living (Matthew 16:3). We should strive to be Scripturally sound but remain open-minded in order to discern "the signs of the times."

Bible prophecy students have for some time debated whether or not the United States is symbolically represented in the prophetic Scriptures. Although answers to the United States question are not clear, there is no evidence of the United States being a major player in the end-time events described in the Bible. Although Babylon the great, described in Revelation 17 and 18, is a great commercial city that thrives during the end-times and resembles the economic success that is currently present in the United States, this prophecy appears to be more aligned with some future city, possibly the city of Rome.

Since the final Gentile world empire will exercise control over Europe, Asia, Africa, and the whole world, the United States must necessarily cease to be the dominant economic force in world affairs. Whether America's demise is brought about by economic collapse, moral disintegration, nuclear war or other unforeseen catastrophe remains to be seen; however, the absence of the U.S. in the end-time picture should be a sobering thought to all Christians living today. Removal of the Christian evangelistic base in the United States would radically change the impact of worldwide evangelism and threaten the basic freedoms enjoyed by many in the Western world.

THE WORLDWIDE KINGDOM **of the Dragon**

. . .

The final worldwide kingdom that is to rule the earth prior to the return of Jesus Christ is described in Daniel 7 and Revelation 13 and 17. In Revelation, the future world kingdom is described as a beast that rises up out of the sea.

> And I stood upon the sand of the sea, and saw a beast rise up out of the sea, having seven heads and ten horns, and upon his horns ten crowns, and upon his heads the name of blasphemy. And the beast which I saw was like unto a leopard, and his feet were as the feet of a bear, and his mouth as the mouth of a lion: and the dragon gave him his power, and his seat, and great authority (Revelation 13:1, 2).

This beast, which is described as having seven heads, ten horns and ten crowns, has characteristics like a leopard, a bear, and a lion. This end-time world government will be different from all previous kingdoms, "and shall devour the whole earth, and shall tread it down, and break it in pieces" (Daniel 7: 23).

Daniel also gives a different view of the same end-time kingdom.

> Daniel spake and said, I saw in my vision by night, and, behold, the four winds of the heaven strove upon the great sea. And four great beasts came up from the sea, diverse one from another. The first was like a lion and had eagle's wings: I beheld till the wings thereof were plucked, and it was lifted up from the earth, and made stand upon the feet as a man, and a man's heart was

given to it. And behold another beast, a second, like to a bear, and it raised up itself on one side, and it had three ribs in the mouth of it between the teeth of it: and they said thus unto it, Arise, devour much flesh. After this I beheld, and lo another, like a leopard, which had upon the back of it four wings of a fowl; the beast had also four heads; and dominion was given to it. After this I saw in the night visions, and behold a fourth beast, dreadful and terrible, and strong exceedingly; and it had great iron teeth: it devoured and brake in pieces, and stamped the residue with the feet of it: and it was diverse from all the beasts that were before it; and it had ten horns (Daniel 7: 2-7).

The fourth beast (end-time world empire) described in Daniel will operate globally in international commerce and will work closely with Satan's team of deceivers to control all buying and selling of merchandise. This composite beast, having characteristics of a lion, a bear, and a leopard, represents the final world Gentile kingdom on earth. This beast, together with the second beast (Revelation 13:11-16), sets up an economic world order that requires a mark in the right hand or on the forehead in order to buy or sell. The underlying feature of this new world commercial system involves the number 666.

And he causeth all, both small and great, rich and poor, free and bond, to receive a mark in their right hand, or in their foreheads: And that no man might buy or sell, save he that had the mark, or the name of the beast, or the number of his name. Here is wisdom. Let him that hath understanding count the number of the beast: for it is the number of a man; and his number is six hundred threescore and six (Revelation 13:16-18).

Today's computer and global satellite system has made commercial transactions commonplace through the use of credit cards, which can carry a vast amount of information from the point of transaction to an overhead satellite, the customer's bank, and back to the satellite and point of sale in a few seconds. Incorporation of this technology permanently under the skin is now taking place in animals and in some cases with humans.

THE FOUR BEASTS of Daniel 7

THE TRADITIONAL INTERPRETATION of Daniel's dream in chapter 7 links the lion with eagle's wings to the Babylonian empire, the bear to the Medo-Persian empire, and the leopard to the empire of Alexander the Great. This interpretation fits in well with the interpretation of Daniel 2 where the first three kingdoms are represented by the Babylonian, the Medo-Persian, and the Alexandrian empires. The fourth kingdom in Daniel 2, the fourth beast in Daniel 7, and the beast described in Revelation chapters 13 and 17 represent the same end-time global empire.

Although some interesting parallels can be drawn from equating the first three kingdoms of Daniel 2 with the first three beasts of Daniel 7, there are also some problems associated with them. First, the four winds striving upon the great sea in Daniel 7 seem to be a spiritual striving that determines the order of the beasts that are to arise on the world scene. It is clear from Daniel's vision that all four kingdoms (or beasts) were still future in Daniel's vision since Babylon had already fallen and Persia had taken over. The distant fulfillment of all of this prophecy is implied by the statement, "These great beasts, which are four, are four kings, which shall arise out of the earth (7:17)."

The Final Kingdom of Antichrist is Judged

After the judgment takes place in the heavenlies (7:9,10), the fourth beast (final end-time kingdom) is judged, destroyed and given to the burning flame (7:11). The judgment of the fourth beast and little horn (antichrist) is followed by judgment of "the rest of the beasts," (i.e. lion-eagle, bear, leopard) who are contemporary with the fourth beast. They have their dominion (power and authority) removed but their lives are prolonged for a period of time (7:12). Since the fourth beast is judged and destroyed before the lion-eagle, bear, and leopard empires whose lives are temporarily spared, all four empires appear to exist at the same time. The kingdoms of Babylon, Medo-Persia, and Alexander the great were not contemporary with each other, are not present today, and will not be present when the fourth beast is judged and destroyed.

In review, the four beasts of Daniel 7 appear to coexist at the same time, strive against each other, and become incorporated into the fourth beast that takes control of the world during the 70th week of Daniel (9:27) (seven-year tribulation) at the close of this age. It is interesting to note that the lion, the bear and the leopard are included in the description of the composite beast of Revelation that rules over the earth; however, the eagle, which was plucked from the lion, is not mentioned.

A Lion, Eagle, Bear and the 20th Century

THE FIRST THREE beasts of Daniel 7 may refer to the major nations that have controlled and influenced commerce and military affairs in the 20th century and have paralleled Israel's return to world status. Up until World War I, Great Britain (lion) was the major world military power that controlled the Great Sea (Mediterranean) and world politics. The United States (eagle), which was birthed from England, has been the dominant nation in the Mediterranean area since World War II. Russia (bear), due to her military strength and nuclear warheads, has been a major factor in world politics for several decades. Although Russia's civilian economy is in ruins today, her military machine is very much intact.

The fourth world empire will be a composite beast made up of 10 kings (horns) which will include a lion (England?), a bear (Russia?), and a leopard (?). Who or what the Leopard may represent is unclear, however it may represent the African nations, the Arab nations, or some Far Eastern nations. It appears that Russia will be a major world military power up until the invasion of Israel that is detailed in Ezekiel 38 and 39. Therefore, it would not be prudent to dismiss Russia's role in world affairs in the foreseeable future.

Although the national media has deceived the American people into thinking that the Cold War ended when the Berlin wall came down, and Russia is no longer a threat to world peace, the United States and European nations keep sending billions of dollars to keep the bear from raising its paw and unleashing its nuclear weapons. The three ribs in the mouth of the bear (7:5), which may represent three nations, or a religious or political alliance controlled by the bear, encourage the bear to "arise and devour much flesh." Obviously, this prophecy by Daniel has ominous implications if its fulfillment is still in the future.

If the lion is represented by England, the eagle is the United States, the bear is Russia, the leopard is yet to be determined, and the fourth beast is the final world kingdom, possibly involving the European Union, we are living in the most exciting time period since Jesus Christ came to earth nearly 2,000 years ago. As stated previously, this is a possible scenario based upon current world events and the prophetic Scriptures and is not a dogmatic assertion. Only God knows the true course of future events.

A Thief in the Night, Peace and Safety, and Sudden

Destruction

THE RETURN of the Lord in the air for His saints will be followed by an unprecedented destruction of the earth's population. We will examine four Scripture passages that are associated with the "blessed hope" or Rapture, when the Lord shall return to take His people away from the earth before judgment is unleashed.

> For the Lord himself shall descend from heaven with a shout, with the voice of the archangel, and with the trump of God: and the dead in Christ shall rise first: Then we which are alive and remain shall be caught up together with them in the clouds, to meet the Lord in the air: and so shall we ever be with the Lord. Wherefore comfort one another with these words. But of the times and the seasons, brethren, ye have no need that I write unto you. For your selves know perfectly that the day of the Lord so cometh as a thief in the night. For when they shall say, Peace and safety: then sudden destruction cometh upon them, as travail upon a woman with child; and they shall not escape. But ye, brethren, are not in darkness, that that day should overtake you as a thief.... Therefore let us not sleep, as do others; but let us watch and be sober .... For God hath not appointed us to wrath, but to obtain salvation by our Lord Jesus Christ, who died for us, that, whether we wake or sleep, we should live together with him (1 Thessalonians 4:16-5:9).

PIERCING THE FUTURE

AND AS IT was in the days of Noe, so shall it be also in the days of the Son of man. They did eat, they drank, they married wives, they were given in marriage, until the day that Noe [Noah] entered the ark, and the flood came, and destroyed them all. Likewise, also as it was in the days of Lot; they did eat, they drank, they bought, they sold, they planted, they builded; But the same day that Lot went out of Sodom it rained fire and brimstone from heaven, and destroyed them all. Even thus shall it be in the day when the Son of man is revealed (Luke 17:26-30).

But the day of the Lord will come as a thief in the night; in the which the heavens shall pass away with a great noise, and the elements shall melt with fervent heat, the earth also and the works that are therein shall be burned up. Seeing then that all these things shall be dissolved, what manner of persons ought ye to be in all holy conversation and godliness, Looking for and hasting? unto the coming of the day of God, wherein the heavens being on fire shall be dissolved, and the elements shall melt with fervent heat. Nevertheless we, according to his promise, look for new heavens and a new earth, wherein dwelleth righteousness (2 Peter 3:10-13).

And take heed to yourselves, lest at any time your hearts be overcharged with surfeiting, and drunkenness, and cares of this life, and so that day come upon you unawares. For as a snare shall it come on all them that dwell on the face of the whole earth. Watch ye therefore, and pray always, that ye may be accounted worthy to escape all these things that shall come to pass, and to stand before the Son of man (Luke 21:34-36).

. . .

TERRY JAMES

Rapture and Rupture

IN THE EXAMPLES GIVEN ABOVE, the return of the Lord is associated with "sudden destruction," "fire and brimstone," "a great noise," "the elements .... melt(ing) with fervent heat," and "a snare" that comes upon the whole world. The context implies economic, business, and social events proceeding as usual during a time of pseudopeace and security which is followed by the sudden return of the Lord for His saints "in the twinkling of an eye," and an associated destruction that impacts the whole world.

How this destructive string of events develops and progresses toward the judgments contained in the book of Revelation is not clear from our vantage point. We "see through a glass darkly" and "know in part" (1 Corinthians 13:12); however, an Old Testament prophecy that might be associated with the "rapture" is given in Ezekiel chapters 38 and 39. The author is not dogmatic concerning this possible scenario, since there is not sufficient Scriptural evidence to fill in the gaps. It is offered only as a possibility based upon the development of world events in recent years and historic prophecies that may be close to fulfillment.

The Russian Invasion of Israel

SINCE THE PROPHECY given to Ezekiel more than 2,500 years ago is yet to be fulfilled, and the stage for its fulfillment is being prepared, we may be closer to a major paradigm shift in world events than is apparent to the casual observer. Ezekiel's prophecy is to take place "in the latter years," and "the latter days," when a large confederacy of nations, made up of Iran (Persia), Ethiopia, Libya, Turkey (Togarmah) and Magog (Russia), invades Israel.

Prior to the 20th century, the Ezekiel prophecy could not have been fulfilled. Israel did not exist as a nation, Russia did not exist as a nation, the military alignment of nations given in Ezekiel did not exist, and the means of coordinating an invasion of Israel was not possible due to primitive communications equipment. All of the hindrances to fulfilling Ezekiel chapters 38 and 39 have been removed. We are now poised for the fulfillment of this remarkable prophecy which may be the major prophetic event that realigns the nations of the world and ushers in the end-time events described in the books of Daniel and Revelation.

An article written for *World Net Daily* (worldnetdaily.com) by editor Joseph Farah, in September 1999, entitled "Is Russia planning Mideast attack?" sheds new light on the possible fulfillment of Ezekiel chapters 38 and 39. Farah's article quotes Joseph de Courcy, editor of the well-respected journal, *Intelligence Digest,* concerning a possible Mideast invasion:

> While NATO congratulates itself on bombing the Serbs into submission, Israel's Mossad and other Middle Eastern intelligence sources have discovered that Kosovo was one humiliation too many for Russia. Now Moscow has agreed to back Saddam's secret plan of revenge. With

> this all-important Russian backing, Saddam is joining with hated Iran and Syria to launch one final war against Israel. Amazingly, Saddam will allow Iranian troops to cross Iraqi territory to join the attack on Israel. And to keep America from interfering, Moscow has given Osama bin Laden and other terrorists the means to attack American population centers with weapons of mass destruction. The threat is real.... and the implications terrifying.

Although the secular press would have us think that Russia is not capable of waging war due to its weak economy, Russia's war machine is poised for fulfilling the prophecy contained in Ezekiel chapters 38 and 39.

Therefore, son of man, prophesy and say unto Gog, Thus saith the Lord God; In that day when my people of Israel dwelleth safely, shalt thou not know it: And thou shalt come from thy place out of the north parts, thou, and many people with thee, all of them riding upon horses, a great company, and a mighty army: And thou shalt come up against my people of Israel as a cloud to cover the land; it shall be in the latter days, and I will bring thee against my land, that the heathen may know me, when I shall be sanctified in thee, O Gog, before their eyes (Ezekiel 38: 14-16).

Russia's Incentive to Invade Israel

In Ezekiel 38:4, the Lord says: "I will turn thee back, and

put hooks into thy jaws, and I will bring thee forth, and all thine army, horses and horsemen." The context implies that Gog, the leader of the nations that invade Israel, will be turned back from his intended plans in order to invade Israel. The phrase "I will turn thee back" might refer to the disastrous economic problems currently being experienced in Russia's civilian economy that tempted the "hungry bear" to "take a spoil" and "take a prey" or it may refer to Russia's military ambitions that are directed towards the Western nations, but for unknown reasons, are to be redirected towards the land of Israel.

Although the actual reason for turning Russia back may not be clear until the event happens, the following scenario is possible. Russia's number one enemy is the United States, due to many factors, including its nuclear arsenal. The shortest distance for Russian nuclear weapons to strike America is not across Europe and the Atlantic Ocean, but directly north across the Arctic Ocean and Canada. If Ezekiel's prophecy implies that Russia will be planning a preemptive military strike towards the north but is turned back by God who puts hooks (incentives) into Russia's jaws (bear jaws) and brings them south into the land of Israel "to take a spoil" and "take a prey," the world may be in for some very disturbing times.

Ezekiel tells us that, "In that day there shall be a great shaking in the land of Israel; so that the fishes of the sea, and the fowls of the heaven, and the beasts of the field, and all creeping things that creep upon the earth, and all the men that are upon the face of the earth, shall shake at my presence, and the mountains shall be thrown down, and the steep places shall fall, and every wall shall fall to the ground" (38:19,20).

God Comes to Israel's Rescue

It is clear from Ezekiel that God will defend Israel from its enemies with "an overflowing rain, and great hailstones, fire, and brimstone" (38:22). Whether the judgments orchestrated by God against the invading forces are God-made, man-made, or a combination of both, remains to be seen. God sent the flood in Noah's day and fire and brimstone against Sodom and Gomorrah; however, He chose to use the Assyrian, Babylonian, and Roman armies and their war machines against Israel when she rebelled.

The possibility of nuclear armaments being present in the invasion seems to be implied due to the special precautions taken during the cleanup and disposal of the weapons and bodies described in chapter 39:9-16. God tells Ezekiel:

> I will send a fire on Magog, and among them that dwell carelessly in the isles: and they shall know that I am the Lord. (39:6) And it shall come to pass at the same time when Gog shall come against the land of Israel, saith the lord God, that my fury shall come up in my face .... For in my jealousy and in the fire of my wrath have I spoken, Thus will I magnify myself, and sanctify myself; and I will be known in the eyes of many

nations, and they shall know that I am the Lord (Ezekiel 38: 17-23).

Since the rapture of the saints is associated with a major destruction and conflagration, it is possible that the Lord's return might immediately precede or coincide with the prophecy given to Ezekiel. The prophecy in 2 Peter and the other passages given above take on a new meaning if they coincide with the prophecy of Ezekiel.

> Seeing then that all these things shall be dissolved, what manner of persons ought ye to be in all holy conversation and godliness, Looking for and hasting unto the coming of the day of God, wherein the heavens being on fire shall be dissolved, and the elements shall melt with fervent heat? (2 Peter 3:11, 12).

Is World War III Around the Corner?

THE UNITED STATES and the other major Western powers will be blackmailed or neutralized militarily prior to or possibly during the confrontation described in Ezekiel, which some have called World War III. Those nations observing this invasion through the modern inventions of television and global communications watch from the sidelines but do not get directly involved. "Sheba and Dedan, and the merchants of Tarshish, with all the young lions thereof, shall say unto thee (i.e. Russia, Iran, Ethiopia, Libya, Turkey, etc.), Art thou come to take a spoil? Hast thou gathered thy company to take a prey? To carry away silver and gold, to take away cattle and goods, to take a great spoil?" (Ezekiel 38:13).

After the earth-shaking fulfillment of Ezekiel 38 and 39, Russia's global agenda will be shattered, and she will cease to be a major world power. With both the United States and Russia out of the way, the stage will be set for the rapid emergence of the fourth beast (final world empire). This final world empire will not be able to control the world financially and militarily until the United States and Russia are removed from their superpower status.

The antichrist, as leader of the global empire, rides on the scene (white horse) in Revelation 6 and meets his ultimate fate (the beast) in the lake of fire burning with brimstone in chapter 19. He will sign a seven-year covenant with Israel either before or after Russia's Mideast invasion. The signing of the covenant with Israel will usher in the apocalyptic prophecies contained in the book of Revelation. He will break the covenant after three and-one-half years and establish his throne in Jerusalem. Antichrist's act of defiance, called the abomination of desolation, will start the events of the great tribulation which encompass the second half of the seven-year covenant.

The kings of the east will begin their march toward Israel during the closing weeks of the seven-year covenant and will be destroyed when the Lord returns to reclaim the earth. Many of the nations from Southeast Asia will be present at the "battle of Armageddon."

And I saw the beast, and the kings of the earth, and their armies, gathered together to make war against him that sat on the horse, and against his army. And the beast was taken, and with him the false prophet that wrought miracles before him with which he deceived them that had received the mark of the beast, and them that worshiped his image. These both were cast alive into a lake of fire burning with brimstone. And the remnant were slain with the sword of him that sat upon the horse, which sword proceeded out of his mouth: and all the fowls were filled with their flesh (Revelation 19: 19-21).

Concluding Remarks

IT IS PERHAPS FITTING that China's national symbol, the dragon, is also the symbol of Satan. In Revelation 12:9 we read, "And the great dragon was cast out, that old serpent, called the Devil, and Satan, which deceiveth the whole world: he was cast out into the earth, and his angels were cast out with him." The final battle, when Christ returns, will involve the kings of the east with China and Satan, representing the dragon in its earthly and spiritual forms.

China, Taiwan, and Japan's rapid rise in world status both economically and militarily in the latter half of the 20th century should serve as a wake-up call that the Asian kings of the East are beginning to prepare for their role in the final confrontation between good and evil. As this spiritual drama continues to unfold before our eyes, we are reminded of the admonition of Luke 21:28, "And when these things begin to come to pass, then look up, and lift up your heads; for your redemption draweth nigh."

6

WHAT ABOUT AMERICA?

BY LARRY SPARGIMINO

INTRODUCTION

Millions of Americans sing about that "Star-Spangled Banner," but is it waving over the land of the free and the home of the brave, or has America become something else?

A TIMELY ILLUSTRATION

A dramatic shift in American values is evident in many places. In his book, *The New Absolutes,* William Watkins speaks about politically correct speech. Even real estate agents are trained to avoid "red flag" words, as the following illustrates:

Red Flag Words	**Reasons to Avoid**
"Executive"	Possibly racist, since most corporate executives are white
"Sports enthusiast"	Could discourage the disabled
"Master bedroom"	Suggests slavery
"Quiet neighborhood"	Could be taken to mean "no children," hence discriminatory against families
"Walk-in closet"	Prejudicial against those who can't walk
"Spectacular view"	Prejudicial against those who can't see
"Convenient to jogging trails"	Perhaps offensive to the disabled
"Desirable neighborhood"	Constitutes racial steering[1]

American society claims to be open-minded. Afraid of sounding dogmatic, most Americans have embraced a new degree of tolerance, and yet, there are "new absolutes." Though these "new absolutes" are presented as proof of tolerance, they are, in fact, absolutes that are completely intolerant. Watkins cites the behavior of some in the homosexual community as a demonstration of his contention that "new absolutes" are oppressing America.

> While homosexuals promote the message that they are victims of an oppressive, heterosexist, homophobic society, nearly a hundred of them terrorized Christians attending Sunday evening church services. Homosexual activists vandalized church property, replaced the church's Christian flag with a homosexual flag, harassed

and scared children, pounded on doors during the service, and hurled eggs and rocks at churchgoers. Activist couples were arrayed in "bondage attire," and many men and women displayed their "bare breasts, bare genitals and buttocks." Some male couples were "totally naked" .... At another church they shouted, "Bring back the lions. Bring back the lions," and they disrupted the guest speaker's talk.[2]

Anarchy and Increasing Regulations

The downward spiral into increasing degeneracy and lawlessness suggests that more controls and government legislation will be necessary. A civil government that allows individual liberty can only exist when individuals exhibit self-control and personal discipline. Edmund Burke has well stated:

> Society cannot exist unless a controlling power upon will and appetite be placed somewhere, and the less of it there is within, the more there must be without. It is ordained in the eternal constitution of things that men of intemperate minds cannot be free. Their passions forge their fetters.[3]

Burke's last sentence reminds us that America's departure from God's standards has set us up for the iron-listed rule of the antichrist. How did we get where we are, and what's next for America?

. . .

TERRY JAMES

A Prophetic Overview

Since the words "America," "United States of America," "U.S.A.," and other specific references are not found anywhere in Scripture, the question, "Is America in prophecy?" is a natural one.

For those who have a high view of Biblical inspiration, the absence of any definite reference to America is significant. Nothing is in the Bible by accident, and it follows that nothing is not in the Bible by accident either. Several years ago, this writer was deeply perplexed by the fact that the Apostle Paul never tells us precisely the nature of his "thorn in the flesh" (see 2 Corinthians 12:7-9). Wouldn't it be nice to know? However, it appears that Paul's lack of specificity was deliberate and the silence of Scripture on the matter is by the wisdom of the Spirit of inspiration. If Paul had revealed in detail his "problem," those not having that specific "problem" might have dismissed the passage as irrelevant.

In the same way, it may be that some of the ambiguities regarding America's place in prophecy create a number of possible applications for both the believer and non-believer. A driver is never as careful as he is on a dark night when the swirling fog makes it difficult to tell where the roadway ends.

Prophecy's Primary Concern

. . .

JOHN F. WALVOORD is not surprised that the Bible does not specifically refer to "America," and he observes that "in keeping with the principle that prophecy is primarily concerned with the Holy Land and its immediate neighbors, it is not surprising that geographical areas remote from this center of biblical interest should not figure largely in prophecy and may not be mentioned at all."[4]

THE EUROPEAN CONNECTION

WHILE THIS IS TRUE, however, there can be some profit in studying the relation of the United States to some of the key world events that are emerging at present. Immediately after the rapture, there will be a time in which a 10-nation federation in Europe will emerge on the scene and the little horn of Daniel 7 will be revealed as the world dictator. In view of this, Walvoord finds America's ties with Europe significant.

Although the Scriptures do not give any clear word concerning the role of the United States in relationship to the revived Roman Empire, it is probable that the United States will be in some form of alliance with the Roman ruler. Most citizens of the U.S. have come from Europe and their sympathies would be more naturally with a European alliance than with Russia or countries of Eastern Asia.[5]

America's recent involvement with NATO in the bombing of Yugoslavia provides further support for a European connection. The United States was one of 19

NATO nations involved in bombing Serbian Christians and supporting the Islamic Kosovo Liberation Army (KLA). Even former Soviet President Mikhail Gorbachev found NATO's air war repugnant. "This war is a disgrace to all of us who tried to build a New World Order based on political methods and a strong role for the United Nations Security Council," said Gorbachev. "Instead we see NATO imposing itself as supreme arbiter, using military power alone."[6]

NATO's sudden and unprecedented air war against Yugoslavia was totally unlike the alliance that was formed during the Persian Gulf War because NATO did not seek cooperation with, or the approval of, the United Nations. As reported by Hutchings and Spargimino, "the pattern and precedent for our Rhodes scholar president was established:

'If there is strife in any quarter, send Americans to bolster up the New World Order.'"[7]

THE OFFICE of the President

AMERICA SEEMS to be fitting into the prophetic picture ever more clearly. The general trends prophesied in Scripture are becoming increasingly more evident in America. According to Peter Jones, one of the most striking events of the 90's has been the election of Bill Clinton as President. Jones writes:

On November 3, 1992, the people of the United States

voted into the most powerful position on earth a president who had smoked pot, dodged the draft, and espoused the sexual morals of the hippie revolution. The anti-establishment, flower-power children of the Sixties entered the halls of political power in the Nineties. Politics will never be the same again. Hippies now with short hair and three-piece suits squat in the White House legally. In the Nineties, the world witnessed 'The second coming of the 60's,' and President Bill Clinton, he who had 'breathed that (60's) era's heady atmosphere, and inhaled deeply,' became, in his capacity as social head of the nation, a metaphor for our times. [8]

George Stephanopoulus spent four years in the White House as Clinton's senior adviser and wrote that Clinton is "a complicated man responding to the pressures and pleasures of public life in ways I found both awesome and appalling."[9]

How much power does this man have whose responses are "both awesome and appalling"?

Stephanopoulus tells of one incident that is particularly revealing. In 1993 Kuwaiti authorities had arrested 14 men for planning the assassination of former President Bush. Their plan was to place a 175-pound car bomb in the path of Bush as he went to receive an award in Kuwait City. President Clinton ordered the FBI and CIA to determine if this assassination attempt had been authorized by Saddam Hussein. When a sure connection had been established between the suspects and the Iraqi Intelligence Service, Clinton decided to retaliate. Several cruise missiles were launched toward Baghdad from the USS

Peterson, a destroyer, and the USS Chancelorsville, an AEGIS cruiser. Clinton told Bush that the plot against him was "an attack against all Americans." "We completed our investigation," Clinton said. "Both the CIA and FBI did an excellent job. It's clear it was directed against you. I've ordered a cruise-missile attack."

Those words - "It's clear it was directed against you. I've ordered a cruise-missile attack" - lodged in Stephanopoulos' mind. He writes: "Along with the vulnerability comes awesome power: the ability to move global markets with a single statement, to obliterate an entire country by ordering the turn of two keys, to avenge an attack on his predecessor by firing cruise missiles under his command."[10]

President Clinton is a globalist with a deep respect for the present role of the U.N. and the belief that the U.N. occupies a key place in the future. On October 17, 1997, in an interview with Argentine reporters in Buenos Aires, Clinton referred to "the globalization of our economy." On November 14 of that same year, when speaking of the crisis created by Saddam Hussein's act of expelling U.N. weapons inspectors, Clinton stated: "Instead of complying with the unequivocal will of the international community, Saddam chose ... to defy the United Nations." It was during this same time frame that the Chairman of the Joint Chiefs of Staff, General Henry H. Shelton, requested the redeployment of U.S. ships to the Persian Gulf, "a prudent measure to demonstrate how seriously the U.S. takes this challenge to the authority of the U.N."[11]

. . .

The Fourth Empire

THESE DEVELOPMENTS MAY NOT SEEM to be of any special significance to the prophetically illiterate, but in the light of some clear biblical prophecies, they are more than unrelated happenings. The European Union, the support of American leaders for globalism, and America's involvement in the NATO alliance are important considerations. Daniel 2 speaks of four kingdoms - the Babylonian, the Medo-Persian, the Grecian and the Roman, or European kingdom. Daniel passes over the first three in a cursory way, but focuses on the fourth, evidently because it is the ruler of this fourth kingdom who makes war against God's people, prevails against them for a time, and is in existence when the Messiah comes to establish His kingdom.

Daniel 2:42 speaks about this Roman part of the image: "And as the toes of the feet were part of iron, and part of clay, so the kingdom shall be partly strong, and partly broken." Hutchings observes "that these ten toes represent a kingdom in the very extremity of the age." He goes on to state that "even though the kingdom would break up into pieces and never cleave together again the pieces themselves are still referred to as a kingdom."[12] Of course, any connection between America and the fourth empire would put America on a collision course with God. According to Scripture, it is the fourth empire that rises to oppose all that honors God.

. . .

Some Other Views

"Tarshish" and "all the young lions thereof"

These words are found in Ezekiel 38:13. The reference to "Tarshish" is open to a variety of interpretations. Some see it as a reference to "Tartessus," a location in Spain, but others, such as Bauman, reject that interpretation because of that location's relative insignificance. "Is it reasonable to believe that some small unknown stretch of beach land in southern Spain or in Cilicia or otherwise meets the demands of the prophecy? I think not." [13] Bauman pursues his point:

> "Tarshish" will be a nation of merchants - "the merchants of Tarshish" (38:13). Could either Cilicia or southern Spain fit this description? Great Britain is the greatest nation of merchants in the world. "Tarshish" is a word that ever carried with it the thought of ship - "the ships of Tarshish" - and of the sea. Surely, this is not true of Spain nor of any part of Spain today .... Great Britain is the greatest maritime nation on the face of the earth ....'Tarshish' will be a nation kindly disposed toward the Jews. Else why the protest against their spoliation? Great Britain is kindly disposed toward the Jew, and holds the mandate for the Holy Land...

Of course, Bauman wrote these words almost sixty years ago. Great Britain has lost much of its empire. But Bauman finds a connection with America in the words "Tarshish, with all the young lions thereof." "If our interpretation is correct," writes Bauman, "then thank God for this divine assurance that Great Britain and her young cubs, Canada, Australia, New Zealand, and America, will be found protesting to the very end of the age against the ravages of the great Bolshevistic colossus of the north and its atheistic allies."[14]

Is America Babylon?

Revelation 18:1-3 speaks about an angel that comes down from heaven who cries out, "Babylon the great is fallen, is fallen, and is become the habitation of devils, and the hold of every foul spirit, and a cage of every unclean and hateful bird. For all nations have drunk of the wine of the wrath of her fornication."

There are many ways in which the 18th chapter of Revelation may be applied to America. In a sense, all nations have drunk of the wine of the wrath of America's fornication. Hollywood has had a corrupting influence on all nations, and the widespread acceptance of false religions in America has made America "the habitation of devils, and the hold of every foul spirit."

Republican Congressman Bob Barr recently wrote a letter to the commander of Fort Hood, located in Killeen, Texas, the largest U.S. military base. Barr was exasperated over the presence of earth-goddess worshippers, Wiccans, some 50 in number, who practice their "religion" on the base. Barr asked: "Will armored divisions be forced to travel with sacrificial animals for satanic rituals?" The only aspect of the Wiccan religion that the Army does not allow is the practice of rituals in the nude.[15]

Other applications to America can also be made. Dr. Bob Glaze, general manager of Southwest Radio Church Ministry, recently observed in a private conversation with this author that the builders of the Tower of Babel were seeking to build a tower reaching to Heaven. As long as they were of one language, they were making rapid progress (Genesis 11:1-9). Dr. Glaze observed that English has now become the international language of the world and that America is the most populous English-speaking nation on planet earth. Is English now the language of the new Babel, America, and will America receive Babylon's judgment?

All these are valid observations and questions. We surely must affirm that God judges wicked nations and that America bears many of the characteristics of both ancient Babylon and the future Babylon of Revelation 18. But is America really Babylon? In answering this question, we must ask a more fundamental one: Who, or what, is meant by "Babylon" in Revelation 18?

In Scripture, "Babylon" is singled out as the source and birthplace of all those "isms" and philosophies that go against God and seek to corrupt God's people. It was on the plain of Shinar, the location of Biblical Babylon, that rebel man first sought to exalt himself against God on a grand scale by erecting the Tower of Babel. In Jeremiah 51:8 God states that the destruction of Babylon would be swift, sudden and total.

The doom of the Babylon of Revelation 18 is described in the same way, especially in verses 17-19. Moreover, Jeremiah 50:40 states, "As God overthrew Sodom and Gomorrah and the neighbor cities thereof, saith the Lord;

so shall no man abide there, neither shall any son of man dwell therein." The city of Babylon continued to prosper after the Medes conquered it. Though Babylon's former glory waned after the Persians lost control of it in 323 BC, the city continued on into New Testament times and was not suddenly destroyed as anticipated by Jeremiah. At present, modern Iraq and her cities are still inhabited, indicating that physical Babylon is still in existence.

All this would strongly suggest that there is a yet future and final destruction of Babylon that will fit the description of its doom found in the Hebrew prophets (see also Isaiah 13:6, 9-11) as well as the picture of her downfall found in the Book of Revelation. It would seem best, therefore, to maintain that there is a literal Babylon of the future, and that while the United States bears many of the marks and characteristics of Babylon, and is therefore ripe for judgment, the United States is not the "Babylon" of Revelation. Those who do make the connection do so out of a realization of the awfulness of America's rebellion against God, but it would seem to this author that they are more motivated by their prophetic slant on the things that are happening in America than by a careful exegesis of the prophetic Word.

First Peter 5:13 indicates that Peter was in "Babylon" when he wrote his letter. Some take this in a figurative way and understand "Babylon" to mean "Rome." Since Babylon was still quite a large city at that time and since the recipients of Peter's letter were at least as close, geographically, to literal Babylon as to Rome, it would have been very confusing to Peter's readers for him to say "Babylon" when he really meant "Rome." Paul wrote a letter to the church at Rome at this approximate time and had no reticence in calling it by its name (Romans 1:7). All of this suggests that "Babylon" means "Babylon" and not something else.

It is hard to understand what is accomplished by identifying "America" with the "Babylon" of Revelation 18. Godless nations are judged by God and Revelation 18 adds nothing new to the general principle that is revealed in many portions of Scripture. If America continues in her impenitence, she too will be judged. Revelation 18 reveals nothing that we don't already know in that regard. But if it does reveal something definite about literal Babylon, then the chapter reveals important information.

Is America the New Home of the Ten Lost Tribes? - British Israelism

Also known as "Anglo Israelism," or "Armstrongism," this view teaches that England and the United States are what is left of the so-called Ten Lost Tribes of Israel, and that the throne of England is the throne of David. Allegedly, when the Northern tribes were captured by the Assyrians, these tribes migrated northward and westward into Northern Europe and are the ancestors of the Saxons who later invaded England. The lost tribe of Dan is followed into Europe, where it supposedly left its tribal name in places like Danzig, Danube and Dnieper. The word "Saxon" is claimed to be a derivative of Isaac-son, and "Britain" is traced to berith, the Hebrew word meaning "covenant."[16]

In the heyday of the British Empire, of which it was

said that "the sun never sets on the British Empire," the proponents of British Israelism affirmed Great Britain's success in subjugating the nations of the world because the British were the inheritors of God's covenantal promises to Israel, and God was exalting His people in the latter times. That the glory of the British Empire has now greatly waned has not daunted the proponents of this theory who maintain that the blessings of the Divine Covenant have now been transferred to the United States of America.

Of all the different views of the place of America in prophecy, this view has the honor of being the most objectionable. It robs Israel of her promises of glory in the future. By transferring them to contemporary England and America, the promises are greatly diminished, for there is no glory in these nations at present. Scripture never gives the slightest suggestion that the "Ten Lost Tribes" went into Europe or that they are even "lost." These tribes are mentioned in 2 Kings 17:3-6, where we are told that it took Shalmaneser three years to capture Samaria. He conquered the city in King Hosea's ninth year (722 BC) and deported many of the inhabitants eastward to Assyria, not westward to Europe. Likewise, 2 Kings 18:9-11 reveals that the Israelites were sent to various locations in the Assyrian Empire. The towns of the Medes, northeast of Nineveh, are specifically mentioned.

Having been dispersed into Assyria and environs, survivors from these northern tribes intermarried with the general population and within a few generations lost their Hebrew identity. But this does not mean that all of the members of the northern tribes were somehow lost forever, or that the division of the tribes was to continue in perpetuity. When the Assyrian and Babylonian captivities were ended, the rivalries between the northern and southern tribes ceased and the Israelites looked forward to a common destiny that was bound up with God's promises to David and with Jerusalem as the capital. The hopes and aspirations of the two kingdoms were unified into a common hope by God. In Ezekiel chapter 37 we read:

> The word of the Lord came again unto me, saying, Moreover, thou son of man, take thee one stick, and write upon it, For Judah, and for the children of Israel his companions: then take another stick, and write upon it, For Joseph, the stick of Ephraim, and for all the house of Israel his companions: And join them one to another into one stick; and they shall become one in thine hand. And when the children of thy people shall speak unto thee, saying, wilt thou not show us what thou meanest by these? Say unto them, Thus saith the Lord GOD; Behold, I will take the stick of Joseph, which is in the hand of Ephraim, and the tribes of Israel his fellows, and will put them with him, even with the stick of Judah, and make them one stick, and they shall be one in mine hand. And the sticks whereon thou writest shall be in thine hand before their eyes. And say unto them, Thus saith the Lord GOD; Behold,
>
> *I will take the children of Israel from among the heathen, whither they be gone, and will gather them on every side, and bring them into their own land: And I will make them one*

nation in the land upon the mountains of Israel; and one king shall be king to them all: and they shall be no more two nations, neither shall they be divided into two kingdoms any more at all (Ezekiel 37:15-22, italics added).

The symbolism of the passage is striking. The prophet Ezekiel is told by the Lord to take two sticks. They are to be marked with the words "For Judah" and "For Joseph." Taylor comments:

These represent the two kingdoms of former days, before Samaria fell to the Assyrians under Sargon II (722/1 BC), and Israel, the northern kingdom, lost her identity. He is to take one of them in his right hand, concealing one end of it in his clenched fist. Then he is to take the other stick and join it to the first one, end to end. His clenched fist will thus grasp the place where the two sticks meet, and it will appear as if he is holding one long stick in the middle.[17]

The meaning of the action is that in the restored Israel, the old divisions of north and south will be abolished and the nation will be united in God's hand.

Ezekiel 37:23-28 are also important in aiding us in assessing the claims of British Israelism. The fact that God's ancient covenant people are one people, that David will be over them and that they will have one shepherd does not fit the basic tenets of British Israelism. Verse 28 is crucial to the argument. "And the heathen shall know that I the Lord do sanctify Israel, *when my sanctuary shall be in the midst of them forever more*" (italics added). Israel's future unity, demonstrated by the central sanctuary which will be the focal point of the nation's life, will be a powerful object lesson to the heathen. British Israelism loses the significance of this and makes the object lesson a failure.

Moreover, British Israelism woefully misunderstands the throne of David. Second Samuel 7:16 speaks about David's "house," "kingdom" and "throne." None of these terms are even remotely compatible with the tenets of British Israelism. David is the Davidic King who is associated with the Jewish or Hebrew kingdom. "Afterward shall the children of Israel return, and seek the Lord their God, and David their king; and shall fear the Lord and his goodness in the latter days" (Hosea 3:5). In this, and in other Old Testament passages, there is not the slightest allusion to "America" or "Great Britain," or "the land of the Saxons." The reference is always to Israel, and David's relationship to the land and the people of that land. Jeremiah 23:5-6 states, "Behold, the days come, saith the Lord, that I will raise unto David a righteous Branch, and a King shall reign and prosper, and shall execute judgment and justice in the earth. In his days Judah shall be saved, and Israel shall dwell safely: and this is his name whereby he shall be called, THE LORD OUR RIGHTEOUSNESS."

THE BEGINNING of the End
   I. The Current Scene in America
   A Nation Richly Blessed

. . .

THE BLESSINGS that America has enjoyed are absolutely phenomenal. Yet, it is hard not to believe that America is ripe for judgment, or that the moral and social chaos, storms, droughts and fires have nothing to do with America's sins. The murder of 40 million unborn babies is enough to secure America's final doom. But why hasn't judgment already come? Why does America continue to enjoy so many of the Lord's blessings when a large segment of the American population is living in open rebellion to the God of the universe?

Though the church in America has not been all that it should and could be, there are, nevertheless, large numbers of Christians who are serving Christ and His people. David Allen Lewis, for example, finds Matthew 24:14 a key for understanding the place of America in the present and in the future. Jesus states, "This gospel shall be preached in all the world for a witness unto all nations; and then shall the end come." Lewis writes, "If one could locate a nation that God is using primarily for the fulfillment of this prophecy, then we will have located a nation of destiny .... This nation is the United States of America."[18] America has its hand in foreign missions and church growth both at home and abroad. The U.S. government allows tax deductions for giving to missions and other Christian causes. No other nation in the history of civilization that has consistently practiced religious freedom.

Lewis believes that in light of Matthew 24:14, "the U.S.A. enjoys a most exalted position in the scheme of events that led up to the end of this age."[19]

Furthermore, American Christianity has, for the most

part, given the Jewish people their proper respect, something that cannot be ignored, for God told Abraham that He would bless those who bless Abraham and his descendants and curse those who do not (Genesis 12:3).

In America, Jews have been allowed to rise in the ranks of society. "Whereas in most Christian and Islamic countries Jews were never able to fully participate in the life of the nation collectively, in America, they were blessed and allowed to become active in almost all spheres of American life. This includes the government, the military, academia, commerce, agriculture, and even space exploration, just to mention a few." [20]

Of course, all of this could change, and, in fact, Victor Mordecai believes it will change because of the importance of what he calls the "petrodollar." Mordecai believes that if Christians and Jews are not supportive of Israel, "Washington will be pro-oil, pro-Arab (as it has always been), and will be ready to sacrifice Israel with all its population, five million Jews and Christians plus three million Moslems." This will cause America "'to look the other way,' while the corporation, big business, petrodollar-backed Moslems close in on the kill of the expendable relatively poorer Israel."[21] If and when this happens, America will find her fortunes reversed. Make no doubt about it, the "petrodollar" is important, and may very well be the consideration, humanly speaking, that brings about the fulfillment of Ezekiel 38 and 39. Vladimir Sakharov, high- ranking Soviet diplomat who narrowly escaped the deadly revenge of the KGB, observes:

The strength of Soviet foreign policy is in its relentless

pursuit of long-term objectives, so that occasional setbacks don't mean much.

For example, in the Middle East, Egypt turned away from the Soviet Union and to the United States under President Anwar Sadat. Overall, however, developments in the Mideast are going according to Moscow's plan, a policy that was being shaped while I was at the Institute preparing to be a Soviet Arabist.

The long-term objective was to cut off the U.S. from the Arab world and its oil. The tactics involved continually fanning the fires of Arab-Israeli conflict. With U.S. support for Israel, and Soviet support for the Arabs and its strong influence over the Palestine Liberation Organization, Moscow made friends while the U.S. was maligned as a colonialist enemy.[22]

A Nation Deeply Troubled

Though our nation has been richly blessed, repeated violations of the standards of decency are having a telling effect. Laws are being modified to conform to patterns of animalistic behavior rather than to patterns of righteousness and truth. Congressman William Dannemeyer describes a most unusual phenomenon. Essentially, they [lawmakers] argued as follows: Everyone is committing adultery, and most men are having homosexual adventures, so how can we possibly outlaw this conduct? You can't have a law that no one obeys. It makes a mockery of the law itself. Therefore, anyone prosecuted for sex acts is doing no more than what everyone else is doing. The only difference is, the others aren't getting caught.

Eventually, lobbyists for the liberalized sex laws began using this argument in quiet conversations with state legislators around the country, pointing to the widespread acceptance of Kinsey as evidence in courts at every level. The result: most states have modified their criminal codes to eliminate such acts as fornication, adultery, and sodomy, while leaving rape and child molestation on the books.[23]

But if Kinsey and his crowd are correct, laws against rape and child molestation will likewise have to be abolished. Fallen man evidently views progress in terms of degrees of increasing perversity. We will have to descend lower to evolve higher. Interestingly, "the move to normalize pedophilia is growing at an alarming rate." Wardell Pomeroy, a former associate with Kinsey and founding board member of SIECUS, has publicly stated that sexual contact between adults and children is not necessarily bad. In fact, such contact "can be a loving and thoughtful, responsible sexual activity."[24]

II. The Gradual Decline of America
The Role of Global Education

THE CONDITIONS that will be on earth during the tribulation find their genesis in the present age in that the events prior to the rapture of the church are setting the stage for what is to follow. Believing "the lie" will be much easier after the seeds of deception are sown through the modern educational establishment in America.

A culture war is taking place in America and the attacks are often injurious to the cause of truth. Certain left-wing groups are mounting a concerted effort to make Christians look dangerous and out-of-touch with reality. In her monumental book, *Cloning of the American Mind*, B.K. Eakman gives an abbreviated list of those organizations most frequently included "in the manuals, pamphlets, and handbooks as 'enemies of education.'" She mentions target groups such as the National Association of Christian Educators, Concerned Women For America, Family Research Council, and others. Eakman writes, "These groups, in turn, are falsely linked by our adversaries to Neo-Nazi groups, like the Ku Klux Klan." [25]

The present struggle between the liberal left and the conservative right involves deception, intimidation, psychological conditioning and other techniques of "psychological warfare." Ancient oriental philosophers as far back as 550 BC "understood that success in war, be it armed or psychological, depends on the ability to confuse and delude while concealing one's true character, weaknesses, strong points, and intentions."[26] Eakman references the ancient maxim of Sun Tzu, author of *The Art Of War*, who wrote, "Those skilled at making an opponent move do so by creating a situation to which he/she must conform - for example, by enticing him with something he is sure to take." Eakman skillfully applies this to a contemporary issue. This is what the opposition has done by declining test scores. By creating a situation in which academic scores were sure to decline, we have been enticed by the bait of "school reform" and nationalized "standards," which we were sure to take. From there it was a short jump to restructuring schools, ostensibly to improve test results. [27]

Perhaps the most effective way to manipulate people is to change their thinking. Liberal commentators often laugh at the term "brainwashing." It is allegedly a favorite term of conspiracy theorists and others regarded as dwelling on the outer edges of the lunatic fringe. However, "manipulation of the masses, or 'collective brainwashing,' has evolved significantly .... Today, it is called, among professionals, 'the science of coercion.'"[28]

This coercive manipulation of large segments of the American population is effectively carried out through the public media which wages a continual "mind game" against Bible-based values. The media seeks to gain control of the psychological environment and can thereby control how people act and react. The basic principles of this psychological manipulation are:

- If people hear the same phrases and slogans often enough, they will come to believe them, or at least accept them;
- If individuals are isolated, undermined, embarrassed, and outmaneuvered often enough, they will give up or become so irrational in presenting their views that no one who is not already in their camp will listen;
- If negative labels are applied consistently, both subtly and blatantly, to certain actions and/or individuals, the connotations inherent in those

labels eventually will become automatic associations in the eyes of the public, leading to a conditioned response.[29]

This latter technique has been blatantly used by evolutionists to discredit the decision of the Kansas State School Board, a decision which allows local school districts to determine whether or not their schools will teach evolution, creation, or both. Unscrupulous, or perhaps woefully ignorant, journalists claim that there is a right-wing takeover. Judging from many of the letters to the editor in some of the major newspapers, ignorance of both science and what the Kansas School Board has really done has gained the upper hand. Comments such as, "There is more proof for Darwin's theory of evolution than for the existence of Adam and Eve" completely miss the point. The Kansas School Board is not suggesting that schools teach the historicity of Adam and Eve. Rather it is simply dethroning evolutionary theory from the place of preeminence that it has had in American education. Such willful ignorance, however, is not surprising. The Scripture states "that there shall come in the last days scoffers, walking after their own lusts .... For this they willingly are ignorant of, that by the word of God the heavens were of old, and the earth standing out of the water and in the water" (2 Peter 3:3,5).

Darwin's monkey empire is fighting back with the only weapons it knows: lies and half-truths.

The Role of Global Government

REVELATION 13 REVEALS that just prior to the return of the Lord Jesus Christ to earth, one individual will have power and authority over the entire earth. This power and authority will be wielded in the political sphere (Revelation 13:7), the ecclesiastical sphere (Revelation 13:8), and in the economic sphere (Revelation 13:17). This power and authority is not taken by this individual, but rather "power was given him." This refers to the place of the beast in the Divine plan. God empowers him to do His will and, as a result, the people of the world willingly give him authority to rule over them.

But what nations form the power base for this coming world dictator? According to Revelation 17:13, "these have one mind, and shall give their power and strength unto the beast." In the context of Revelation 17, verses 7-12, these nations are part of the Revived Roman Empire and fit in with the end-time prophecies of Daniel 2 and 7 and, by virtue of America's European connection, discussed earlier, could very well place the United States in the center of this end-time picture.

Malachi Martin has observed that the emerging new world order "is the most profound and widespread modification of international, national and local life that the world has seen in a thousand years." Who will be the supreme leader of this global arrangement? The competition for this pivotal role Martin calls "the millennium end-game."[30]

This "millennium end-game" has been in progress for the last 100 years. Dennis Cuddy traces the influence of

Cecil Rhodes who, in 1890, stated that he would start a movement which, in 100 years, would bring in world government and guarantee the total absence of war and the implementation of one universal language. Cuddy shows how Rhodes scholars have been working through the Council on Foreign Relations, the United Nations, the International Monetary Fund, the U.S. Congress and various branches of the American federal government. President Clinton, himself a Rhodes scholar, has appointed some 22 Rhodes scholars to positions of great importance in his administration.[31] The unholy ones in high places have a vice-like grip on America. Dan Quayle comments:

> There are in America various groups of people enjoying almost earthtaking privilege, each one of which is dominated by individuals who got the major issues of the 60's wrong. The members of these groups generally enjoy enormous wealth and virtual unassailable professional security. They answer either to no one (in the case of federal judges and tenured university faculty) or to only a few like-minded people (in the case of producers, directors, and senior editors). A numbing near-uniformity of opinion and taste has settled over these specially privileged groups. Their collective mindset is significantly to the left of the political center in this country, and that simple fact has tilted the country's culture in a direction that is counter to middle-class values.[32]

This "numbing near-uniformity" has hardened like

concrete because the major media outlets are controlled by globalists. This includes the television networks, major magazines and wire services, plus the major newspapers. The news that comes from the *Associated Press, United Press, Reuters, Time, Life, New York Times* and others comes to readers and viewers through filters erected by groups sympathetic to causes that Christians oppose. Furthermore, the government news releases are written by "spin doctors" to give the news just the right slant. As a result, the American public sees and hears all the news that's fit to see and hear as determined by the elitist few who have taken to themselves the privilege of judging what's good for the public. Christians would do well to consult alternate news sources.

III. The Final Countdown for America
Denials We Foolishly Believe

THE POLLS SUGGEST that America is in a condition of denial. What does the average man on the street (if there is such a creature) think of prophecy, Armageddon, and the end of the world? A recent report states:

> Americans overwhelmingly believe the world, as we know it, will come to a sudden and apocalyptic end as predicted in the Bible, but despite the predictions of doomsday cults fixated on the coming of a new millennium, Americans don't think the world is going to end soon, according to a poll of 1,027 adults conducted

by Scripps Howard News Service and Ohio University. Most Americans discount imminent end-of-the-world predictions as irrational. The survey found that only 15 percent said they believe it is either "very likely" or "somewhat likely" that "the arrival of the millennium means that the world will come to an end." Two-thirds of the respondents in the poll said they believe looming global demise is "very unlikely."[33]

We have AIDS, the threat of nuclear warfare and biological terrorism, wars on almost every continent, devastating earthquakes and storms, rank immorality in every strata of society and government, the increasing erosion of human rights in America and abroad, school violence, the virtual demise of American sovereignty, and so on, but basically, people think that things will continue as always. It sounds like 2 Peter 3:3-4:

> Knowing this first, that there shall come in the last days scoffers, walking after their own lusts, And saying, Where is the promise of His coming? for since the fathers fell asleep, all things continue as they were from the beginning of creation. The recurring patterns in the natural world have lulled these scoffers into a false sense of security.

"All things continue as they were from the beginning of creation." In other words, "Nothing has changed. It is business as usual." Our Lord spoke of this when He said: "For as in the days that were before the flood they were eating and drinking, marrying and giving in marriage, until the day that Noah entered into the ark, and knew not until the flood came and took them all away" (Matthew 24:38-39).

Recently a national magazine reported on two baby girls who were accidentally "switched" at birth. A lawsuit is pending against the makers of the identification bracelets used to keep track of patients. Allegedly, the babies' bracelets were so loose that they slipped off of the babies' wrists and ankles. The article added, "This month the medical center will begin to implant electronic belly-button chips on newborns. Alarms will sound if a baby is taken through restricted doors."[34] Our ministry reported on this and enumerated possible prophetic implications.

Some of our callers felt sure that these belly-button chips would be optional and nothing to be concerned about.

One listener sent an e-mail that said: "A closer reading of this article turns up the possibility that the chips are implanted on the umbilical stump, which falls off a few days after birth." But "a closer reading of this article" reveals no such thing. "Umbilical stumps" were never mentioned.

While it is all too easy to believe that nothing is amiss, denial turned deadly at the Columbine High School in Littleton, Colorado. How could that awful tragedy have happened unless people were denying the obvious and believing their own denials?

In recent years there have been enough school massacres to put school officials and parents on "red alert." In March 1998, two boys, age 11 and 13, shot and killed a teacher and four students in Jonesboro, Arkansas.

That was just one of a series of incidents at U.S. high schools in which at least 14 people were killed and more than 40 wounded in less than two years. Could it happen again? After Jonesboro and several other tragedies too numerous to mention, reasonable people should have realized that it could. There had been many indications that Eric Harris and Dylan Klebold were going to do the unspeakable. *Time* magazine for May 3, 1999, states that the "Trench Coat Mafia" had been giving off many dangerous signals. They made a video for class - a tale of kids in trench coats hunting down their enemies with shotguns. The graffiti in the boys' bathroom warned, "COLUMBINE WILL EXPLODE ONE DAY. KILL ALL ATHLETES. ALL JOCKS MUST DIE." Why didn't school officials do something despite all of the warnings?

There are many possible reasons. People are afraid of being viewed as alarmists. School officials are often afraid of opening themselves to lawsuits. "What? My son might be planning to commit a crime? Where did you get such an outlandish idea? I'll see you in court!" People are already so busy holding down two jobs so that they can maintain their expensive life-styles, taking the kids to ball practice, band rehearsals, ballet lessons, and attending church suppers and a variety of community activities, that they are generally reluctant to break out of their busy patterns to deal with a potential problem. By going into denial, they avoid spending extra time and money on all of these possible adverse reactions. But, of course, as in the case with the Columbine massacres, the consequences of denial are often tragic.

The lessons here reach far beyond school massacres.

For years, America has been in denial about key issues in critical areas of national survival. Lulled into carnal security by soaring Dow Jones reports, many Americans have found it easy to deny the importance of integrity in national leaders. We have found it economically attractive to ignore the blatant sins of our leaders and have elected leaders who promise to provide us with creaturely comforts.

Through its legal system, America has endorsed the murder of millions of unborn babies. Cries of indignation have been raised. Warnings have been sounded. But what has been the result? A total denial of the gravity of America's murderous sins by electing a president who has vetoed the partial birth abortion ban. Predictably abortion has now been credited with the reported nationwide drop in crime. As initially reported in the *Chicago Tribune*, "two researchers have concluded that legalizing abortion in the United States in the 1970s led to the drop-in crime scene in the country two decades later." The report stated that "because the unwanted offspring of poor, teenage minority women were aborted at a disproportionately high rate in the 1970s, the pool of young potential troublemakers now reaching adulthood has been thinned."[35]

When the movies began to thrive on sex and violence, many pulpits rightly sounded the alarm that disastrous spiritual and moral corruption would follow. The result? More denial. At present, America has ignored President Washington's warnings against entering entangling alliances. These warnings have been sounded again and again, but despite these warnings America becomes more deeply involved in military actions that further the globalist agenda. Proverbs 29:1 states, "He that being often reproved hardeneth his neck, shall suddenly be destroyed, and that without remedy."

America has lost its soul because it has denied that it ever had one. How much longer can America exist in its chronic condition of denial?

Warnings We Dangerously Ignore

THOSE WHO LIVE in denial shrug off warnings - often to their own hurt. Propelling America to a critical meltdown is one of the many Presidential Executive Orders which could be invoked in a time of national crisis. These Executive Orders suspend our rights and privileges and make the President of the United States a law unto himself. *The Los Angeles Times* (7/4/98) commented:

> The latest series of executive orders is illustrative of a president who has used his unilateral authority more robustly and frequently than almost any of his predecessors. Clinton has rewritten the manual on how to use executive power with gusto. His formula includes pressing the limits of his regulatory authority, signing executive orders and using other unilateral means to obtain his policy priorities when Congress fails to embrace them.[36]

Times of crisis, whether real or manufactured, are convenient pretexts for a tyrannical power grab. If a tyrant feels the time is right, why not generate a crisis to further one's aims? And might such dastardly motivations tie in with the expanding role of the Federal Emergency Management Agency (FEMA)?

Though serving the needs of disaster victims in Hurricane Carla (1962), the Alaskan Earthquake (1964), Hurricane Betsy (1965), and other disasters, FEMA was given a radically- expanded authority when President Carter, in 1979, issued an executive order that merged many of the separate disaster- relief agencies into FEMA. "At that time," writes Veon, "FEMA began the development of an Integrated Emergency Management System with an all-hazards approach that includes direction, control, and warning systems that are common to the full range of emergencies from small isolated events to the ultimate emergency - war."[37]

It is more than a mere coincidence that the realization that "these are terrible times" fraught with problems beyond solution by nonglobal entities is also creating the alleged need for a new conception regarding the home. In her book, *It Takes A Village*, "Hillary Rodham Clinton argues that these are 'terrible times when no adequate parenting is available and the village itself [i.e., the state] must act in place of parents. The village accepts those responsibilities in all our names through the authority we vest in government.'"[38]

IV. A Word for God's People in America

. . .

PROPHECY IS NEVER to be studied in a merely detached and academic manner. Those who claim that the study of prophecy is necessarily irrelevant because it deals with the future do not understand prophecy. Both Paul and Peter addressed prophetic issues, but they clearly made the application to their readers in their present circumstances (1 Thessalonians 4:18; 2 Peter 3:11).

BETRAYED and Bewildered

IT IS this author's belief that America has been the greatest and most wonderful country on the face of the earth. Multitudes have flocked to our shores to find freedom, opportunity, and yes, to find Christ. Religious liberty has been enjoyed for years. Many churches are faithfully proclaiming the Gospel, and yet America has changed drastically, and may change even more drastically in the immediate future if the Lord tarries. As a result, many Christians in America are feeling betrayed and bewildered. It is easy for a Bible-believing Christian to fall into that trap. Our country has elected a liberal President who has appointed liberal judges and cabinet members. We have engaged in an illegal and immoral war in the Balkans and yet hardly anyone seems to protest. Our government seems to be gradually becoming more hostile to Christian values by the day. Has America let us down?

First Peter 4:7 gives a timely exhortation, "But the end of all things is at hand: be ye therefore sober and watch unto prayer." The word "sober" means something like "clear-headed." We are to be clearheaded and to "watch unto prayer." Feeling resentful and betrayed will interfere with keeping Peter's exhortation. We will only feel that America has let us down when we forget that our citizenship "is in heaven; from whence also we look for the Saviour, the Lord Jesus Christ" (Philippians 3:20). If America has let you down, it might be that you have put too much hope in America.

Faithful and Rewarded

Trusting Christ for salvation is a simple response of faith. No works are required to earn salvation, but once an individual is saved, that person is a new creation (2 Corinthians 5:17) and God addresses the believer as a responsible individual. Those who meet the Lord's expectations are rewarded. Those who fail to live up to their potential in Christ fail to receive a full reward (2 John 8).

In a sense, we live in "the best of times" as well as "the worst of times." Opportunities for service to our Lord abound, but Satan knows that he has but a short time and is seeking to destroy the work of God (see Revelation 12:12). It's a mad, sad world - but things will improve, and God will have His way.

7
JUDGMENT AT JERUSALEM

BY DAVID ALLEN LEWIS

THE JUDGMENT OF THE SHEEP AND THE GOATS HAS LONG been a source of intrigue to theologians and Bible students. Misappropriation of this important passage of Scripture leads to doctrinal fantasies that affect the quality of one's eschatological views concerning the end of this age.

On the other hand, a clear understanding of Matthew 24:31-46 has a most salutatory effect on our appreciation of our position in Christ as well as giving us answers to some of the most intriguing questions presented to our minds as we approach the time of the Lord's Coming.

Some of the things that we will try to answer in this essay are:

1. When does the judgment take place in relation to other prophetic events?
2. Who are the nations: the sheep and the goats?

3. What does the outcome of this judgment show us?
4. Who are the Shepherd-King's (Christ's) brethren (the recipients of good deeds)?
5. Is this a parable or a prophecy?
6. What comes after this event?

The Revelation of the Son of Man

"When the Son of man shall come in his glory, and all the holy angels with him, then shall he sit upon the throne of his glory" (Matthew 24:31).

This passage does not describe the rapture of the church nor does it describe the great White Throne Judgment. It refers to the visible second coming of Jesus Christ which takes place at the end of the 70th week, designated as the tribulation. The judgment of the sheep and goats takes place at the end of the tribulation to determine who of earth's natural folk will be allowed to enter the millennium to rebuild the earth after the calamitous ruin of the wars and plagues of the great tribulation. The sheep are the people who will repopulate the planet during the visibly manifested kingdom of God of 1,000 years duration.

The Nations

. . .

"And before him shall be gathered all nations: and he shall separate them one from another, as a shepherd divideth his sheep from the goats" (Matthew 24:32).

It is singularly important at this juncture that we identify what is meant by nations (Gr. ethnos). It is the conclusion of this author that nations, as such, are not referred to in this passage of Scripture. The Greek word ethnos is used in the New Testament 164 times. The word is translated variously as follows: "Gentiles" 93 times; "nations" 64 times; "heathen" 5 times; "people" 2 times. In general, the term "nations" is commonly used to describe the human race.

In addition, it is interesting to note that the Hebrew equivalent of ethnos (goyim) is translated into the word "nation" 374 times; "heathen" 143; "Gentiles" 30; and "people" 11. We will demonstrate in the exposition of this text that the word is used here, not as the general concept of nations, but rather as people. So, we would understand the meaning of verse 32 to be: "And before him shall be gathered all people comprising the nations of this world." One can only conclude that it is individual people and not whole nations that are being judged.

Blessed Sheep

"And he shall set the sheep on his right hand, but the goats on the left. Then shall the King say unto them on his right hand, Come, ye blessed of my Father, inherit the kingdom prepared for you from the foundation of the world" (Matthew 25:33, 34).

One thing is sure: No one will inherit the kingdom and everlasting life because he is a Norwegian, a Scot or an African. By the same token, no one will be sent to hell because of a national identity. God does not have two ways of salvation. People are saved not by works, but by the grace of God through the redeeming work of Calvary.

The sheep on His right hand are those individuals who are saved as a result of the witness of the 144,000 and comprise a company of people so vast that no man can number them. See the seventh chapter of Revelation.

Obviously, the antichrist will murder many who resist him, but the beast is not as powerful as some have thought him to be. Many new post-rapture tribulation believers will escape out of his hand. These new believers are the sheep in this future judgment. The sheep receive salvation, not because of their national identity, but because they will receive Christ as their personal Savior. Their good deeds are a product of their transformed hearts. Salvation is not a reward for good deeds.

Christ's Distressed Brethren - Hungry, Thirsty, Naked, Sick, in Jail

For I was hungered, and ye gave me meat: I was thirsty, and ye gave me drink: I was a stranger, and ye took me in: Naked, and ye clothed me: I was sick, and ye visited me: I was in prison, and ye came unto me. Then shall the righteous answer him, saying, Lord, when saw we thee and hungered, and fed thee? or thirsty, and gave thee drink?

When saw we thee a stranger, and took thee in? or naked, and clothed thee? Or when saw we thee sick, or in prison, and came unto thee? And the King shall answer and say unto them, Verily I say unto you, in as much as ye have done it unto one of the least of these my brethren, ye have done it unto me (Matthew 25:35-40).

In the traditional mode of interpretation in this fascinating passage, the sheep and goat nations are generally identified as literal nations. We think that seeing the sheep and goats not as national entities but as the individuals who comprise the nations is much more reasonable and in line with the context of the entire Bible. Thus, the sheep are those people who treated Christ's brethren with mercy and true Christian charity.

Tribulation Brethren of Our Lord, the King

Christ's "brethren" refers to the 144,000 Israelites, 12,000 from every tribe of Israel, a mighty company of tribulation witnesses for the Lord. The post-rapture converts from all the Gentile nations will react with goodwill and kindness to the 144,000 Jewish evangelists. This is a natural reaction, amplified by the Holy Spirit's anointing and guidance upon the new believers.

The reason we identify Christ's brethren primarily as Jews will be apparent. The only recognizable human groups on earth during the tribulation are:

1. Israelites, including 144,000 Jewish preachers of the Gospel. Scripture regards all of Israel to be Christ's brethren according to the flesh. (See Romans 9:3-5.)
2. The tribulation-time Gentile converts. Saint Paul describes born-again people as former Gentiles. (See 1 Corinthians 12:2, Ephesians 2:11-12.)
3. The goyim, or unsaved, pagan Gentiles.

ONLY PEOPLE in categories one and two could ever qualify as Jesus' brethren. Never, in any age, would unbelieving pagan goyim be thought of as Christ's brethren.

Salvation by Nationality? By Works?

THIS ENTIRE ACCOUNT of the judgment of the sheep and goats proposes a problem as it is normally translated in our English Bibles. On the surface, it seems that the passage teaches that salvation is received because of national identity (sheep nations), through good works.

Even more distressing is the idea that people who are part of a goat nation are damned to eternal hell because of their nationality and because everyone in that goat nation has neglected the works spoken of by the Son of Man who sits upon the throne.

. . .

Salvation by Faith

Nothing could be further from the truth. To think that salvation comes by any means other than God's merciful grace through faith is not recognizable as being a Biblical teaching. It is absolutely grotesque!

St. Paul teaches, "For by grace are ye saved through faith; and that not of yourselves: it is the gift of God: Not of works, lest any man should boast. For we are his workmanship, created in Christ Jesus unto good works, which God hath before ordained that we should walk in them" (Ephesians 2:8-10).

Works Are Important, Too

The great apostle of faith advocates our premise exactly. The phrase, "created in Christ Jesus unto good works," can be applied to Jesus' teaching in the prophecy of Matthew chapter 25 regarding the sheep and goats. The people who will treat Christ's brethren with kindness do so because they are saved. It is not the reverse, to wit, they are not saved by their mitzvot (good deeds).

Doomed Goats

Then shall he say also unto them on the left hand,

Depart from me, ye cursed, into everlasting fire, prepared for the devil and his angels: For I was an hungered, and ye gave me no meat: I was thirsty, and ye gave me no drink: I was a stranger, and ye took me not in: naked, and ye clothed me not: sick, and in prison, and ye visited me not. Then shall they also answer him, saying, Lord, when saw we thee and hungered, or athirst, or a stranger, or naked, or sick, or in prison, and did not minister unto thee? Then shall he answer them, saying, Verily I say unto you, in as much as ye did it not to one of the least of these, ye did it not to me (Matthew 25:41-45).

Entire Nations in Hell?

At this juncture we note again that one is not damned because of his nationality, so it is individuals and not entire nations that are being judged. If the traditional mode of interpretation were followed, we would have entire nations being cast into hell with individuals having no opportunity to accept or reject Christ.

Serious Consequences

"And these shall go away into everlasting punishment: but the righteous into life eternal" (Matthew 25:46).

This is no parable. It is a prophecy of definite future events! Verse 46 powerfully drives home the fact that this passage is set in a post-tribulation scenario in which Jesus judges the people of planet earth. Every living person on earth at the end of the tribulation is sent into hell, or is granted entry into the millennial kingdom, saved forever.

The subjects of the judgment are twofold. First of all, there are the goats that are damned for eternity. This damnation results from a rejection of God's plan of salvation. They are incorrigible rebels who have slavishly followed the beast, have received his mark and worshiped his image. Their neglect of good deeds is a testimony of their hatred for the chosen people, the Jewish nation, and it reflects the unredeemed condition of their souls. No one is damned because of his or her national identity.

The second group is the sheep, representing those who will be saved in the tribulation and who survive the wrath of the antichrist. These survivors stand as redeemed individuals before the Judge and are rewarded with entrance to the kingdom because they accepted Jesus Christ as personal Savior and Lord. Their good deeds are displayed as evidence that they truly know Jesus as their Savior.

MILLENNIUM **after the Judgment**

THE TRIBULATION-REDEEMED people (who survive martyrdom) will be subjects of Christ's kingdom during the 1,000-year reign of Jesus on the throne of David in Jerusalem.

The millennium, however, is an idyllic age, not a

perfect age. There will be occurrences of sin, rebellion, death and punishment (Zechariah 14)!

You may wonder how saved people, living in the millennium under the reign of Jesus Himself could possibly become rebels? After all, was not their reward eternal life (verse 46)? The answer is very simple. They cannot and will not rebel.

The original earthlings who are allowed entrance into the millennial kingdom are all saved people. They are saved after the rapture of the church. They hide from the antichrist and are not beheaded by the henchmen of the beast. They stand in the judgment when everyone living on earth at the end of the tribulation will be called before the judgment throne.

How Can it Be?

THE SHEEP PEOPLE who enter the millennium may be few in number. Having passed the test in the Matthew 25 judgment, they have eternal life and cannot and will not rebel against Jesus, but they will have children and grandchildren and greatgrandchildren. Ideal living conditions characterizes the earthly kingdom. Poverty and hunger are a thing of the past. There will be no wars. Under this umbrella of physical grace, the population could easily reach 20 billion in 1,000 years.

Those born in the millennium will hear the preaching of the Gospel and must decide whether or not to accept Jesus as Savior. Even under the wonderful conditions on planet earth when no one will be hungry and there will be more than adequate housing for everyone, when wild animals will be tame and peace prevails everywhere, Jesus has to rule with an iron scepter to keep order (Psalm 2:9; Revelation 12:5; 19:15).

"Never again will there be in it an infant who lives but a few days, or an old man who does not live out his years; he who dies at a hundred will be thought a mere youth; he who fails to reach a hundred will be considered accursed" (Isaiah 65:20 NIV). A thousand years' worth of generations will build the greatest civilization earth has ever known. However, the offspring of the early pioneer millennialists will not be coerced to except Christ as Savior. The purpose of the millennial age is to finally prove that the fallen human heart inclines toward evil, unless the individual calls upon God for salvation. Even with Satan bound up during the 1,000 years and Jesus ruling the earth, there is rebellion, especially at the very end of the millennium. See Revelation 20.

Except a Man Be Born Again

God has no grandchildren. He only has sons and daughters. Jesus' dialogue with Nicodemus as recorded in John's Gospel expresses it this way, "Jesus answered and said unto him, Verily, verily, I say unto thee, except a man be born again, he cannot see the kingdom of God" (John 3:3). (Also see John 3:7, 1 Peter 1:23.)

. . .

Only One Plan of Salvation

Let us emphasize one more time that God does not have two or more plans of salvation. The only salvation is provided for us by the death of Jesus on the cross and empowered by His victorious resurrection from the dead. This provision applies to pre-Christian, Old-Covenant believers as well as all who are saved in the Church Age and further to all who will be saved in the tribulation and in the millennium. Isaiah points out that the kingdom age will be the greatest time of bliss for humanity since the fall from Eden.

A curious fact is that the Hebrew prophets, with their Near East mind-set did not, in many cases, manifest a high regard for chronological arrangement of ideas. This challenges our Western mode of straight-line thinking. We seem to be fanatics for chronology. Isaiah 65 is a good example of Oriental construction and expression of ideas:

> Behold, I will create new heavens and a new earth. The former things will not be remembered, nor will they come to mind. But be glad and rejoice forever in what I will create, for I will create Jerusalem to be a delight and its people a joy. I will rejoice over Jerusalem and take delight in my people; the sound of weeping and of crying will be heard in it no more (Isaiah 65:17-19).

This portion of Isaiah's prophecy refers to the eternal state of the redeemed. In verse 20 he reverts to predicting millennial conditions, many of which are temporary:

Never again will there be in it an infant who lives but a few days, or an old man who does not live out his years; he who dies at a hundred will be thought a mere youth; he who fails to reach a hundred will be considered accursed. They will build houses and dwell in them; they will plant vineyards and eat their fruit. No longer will they build houses and others live in them, or plant and others eat. For as the days of a tree, so will be the days of my people; my chosen ones will long enjoy the works of their hands. They will not toil in vain or bear children doomed to misfortune; for they will be a people blessed by the LORD, they and their descendants with them. Before they call I will answer; while they are still speaking I will hear. The wolf and the lamb will feed together, and the lion will eat straw like the ox, but dust will be the serpent's food. They will neither harm nor destroy on all my holy mountain," says the LORD (Isaiah 65:20-25).

Verse 25 beautifully describes the taming of all wild beasts and indicates the fact that peace will prevail on God's earth. While it is not specifically mentioned that this is the 1,000-year phase of the eternal kingdom, premillennialists will agree that this is the case.

We know that many unredeemed people born in the millennium will be deluded when Satan is loosed from the abyss and goes abroad throughout the world deceiving vulnerable, unsaved people who have already begun to question the person and authority of Jesus. This, not Armageddon, is absolutely the final conflict of the ages.

No General Judgment

SCRIPTURE DOES NOT TEACH a general judgment for all humanity. But let me tell you briefly about two other judgments that lie in the future. (For more information, see Chapter 12, *Believers Bow Before the Bema*.) One is the Bema judgment when, after the rapture, all believers from Adam until the rapture (some say only church believers) will be evaluated according to their works, not to determine whether they are saved or lost, but to determine what works they have done which deserve rewards. Everyone in this Judgment is saved before he arrives there. Some receive great rewards. Some receive no rewards, but they are saved:

> Now if any man build upon this foundation gold, silver, precious stones, wood, hay, stubble; Every man's work shall be made manifest: for the day shall declare it, because it shall be revealed by fire; and the fire shall try every man's work of what sort it is. If any man's work abide which he hath built thereupon, he shall receive a reward. If any man's work shall be burned, he shall suffer loss: but he himself shall be saved; yet so as by fire (1 Corinthians 3:14-15).

This Bema judgment of believers takes place right after the rapture of the church. Paul speaks of it as "The

PIERCING THE FUTURE

judgment seat of Christ" before which all believers must appear.

BACK ON EARTH

WHILE THIS IS GOING on in heaven, the seven-year tribulation unfolds on earth. At the end of the tribulation, Jesus will come back to earth with all the holy angels and with the raptured, glorified church in His entourage. (See Revelation 19:8, 14.)

In Revelation 19 and 20, the writer, John, describes how Messiah defeats antichrist at Armageddon. Satan, the false prophet and the antichrist are incarcerated in the lake of fire. "And the beast was taken, and with him the false prophet that wrought miracles before him, with which he deceived them that had received the mark of the beast, and them that worshiped his image. These both were cast alive into a lake of fire burning with brimstone" (Revelation 19:20). And the devil that deceived them was cast into the lake of fire and brimstone, where the beast and the false prophet are, and shall be tormented day and night for ever and ever (Revelation 20:10).

AFTER TEN CENTURIES of Peace

THE JUDGMENT of the sheep and goats takes place. The millennium begins. At the end of the 1,000 years, Satan is loosed for a season. He deceives many, builds an army, attacks Christ at Jerusalem, and is defeated, nevermore to have access to planet earth. The Second Resurrection of all the wicked dead takes place.

The Great White Throne Judgment

THE MILLENNIUM COMES TO AN END. The battle of Gog and Magog II is over. Satan is cast into the Lake of Fire. Now it is time for the final and last of all judgments: the great White Throne judgment.

> And I saw a great white throne, and him that sat on it, from whose face the earth and the heaven fled away; and there was found no place for them. And I saw the dead, small and great, stand before God; and the books were opened: and another book was opened, which is the book of life: and the dead were judged out of those things which were written in the books, according to their works. And the sea gave up the dead which were in it; and death and hell delivered up the dead which were in them: and they were judged every man according to their works. And death and hell were cast into the lake of fire. This is the second death. And whosoever was not found written in the book of life was cast into the lake of fire (Revelation 20:11-15).

This is not a judgment to decide who is saved and who is lost. That has already been decided by each individual, in this life, on this earth. Since all redeemed persons are already resurrected in the first resurrection, this is a judgment of the damned. This event is to reveal the degree and intensity of punishment each sinner will endure in the Lake of Fire.

Eternity Dawns
No More Wars, Poverty, nor Death - Never Again

AND I SAW a new heaven and a new earth: for the first heaven and the first earth were passed away; and there was no more sea. And I John saw the holy city, new Jerusalem, coming down from God out of heaven, prepared as a bride adorned for her husband. And I heard a great voice out of heaven saying, Behold, the tabernacle of God is with men, and he will dwell with them, and they shall be his people, and God himself shall be with them, and be their God. And God shall wipe away all tears from their eyes; and there shall be no more death, neither sorrow, nor crying, neither shall there be any more pain: for the former things are passed away. And he that sat upon the throne said, Behold, I make all things new. And he said unto me, write: for these words are true and faithful (Revelation 21:1-5).

The Great Invitation

. . .

BEHOLD, I come quickly: blessed is he that keepeth the sayings of the prophecy of this book. And, behold, I come quickly; and my reward is with me, to give every man according as his work shall be. And the Spirit and the bride say, Come. And let him that heareth say, Come. And let him that is athirst come. And whosoever will, let him take the water of life freely.

He which testifieth these things saith, Surely I come quickly. Amen. Even so, come, Lord Jesus. The grace of our Lord Jesus Christ be with you all. Amen (Revelation 22:7, 12, 17, 20, 21).

PART II
GAZING INTO YOUR FUTURE

8

YOUR FUTURE AND YOUR MONEY

BY TOM CLOUD

Whenever believers begin to think or read about the future rapture, or tribulation, timing often comes to mind. It is difficult to write about those "last days" without leaning toward a particular notion concerning end-times. It is not my intention in this chapter to favor pre-, mid-, or post-tribulation, but to look at world economies with a view of finances from a prophetic stance. I will use God's Word to shed light on different demands, commandments, and investment beliefs that impact our lives daily.

Very few subjects command more attention than finances. Of utmost importance should be serving as good stewards of the money that God has entrusted us with while we are on earth. In the following paragraphs I will take a look at some very pointed subjects concerning finances — subjects ranging from the so-called prophets that are revered by the secular world all the way to the words of our Lord and Savior Jesus Christ. I will discuss what the Bible has to say about the antichrist and finances in the "last days."

Christians must be wary of the so-called prophets that are revered by the secular world, especially the so-called prophets that can deceive even the elect. Nostradamas, a well-respected prophet for the past few centuries because of his predictions, spoke of President Kennedy's assassination, World War II, and Adolf Hitler hundreds of years before events concerning these people occurred. How did he and others like Edgar Casey and Jeane Dixon know some of their predictions would come true?

Satan gives some people a glimpse of the future just as God gives the gift of prophecy. Satan knows the truth (James 2:19) but is the father of lies and does not stand in the truth (John 8:44). From the thirteenth chapter of the last book in the Bible, Revelation, Satan will give powers to the future antichrist and false prophets. The antichrist is also referred to as "the son of perdition," "the man of lawlessness," "the little horn," "the beast from the sea," "the king of fierce countenance," "the rider of the white horse," and other names mentioned in the Bible. God told us how Satan could affect people through numerous examples in the Bible, starting with Adam and Eve in the Garden of Eden, to Job, and ending in the chapters of Revelation. As we enter the 21st century, many in the secular world are asking whether Satan gave Nostradamas the ability to interpret that one would come who would be a visionary. Two thousand years ago, Jesus warned us, "for false Christs and false prophets will arise and will show great signs and wonders, so as to mislead, if possible, even the elect" (Matthew 24:22). Certainly, Jesus is talking about the "last days" in this verse. In addition to being surprised, shocked or even fearful of these occurrences, Christians should expect and pray about these incredible times when we will come face to face with the King. If the Truth tells us that we will see individuals perform great signs and wonders so as to mislead, then believers should prepare their verbal testimonies and spend time in prayer to soften their hearts in anticipation of this incredible time in God's plan.

Before we get into specifics about God's Word on finances for our future, it is also important to remember that accountability runs hand-in-hand with money and finances. In our spiritual fives, we find inaccurate information from the secular world that is not Biblical. One of the easiest ways to see if someone dealing with the money of others is empowered by God is to look no further than Matthew 7:12 - the Golden Rule. Accountability to God, our families, and ourselves is something we look at from a personal view. We should expect the same from those people who deal with our finances. Accountability is the most overlooked aspect of financial planning and money management from both a personal and professional standpoint. Satan hates accountability more than anything and being accountable is what he avoids at all costs. Accountability wears down one's pride, bringing a person to repent and turn to Jesus Christ. If a prophet or a counselor teaches that every human is a sinner and accountable to God, this is the Truth (Romans 3:19). Any prophet, financial planner or other person who deals in finances who avoids the topic of accountability should be held in suspicion. Ultimately, accountability is what separates Christianity from every other world religion, and so it is in finances.

To truly be accountable, we must look directly ahead diligently, seeking the proper way to diversify our holdings. This is not an issue that was resolved when Y2K died; instead, it is an event that will impact our finances for months and possibly years. If a recession does come, it will become even more important for Christians to look to God's Word to determine how to diversify investments (Ecclesiastes 11:2) in both turbulent times and times of peace.

There are two primary reasons I believe there will be a recession. Companies around the world spent large sums of money to prepare for potential Y2K problems. The vast amount of money spent on computer repairs, re-training employees on new equipment/software, overtime, inventory, and working with suppliers to guarantee future inventories has caused a surge in growth around the world. Subsequently, the first reason I anticipate a recession will be the contraction of these areas. All of the preparation in anticipation of Y2K problems has created jobs both in the U.S. economy and around the world. As Y2K concerns subside, there could be a sharp cutback early in the year 2000. A second reason for a world recession pertains to inventories. Inventories grew throughout 1999 as companies looked to the probability of Y2K-related problems and the interconnectivity that could be a problem in the first half of the year 2000. Inventory stocking should fall off quickly in the year 2000 and return to normal inventory levels as the year progresses. U.S. companies which have been obtaining this excess inventory have been importing their goods predominately from other countries. This is obvious when one looks at the current trade deficit in the U.S. Trade deficits in 1999 were the highest in American history. While part of that figure can be attributed to Y2K, Americans must now pay for it through a recession or perhaps a sharp drop in the value of the dollar. Understanding trade balance is important in any financial discussions due to the value in different world currencies.

If the world is heading toward the end-times, Christians must ponder another question: Will the world leader who is forthcoming have financial systems set up that will make it easy for him to rule and to deceive many? All one has to do is pick up a *Wall Street Journal* and go into the "Money and Investing" section. Compare the Dow Jones Industrial Average (USA) and the DJ World Stocks Index (excluding the USA). Since the problems in Asia in 1997, these markets have performed almost identically. This is not by accident. The world financial system is already in place for a one-world political and religious leader to take over. To further understand how this could happen, take a look at the world as a "piggy bank" and call it the International Monetary Fund (IMF). The IMF acts as a place for the most powerful countries in the world to store their reserves and as an emergency fund to bail out other countries. No doubt that the coming world leader, or "little horn" as the Bible refers to him, will have complete control over the IMF. In fact, the future "666" money system could be linked or controlled by the IMF. Revelation 13:16-18 tells us:

> ...he calls us all the small and the great, and the rich and the poor, and the free man and the slaves, to be given a mark on their right hand, or on their forehead, and he provides that no one should sell, except the one who has the mark, the name of the beast or the number of his name. Here is wisdom. Let him who has understanding calculate the number of the beast. For the number is that of a man; and his number is six hundred and sixty-six.

This verse must be viewed in context of the interesting times in which we live.

A one-world currency will not be created by the beast from the sea or antichrist, but by the beast from the earth, the false prophet. The beast from the earth is the final component of the evil trinity (Satan, antichrist, and false prophet) and is the last to appear on the scene. The false prophet is a religious leader, unlike the man of lawlessness who is a political leader. The false prophet will perform great signs and wonders.

Many have postulated that a monetary crisis could usher in the antichrist because of the economic havoc that could be heaped on the world, but the Scriptures point to war as the reason. Jesus said, "And you will be hearing the wars and rumors of wars; see that you are not frightened, for those things must take place, but that is not yet the end" (Matthew 24:6). It would be impossible to finish the above thought without considering what God says in Revelation about the false beast which, as the son of perdition, will bring false peace to the world (Revelation 6:2). The white horse he is riding represents this false peace.

Why will the world follow this individual? We are told that he will have a fatal wound that is healed (Revelation 13:3-12) and his partner, the false prophet, will "perform great signs, and so that he even makes fire come down out of heaven to the earth in the presence of men" (Revelation 13:13).

As Christians have looked at the behavior of the leaders of the United States during recent history, the world has been winning. Accountability, unfortunately, seems to have become a thing of the past. The kind of behavior that Christians have condemned for decades is now being accepted "as the way things are." This lack of accountability alone will be evident as the antichrist rises from the old Roman Empire area, according to Daniel in the Old Testament. The world is being prepared for these incredible beliefs. The centerpiece to the coming evil trinity is that there will be little, if any, individual accountability.

The new one-world currency that will evolve under the leadership of this coming world leader will not necessarily be a number. The mark possibly could be the name of the new one-world currency. The name and number of the false prophet because he gets all his power from Satan will be a riddle that pertains to the origin of the fall of man - "for the number is that of a man." Six hundred and sixty-six is representative of man. It is the opposite of God. Look back at the size of Nebuchadnezzar's statue. Six- six-six is short of complete, which is represented by the number seven. Just as words are not enough to save us, 6-6-6 is a number for a currency that will not be quite enough to save the world from a financial collapse.

The prophet Daniel spoke directly to the saints about finances and investments worldwide when he wrote:

> And he shall speak great words against the Most High and shall wear out the saints of the Most High, and think to change times and laws: and they shall be given into his hand until a time and times and the dividing of time (Daniel 7:25).

Here Christians are told that the "little horn" shall speak great words against the Most High, shall wear out the saints of the Most High, and think to change times and laws. From a financial aspect, laws would have to be changed worldwide for a one-world currency. In speaking with 29 to 30 people a week, I have learned that a person's identity is more and more becoming dependent on money and not on Christ Jesus. In 2 Timothy 1:2, God tells us that in the last days, "men will be lovers of money." Certainly, there is no truer statement about the U.S. today. We are lovers of money! Never in the history of mankind has there been as much wealth (as widely distributed) as today. Yet man and his sinful nature still are not satisfied.

There are three or four areas in which "lovers of money" are impacting the world financial picture. They are (1) improper asset allocation (Ecclesiastes 11:2), (2) lack of savings, (3) soaring debt worldwide, and (4) not giving back to God the just part that He has mandated Christians to give. I will discuss the first three in more detail and I always encourage the fourth, tithes and offerings, in accordance with God's commandments.

Improper Asset Allocation

IMPROPER ASSET ALLOCATION is the area in which there is too much speculation, and investors are falling into the world system rather than looking at the whole duty of man according to God. Ecclesiastes 11:2 tells us to, "give a portion to seven, and also to eight: for thou knowest not what evil shall be upon the earth." In Ecclesiastes 12:13, 14 we are told, "let us hear the conclusion of the whole matter: Fear God and keep His commandments: for this is the whole duty of man. For God shall bring every work and due judgment with every secret thing, whether it be good or whether it be evil." There is no area in which we fail in our duty more than when we try to outguess markets and allocate large percentages to one area in our investment lives. For 23 years I have written and spoken about the fact that the money God entrusts us with on earth should be managed His way - not by the ways of the world. The biggest potential for "alterations" and "loss" is in the area of the stock market. Over the past several years, articles have been written leading many to fall into the trap of investing large percentages of money into the stock market because of large increases over the past 17 years. From 1996-1998, these averages were around 25 percent annually. Many arguments have been made by the powers that be at brokerage firms that these rates are sustainable even though interest rates have been dropping for 17 years. A few of the symptoms that have kept such large percentages of clients' portfolios in the stock market have been:

- Lower price earnings multiples are accepted because interest rates are low.
- High inflation has gone to low inflation.
- Heavy traffic of online trading has caused new momentum.
- Baby boomers are spending more and some say they are saving more, therefore, they are driving the GDP and/or they are driving the stock market.

Common sense tells us that baby boomers cannot spend more and save more at the same time. I also hear that earnings are no longer important. I've seen articles inferring that interest rates no longer matter because they are going to be low from now on. Direct-deposit checks flowing into the stock market and 401 (k) plans, and certainly foreign investments coming into America as a safe haven, impact our economy. While the above symptoms could be argued as valid reasons for the market going up, they certainly give us Christians no reason to turn our backs on a mandate of dividing our wealth seven or eight ways and being good stewards with what we have been given. Given the levels of wealth around the world today, one would think that the world would be satisfied. However, it moves us to the real motive of "alterations and laws." The motive, of course, is greed. In 1984, 22 percent of the average household assets were represented by equities.

Today, that number is close to 45 percent. Also, today, we see most of the investments and net worth of Americans tied up in equities and real estate. These two asset categories should be in a well-diversified, mandated portfolio that God has given us. However, bonds, fixed-income products, foreign-currency investments, precious metals, and cash and money markets should also be included. While many stories in the Bible teach us to make a return on what God has entrusted us with, Christians are also told to preserve wealth and to spread investments out, as mentioned earlier. It is critical to properly allocate our assets when dealing with God's money.

Savings by Americans continue to fall while equity markets continue to rise. Studies have shown that the ratio of U.S. household equity and mutual fund holdings, as compared to disposable personal income, is now more than 130 percent. People are speculating with their homes, borrowing money and putting it in equity markets, thinking the increases of the past several years will continue. The total U.S. consumer and mortgage debt outstanding shows that nearly 100 percent of the personal disposable income of the average American is tied up. The facts are in: we have never had less personal savings than we have currently. The number for 1999 was down to slightly over 2 percent. As this speculative bubble grows with the lack of savings, and the "get rich" mentality of investors today, becomes the mindset, we must look to Scripture for our examples:

- Save your money regardless of what any

government or ruler may tell you (Proverbs 6:6-8).
- Save your wages with money you earned honestly (Proverbs13:11).
- Invest your earnings as the wise do and do use all your resources (Proverbs 21:20).
- Live below your means just as the ant does, so when difficult times come you will be able to meet your needs (Proverbs 30:25).
- Do not invest your savings in a risky way or you will not have anything left to support your family (Ecclesiastes 5:13-14).

While the lack of savings certainly is a major problem in God's eyes, another area closely tied to a lack of savings is the area of explosive debt. Debt is clearly a handle by which the future antichrist and the false prophet can take control of people's lives. What does the Lord say about debt?

- Only the wicked borrow and do not repay (Psalm 27:31). Look at the bankruptcy level in the U.S.
- Do not say to your lender that you will pay him tomorrow when you have it today (Proverbs 3:28). Is that not what Americans are doing with credit cards? Forty-one million, or 14 percent of Americans, applied for credit cards in 1998. For most, this was their second to fifth credit card. Sixty- seven percent of the applications were for platinum cards. Also, in

1998, 51,200 people charged their federal income taxes, according to Reuter's on April 7, 1999.
- Do not take out a loan or borrow against your sureties or well-being (Proverbs 22:26, 27). The level of home equity loans and margin trading is currently astronomical.
- Continue to pay a debt until it is paid off (Romans 13:8).
- The borrower is servant to the lender (Proverbs 22:7). Here is the verse that literally tells us how laws can be changed to allow the antichrist to rule a person's life.

No doubt the level of individual and government debt, which is now over $25 trillion in the U.S., could play a major role in when the antichrist enters the world scene.

With debt increasing and savings decreasing, it is obvious that the idea of stock prices increasing due to savings can be dismissed. Also, increased salaries have been given as one of the main reasons for the eleven-fold increase in stocks over the past 17 years. Certainly, increased salaries are not a major reason for the movement of the stock market.

Improper Asset Allocation, Within Stocks

. . .

NINETY-FOUR PERCENT of shares in the U.S. stock markets are owned by entities with a choice of allocation. While the government invests six percent in U.S. stock shares, the remainder is invested by individuals, insurance companies, pension plans, and mutual fund managers. The average 401 (k) plan invests 71.09 percent of its funds in equities, according to Hewitt and Associates. Ed Larson, chief equity officer for AIM, said in the *Wall Street Journal* in April of 1999, "From a decade-long belief in wrongly diversified portfolios, the table shows thinking shifting first to a 100 percent S&P 500-based portfolio and, now to belief in the holding of a single hot stock." Larson goes on to state that mutual fund managers must buy the hot stocks, or they will not perform well and will not be rated high among the rating services.

Another reason for a move to improper asset allocation is referred to as index manipulation. This is when stocks are changed within all indexes to make the index perform better. The S&P 500, the most broadly used index to measure stock-market performance, is now being changed constantly so the hottest stocks are being given the greatest weight. Since 1984, the S&P 500 has become increasingly weighted with "new economy stocks." These include telecommunications, technology and consumer services. In 1994, new economy stocks represented only 60 percent of the S&P 500. Today, new economy stocks represent 75 percent, according to the *New York Times* in an article written in 1999. For the 12-month period ending in December 1998, the top ten stocks in the S&P 500 accounted for 43 percent of the indices' gain. For the 12 months ending February 28,

1999, the top ten stocks contributed 49 percent of the S&P's advance.

Then there are what Solomon Brothers calls the Laggard's indicator, which measures the number of stocks trailing the S&P 500 Index by 15 percent or more. In the second quarter of 1999, 75 percent of all of the 500 stocks in the S&P were trailing by over 15 percent. This was the highest number recorded since the severe recession of '73 and '74. The most impressive of all these figures occurred in the first quarter of 1999, when 18 of the hot stocks and new economy stocks accounted for 100 percent of the S&P 500's increase. These statistics are included to better explain the index manipulation that has taken place strictly as a way to "take" the average client/investor who simply doesn't have the time to do the research into what the real indexes are. Government and stock-market firms realize that America has become consumed with accumulating money and improving status. When one evaluates the index manipulation, the debt binge and the toppling of savings, it is easy to see how economists like Ed Yardeni are predicting a 30 percent contraction in the stock market in the year 2000.

A lot has been written about the circuit breakers and trading restrictions that were revised in May '99 as to how the stock market exchange will shut down in each level of drops in the indexes. It is therefore easy to see that any sharp drop in the stock market would leave most households 35 percent short of being able to pay off their consumer debts if this correction takes place as this writer and many others believe. If this scenario plays out and loan defaults start, the world economy could go into a severe recession for the first time in 26 years. With any sharp downturn in world stock markets, or recessions worldwide, Christians can certainly see a time outlined in the Bible. The world is set up for the antichrist to control the world's "piggy bank" and use it to manipulate stock markets, investments, and all aspects of economies around the globe. A statement released by the IMF in March of 1999 plainly shows the impact the IMF will exert in individual finances during the new world economy.

The IMF and the Private Sector

THE IMF IS EXAMINING the important and complex issues associated with involving the private sector in forestalling and resolving financial crisis. By formally involving private creditors and private enterprises in crisis fighting, the international community aims to limit both moral hazard "the perception that international rescues encourage risky investments" and a "rush for the exits" by private investors during a crisis.

Efforts to better involve the private sector in crisis resolution serve a number of purposes. By reducing outflows that occur in the context of members programs, private sector involvement can make the adjustment process more orderly. Such involvement is thought appropriate in order to share the burden of crisis resolution equitably with the official sector, strengthen market discipline, and in the process, increase the efficiency of international capital markets and the ability of emerging market borrowers to protect themselves against volatility and contagion. An additional goal is avoiding moral hazard - the encouraging of imprudent or unsustainable behavior by creditors or debtors that can't increase the potential magnitude and frequency of future crisis.

This statement infers that each individual will be responsible, financially, for the whole. Of particular interest is the part that says, "rush for the exits" and "strengthen market discipline." They are emphatically saying they will manipulate the market if private investors try to get out in a "crisis" and one of their purposes is to encourage the "buy and hold theory." The level of control the IMF will have over individual investors at that point would have been difficult to imagine just a few short years ago. How does this stated future market manipulation relate to us as individual investors here in the United States? There is one thing I want to make clear: Investing in the stock market is not the problem. The problem is improper asset allocation. It's putting too much into one basket and believing that one can outguess all the markets. This is an individual's responsibility. Remember that individuals own 48 percent of the stocks in U.S. markets. It is certainly understandable that the IMF would not allow a "rush to the exits."

To elaborate further on the possibility that there could be a burst in the American stock market, if there is a market correction of only 20 percent, there will be mutual fund liquidations, insurance companies forced to sell stocks, and 401 (k) plans moving from stock holdings to either money markets or bond portfolios. The "alterations of laws" not only might come true but should be expected.

Another example that may hit home is the debt that has been amassed by the improper management of our government. The budget to run the U.S. government was $500 billion in 1980. Today, only 20 short years later, the fiscal 2000 budget is $1.8 trillion, representing a 350 percent increase in the size of government. The American public continues to fall into the trap of believing that the budget has been balanced. That, most assuredly, is not the case. In viewing the website of the Bureau of Public Debt, the deficit grows monthly when the budget is not manipulated or when funds borrowed from the Social Security trust fund are not counted as debt. This is important for investors to realize because now, $25 trillion of debt has been amassed throughout the sectors of the government, real estate, consumer, municipal, and bond debt. Until there is a sharp contraction and money by decree disappears, world economies will have a hard time growing. The engine that has driven this massive debt has been the move from inflation to disinflation over the past 18 years. In all probability, the world will have to reinflate starting after the next recession. At that point, asset categories will change. One should go back to review what investments did in the '70's and '80's. Using God's mandate in Ecclesiastes 11:2, Americans desperately need to take the advice of the Lord before it's too late: "Divide your wealth seven, even eight, for you do not know what misfortune may occur on the earth."

Christians should not feel anxious about the future, as we cannot be defeated because of the victory that Christ brought us from the grave. We must eye Israel as a place to look for investments in the future. Israel has caught the eye of many investors, including myself, over the past 12 months. Its interest rates have decreased, and its stock market has increased at double the rates of the U.S. In Deuteronomy 30, Ezekiel 36, Ezekiel 37:25-29, Isaiah 51, and Jeremiah 33, God tells us that He will restore Israel. There are a myriad of verses concerning the restitution of the "Holy Land" that readers might challenge themselves to find. Israel, as we move to end-times, will be more profitable than ever before in the history of civilization.

On March 5, 1999, the *Wall Street Journal* published an article entitled "Investors, Amid Battered Emerging Markets, Shift Attention to Israel, Other Unexpected Places." This article states, "Investors seek potential in Israel, citing falling interest rates, and proving consumer demand and economic restructuring... The falling interest rates are driving stocks higher in Israel where the benchmark rate has dropped and is expected to drop further." The part of the article that also fits with Scripture is that the economy is growing, and it is expected to grow stronger for the next several years. Israel has been transformed from a barren land to being the third largest exporter of food in the world currently (Isaiah 27:6).

The Televiev 100 (TASE) increased 44 percent in the first half of 1999, which was more than double the rate of the DOW Industrials. Knowing what God says about the future of Israel, and especially Israel in end-times, it is interesting to look at Israeli stocks as the next place to moderately diversify one's portfolio, as evidenced in Ecclesiastes 11:2. The strongest stock sectors in Israel currently are food, oil, and technology. For further information, visit the TASE website (the address is www.tase.co.il). With many people trying to figure out how someone would want to invade Israel when they aren't looking at God's Word, the answer could lie in the oil reserves. Oil from Israel is another area that is suitable for consideration (as a small percentage of a diversified portfolio).

In looking at the continual growth and restoration of Israel, it is interesting to review Jeremiah 33:9, where the Lord says that, "All the nations of the earth, shall fear and tremble because of all the good and all the peace that I make for it." Nations do not fear powerless nations. In other verses, God says He will restore Israel's fortune specifically through oil and food. Here are several of the food and oil-related verses that show the way Israel's land was before and that describe God's blessings:

Job 29:6
- Isaiah 45:3
- Deuteronomy 32:13
- Ezekiel 16:55
- Jeremiah 31:12
- Ezekiel 16:53
- Deuteronomy 33:13, 19
- Genesis 14:10
- Isaiah 60:1-5
- Isaiah 35:1, 2
- Ezekiel 36:6, 9, and 30
- Isaiah 61:3
- Genesis 13:10

Genesis 19:24, 25, 28-29
Zechariah 14:14
Jeremiah 33:6, 7, and 9
Ezekiel 37:7-10
Genesis 49:25
Job 28:3-4
Job 28:9-10

Reading these verses has convinced me that Israel will become powerful, have oil, have fruitful fields, and be one of the wealthiest nations in the world. Currently Venezuela and Saudi Arabia provide the U.S. with over 30 percent of our oil imports, and if another country which relies more heavily on Venezuela and Saudi Arabia for oil sees that Israel is a major producer in oil, wealth could come to an area that literally only a few decades ago was a barren land with little possibility of ever having a major impact on world events - unless of course we believe what God told us. Once Israel becomes a major refiner of oil to the world, they will become very prosperous, thus fulfilling prophecy - especially for those companies planning to drill in Israel in the year 2000. Ezekiel 38:10-16 states that Gog will attack Israel in the last days to steal its fortunes. It is an intriguing possibility that oil might indeed be the "fortune." Many believers are now pondering the potential events that may unfold that would lead to such an invasion.

My hope in writing this chapter is that you will take a close look at a subject that God has more to say about than any other subject in the Bible. As we look at stewardship, investing, savings, and debt, many verses offer us direction. In 1 Timothy 6:9-11, Christians are told that the love of money is the root of all kinds of evil and yet we are instructed to invest our money (see Proverbs 13:11, Proverbs 21:5-6, Proverbs 16:20, Proverbs 28:20, Ecclesiastes 5:13-14, and reread Matthew 25:14-30). Christians must seek true wisdom when dealing with the wealth that God has bestowed upon us. Financially speaking, no area is more critical than dividing wealth as is mandated in Ecclesiastes 11:2. Even though there are possibilities that by moving into different areas one or two may fall in value, investors still must move forward to properly invest without overly speculating.

At Cloud and Associates, we genuinely try to realize at all times that God is first. We realize that all creation is under the authority of the Lord Jesus Christ. With that understanding, we attempt to glorify God in everything we do. We believe the Bible teaches financial stewardship. It is our first priority to help others, through Biblical teachings, to be wise stewards. If our clients don't succeed, we have not succeeded. We therefore make every effort to help our loyal clientele reach their financial investment goals. We make available, at no charge, relevant information about trends in the economy and investment options through newsletters, websites, e-mail updates, media, books, and many other outlets. We also feel that financial integrity is important to give our clients the best opportunities to realize profitable returns, and we retain the lowest margins possible on all products we offer.

Of all of our goals and objectives, however, we believe the most important thing in life is a personal relationship with the Lord Jesus Christ. Conveying all the wisdom in the world on economics and finances is pale in comparison to this fact. If you have never made a personal commitment to the Lord, we encourage you to seek out the Truth in the Bible. My staff at Cloud and Associates and I always stand ready to answer any financial or spiritual questions and will gladly share our convictions and beliefs with you at any time.

9

YOUR FUTURE AND TECHNOLOGY

BY CHUCK MISSLER

"It was the best of times and it was the worst of times..."
—Charles Dickens

AMERICANS TODAY LIVE in a luxury which Solomon could not begin to imagine. Solomon traveled at the speed of horseback. He communicated by means of a foot messenger. He clothed himself with the technology of an agrarian society.

George Washington, 2,700 years later, still traveled at the speed of horseback, communicated by hand-carried messages, and clothed himself with the technology of an agrarian society. The minor improvements in technology over those three millennia we would regard as trivial. Their decisions in life were constrained by the natural resources available.

Only two centuries later, we now travel at the speed of

sound, communicate at the speed of light, and clothe ourselves with molecules that are designed in laboratories. The resources available to us appear to be the result of our own decisions and commitments.

We now live in a technology-worshiping culture that has led us to a presumptive pride in mankind's achievements which is also unparalleled in human history.

This astonishing progress in our technology has been accompanied by an embracing of the most irrational myths imaginable. Instead of kneeling in reverential awe before the incredible craftsmanship evident in every nook and cranny of our amazing universe, we ascribe it all to the random occurrence of some kind of cosmic accident!

The conjectures popularized by Charles Darwin have not only set mankind's course in biology and anthropology, they have also led to the psychiatric constructs of Sigmund Freud and the social and economic premises of Karl Marx.

While the pagan tribes of the past attributed their fortunes to gods of wood and stone, modern technological cultures have invented the most insulting "god" of all: random chance. Reluctantly acknowledging that the universe had a beginning, cosmologists continue to patch their various versions of the Big Bang: "First there was nothing, and then it exploded!?"

Thus, our pseudo-science and technology have also led to a flight from any accountability to a Creator, and to a hedonism that rivals the worst of the pagan past and reveals a moral depravity unvarnished by the centuries.

Even so, let's take a brief survey, from a Biblical

Weapons Technology

The 20th Century is recognized as the bloodiest century in recorded history. Technology has brought us to the brink of the very precipice that Jesus warned us of:

> Except those days be shortened, there should no flesh be saved. But for the elect's sake, those days shall be shortened (Matthew 24:22).

It is only in our generation that this famous prediction is technologically feasible. In a world of rifles and bayonets, it was hard to visualize this as a realistic threat, but with the technology of modern warfare, it appears timely, indeed. The threat of a nuclear cloud hangs over every major geopolitical decision of our present day.

Every prophecy buff has examined the remarkable predictions of Ezekiel chapters 38 and 39. Here we see Magog (an ancient tribal term for the Scythians, the ancestors of the modern Russians), with a group of allies, arming and leading an ill-fated invasion of a regathered Israel. What makes the passage so well-known are two key factors:

1. It is the occasion that God intervenes on behalf of Israel and decimates the invading forces; and

2. The passage appears to suggest the use of nuclear weapons.

We note that after the battle, the leftover weapons will provide all the necessary fuel for Israel for seven years. Furthermore, the Jews will hire professionals who will wait seven months before entering the area, and then spend seven months clearing the area, taking all the debris they find and burying it all east of the Dead Sea — read that "downwind." Ezekiel even notes that later, if a traveler is passing through the region and finds something that the professionals have missed, he doesn't touch it! He marks its location and lets the professionals deal with it. To anyone who has reviewed the procedures for "NBC Warfare" (Nuclear-Biological-Chemical), this is all too familiar, even though this was penned by Ezekiel over 2,500 years ago!

Another provocative glimpse of modern warfare technology occurs in Zechariah:

> And this shall be the plague wherewith the LORD will smite all the people that have fought against Jerusalem; Their flesh shall consume away while they stand upon their feet, and their eyes shall consume away in their holes, and their tongue shall consume away in their mouth (Zechariah 14:12).

This seems to be highly suggestive of a neutron bomb. It is possible to tailor the design of a nuclear weapon so that its primary effect is an intense dispersion of neutrons, which can pass through buildings and other obstacles, and only destroy proteins. It would appear to be an ideal antipersonnel weapon, leaving the real estate and other tangible property intact.

(Although it was believed that only the United States and Israel had access to neutron bomb technology, recent espionage scandals appear to have conveyed this and other strategic technologies to both the Chinese and Russian military establishments.)

But other technological advances not only are impacting us daily, but also have some surprising Biblical relevance.

Communication Technologies

It is interesting that the Bible clearly describes a round earth. Furthermore, Jesus also warns that "all who are in Judea" are to flee when they "see" what will be going on inside the Holy of Holies of the (rebuilt) Temple. How can someone at home in Judea be able to observe what is going on inside the Temple - in fact, in the very inner sanctum of the Temple? On CNN, of course! It will be a cataclysmic event of global import. (Many of us remember being eyewitnesses to the assassination of Lee Harvey Oswald in Dallas in 1963. We do live in a highly visible world.)

The astonishing advances in electronics are, of course, impacting every aspect of our daily lives. The advent of electronic transactions, with debit and credit cards, bar codes and the like, are all too familiar to each of us. Now there are even developments of insertable microchips and other techniques being used for identification, prevention of fraud, etc.

The potential of these devices would appear to be a prerequisite for the kind of political (and religious) controls destined to be exploited by the coming world leader and his cohorts. So much has been conjectured about these techniques - and the notorious "666" - that we needn't dwell on these here.

The Information Age

Daniel prophesied a day when "many shall run to and fro, and knowledge shall be increased." (While many apply this to knowledge in general, the author believes that this primarily applies to knowledge about the Word of God.) In any case, the explosive growth of knowledge is clearly a primary characteristic of our times. In fact, if, as some estimate, all accumulated knowledge doubles every decade, then half of all that we now know was determined in the past ten years. It does appear that the impact of many of these astonishing new discoveries are validating much of what the Bible has portrayed all along over the centuries.

Decoding Life Itself

. . .

Many of the discoveries of recent decades have overturned the most cherished presumptions of the past. Certainly, in the fields of microbiology and quantum physics, our entire concepts of reality have been challenged. The discovery of DNA has revealed that our entire process of life is based on a three-out- of-four digital code, and that puts the final nail in the coffin of Darwin's theory of evolution as an explanation of biogenesis and the origin of life. A digital language, and the engines that process it, can't possibly "evolve" without astonishingly skillful design and very deliberate precision. The very digital nature of these codes designates the differentiation of the species so specified in Genesis, while also signifying that they all originated with the same Software Designer.

Discovering Our Digital Universe

Whether one gazes through a telescope or a microscope, one can't escape the presumption that there are no limits - large or small - to the universe in which we find ourselves. Yet, in the macrocosm of astronomy, we are now astonished to discover that the universe is finite. It has a limit and it had a beginning.

In the microcosm, too, we also find disturbing surprises. We would assume that if we take any length of something - anything - we could, of course, cut it in half. We assume that we can take one of the remaining segments and cut it in half again. And again. And so on, infinitely. But it turns out that this is not so! We eventually encounter an indivisible quantum that cannot be divided! A length of 10-33 centimeters, or a unit of 10-43 seconds, cannot be divided; it will cease to exist.

There are so many strange contradictory discoveries in particle physics that have challenged our very conceptions of reality. Perhaps most astonishing is that subatomic particles have "no locality," and that all such particles appear to be immediately interconnected. The implications of these disturbing discoveries have put our most solid of the sciences - physics - in a total turmoil. Even our atheistic scientists have suggested that it appears that our entire physical universe may be nothing more than "a thought in the mind of God!"

The realization that we apparently live in a ten-dimensional universe, rather than the three-dimensions we've been used to, requires more background than we can address in this brief article. A discussion of the bizarre implications of recent discoveries in quantum physics would go far beyond the opportunity here. Suffice it to say, most of our concepts of physical reality are in a rapid state of drastic revision!

The Social Impact of Communication

The technologies of improved communication continue to have deep impacts on our society. The ready exchange of video tapes was ostensibly a major factor in bringing down the Berlin Wall. The pervasiveness of facsimile machines and email are challenging the control of governments. (Many view the concentration of economic and political power in control of the mainline media as a major challenge to a free society, but the emergence of the alternative press, including talk radio and private newsletters, is viewed as the last bastion to preserve free speech in America.)

But no development is as far-reaching as the emergence of personal computers and the Internet.

The Internet

ONE OF THE most profound impacts of technology on our society is the availability of the astonishing resources of the Internet. Packet switching, the technology underlying the Internet, has not only plunged the cost of communication, it has made it independent of distance. With the pervasive personal information appliances and the Internet, one can browse a library in Europe or Israel as casually as the library down the street.

As an example, one can plunge into the Blue Letter Bible, an offering on the Internet, and explore a completely hyper- texted Bible - in English, Greek, or Hebrew - along with dozens of commentaries (both classical and contemporary), dictionaries or encyclopedias, all word-searchable and all for free of charge! One has available, in the comfort of one's own study, more complete resources than adorn the shelves of most seminaries.

The incredible resources that are now available on the

Internet are dramatically changing our society, and some of the biggest impacts are still ahead. The technology of the Internet has also opened additional new windows of opportunity, especially to those that cherish freedom of expression and fellowship.

Secrets of Your Own

Anyone who has seen the movie *Enemy of the State* has been sensitized to the implications of current surveillance technology which can be exploited against an individual citizen. With the increasing persecution of Christians throughout the world, and with Biblical Christianity becoming increasingly "politically incorrect" in the United States, many Christians are getting increasingly apprehensive. Many are pondering techniques which could assist churches which may be ultimately driven "underground." Fortunately, there are some pleasant surprises in emerging "counter-technology" that may prove of substantial value to all of us who value privacy.

Advances in Cryptography

The interception and breaking of secret codes have tumbled proud thrones and determined the outcome of major wars since the dawn of history. The deciphering of hidden messages has turned the tide of history on more occasions than one can enumerate. And even today they continue to have more of an impact than any of us can possibly imagine. Hardly a day goes by when we don't read about some computer code being compromised or secrets being stolen. Yet, one of the great ironies of our present age is that one of the most advanced cryptographic techniques is now available in any office supply store. It is relatively easy to enjoy virtually impregnable security in anyone's computer system. The availability of really secure communication capability may prove to be of very substantial value to the "underground church," so let's begin at the beginning.

Cryptography is the science of writing messages that no one except the intended receiver can read. Cryptanalysis is the science of reading them anyway. Most cryptographic methods employ complex transposition and transformation procedures under the control of a key, the protection of which is essential to the security of the entire process. (A contemporary example is the National Bureau of Standards' Data Encryption Standard [DES] which involves a 64-bit key that controls 17 stages of polyalphabetic substitution, each alternated with 16 stages of transpositions. Cryptanalysis involves an exhaustive search of all 264 keys. In the opinion of many experts, the DES is not adequately protective as the key is too short.)

The only truly unbreakable cipher requires a key which is...

1. as long as the message;
2. totally random; and

3. never reused.

Such a system is called a one-time pad because of the typical way it was implemented. While theoretically ideal, it proves unmanageably cumbersome in actual practice. Fortunately, a remarkably practical alternative has emerged in recent years.

One-Way Keys

In 1976, Whitfield Diffie and Martin E. Heilman of Stanford University forever changed the cryptographic landscape with their open publication of one-way keys. In conventional cryptosystems, a single key is used for both encryption and decryption. Such systems are called symmetric. The weakness of these systems is their requirement of protecting any exchange of such keys over a secure channel, which is inconvenient at best. (If a secure channel were available, why use encryption in the first place?)

The introduction by Diffie and Heilman to asymmetric keys has made possible the concept of "public key cryptography" which allows the participants to communicate without requiring a secret means of delivering the keys. It is possible to have a system in which one key is used for encryption and a different key is required for decipherment. One can publish the encryption key widely for those who would send a message. The encryption key is useless for decipherment. When the message is received by the intended recipient, his private complementary key is used for deciphering the message. This private key is, of course, made available to no one.

These asymmetric cryptosystems are based on mathematical techniques that are easy to compute in one direction, but excessively onerous and slow to solve in the reverse. The main public-key algorithms are the Diffie-Helman and RSA (developed at the Massachusetts Institute of Technology by Ronald L. Rivest, Adi Shamir and Leonard M. Adleman). A fairly advanced form of encryption technology is known as "PGIJ" for "Pretty Good Protection," and is readily available in most office supply stores or over the Internet. Many are beginning to use these techniques among business partners, clubs, and among various associates simply to gain experience in the practical implications of these techniques in anticipation of more serious requirements.

Symmetric systems are still the most efficient, and the public key techniques, while involving more substantial computational loads, make the conveyance of the necessary keys secure. The ability to share extensive, dynamically changing keys, accompanied by the necessary sophisticated software at both ends, makes practical protection readily available to anyone.

INVISIBLE TRANSACTIONS

THE WORLDWIDE INTERNET has already enabled the geographic separation of markets and their suppliers. A non-obvious implication of asymmetric encryption systems is that they can also be adapted for authentication, verification, and for electronic "signatures" for approving documents, contracts, and the like over e-mail. These techniques can thus also lead to the emergence of "cybercurrency," with the opportunity to conduct invisible commerce on a worldwide basis.

The advent of open, secure, asymmetric encryption is also leading to invisible (and thus non-taxable) transactions, eroding the restrictions of commercial borders and the surveillance and control of governments. There are those who look toward a day when governments will have to compete for - rather than exploit - "sovereign individuals" as citizens. The open availability of this technology leaves those who abhor privacy - especially governments and so-called "liberals" - very uncomfortable.

OTHER TECHNIQUES

MOST ENCRYPTION TECHNIQUES envision communication over a passive channel between the sender and receiver. However, the Internet is a dynamic, multi-node global network embedded with virtually unlimited databases. The exploitation of a dynamic data base - masquerading as a parts list or some similarly cryptic list - can be used as the equivalent of the proverbial one-time pad, and thus provide virtually "bulletproof" security to an "inner circle" or private group seeking privacy from prying eyes.

(We anticipate that the increasing persecution of

believers throughout the world may render some of these techniques of unique value to the leadership of fellowships in the years ahead. Now may be the time to acquaint yourself with their use, characteristics, and limitations if you anticipate darker days ahead.)

And there do seem to be some darker clouds looming on the horizon.

Hosea's Challenge to America

Hosea was the prophet who was called to declare God's indictment against the Northern Kingdom. (Almost a century later, Jeremiah would be called to render a similar service to the Southern Kingdom.)

Their Predicament

The kingdom divided after Solomon's death into two kingdoms: Judah, and Jerusalem in the south, under Rehoboam, Solomon's successor, and which, in large measure, remained faithful to God and the temple worship; and the Northern Kingdom under Jeroboam, called Israel, which plunged into idolatry.

The Northern Kingdom, with a successful standing army, had recovered all the territory lost by the United Kingdom (Judah and Israel), even the possession of Damascus. They enjoyed material prosperity unequaled since the days of Solomon. It was, indeed, "the best of times." At least, so it seemed from their own point of view.

However, they also had sunk into their lowest ebb of immorality and idol worship. In addition to idolatry, other sins denounced by Hosea included social injustice, violent crime, religious hypocrisy, political rebellion, dependence upon foreign alliances, selfish arrogance, and spiritual ingratitude. It was also, indeed, "the worst of times" - particularly from God's point of view.

Hosea's Message

This is the burden of Hosea: that although a loving and caring God had provided the Northern Kingdom's abundance and prosperity, its sin, disloyalty and abandonment of Him would force Him to vindicate His justice with judgment. After detailing the indictments against the nation, Hosea then declared that God would use its enemies as His instrument of judgment. Shortly it would be history.

An Uncomfortable Parallel?

The parallels with America are very, very disturbing. We, too, are experiencing unprecedented prosperity. The Dow stock index has been caressing 12,000. People are purchasing their third and fourth cars. Almost every home has a computer. It's difficult to find a pedestrian without a cellular phone in his ear or on his belt. Fuel for our cars costs less than a bottle of water. It is, indeed, "the best of times." Or so it seems.

And yet we have sunk to moral depths lower than could have been imagined only a generation ago. We are so "sophisticated" that we condone homosexuality as an "alternative lifestyle." We murder babies that are socially inconvenient. We change marriage partners like a fashion statement. We have abandoned the sanctity of commitment in our marriages and in our business enterprises. Our entertainment industry celebrates adultery, fornication, violence, and aberrant sex practices and every imaginable form of evil. We have become the world's leading exporters of all that God abhors. It certainly is "the worst of times" from His point of view.

God rebuked the people of Israel for their brutality: There was murder, there was violence, and there was warfare. We, too, have had Waco and Columbine High School. New York City has recorded more crimes than England, Scotland, Wales, Ireland, Switzerland, Spain, Sweden, the Netherlands, Norway, and Denmark, combined. And we, too, have had Vietnam, Kosovo, et al. We should have been sending Bibles, not bullets and bombs - missionaries, not missiles.

Immorality and deceit have come to characterize the highest offices of our nation as well. Our politics have condoned and covered up more murders than we dare list. Our public enterprises have been prostituted to the convenience of the elite. We have clearly disconnected character from destiny.

There is nothing new in the "new morality." They practiced it in 700 BC and were ultimately destroyed as a result. And so, may we be.

Israel had neglected the Word of God for 200 years. So, have we.

All this is but a mirror of the American soul. Behind all of our problems is the big problem: we are not recognizing God. We are virtually ignorant of God's Word.

We have outlawed Him from our schools and exiled Him from our lives.

The minute you get away from the Word of God, you are doomed to failure in both your Christian life and your national life.

The Rise of Paganism

It is hard to understand the insanity of paganism. Who can tally the blood that has been spilled upon the altars of stone of the gods who are not and the demons who are? When the knowledge of the True and Living God is refused, false gods inevitably fill the vacuum, and we become like the gods we worship!

Are idols of stone cold, unresponsive, impersonal? If you worship them, you, too, will become cold, unresponsive, impersonal.

Is the world materialistic, harsh and unforgiving? If

you worship the world, you, too, will become materialistic, harsh, and unforgiving.

And if you worship Christ, you will become like Him! Ah! Devoutly to be wished!

The Prognosis for America

"It could never happen here." That was the cry in Eastern Europe, doubting that atheistic Communism would ever take over. Yet it did. This also is the presumption that pervades our own country regarding God's judgment. It is the slogan of a fool in ignorance of God's nature and His commitments.

Yet, let's take an honest, hard look at ourselves. Covetousness and greed (also called idolatry) are now the gods of America, too.

Furthermore, we are also hated by major segments - one might say most - of the world's population. As you read this, alliances are being formed between Russia, China, and Islamic countries against us. Weapons of mass destruction are increasingly available while America's defenses are rapidly being depleted, dissipated, and appearing increasingly inadequate.

We would seem to be ripe for judgment. Have we crossed the Rubicon? Is it too late? Some think so.

Remember Nineveh

. . .

YET, remember Nineveh. This pagan capital ruled the world for several centuries, and it was scheduled for God's judgment. It was 40 days from "ground zero!"

And God called Jonah, the Reluctant Prophet. He wasn't excited about the assignment until God explained it to him a bit more clearly. And Jonah wasn't very tactful in his message: "Forty days and you get yours!"

And then the biggest miracle in the Old Testament occurred: within those forty days, from the king on down, all repented!

(And they repented on speculation! They had no apparent basis to assume that judgment could be averted!)

And yet their kingdom was spared for almost another century! God, we must remember, is in the miracle business.

> God has also declared His clear and exciting principle:
>
> If my people, who are called by my name, shall humble themselves, and pray, and seek my face, and turn from their wicked ways; then will I hear from heaven, and will forgive their sin, and will heal their land (2 Chronicles 7:14)

(The purist will declare that this commitment was given to Israel, not America. Denotatively, they are correct. However, God is also declaring a principle and our immutable God changes not!)

This is not addressed to our President, our Congress, or our population in general. It is addressed to "My people, who are called by my name." It is addressed to the Body of Christ. If we will humble ourselves, and pray, and seek His face, and turn from our wicked ways - then He will forgive our sin and heal our land.

We need a national revival - but it must begin with you and me. It is our sin that is standing in the way of what God would prefer to do: to have America continue as a beachhead for the Gospel to a hurting world. It's up to us. It's high time we got serious about it.

It isn't technology that will provide the peace and prosperity that we seek for our children and grandchildren; it is a return to the heritage and spiritual values that have come to us as such a high price. I believe we will each be held accountable before the Throne of God for our stewardship of the mandate that is before us.

And, fortunately, God is, indeed, in the miracle business. Our most important technology is a 24-hour "hot line" to the Throne Room of the Universe. Let's take full advantage of it and praise His Name! And our most important message was that love letter, written in blood on a wooden cross erected in Judea almost 2,000 years ago.

10

YOUR FUTURE LIVING CONDITIONS

BY PHILLIP GOODMAN

Love, peace, and harmony weren't to be had in our current state of affairs. This is the way Joyce saw things back in 1976. Several years ago, I had occasion to recall our many discussions about her views when her picture showed up on the front page of the newspaper. Not just the local paper, but the story spilled out across the nation, and then in *Time, Newsweek,* and *People* magazines, the evening news, and many other programs as people sought to understand the mass suicide of the Heaven's Gate cult.[1]

Behold — the Gatecrashers

Thirty-nine people had followed Marshall Applewhite, the leader, into a carefully planned "journey to the other side." At first, they had sought inner peace. Then, through a sort of self-induced "new age enlightenment," they sank deeper into the abyss of cult deception. They gravitated to looking for a deliverer. Originally, this "messiah" was Applewhite himself: later it became angelic aliens from somewhere in space.[2]

They were not originally "fringe" people. As I read their personal stories, it was clear that most of those sucked in by the deceptions of Heaven's Gate had come from the ranks of very normal and successful "mainstream" people.[3] Joyce herself had been successful as a television news reporter and commentator. It was her sharp mind and bright personality, as well as a kind of perpetual energy, which convinced me when I interviewed her for a job in 1974 that she was the right person. The community education position required her kind of innovative and creative thinking. I hired and supervised her in what turned out to be her last real job in the "real world," and for over a year she was an outstanding community education specialist, setting up many beneficial programs in the neighborhoods of Tulsa.

When Joyce came to me in the spring of 1976 to offer her resignation, it was on the best of terms. I regretted losing this talented individual. I knew I would miss her pleasant personality. I was disappointed and perplexed when I learned a few weeks after her departure that this seemingly ideal single parent had abandoned her two teenage daughters to join "some kind of meditation group" up north somewhere. Now 21 years later, poring over the news reports, it all came together.

Joyce and the 39 members of "Heaven's Gate," after years of reclusive existence, had attempted to pierce the future! They sought to "fast-forward" their way into better living conditions - an abundant life! When the spectacular - and fateful - Hale-Bopp Comet passed over in the spring of 1997, Applewhite gave the word: their "alien messiah" was here. Deliverance was at hand. Thirty-nine dead bodies were evidence to prove the point.[4]

BEHOLD - THE DOOMSAYERS

COUNTLESS CALLS HAVE BEEN ISSUED to the spiritually deceived and the down and out - even to seemingly normal people - to take stock, cash in, and "head for the hills" because someone with "special insight" has declared that "the time is at hand" for the end of the world. Richard Abanes thoroughly documents some 2,000 years of such prophetic bantering in his book *End-Time Visions*.[5] He logs the prophetic meanderings of alarmists from as early as 60 AD, to Nostradamus, through the Millerites and Jehovah's Witnesses, down to current-day quasi-evangelical doomsayers. Unfortunately, he oversteps the legitimacy of his argument when he seems to lump all contemporary teachers of a literal reading of Biblical prophecy into this broad array of perennial false alarmists. For example, Abanes has this to say about the current scene:

> Despite centuries of failed predictions about doomsday coming in a particular year or on a specific occasion, innumerable individuals continue to assert that the end

> of the world is undeniably at hand. The assumption that seems to appear most frequently ... is that Armageddon's immediacy is reflected in current events. In *Countdown to the Second Coming,* for example, Dave Hunt declares that, "the antichrist is almost certainly alive ... based upon sober evaluation of current events." He continues: "The present generation - unlike any generation before it - has more than sufficient reason for believing that the second coming is very near."[6]

Abane's reasoning, then, seems to be like this: For 2,000 years alarmists have cried "The time is at hand;" they have all been wrong. Therefore, those today who say that the return of Christ is near must also be wrong. But the validity of any particular view on end-time prophecy must be tested by the Bible, not by the miscues of overzealous doomsayers, no matter how long and consistently wrongs their track record has been.

Abanes, a professed Christian, ought to know that he is actually recording fulfilled Biblical prophecy when he documents two millennia worth of doomsayers. Jesus said one of the characteristics that would prevail during the period between His first and second coming would be that "many will come in My name, saying, 'I am He.' and 'The time is at hand'; do not go after them" (Luke 21:8). The rise of various doomsayers is in itself a fulfillment of Biblical prophecy.

Behold - the Naysayers

. . .

WHAT ABANES HAS DONE, by dumping into the same category with these doomsayers those who believe that prophetic signs are appearing in our day, which show that the second coming of Christ is near, is lend credibility to a world already full of naysayers. The naysayers' monotonous refrain asking, "Where is the promise of His [Jesus'] coming?" is also a prophesy whose fulfillment is even more obvious today. These naysayers are specifically predicted in 2 Peter 3:3,4 to proliferate in the last of the "last days."[7]

In fact, these two mind-sets will predominate as the end-time nears. On the one side, alarmists by the gross, fanning the heat and crying, "The time is at hand." Standing opposite, an even more abundant array of mockers and skeptics asking, "Where is the promise of His coming?" Even some respected theologians, who are supposed to be guardians of the faith, have made high-sounding noises that actually sound like a denial of the second coming of Christ! Note this appraisal of respected Christian apologist R.C. Sproul's recent book *The Last Days According To Jesus,* as reported by the Pre-Trib Research Center:

> While Dr. Sproul sees Matthew 24 as a prophecy that was fulfilled in the first century, liberal preterists join him in giving a naturalistic explanation even though from a different framework. But they both deny that our Lord prophesied a supernatural, bodily, visible return of Christ in fulfillment of Matthew 24.8.

This is disappointing, that shepherds among us have

been blown by the winds of time's passage toward the naysayers. Jesus foresaw this in the prophetic parables of Matthew 24 and 25. He warned about impatience and unfaithfulness. He even intimated that His return may be a long time in coming when He made such statements as, "My master is staying away a long time" (24:48); "The bridegroom was a long time in coming" (25:5), and "After a long time the master of those servants returned" (25:19). But the sure Word and the rock of Biblical prophecy does not bend with the winds of time, nor does our eternal, unchanging God:

I AM GOD, and there is no other; I am God, and there is none like me. I make known the end from the beginning, from ancient times, what is still to come.... What I have said, that will I bring about; what I have planned, that will I do (Isaiah 46:9-11).

BEHOLD - THE SIGNS of the Times

WITH DOOMSAYERS and naysayers compounding the spiritual confusion of our time, did Jesus give us a reason to believe that any generation could know anything about the nearness of His coming? Listen to Abanes: "Scripture plainly teaches that we will never know when, or even about when, the apocalypse will occur." [9]

The first part of his statement is true. But the second part is not. What Jesus said is that (1) We cannot know the exact time of His coming (Matthew 24:36), (2) nor can we know the "times and epochs" [the time spans and historical events] leading up to the period which will set the stage for His millennial kingdom, (Acts 1:7); and (3) but when that period does arrive, and "...you see all these things [the events of the end time period], recognize that He [Christ] is near, right at the door" (Matthew 24:33; emphasis mine). That is, we can - we are commanded to - know something about the time of the second coming. We are counseled by the Lord Himself to recognize the signs of the nearness of His coming. He goes on to say that "this generation [that sees these events] will not pass away until all these things take place" (Matthew 24:33,34). We cannot know more than the Lord has revealed, but we ought not to know less.

The Lord employed the same metaphor given to the generation that witnessed His first coming to the generation which would witness His second coming; He said the signs that would precede His coming would be just as obvious as the signs of approaching changes in nature:

NOW LEARN this lesson from the fig tree: As soon as its twigs get tender and its leaves come out, *you know* that summer is near. Even so, when you see all these things, *you know* that it is near, right at the door (Matthew 24: 32, 33; see also 16:1-3, and Luke 12:54-56; 19:43, 44; emphasis mine).

BEHOLD - THE SIGN

. . .

Dave Hunt's contention that "The present generation - unlike any generation before it - has more than sufficient reason for believing that the second coming is very near" is placed by Abanes in the same context with that of the following third-century remarks made by Cyprian in an attempt to make the point that, since Cyprian was wrong, Hunt's similar remarks must also be off-base:

> That wars continue to prevail, that death and famine accumulate anxiety, that health is shattered by raging diseases, that the human race is wasted by the desolation of pestilence, know that this was foretold; that evils should be multiplied in the last times, and that misfortunes should be varied; and that the day of judgment is now drawing nigh.[10]

But it is a mistake to make this association. Cyprian could not see, touch, or walk the cobblestone streets of a Jewish- controlled Jerusalem in a reborn state of Israel. Today we can. The objective reality of the reassembled sovereign state of Israel, combined with the objective arrangement of the ink strokes on the pages of Scripture predicting its rebirth in the end days stares us in the face. The reappearance of national Israel as a distinct people regathered from the nations is the centerpiece of Bible prophecy. This is a clear teaching of the Bible that, sadly, is often anticipated by the non-Christian world even more that the professing church. The following remarks made in a secular publication are typical;

remarks which most of today's church would consider too literal:

> Like no other place on earth, Jerusalem is ground zero for the apocalypse. The city is the center of biblical prophecy and esoteric lore, with the Mount of Olives and the Temple Mount, the site of Solomon's Temple, as possible touchdown sites for the Lord.[11]

That all of the events leading up to the return of Christ interplay with a revived Israel is a fundamental fact of prophecy which we cannot escape. The Scriptures say, in very plain language, that when the final antichrist, spoken of by the prophet Daniel, institutes the great tribulation — a yet-to-be tribulation "such as has not occurred since the beginning of the world until now, nor ever shall," - then the Jews who observe the very Jewish Sabbath are to flee their homes which happen to be located in the land of Jewish Judea-Israel (Matthew 24:15-21).

Israel is the prophetically accredited sign which sets apart a particular generation in the last days. It is our generation which has seen this astonishing event. One respected observer of prophetic events in our day writes, "While mankind's achievements are remarkable, one specific event outshines all others in history, save the Word becoming flesh: the reestablishment of the nation of Israel in the Promised Land .... We can't talk about prophecy without targeting the prophetic nation of Israel."[12]

It defies circumstance that we are also seeing a host of other long-prophesied events converging on the very moment of history which has seen the rebirth of Israel.[13] We are greatly remiss if we do not "look up and see our redemption drawing near" (Luke 21:28).

Deluded gate-crashers cannot pierce the future. Overzealous doomsayers cannot preempt the future. Nor can the humanist naysayers program the future through the best efforts of their "futurists" - futurists who are consistently inconsistent with their hit-and-miss predictions. The future will be played out by the sovereign hand of the God of Abraham, Isaac, and Jacob and Jesus - who knows the "end from the beginning." Furthermore, He "does nothing unless He reveals His secret counsel to His servants the prophets" (Amos 3:7). The "secret things" [the day and the hour of Christ's return] belong to God, "but the things revealed [the signs that "He is near, even at the door"] belong to us" (Deuteronomy 29:29). The Lord has pierced the future. He has preempted Satan's evil plans, and He has programmed a future without end for "all who have loved His appearing" (2 Timothy 4:8). Beyond this, He has revealed this future to us in the prophecies of the Bible. They tell us much about the living conditions we will encounter as we enter those days - days of both peril and a bright new dawning.

BEHOLD - PERILOUS DAYS

WE KNOW, then, not only that the prophetic signs of the coming of our Lord have appeared in objective, "hard copy" form (Israel, Jerusalem, Europe, etc.), but that radical changes will impact our lives as those signs continue to mature in our time. What will our future living conditions be like? We have no way of knowing any individual's future, so we must rephrase this question in two parts: "What will be the future conditions of the world?" and "Who will live in those future conditions?" About both of these issues, the Bible has much to say. In fact, world conditions will markedly degenerate.

Prophetic Scripture reveals a pervasive principal which will weigh heavily on living conditions for everyone as this age winds down: Things will proceed from bad to worse. This slide from "bad to worse" was characteristic of the "days of Noah" and the "days of Lot." Our Lord says that the final generation, on a much wider, global scale, will essentially be a rerun of those evil days, as world conditions "proceed from bad to worse" (Luke 17:26-30).

BEHOLD - GLOBALISM

AS WORLD CONDITIONS DEGENERATE, so will personal freedom, and even "personhood" itself. The factor having the greatest impact on the loss of personal identity and freedom, according to the prophecies, will be the rise of a one-world government. America and all of the countries of the world are now on an irreversible path of economic globalization. Political unity via supranational organizations is also on the same fast track to "a new world order."

The most significant region embracing globalism in

both end-time prophecy and today's headlines is Europe. Europe has embarked on a course of unification under the flag of the European Union. The European Union is expanding eastward. In the process, a new Roman Empire is shaping up fast. Biblical prophecy says that New Rome will eventually be dominated by ten "kings," or rulers. During the term of their rule, Jesus Christ will return (Daniel 2:44)! But before that, personal freedom will be axed. The process of European unity is extremely significant, and indeed sobering, and bears close watching.

Many European leaders are making clear they see the crisis [the 1999 Kosovo war] as a decisive test of their ability to purge Europe of its old nationalistic demons and present a common front to the world in the coming century. Joschka Fischer, the German foreign minister, has gone so far as to describe the hostilities over Kosovo as a "unifications war" that will lead to a much more united Europe.[14]

The prophecies forecast a "new world order," driven by an illusion of worldwide peace and optimism, which suddenly takes a dramatic turn to a totalitarian world order. But according to the Bible, globalization is not the process of the arrival of the antichrist, it is the preparation for the arrival of the antichrist. Looking ahead, we see that his rise actually begins as an insignificant blip on the historical flow chart. The planet has already gone "global," as seen in the singular "kingdom" of the ten kings of New Rome, who precede the antichrist to power.[15] But his arrival as the antichrist comes quickly and violently. The world is literally jolted into a paradigm shift, hypnotized into a lock-step conformity with the iron will of this

PIERCING THE FUTURE

dark character. His burst onto the international stage freezes humankind in its collective tracks. His arrival is sudden. It is stunning. And it comes in clearly discernible stages.[16]

First, the ten kings of New Rome arise in the same generation that produces the antichrist.[17] They precede him to power.[18] They rule as coregents; that is, they reign over a single empire, indicating a global-bound world already exists.[19]

Second, a ruler of seemingly minor political stature (the antichrist) eases in among them as an eleventh king in New Rome.[20]

Third, his contemporaries misjudge him. In an astonishing stroke, he underwrites a security agreement which appears to solve the ever-elusive Middle East peace problem and allows the rebuilding of the Jewish Temple in Jerusalem.[21]

Fourth, his political stature rises sharply.[22] In a swift move, he executes a bloodless coup on three of the ten kings of New Rome, installing his own proxies in their places.[23]

Next, he emerges victorious from a firestorm of horrific warfare.[24] The crushing collapse of a Russian-led allied force on the mountains of their intended victim, Israel, catapults him onto a whirlwind of short-order but decisive military triumphs.[25] He emerges with supreme military power from the center of this planetary blowout of "nation against nation and kingdom against kingdom." The world rises in adulation, exclaiming, "Who can make war against him?"[26] This statement alone says a lot!

Fifth, the ten kings of New Rome cap his rise to planetary enthronement when they hand him the "keys to the kingdom." All ten continue as his proxies. [27] The rest of the world either comes under his boot or bows the knee, with the collective refrain of "Who is like the beast?" [28] Again, a revealing sentiment - coming from the whole world!

Meanwhile, new believers, born again after the rapture (see chapter 11 for reasons the rapture will occur before these events of the final seven years), resist this promise-maker. They resist his false enthronement and his bogus "millennial kingdom." The ten kings and war-weary globalists see this resistance as an age-long malignancy of religious intolerance left over from the "old order," and a lethal threat to the imminent "new order." The antichrist embarks on the great tribulation against those who belong to Christ.[29] Jewish believers first, and then Gentile believers are committed to systematic genocide.

What happens next is unbelievable, but it happens! "All inhabitants of the earth will worship the beast - all whose names have not been written in the book of life belonging to the Lamb that was slain from the creation of the world."[30]

We see from this chain of events that the world, then, is already "global" to a great extent, before the rise of the antichrist. The ten kings of New Rome reign in tandem over a single kingdom, and the embryo of that kingdom is the European Union!

In 1997, the 40th year since its founding, the European Union appeared successful beyond the dreams of its founders: The world's largest economic superpower, a gigantic market of over 370 million people in 15 nations with even more countries aspiring to join.[31] And then there is this:

> With the end of the war in Kosovo, the conflict is acting as a catalyst for Europeans to consider bold ideas, from bolstering and *unifying* Europe's armies to reconstructing the Balkans and expanding the European Union to the East.... [and they] are now seriously discussing the need for a *common* EU foreign policy and a bulked-up, more *unified* European defense[32] (emphasis mine).

It may be the twin pillars of the Internet and the one-world economy which are driving the planet toward globalism, but, as seen above with reference to the war in Kosovo and its rallying impact on European unity, it will be the last world war which will catapult the antichrist into power and tie the final knot on globalism. Rather than shattering the world into irretrievable pieces and irreconcilable kingdoms, a planetary war at the end time involving "kingdom against kingdom" will drive the world to an iron-fisted global unity under him who will be "given authority over every tribe, people, language and nation" (Revelation 13:8). *Gone will be personal freedom!*

Behold - A Great **Sword**

Many "dominion," or "reconstructionist" theologians think that Christians will convert the world to the extent that tragedies such as warfare will give way to a worldwide "king- dom-now" type of Utopia, but the Bible shows just the opposite. Through the witness of faithful believers, Christ Himself "will build [His] church, and the gates of Hades will not overcome it" (Matthew 16:18). Then all true believers (the church) will be taken to heaven in the rapture, after which there will be such a time of tribulation on the earth that it is said to be "the tribulation, the great one," (literal rendering) "unequaled from the beginning of the world until now - and never to be equaled again" (Matthew 24:21). Which way, then, is the modern world headed? Toward a Christianized, man-made, "Thy kingdom come" type of utopia, or toward the "days of distress" that the prophets warned us about?

> There have been about 60 wars since 1945 .... The tempo of wars is increasing. In the 1950's, the average number of wars was 9 a year; today it is 14 .... this ominous trend continues.[33]

When the Bible tells us that in the later days "nation will rise against nation" (Luke 21:10), and at that time "many countries will fall" (Daniel 11:41), including even "the mightiest fortresses" (Daniel 11:39), all because the antichrist will be "given power to take peace from the earth and to make men slay each other [and] to him [will be] given a large sword" (Revelation 6:4), so that "those who destroy the earth" (Revelation 11:18) might be "given power over a fourth of the earth to kill by sword, famine and plague, and by the wild beasts of the earth" (Revelation 6:8), shall we say it differently? Even the Bible-oblivious media and education establishment see the writing on the wall:

> The nuclear payload carried by a single Trident submarine is equivalent to eight times the total firepower expended during World War II. Today's nuclear arsenals contain the combined potential firepower of over one million Hiroshimas .... Enormous ingenuity has been expended to ensure that nuclear warheads land on particular sites or cities ... [enough megatonnage] to destroy all the world's cities.[34]

In light of this, Winston Churchill's post-World War II statement carries even more apocalyptic overtones for our time:

> The stone age may return on the gleaming wings of science, and what might now shower immeasurable blessings upon mankind may even bring about its total destruction. Beware, I say; time may be short.[35]

Amid all of this foreboding darkness and gloom, there comes a Great Light into our prophetic generation, just as there came a Great Light into the prophetic generation at the first coming of Christ: "The people walking in darkness have seen a great light; on those living in the land of the shadow of death a light has dawned" (Isaiah 9:2).

That is the direction we are headed in this essay, for as the compiler and editor of this book has previously stated, "this essay, like this book in its totality, is intended to point to the glorious light at the end of the long, sin-darkened tunnel we call human history. That light, toward which all mankind is streaming, is none other than God, Who personally came to dwell among fallen man ... [in the form of His Son] Jesus Christ..." our soon coming Deliverer and Savior.[36]

> Until then - except for a short period of false security –
> *Gone will be peace!*

Behold - Plague and Pestilence

When this "Great Light" came at the beginning of the first century into the countryside of Galilee, He went about "healing every disease and sickness among the people" (Matthew 4:23). It would seem today, however, that it is modern medicine that will come "healing" with a permanent cure, many predicting that science is on the brink of conquering disease and mastering human health. There is even the haughty idea among serious thinkers that mankind has now actually "evolved" the capability of directing and managing "human evolution." The entire matrix of the human genetic code (DNA) has virtually been "mapped."[37] Mutated genes which are the cause of specific diseases have been identified and are being corrected or replaced with laboratory-nurtured healthy genes. Animals have been cloned through the manipulation of genetic material and reproductive processes. Even the notion of "designer babies" for humans has been elevated from the tabloids to the laboratories to the "ethics" agendas of social manipulators.

Is it possible, as many are confidently predicting, that a healthy and disease-free human race can be guaranteed by man himself within the foreseeable future? Not according to the scenario of the latter-day world found in the prophecies of Scripture, or even the lessons of recent experience. Let's note three basic facts regarding health conditions in the end-time world.

First, the Bible foretells of plagues and pestilence that will beset humankind in the latter days. The Amplified Bible says the "pestilence" mentioned in the scene found in Luke 21:11 means "plagues: malignant and contagious or infectious epidemic diseases which are deadly and devastating."[38] Vine says of the same term "any deadly infectious malady."[39] In the last days, there will be a health crisis in need of a cure.

Second, God's sovereign will, and power still operates over and above any achievements and pronouncements of science. It is unfortunate that alongside the magnificent benefits we have reaped from scientific discoveries in the 20th century, we have raised up out of the scientific schools and academies such a broad consensus as that expressed by one eminent scientist: "I think a case can be made that faith is one of the world's great evils, comparable to the smallpox virus but harder to eradicate."[40] In the last days, there will be an entrenched scientific establishment lacking the humility to court divine assistance for a health-crisis cure.

Third, plagues and pestilences sent as a judgment of God means they involve either the removal of divine restraints on the degenerative tendencies of sin-oppressed nature (Colossians 1:17, coupled with Romans 8:19-22, shows that the creation is sustained and held together by the Creator, or it would be a cesspool of disease and decay, ultimately disintegrating altogether), thus releasing plagues and pestilence upon a sinful world, or that divine intrusion comes as a direct judgment upon mankind. Either way, there are not enough scrawled prescriptions, drug stores, or medicine cabinets in the universe to withhold the plagues and pestilence in the prophetic days to come. God is still Lord over both eco- and bio-systems, including human welfare and health. Gross sin breeds gross consequences. In the last days, there will indeed be a health crisis without a cure!

One of the great blind spots of this sick generation is its inability to connect the AIDS plague to the gay parade. The time of the Return of Christ is to be like the days of Sodom (Luke 17:28-30), which also had a gay-rights parade (Genesis 19:4, 5). Sodom was destroyed because of its degenerate lifestyle. But its wicked memory is retained, not only in its etymological offshoot word, "sodomy," but also in the public legitimacy extended to the lifestyle that word represents. [41]

Gone will be health and well-being!

BEHOLD - THE BEAST - the Net

. . .

PIERCING THE FUTURE

THE INTERNET HAS BECOME "the world's largest communications network," and literally drapes the planet[42]

In just a few short years, the Internet and the Web have quite literally transformed the way millions of people go about their daily lives .... Almost unheard of before 1989, the Internet has entered the vocabulary of most Americans and the homes of a large number of them.[43]

This massive interlinking system of communication is aptly termed "the Net." The Net will become a snare as it spins its "Web" into what some analysts have termed a global "electronic skin," draping the glove in a shroud of lightning-like info-flow. [44]

Hundreds of thousands of PCs working in concert have already tackled complex computing problems. In the future, some scientists expect spontaneous computer networks to emerge, forming a "huge digital creature" .... Ten years from now, there will be trillions of such telemetric systems, each with a microprocessor brain and a radio ... by 2010 there will be 10,000 telemetric devises for every human being on the planet.[45]

The inevitable effect of such a system, so vast and complex and potentially invasive, will be to crowd out personal privacy and individual liberty.

In our age of the global marketplace, the value of global telecommunications systems is their immense capability to simultaneously shrink time and distance while expanding outreach/output capabilities by quantum leaps. The Bible shows much evidence of this kind of world during the final days leading to the return of Christ.[46] For example, within a condensed time span of less than a week, the bodies of the two witnesses are viewed by people from every country as they lay slain in the streets of Jerusalem. Before the end of that short period, the whole planet is involved in reacting to that event through massive celebrations, gift-sending, and trans-communications, an event which could not be imagined before the advent of modern telecommunications. [47]

Furthermore, the prophetic Scriptures depict the outbreak of a global war which, together with its aftereffects, will claim the lives of one-fourth of the world's inhabitants, all within the short span of just over three years. [48] Then there is the convergence of the armies of all the nations of the world - troops, gear, support units and all - into the Valley of Armageddon on the short notice of an order sent forth by the antichrist at the end of the tribulation period. [49] There is no possibility for events of such magnitude to occur within such narrow time frames except in our era of high tech.

But it is an action at the start of the last three-and-one- half years that astounds us and alerts us to the path civilization is on. And that path is being laid by the twin pillars of globalism - high-tech and the one-world economy. These two factors are integral to our assessment of the conditions of the future world and its livability.

Meanwhile, with the pervasive "electronic skin..."

Gone will be personal privacy!

Behold - the Beast - the Mark

Now we will consider what is undoubtedly the most remarkable - and foreboding prophecy of living conditions at the end-time:

> Then I saw another beast [the antichrist's assistant, the False Prophet], coming out of the earth. He had two horns like a lamb, but he spoke like a dragon. He exercised all the authority of the first beast on his behalf and made the earth and its inhabitants worship the first beast, whose fatal wound had been healed. And he performed great and miraculous signs, even causing fire to come down from heaven to earth in full view of men. Because of the signs he was given power to do on behalf of the first beast, he deceived the inhabitants of the earth. He ordered them to set up an image in honor of the beast who was wounded by the sword and yet lived. He was given power to give breath to the image of the first beast, so that it could speak and cause all who refused to worship the image to be killed. He also forced everyone, small and great, rich and poor, free and slave, to receive a mark on his right hand or on his forehead, so that no one could buy or sell unless he had the mark, which is the name of the beast or the number of his name (Revelation 13:11-17).

Here we see a worldwide economy under the ironclad control of the antichrist. This control is systematically applied and enforced over every person in every nation and corner of the globe (if they want to eat!) within the short time span of 42 months. This is high-tech indeed! This kind of monolithic control could only be possible by means of a global technology with a capacity to systematically control the inventory and flow of goods and services, track and arbitrate the personal activity of billions of individual consumers, and order up personalized feedback from, and personal profiles on, each of them. Is this possible? Yes, it is, and will be, on a rapidly escalating scale. Look at the cutting edge of cyberspace taking place in Finland:

> But in the realm of communications, looking at Finland is very much a glimpse into the future .... Despite its small size and relative isolation in the Arctic Circle, this Nordic nation is leading the pack in mobile phone technology and its applications .... The result is that Finland, in a few years' time, will pioneer the use of so-called "Third Generation" mobile phones that boast lightning-quick access to the Internet. [50]

Considering the cutting-edge wireless phones in Finland, we see three aspects of end-time technology, about which God spoke long ago, materializing before our eyes:

1. "He ... made the earth and its inhabitants worship the first beast [the antichrist] ... [and] all who refused to worship the image [of the beast] to be killed" (Revelation 13:12-15). There will be a global system with the capacity to

monitor individual people, solicit instantaneous feedback, and require personal responses to central monitoring sources. To monitor and enforce all of this, people must be located and watched. Today in Finland you can use your phone to "send text messages to other users instead of calling them. SMS (Short Message Service) is exploding." In the near future there will be "locator-based services, which amount to your phone acting like a global positioning system for service providers." One expert says "Your phone will know where you are at all times. It will provide you information based on your profile." Which means, of course, it would be capable of doing just the opposite - provide an "oversight committee" with "information based on your profile."[51]

2. There will be in place a system with the capacity to make "an image in honor of the beast ... [and] to give breath to the image of the first beast, so that it could speak" (Revelation 13:14, 15). At this moment, these wireless, hand-held phones in Finland permit you to "send instant postcards of yourself by shooting a picture [image] with a digital camera, uploading it to a mobile phone with Internet access, then sending it to Sonera [a service provider], which ... prints the image with your message and mails it .... The future ... includes phones that would take advantage of high-

speed data connections to provide video conferencing. "[52]

3. "He also forced everyone, small and great, rich and poor, free and slave, to receive a mark on his right hand or on his forehead, so that no one could buy or sell unless he had the mark, which is the name of the beast or the number of his name" (Revelation 13:16,17). There will be a system capable of informing, tracking, and monitoring the personal activity of every individual in the world to "buy or sell." Today we have a system in place, in the form of the international acceptance of credit cards. But the wireless nation of Finland shows that the super-enhancement of such a tracking system is poised at the doorstep of a world ready to fulfill the prophecies. "Finland will hit 100% penetration by late 2000," says one analyst, predicting, "For the average person, having a mobile will mean not having to carry an ATM card. It will be your cash, your access to the Net and more."[53] As one expert observes, "In a mobile society, your phone is your virtual you."[54]

Until then, we can expect the "global preparation" occurring before the eyes of our generation to continue full-speed- ahead - literally, at the "speed of light:"

We are laying the foundations for an international information highway system. In telecommunications we are moving to a single worldwide information network, just as economically we are becoming one global marketplace. We are moving toward the capability to communicate anything to anyone, anywhere, by any form - voice, data, text, or image - at the speed of light.[55]

Communicate anything, to anyone? Anywhere, by any form - voice, data, text, or image? At the speed of light? Yes! The new technology already includes all of this. The system of the antichrist will transmit data, especially the ultimate PIN number, 666. Every person will be compelled to worship an image of the antichrist, one that even speaks with a voice to them. Transmissions of text will instantaneously convey the orders of the day. The speed of the electron - virtually the speed of light - will be at the fingertips of the antichrist. All of this used to sound like so much science fiction and speculation. But here we are, watching high technology spin the web that knits our world into the one world order, all spelled out quite literally in the prophecies of Revelation. Arno Froese, a respected observer of Bible prophecy in the headlines, voices a sentiment common among prophecy watchers when he says, "We are overwhelmed by the speed of technology, particularly when it comes to communication and identification."[56]

Based on current trends, a beast-mark made possible through "biometrics" will surely be scanned into a wireless system. It will come from a mark bio embedded on the right hand or forehead of every individual who rejects Christ, as most will (See Matthew 7:13, 14; 22:14; Luke 13:23-4). Then, by means of a global computer network, which is actually predicted by experts to "become invisible" in the very near future, no one will be able to 'buy or sell" without the "mark of the beast."[57]

Gone will be control over your own dinner table!

Behold - Scorched Earth

A casualty of the blind rush into globalism is the environment. In short, this green and blue biosphere has become the "endangered planet."

The world's preoccupation with defense and the Cold War, which is receding, is being replaced by concern about the destruction of our natural environment, now our most important common problem.[58]

Few outside of Bible believers recognize the relationship of environmental health to man's moral behavior, but most readily see the more obvious aspect:

> The living world, or biosphere, stretches around our planet in a film as thin as the dew on an apple .... At the present rate of "progress," and unless something is done quickly, disaster stares us in the face. Erosion, desertification and pollution have become our lot. It is a weird form of suicide, for we are bleeding our planet to death.[59]

The American public first began to take stock of

nature's collapse going on around them in the early 1970's.[60] Like all of the other trends associated with globalism, the deterioration of the environment is slotted in the same generation which has seen the rebirth of Israel. Furthermore, it is prophesied that the initial phases of environmental collapse will be caused directly by man himself.

> The nations were angry; and your wrath has come. The time has come for judging the dead, and for rewarding your servants the prophets and your saints and those who reverence your name, both small and great - and for destroying "those who destroy the earth" (Revelation 11:18).

The sequence of the environment's final devastation is seen in the "four horsemen of the apocalypse" in Revelation 6. First, there begins a nature-dissolving chain reaction set off by the effects of the war of all wars:

> When the Lamb opened the second seal, I heard the second living creature say, "Come!" Then another horse came out, a fiery red one. Its rider was given power to take peace from the earth and to make men slay each other. To him was given a large sword (Revelation 6:3,4).

The massive ecological imprint of war is pointed out by experts in human geography:

> Many political actions and decisions have an ecological impact, but perhaps none as devastating as warfare.

> "Scorched earth," the systematic destruction of resources, has for millennia been a favored practice of retreating armies. Even military exercises and tests can be devastating. Certain islands in the Pacific were rendered uninhabitable ... by American hydrogen bomb testing in the 1950's .... General Patton's tank exercises in the desert of southern California over 50 years ago damaged the natural vegetation so extensively that only about a third has since recovered.[61]

The Bible then predicts that in the wake of war will come worldwide famine.

> When the Lamb opened the third seal, I heard the third living creature say, "Come!" I looked, and there before me was a black horse! Its rider was holding a pair of scales [the historical symbol of economics] in his hand. Then I heard what sounded like a voice among the four living creatures, saying, "A quart of wheat for a day's wages, and three quarts of barley for a day's wages [grossly inflated cost indicating a scarcity of basic food staples], and do not damage the oil and the wine [the sparing of these costly luxury items indicating a society with a deep gulf between the haves and the have- nots]!" (Revelation 6:5,6).

The division of people into "haves" and "have-nots" is an end-time backdrop already on the world stage. According to authoritative sources, "The world's 200 richest people make more money that the world's 2 billion poorest people."[62] Phenomenal!

Experts say that the deterioration of the environment will lead to "increased numbers of hot days," that is, deep heat spreading to normally moderate regions of the world. Better known as "global warming," it "produces a domino effect that can spell environmental disaster ... Changed weather patterns can have a severe impact on crops and other forms of vegetation."[63]

The "four horsemen" environmental chain of catastrophe continues in the destruction of life, from plants to animals to humans - right up the food chain:

> When the Lamb opened the fourth seal, I heard the voice of the fourth living creature say, "Come!" I looked, and there before me was a pale horse! Its rider was named Death [people], and Hades was following close behind him. They were given power over a fourth of the earth to kill by sword, famine [plants] and plague [viruses, bacteria, insects], and by the wild beasts of the earth [animals] (Revelation 6:7, 8).

It is astonishing the number of apocalyptic-like scenarios which are today being taken seriously by a world oblivious to Biblical truth - scenarios which couldn't be more descriptive of those found in the prophecies of Revelation. For instance:

> As the human species creates around it a constantly growing desolation, it is in danger of finding itself isolated on a desecrated planet. Its only companions will be the cowed species it has domesticated and the rodent

survivors, wily and vicious, that have resisted its assault.[64]

Here we see a revolt of nature, and in essence, a revolt "by the wild beasts of the earth." Massive disruption of the bio- diverse food chain will spell disaster.

Another outgrowth of the destruction of biodiverse habitats is the onslaught of pestilence and plague: "Rising temperatures [from global warming] also enable insects and fungal pests to migrate to previously unaffected regions," where they would carry disease alien to that region.[65]

The conditions of the latter-day world and its attendant "livability" will undoubtedly be sort of "phased in," since prophetic signs generally cast "pre-signs" before their actual fulfillment comes. Thus, we should expect the great famines, earthquakes, and pestilence mentioned in the Bible to be foreshadowed by incremental and steadily escalating tragedies of the same type. For instance, the clear allusion to a population explosion at the end time in Revelation 9:16 is foreshadowed by the official count of a phenomenal six billion people on the earth as of October 12, 1999.[66] And indeed, environmental conditions have continued to degenerate in our day as never before in history.

Gone will be earth's life-support systems!

BEHOLD - THE HARLOT

OTHER FACTORS AFFECTING future living conditions are linked together by what is undoubtedly the most neglected - and fundamentally the most godless - sign of the end days: philosophical evolutionism. Yet the Bible provides a clear picture of a generation gone degenerate as it sells out to the monolithic establishment of evolutionism. The story of this step-by-step expulsion of God from His creation begins in the prophecies of Peter.

In 2 Peter 3:3-7, we read that in the last of the last days, a deliberate and willful "forgetting" will take place: People will choose to reject the Bible's historical account of a supernatural six-day creation as well as a cataclysmic worldwide flood judgment as recorded in the book of Genesis.[67] That is, as the end time approaches, a flat-out rejection of the foundation of God's revelation to man, found in the first 12 chapters of Genesis, will occur. It will mimic the original denial of God's Word-the proto-denial given by Satan in the garden when he proposed to Eve, "Indeed, has God said...?" With that first rejection of God's Word as a theological benchmark, all of the variety of false religions were born out of a single harlot religion at Babel. And out of the latter-day rejection of foundational Biblical truth found in Genesis, and under the banner of pantheistic-evolution, the many and varied religions will return to the "mother of harlots" as a united religious body.

> At the end time, the religions of the world, in particular the five great religions - apostate Christianity, Islam,

Judaism, Hinduism, and Buddhism, as well as the gnostic umbrella religions, the New Age Movement, and various occult offshoots - will reconvene at the site of their primal origin in an unprecedented unity movement in rebuilt Babylon .... As a result of God's judgment on the degenerate primal religion at Babel, it became the fountainhead (mother) of false religions (harlots), all displaying a common root, which were fanned out across the earth in the ensuing confusion of languages and dispersion of peoples (Genesis 11). Through the centuries, a resurgent Babylon continued to be a primary source of new religious seedlings, but they all reveal a more ancient common genesis. In the end days, the world's religions will reconvene at a rebuilt Babylon in a sort of "family reunion," as harlot daughters returning to the "Mother of Harlots," and the cryptic Revelation 17 will suddenly make amazing sense![68]

Today's movement to merge the world's religions involves a strange partnership with science, particularly within the melting pot of the New Age movement. As people flock to a smorgasbord of New Age groups, they are finding solid support for their evolutionary and pantheistic beliefs through the compatible metaphysical-quantum-punctuated-chaos-ad infinitum dreamland speculations of what used to be regarded as science fiction. However far outside the parameters of the scientific method these fantasies may be, such "theories" are no longer considered to be on the fringe. The blending of science and New Age beliefs is a portent of the one-world church to come.

Gone will be a Biblically rooted belief in the Creator!

BEHOLD - HAPPENSTANCE SCIENCE

PETER FORESAW the next link in this chain of apostasy to be the humanistic reasoning that, since God was not involved in either the creation of the universe and its life forms, or in any supposed world-destroying flood judgment, then men will suppose "all continues just as it was from the beginning of creation" (v.4). That means, of course, that in a godless cosmos, the creation itself must be eternal. The universe and the earth must just kind of "continue" on their evolutionary-merry way by pure chance, happenstance, something or another — very scientific indeed! And indeed, the very foundation of modern science is something called the "theory of uniformitarianism," or, in a word, "all continues just as it was from the beginning by pure chance, happenstance, something or another." This, of course, is not science. It is faith! And it is a faith which is pure and simple, godless. Remarks from four of this generation's leading gurus of "religion disguised as science" make this abundantly clear.

The late Dr. Carl Sagan of Cornell University has said, "The cosmos is all there ever was, all there is, and all there ever will be." Then there is the remark from Dr. Stephen J. Gould of Harvard University, a leader of the evolutionary think tank: "Scientific creationism [the Genesis account of creation verbatim] is a nonsense term." The late Isaac

Asimov, a prolific author who has written numerous books used in science classes, states, "I don't have the evidence to prove that God doesn't exist, but I so strongly suspect He doesn't that I don't want to waste my time." Joining this esteemed group is the celebrated physicist Dr. Stephen Hawking of Cambridge University, who says that if the universe is completely self-contained (which he believes it is), "what place then for a creator?"[69]

These are some of the key individuals who not only set the tone for the education of our children, but who unfortunately are beckoned by the church to provide its commentary on those parts of the Bible which touch upon science, origins, and the book of Genesis. Where the foundational book of Genesis goes, so goes the rest of the Bible.

Gone from the halls of learning will he scholastic integrity!

Behold - The Ring of Truth

With no Genesis, no Bible, and no God, as the line of reasoning continues in Peter's prophesy, "Where is the promise of His coming?" makes a lot of sense (v.4). The latter-day world will reject any idea of a second coming of Christ, and a coming prophetic day of judgment. The rejection of the coming of Christ is aided and abetted by the acceptance of the theory of evolution, in whatever form, be it atheistic or theistic. [70] A denial of the second coming is essentially a denial of Christ! To deny Jesus Christ is, in turn, a denial of God - for "No one who denies the Son has the Father" (1 John 2:23).

The next link in this chain of denial is picked up in the Holy Spirit-inspired writings of Paul. We see in Romans 1 that even though the "ring of truth" about God is innate knowledge to every individual, since all have the built-in common sense to know that "The heavens declare the glory of God [and] the skies proclaim the work of his hands" (Psalm 19:1), evolutionary-enamored men will still "suppress the truth by their wickedness" (Romans 1:18). This is truly amazing, since what may be known about God is plain to them, because God has made it plain to them. For since the creation of the world God's invisible qualities - his eternal power and divine nature have been clearly seen, being understood from what has been made, so that men are without excuse (Romans 1:19, 20).

In view of the fact that knowledge about God is ingrained in the reasoning powers of every person, it is clear that modern science has had to make a grand effort to wrench God from His creation and from the laboratory. [71] And the evolutionary-scientific establishment will continue with equal fervor to raise up a generation of rootless offspring who will grow up eager to search with great gusto for some sign of "evolved aliens" in outer space, while in the same breath of rational abandonment they "will come with their mocking, following after their own lusts, and saying, 'Where is the promise of His coming?'"

Gone will be the admittance of self-evident truth!

Behold - Rootless Education

The slippery chain of events continues as the world of "science falsely so-called" (1 Timothy 6:20) passes its legacy of evolutionism on to the classroom. Few science textbooks have not "exchanged the glory of the immortal God for images made to look like mortal man and birds and animals and reptiles" (Romans 1:23), displaying them in charts as creeping creatures that prance four-legged through eons of time, eventually achieving a semi-gaited slump-shouldered club-footed walk that is supposed to be passed off as the emergence of "man." Making this evolutionary scenario seem feasible is the aforementioned hit-and-miss "pure chance-happenstance something or another" idea; magic camouflaged as science behind the high-sounding term "uniformitarianism." Several generations of kids have now grown up believing this stuff.

Furthermore, this "evolved universe" backdrop for the denial of the return of Christ will lead to a drastic rewriting of history - one where Jesus Christ is intentionally written out! All connotations and allusions to the God of the Bible and His son Jesus will be removed from the halls of education - and all of mankind's institutions when the antichrist "will speak against the Most High and oppress his saints and try to change the set times and the laws" (Daniel 7:25).

The changing of "times and laws," in this context, must mean the ultimate "times and laws." The ultimate "times" is the centering of history around the birth date of Jesus Christ - the Christian calendar organized around BC (before Christ) and AD (Anno Domini, Latin for "in the year of the Lord").

The changing of the ultimate "laws" would be those set forth in the Word of God, rooted in the Ten Commandments, the very basis of Western law and ethics. The antichrist will attempt to rewrite history. He will write God, Jesus Christ, and anything related to Biblical truth out!

This rewriting of history began in our Christian culture with the advent of Darwin and godless evolution. From that point on, there has been a steady de-Christianizing of culture in the West. Government, the courts, and the education elite have all been in the deep middle of this rewrite on the Judeo- Christian history and value base of America. This will continue right up to the day that the antichrist orders the ultimate reinvention of truth.

But we have a Champion in all of this. Note that the passage says the antichrist will "try to change the set times and the laws." He will not succeed. There is a limit to how far God will permit the denial of truth to proceed. But in the meantime, the rewriting of history is already into the textbooks, TV programs, and media of the world, and it began where Peter said it would - the denial of God's bedrock truth set forth in the first 12 chapters of Genesis. As well-known prophecy expert and author, William Terry James, has written regarding the prophecy of 2 Peter 3: 1-7, "God is, in very specific terms, warning us through the Apostle Peter's words that there will, near the close of this present age, be an intensive effort to reinvent truth."[72]

Gone will be a legacy of Christian education for our children!

BEHOLD - RELATIONSHIPS

THE CHAIN of godlessness quickly links up with its logical outcome - the chain of depravity.[73]

Therefore God gave them over in the sinful desires of their hearts to sexual impurity for the degrading of their bodies with one another. They exchanged the truth of God for a lie .... Because of this, God gave them over to shameful lusts. Even their women exchanged natural relations for unnatural ones. In the same way the men also abandoned natural relations with women and were inflamed with lust for one another. Men committed indecent acts with other men and received in themselves the due penalty for their perversion.

They have become filled with every kind of wickedness, evil, greed and depravity. They are full of envy, murder, strife, deceit and malice. They are gossips, slanderers, God-haters, insolent, arrogant and boastful; they invent ways of doing evil; they disobey their parents; they are senseless, faithless, heartless, ruthless (Romans 1:24-31).

Other passages tell of the same wicked way of mankind in the last days. Jesus said that during that time,

"Because of the increase of wickedness, the love of most will grow cold" (Matthew 24:12), and the Holy Spirit forewarned through the Lord's apostle, Paul:

> But mark this: There will be terrible times in the last days. People will be lovers of themselves, lovers of money, boastful, proud, abusive, disobedient to their parents, ungrateful, unholy, without love, unforgiving, slanderous, without self-control, brutal, not lovers of the good, treacherous, rash, conceited, lovers of pleasure rather than lovers of God ... having a form of godliness but denying its power. Have nothing to do with them (2 Timothy 3:1-5).

Relationships - a key to the happiness of us all. Certainly, it is a key factor in determining the quality of living conditions. Perhaps the quality of relationships within our family, among our neighbors, and at our workplace is the most important factor. But as with the other aspects of future living conditions, relationships will "proceed from bad to worse" as the dawning of the end peers over time's horizon. Brother will betray brother to death, and a father his child. Children will rebel against their parents and have them put to death. All men will hate you because of me, but he who stands firm to the end will be saved (Mark 13:12,13).

Gone will be love!

Behold - Jesus!

BUT IT IS NOT for Christians to become depressed and despondent, as we surely would be if we quit here. Note the quote from Jesus above. He said the deterioration of relationships, even within families, will be "because of me." That is, during the great tribulation, when under threat of death people will be required by the antichrist to choose publicly between himself or Jesus Christ, families will divide between believers and unbelievers. The opposite is also true; those who have received Jesus as their personal Savior will find unity and joy in Him, and through Him, among one another. It was the Lord's desire that believers might all be one in Him: "My prayer is not for them alone. I pray also for those who will believe in me through their message, that all of them may be one" (John 17:20-21).

The key word, then, is not "relationships," plural, but rather, "relationship" singular! In fact, our relationship to God through Jesus Christ will be the sole factor that will determine our future living conditions. All of the aforementioned problems we may encounter here on earth as our generation stands on the precipice of that time known as the "end time" will ultimately be in our favor if we are in Christ Jesus, for "we know that in all things God works for the good of those who love him, who have been called according to his purpose" (Romans 8:28).

Present will be expectant hope and joyful anticipation for those in Christ!

Behold - Our Great **God and Savior**

We know that "In this world [we] will have trouble," but we also know that "God did not appoint us to suffer wrath but to receive salvation through our Lord Jesus Christ" (John 16:33; 1 Thessalonians 5:9). Actually, Jesus prayed specifically for believers when He asked, "Father, I want those you have given me to be with me where I am, and to see my glory, the glory you have given me because you loved me before the creation of the world" (John 17:24). Do we for a moment think that the Father in heaven will not answer this prayer of Jesus? The Scriptures already provide the answer in perhaps the greatest of all the end-time prophecies, when it says:

> For the Lord himself will come down from heaven, with a loud command, with the voice of the archangel and with the trumpet call of God, and the dead in Christ will rise first. After that, we who are still alive and are left will be caught up together with them in the clouds to meet the Lord in the air. And so we will be with the Lord forever (1 Thessalonians 4:16, 17).

The passage goes on to say, "Therefore encourage each other with these words." And this we are compelled to do. You see, if you have given your heart to Jesus, and believed in Him as your Savior (If you haven't, you can ask Him into your heart right now), you will be - dead or alive - a participant in the above scene of those taken to be with Jesus in heaven. It is a personal prophecy for all of those saved by the death and resurrection of Jesus. And you will be taken before the advent of the antichrist! What a blessed prospect, for the conditions of that world will be, well, "No eye has seen, no ear has heard, no mind has conceived what God has prepared for those who love him" (1 Corinthians 2:9).

Behold - Our Future Living Conditions

Globalism? Yes; the kingdom of Christ "will be an everlasting kingdom, and all rulers will worship and obey him ... [and it will fill the whole earth" (Daniel 7:27; 2:35).

High-tech telecommunications? Yes; "Before they call I will answer; while they are still speaking I will hear .... Whether you turn to the right or to the left, your ears will hear a voice behind you, saying, "This is the way; walk in it" (Isaiah 65:24; 30; 18).[74]

Economic prosperity and the "mark?" Yes; for "No longer will they build houses and others live in them, or plant and others eat... the reaper will be overtaken by the plowman and the planter by the one treading grapes. New wine will drip from the mountains and flow from all the hills .... His name shall be on their foreheads" (Isaiah 65:22; Amos 9:13: Revelation 22:4).

Truth in religion? Yes; for, "we will walk in the name of the Lord our God for ever and ever ... and [we] shall be

His people, and God Himself shall be among [us]" (Micah 4:5; Revelation 21:3).

Education with roots? Yes; "for the earth will be full of the knowledge of the Lord as the waters cover the sea" (Isaiah 11:9).

War and strife? No; because "Nation will not take up sword against nation, nor will they train for war anymore .... He will proclaim peace to the nations"[75] (Micah 4:3; Zechariah 9:10).

Safe environment? Yes; because "The burning sand will become a pool, the thirsty ground bubbling springs .... Never again will they hunger; never again will they thirst. The sun will not beat upon them, nor any scorching heat" (Isaiah 35:7; Revelation 7:16).

And health - mental, spiritual, and physical? Yes; for "He will wipe every tear from their eyes. There will be no more death or mourning or crying or pain, for the old order of things has passed away" (Revelation 21:4).

Behold - Life!

11

YOUR FUTURE AND RELIGION

BY ED HINDSON

NEW AGE "THEOLOGY" REPRESENTS A DO-IT-YOURSELF form of religion. One can pick and choose whatever ideas, beliefs, concepts and concerns happen to appeal to him personally. The rest can merely be set aside; they need not be rejected.

The bottom line is obvious. New Age theology rests upon pantheism:

> All is God,
> God is all,
> Man is part of it,
> Therefore, man is God.

The only thing separating man from God is his own consciousness, not his sin. Thus, New Agers propose finding God within oneself by altering one's consciousness through meditation, chanting, channeling, sensory expansion, ecstatic dancing and even fire-walking! The

New Age approach to spirituality is more a matter of experience than belief. Altered conscience leads to self-realization, which results in personal transformation (the New Ager's "salvation"). In this process, personal experience becomes the final authority to define one's spiritual journey.

In his very helpful book, *A Crash Course on the New Age Movement,* Elliot Miller defines the New Age movement as an informal network of individuals and organizations bound together by common values (mysticism and monism) and a common vision (coming New Age of Aquarius).[1]

Within the New Age network are several separate strands that interconnect:

1. **Consciousness movement:** those advocating the expansion of human consciousness by altered mental states, resulting in the expansion of human awareness.
2. **Holistic health:** those encouraging better food and diet for better mental and spiritual development.
3. **Human potential:** the self-help psychology of self-awareness, self-actualization, and self-improvement.
4. **Eastern mysticism:** various gurus advocating transcendental meditation, astral projection, reincarnation, and various Hindu doctrines that view the material world as illusionary.
5. **Occultism:** pseudoscientific return to

witchcraft, satanism, shamans, mediums, palm readers, and Tarot cards.

THE BLEND of these various elements varies with every individual and every subgroup within the New Age network. Some lean toward ecological issues (save the planet); others lean toward global peace issues (make love, not war); and still others prefer a mystical orientation that mixes meditation, yoga, ESP, and astrology with a strong belief in reincarnation. The combinations of any of these elements are like fingers of an intellectual hand reaching out to potential followers.

Miller states, "New Agers tend to be eclectic: they draw what they think is the best from many sources. Long-term exclusive devotion to a single teacher, teaching, or technique is not the norm. They move from one approach to another in their spiritual quests."[2] Thus, the subjective guides of experience and intuition are the final authorities for New Age thinkers. The Bible and the Gospel message are vehemently rejected. Because there is no objective truth, the New Ager creates his or her own subjective truth. Therefore, the uniqueness of the Gospel of salvation through Jesus Christ can be easily rejected with, "That's your truth, but it's not for me."

SCIENTIFIC MYSTICISM

. . .

MODERN MAN HAS REACHED the point where he does not want to face the logical consequences of a secular world without God. But instead of repenting of his rebellion against God, he has now turned to a kind of scientific mysticism that has been popularized as the New Age movement.[3] Modern New Age mysticism is a combination of transcendentalism, spiritualism, Oriental mysticism, and transpersonal psychology. It rests upon the humanist psychology of Abraham Maslow, Fritz Perls, Carl Rogers, and Rollo May, all of whom emphasized the elevation of personal growth as the highest good and placed the transcendent at the top of the list of man's hierarchical needs.

The New Psychology, as it came to be called, developed a trend in therapy toward deification of the isolated self and the rejection of traditional morality as moral blindness in favor of holistic psychic health. Thus, it developed hand-in-hand with the whole Human Potential movement. Key elements of New Age thought include restructuring the mind through meditation, sensory deprivation (for example, flotation therapy), and the self-tuning of the mind and body to become receptors and transmitters of cosmic forces. Psychic therapies claim to manipulate "life energies" to provide inner healing of individuals and to promote human relationships in harmony with cosmic forces.[4]

David Hunt is certainly correct in his observation that the whole of New Age mysticism is based upon Teilhard de Chardin's concept of the evolution of the soul. [5] Teilhard was a French Catholic priest, paleontologist, and theologian who attempted to "Christianize" evolution with a theistic view in which the soul emerged as the driving force of evolution. This evolution would lead to a collective super consciousness of humanity, which in turn would result in a new age of life on earth.[6]

Teilhard's mysticism is expressed most clearly in his now popular Hymn of the Universe, in which he advocated the concept of centrism, or the tendency of things to converge and move to the center, resulting in the totalization of all phenomena. [7] This end result of spiritual evolution will be realized in a collectivism of all reality, by which everything will become a part of a new organic whole. Present human consciousness (noosphere) will culminate in a Theosphere when converging human spirits transcend matter and space in a mystical union called the omega point.

It is this merging of scientific mysticism with a rejection of materialistic secularism that has resulted in New Age thinking. This thinking then couples with the human potential movement, which offers a number of techniques for advancing one's metaphysical evolution. Since all ideas have political consequences, we should not be surprised to discover that the political agenda of New Age thinking includes ecological concerns, sexual equality, and the unification of the world order by the transformation of the current political order through a "planetary consciousness."

The New Age transformationalists seek the total transformation of society along ideological lines consistent with their own beliefs. By challenging the "myths" of matter, time, space, and death, New Agers believe they will release our untapped human potential to create a new and better world.

The End of the Intellectual Rope

Twentieth-Century man has come to the ultimate conclusion that he needs hope beyond himself to solve the problems of life. His choices are relatively few indeed. He can turn to God, himself, others, nature, or a mystic collective consciousness, but in reality, he has only two choices: himself or God. Ironically, man's rationalism has driven him to irrationality. Either he must accept the logical consequences of living in a world without God or he must turn to God. All other options are merely wishful thinking.

Modern Americans, however, usually find it difficult to throw God away altogether. We always seem to rely on some popular myth that Superman (or someone like him) is going to come from outer space to save the world. Unfortunately, our own scientific rationality ought to tell us that this isn't so.

The great danger in New Age thinking is its unwillingness to face the facts. There is no scientific proof for the mystical claims of reincarnation, spirit guides, astral projection, time travel, or a dozen other ideas popularized at New Age psychic fairs. When the process of mystification is complete, it leaves man dangling at the end of his own intellectual rope - with nowhere to turn!

The spiritual void caused by the rejection of Christianity has left modern man desperately looking for a spiritual reality beyond himself. New Agers argue that our overemphasis on rationality has caused us to lose our intuitive awareness. Like the old Jedi warrior in *Star Wars*, New Agers advise people to let their feelings guide them. The collective "force" of humanity (past and present) will guide you better than following mere objective facts.

In the end, objectivity is thrown out the window by New Agers. In turn, they want to blame the rest of the world for its collective intellectual blindness. This leads to the great paradigm shift, or new way of thinking about old problems. Leading the vanguard of New Age thinkers is Fritjof Capra, who argues that the old mechanistic perspective of the world must be replaced by the view that sees the world as one indivisible, dynamic whole whose parts are interrelated in the cosmic process.[8]

Following the earlier ideas of Austrian Ludwig Von Bertalanffy and South African Jan Smuts, Capra promotes a holistic approach to solving social problems based upon the General Systems Theory (GST), which calls for the unification of the physical and social sciences to produce a great global society.

Selling it to the Public

In order to intellectually promote the idea of a New World Order, New Agers turn to mysticism as an ally to the systems movement. Synthesis replaces analysis of scientific data. The intuitive ability to recognize "wholes" replaces the need to analyze all the "parts." Capra clearly states, "The systems view of life is spiritual in its deepest essence and thus consistent with many ideas held in mystical traditions." [9]

New Agers tie their concepts of an emerging world order to the concept of purposeful and creative evolution. Following the ideas of German philosopher G.W.F. Hegel, they view God as a process rather than a person. Thus, for New Agers, evolution is "God in process." Elliot Miller observes, "Without such faith in evolution, New Agers would be incapable of maintaining their distinctive optimism." [10]

Consequently, New Agers believe in the evolutionary emergence of a new collective consciousness that will result in a new humanity. They will solve the threats of nuclear war, ecological disaster, and economic collapse by an intuitive and mystical approach to life. New Age thinker Donald Keys put it like this: "A new kind of world - the world into which we are already moving - requires a new kind of person, a person with a planetary perspective." [11]

To make this hopeful human improvement work, New Agers propose a "quantum leap" forward in evolution. John White says, "We are witnessing the final phase of Homo sapiens and the simultaneous emergence of what I have named Homo Noeticus, a more advanced form of humanity .... As we pass from the Age of Ego to the Age of God, civilization will be transformed from top to bottom. A society founded on love and wisdom will emerge."[12]

All of this may seem like intellectual wishful thinking in light of the human tragedies of crime, war, drought, and starvation. But to the New Agers, it is a religion - with faith in evolution as the process and the worship of the planet as God. Teilhard himself, though a Jesuit Catholic paleontologist and philosopher, suggested that the planet earth was itself a living thing. Today it is called "Gaia" or "Terra," the mother-earth goddess of ancient mythology. It is further suggested that the mind of Gaia, in turn, must participate in some universal or cosmic mind. On this basis, New Agers call upon everyone to surrender their personal agendas to the ecological well-being of the living earth - Gaia. "Save the planet" is the evangelistic cry of the New Age movement.

A Return to Paganism

THE NEW AGE worship of the earth and the deification of the planet represent a return to primitive paganism. According to Margot Adler, a practicing witch and coven priestess, "the modern pagan resurgence includes the new feminist goddess worshiping groups, certain new religions based on the visions of science fiction writers and attempts to revive the surviving tribal religions."[13] Judeo-Christian patriarchal religions with a Father-God figure are vehemently rejected in favor of goddess religions and witchcraft (or Wicca), which promote a spirituality of ecological wholeness and human pleasures.

While goddess religion has gained popularity because of its alignment with feminism, shamanism has exploded in popularity with men. Blending animism (spirit contact through natural objects; e.g., sacred trees or mountains) with pantheism (belief that all is God), shamans try to harmonize the natural and spiritual worlds. Following Native American tradition, shamans view themselves as spiritual masters rather than mere medicine men.

Shaman is a term adopted by anthropologists who studied the Tungus people of Siberia. It is equivalent to "witch," "witch doctor," "medicine man," "sorcerer," "wizard," and so on. Shamanism is the most ancient system of mind-body healing known to humanity. It represents false religion that is under the influence of "the god of this world" - Satan!

Dave Hunt expresses a strong concern that modern shamanism is creeping into today's churches under the guise of psychological terms and labels.[14] The techniques of visualization, guided imagery, and inner healing have all been practiced in shamanism for thousands of years. But today they have been redefined as a part of the New Age language of transpersonal psychology. Some like Morton Kelsey have gone so far as to suggest that Jesus was the "greatest of all shamans."[15] He equates clairvoyance, telepathy, out-of-body experiences, ESP, and psychokinesis with manifestations of the power of God.

It is this kind of mental gymnastics that enables New Agers to redefine the terms and concepts of spirituality. They are ready to accept the earth or the self as God. They believe in extra-terrestrial beings, angels, demons, witches, and wizards. Their influence can be seen in movies like *Star Wars, Ghost, Field of Dreams, E.T., Jewel of the Nile,* and *Dances with Wolves.* They see great spirituality in Native American medicine men, Hindu gurus, Tibetan lamas, Sufi mystics, Zen teachers, and Oriental hermits. But they are united in their rejection of God the Father, the deity of Christ, and the personality of the Holy Spirit.

THE COUNTERFEIT CHRIST

WHILE NEW AGE thinkers buy into Eastern mysticism, they clothe it in Christian terminology. Growing up in the Western world makes it difficult for some people to totally shed their religious heritage. So, they repackage it to make it more acceptable to the Western mind. Douglas Groothuis of Probe Ministries notes that:

> New Age spirituality takes on a distinctive Western identity. Because the West still remembers its Christian heritage, traffics in Christian images and bandies about Christian words, Christian symbols serve as a good medium for advancing the cause. The semantic rail system has already been laid by hundreds of years of Christian tradition, and the message is now steaming full speed ahead.[16]

The Christ of the Bible is totally reinterpreted and repackaged as the New Age Jesus. New Agers separate the historical Jesus of Nazareth from the Christ-consciousness which He came to attain. Jesus is not the Way, the Truth, and the Life; He is a way-shower. He is one of the Ascended Masters who realized oneness with God, but He is not viewed as the unique and divine Son of God. To

New Agers, Christ is one of the monistic masters in a whole pantheon of deities.

Actress Shirley MacLaine, a prominent New Age promoter, has said Jesus "became an adept yogi and mastered complete control over His body and the physical world around Him ... [He] tried to teach people that they would do the same things if they got in touch with their spiritual selves and their own potential power."[17]

New Agers like MacLaine leap to this conclusion by suggesting that Jesus traveled to India during His silent years before His public ministry. There He supposedly came under the teachings of the Hindu masters - teachings which He unsuccessfully attempted to communicate to the Jewish community when He returned to Israel.

The counterfeit Christ of the New Age movement is being repackaged as a tolerant, broad-minded, nonjudgmental teacher. He is a way-shower who points men toward the god within themselves. As the cosmic Christ, He is now one of the Ascended Masters who continues to reveal Himself as an emissary of the kingdom of light.

In his very thorough study *The Counterfeit Christ of the New Age Movement*, Ron Rhodes of the Christian Research Institute points out that orthodox Christian beliefs are explained away by new Agers in one of three ways:

1. Supposed discoveries of hidden writings about Christ (e.g., Gnostic Gospels).
2. New revelations of truth about Jesus from psychics and channelers.
3. Esoteric interpretations (deeper meanings) of Scripture.[18] The details about Jesus may vary

> from one New Age teacher to the next. [19] David Spangler believed Jesus merely "attuned" to Christ and became His channel. Edgar Cayce taught that Jesus became the Christ in His thirtieth reincarnation. Levi Dowling believed Jesus became the Christ through ancient Egyptian initiation rites. Elizabeth Clare Prophet believes Jesus traveled to India as a child and eventually ascended to Christhood and returned to His homeland.

However, the particular details may vary, all New Age thinkers agree that Christ is only one of many Ascended Masters who may serve as guides to the truth. New Age Christology is drawn from a vast array of existing religious and philosophical concepts that are eclectic and syncretistic to the extreme. In a do-it-yourself religion, one ought not be surprised to find a make-your-own Jesus!

Voices from the Dark Side

New Age thinking is rooted in the hippie counterculture of the '60's and '70's. Though the hippie movement died out after the Vietnam War, its ideas remained behind. Elliot Miller observes that New Agers are primarily baby-boomers (born shortly after World War II) who have recycled, but not rejected, the ideals of the hippie counterculture:[20]

1. Anti-materialism
2. Utopianism
3. Exaltation of nature
4. Rejection of traditional morality
5. Fascination with the occult

THE NEW AGE movement is not a passing fad. It has been gaining momentum for three decades. It represents a cultural revolt against the spiritual void of secularism. It was not until the late '80's that the general public became aware of the popular appeal of New Age thinking. Actress Shirley MacLaine's autobiography *Out on a Limb* and several subsequent books openly promoted New Age ideals: "I am God," reincarnation, seances, crystals, and pyramid power. In August 1987, 20,000 New Agers gathered at various "sacred sites" around the world for the "Harmonic Convergence," a supposed cosmic event of great significance. By December 7, 1987, the New Age movement had made the cover of *Time* magazine.

Miller refers to the New Age subculture as "another America" existing alongside the secular and religious establishments and competing with them for cultural dominance.[21] He characterized New Agers as sincere, intelligent, optimistic, and humanitarian. Unlike traditional Eastern mystics, New Agers are positive about life and their involvement in the world. They embrace the future while promoting the ideals of global peace, economic prosperity, political unification, and ecological balance.

New Agers have been variously described as "Western mystics," "hippies come of age," "secular prosperity theologians," and "secularized spiritualists," but it is their combination of subjective spirituality and secular morality that leaves them so vulnerable to astrological and occultic influences.

AGE OF AQUARIUS

NEW AGERS HITCHHIKE MUCH of their ideology on the concepts of astrology, especially the idea of the "Age of Aquarius." New Agers believe that a spiritual age is now upon us in which many people are evolving into advanced stages of spiritual consciousness. They further believe that personal transformation must precede planetary transformation. This means that New Agers are committed to the proselytization of new "converts" to their cause. They are out to win over people to what some, like Marilyn Ferguson, have called "The Aquarian Conspiracy." [22]

Astrologers believe that human evolution is progressing in cycles corresponding to the signs of the zodiac. Each cycle allegedly lasts about 2,000 years. Following the beliefs of astrologers, New Agers believe man is now moving from the Piscean (intellectual) Age into the Aquarian (spiritual) Age.

On April 25, 1982, millions of people in 20 major

cities around the world were stunned by a large, full-page newspaper ad boldly proclaiming:

> THE WORLD HAS HAD ENOUGH - OF HUNGER, INJUSTICE, WAR. IN ANSWER TO OUR CALL FOR HELP; AS WORLD TEACHER FOR ALL HUMANITY.
> THE CHRIST IS NOW HERE. [23]

THE ADVERTISEMENT WENT on to announce that since July 1977, the Christ has been "emerging as a spokesman" for the world community. "Throughout history," the notice continued, "humanity's evolution has been guided by a group of enlightened men, the masters of wisdom." The public notice went on to announce that the world teacher who stands at the center of this great spiritual hierarchy is Lord Maitreya, known to Christians as the Christ. Christians await the return of Christ, Jews await the coming of the Messiah, Buddhists look for the Fifth Buddha, Hindus expect the Lord Krishna, and Moslems await the Imam Mahdi. "These are all names for one individual," the notice proclaimed, assuring the readers of a New World Order of peace and prosperity.[24]

The "Christ Is Now Here" ad campaign was engineered by New Ager Benjamin Creme, an English esotericist who was a disciple of Theosophy's Helena Blavatsky and Alice Bailey.

Miller notes that if Blavatsky was the "grandmother" of the New Age movement, Alice Bailey would be its "mother." [25] She, more than any other individual, took the ideas of spiritualism and repackaged them into the basic tenets of the New Age movement. Creme, in turn, hit the road like an evangelist to promote these concepts on a nonstop, worldwide tour.

Constance Cumbey, a Christian attorney from Detroit, Michigan, first alerted the evangelical community to what she called *The Hidden Dangers of the Rainbow* in her 1983 book. While many feel she overreacted to the conspiracy threat from the New Age movement, no one can doubt her sincerity in attempting to alert the Christian public to what she discovered in New Age books, seminars, and lectures. Even Elliot Miller admits, "There is an 'Aquarian Conspiracy' - a conscious effort by a broad-based movement to subvert our cultural establishment so that we might enter a 'New Age' based on mysticism and occultism." [26]

NEW AGE ACTIVISM

SINCE THE PUBLICATION of Mark Satin's *New Age Politics* in 1978, it has been clear that New Age activists intend to continue promoting a political agenda for a united global community under the control of a one-world government. In order to convince society of the need for this New World Order, New Agers have adopted several promotional techniques:

Psychic healing-Using man's inner psychic energy to heal his emotional conflicts and distress.

Holistic health-Combining diet and inner dynamic

force to produce a healthy and productive life.

Transpersonal education - Also called holistic education, it targets public education as the medium to combine humanistic and mystical approaches to learning.

Values clarification - An educational technique that emphasizes that one's values emerge from within himself and not from external codes, such as the Ten Commandments.

Human Potential - Thought-reform techniques promoting the use of guided imagery and visualization through organization development (O.D.) and organization transformation (O.T.) seminars. Used to bring humanistic psychology and Eastern mysticism into the workplace.

NEW AGERS PROMOTE the basic human values as 1) survival, 2) interdependence, 3) autonomy, 4) humanness. This leaves little or no place for Biblical Christianity. In fact, the occult connection with New Age thinking is essentially anti-Christian. A New World Order based upon New Age ideology would likely view evangelical Christianity as bigoted, divisive, and sectarian. This could easily set the stage for justified persecution of Christians as rebels against the Aquarian regime. Elliot Miller warns, "Christian dogmatism could easily be viewed (in fact, already is) as antirevolutionary - a threat to the global unity necessary for racial survival. And when survival dominates over all other values, the elimination of any perceived threat to it could easily be 'justified.'" [27]

. . .

New Age Spiritism

THE GASOLINE that drives the New Age engine is spiritism, which is the practice of communicating with departed human spirits or extra-human intelligences through a human medium by the process of channeling. In his recent book *Channeling,* Jon Klimo claims that channeling involves a human being who is possessed by an external force, power, or personality.[28] This entity exercises control over the perceptual, cognitive, and self-reflective capacities of the person who has relinquished himself to the external force.

The Bible clearly warns against involvement with witchcraft, seances, and mediums. Deuteronomy 18:10-12, commands, "Let no one be found among you ... a medium or a spiritist or one who consults the dead. Anyone who does these things is detestable to the Lord." The prophet Isaiah warned, "When men tell you to consult mediums and spiritists, who whisper and mutter, should not a people inquire of their God? Why consult the dead-on behalf of the living?" (8:19, 20).

Scripture acknowledges the reality of demonic spirits and their attempts to communicate through human mediums (see 1 Samuel 28:6-14; Acts 16:16-19). It always presents them as evil, deceptive, and malevolent. They are channels to Satan's lies, not to God's truth.

The Ultimate Seduction

. . .

ELLIOT MILLER OBSERVES that the varied messages of the channels are ultimately the same: We are gods; we don't need a savior other than ourselves; there is no sin or death; we create our own reality. New Agers imply there is no objective truth, only subjective "truth." Since we create our own truth, we create our own reality. Miller writes, "Once the New Ager accepts this premise, an almost insurmountable barrier to Christian penetration is erected."[29] No matter what appeal the Christian makes, the New Agers will tend to dismiss it as irrelevant to his own personal "reality."

Desperately seeking answers to the great human problems of inner spirituality, personal growth, true peace, and security, the New Ager turns to himself, the planet, the forces of nature, and the spirit world for help. In all this quest, he misses the true Christ, the real source of the peace, security, and stability he seeks.

In the meantime, New Agers are left hoping for some great cosmic deliverer to rescue the world and preserve its peace. Constance Cumbey is right when she says, "For the first time in history there is a viable movement - the New Age movement - that truly meets all the Scriptural requirements for the antichrist and the political movement that will bring him on the world scene."[30]

The stage has certainly been set for a New World Order based upon a subjective view of reality. It will only be a matter of time until the objective standards of truth will be totally eroded in the modern world. We are getting closer to the end. The only real question left is this: How much time do we still have until it's too late?

12

WHY I BELIEVE THE BIBLE TEACHES RAPTURE BEFORE TRIBULATION

BY THOMAS ICE

CHURCHES TODAY OFTEN NEGLECT THE STUDY AND preaching of Biblical prophecy because they consider it a controversial and impractical topic. At the same time, many bemoan the apathy of believers and struggle to encourage people toward holy living. Churches caught in this trap need to consider that the teaching of the rapture, woven throughout the fabric of the New Testament, addresses these issues and can provide motivation for godliness. No single Bible verse says precisely when the rapture will take place in relation to the tribulation or the second coming in a way that would settle the issue to everyone's satisfaction. However, this does not mean that the Scriptures do not teach a clear position on this matter, for they do. As we will see later, the Bible does promise that the church will not enter the time of God's wrath, which is another term for the tribulation. Many Biblical passages teach the pretribulation rapture of the church.

Many important Biblical doctrines are not derived

from a single verse but come from a harmonization of several passages into systematic conclusions. Some truths are directly stated in the Bible, such as the deity of Christ (John 1:1; Titus 2:13). Other doctrines, like the Trinity and the incarnate nature of Christ, are the product of harmonizing the many passages that relate to these matters. Taking into account all that the Bible says on these issues, orthodox theologians, over time, concluded that God is a Trinity and that Christ is the God-Man. Similarly, a systematic, literal interpretation of all New Testament passages relating to the rapture will lead to the pretribulation viewpoint - that at the rapture, all living believers will be translated into heaven at least seven years before Christ's second coming. This is what I believe the Bible teaches.

Foundational Issues

Four affirmations provide a Biblical framework for the pretribulation rapture: They are (1) consistent literal interpretation; (2) premillennialism; (3) futurism; and (4) a distinction between Israel and the church. These are not mere suppositions, but rather are important Biblical doctrines upon which the doctrine of the rapture is built.

Literal Interpretation

. . .

CONSISTENT LITERAL INTERPRETATION is essential to properly understanding what God is saying in the Bible. The dictionary defines literal as "belonging to letters." Further, it says literal interpretation involves an approach "based on the actual words in their ordinary meaning ... not going beyond the facts." "Literal interpretation of the Bible simply means to explain the original sense of the Bible according to the normal and customary usage of its language." How is this done? It can only be accomplished through the grammatical (according to the rules of grammar), historical (consistent with the historical setting of the passage), contextual (in accord with its context) method of interpretation.

Literal interpretation recognizes that a word or phrase can be used either plainly (denotative) or figuratively (connotative). As in our own conversations today, the Bible may use plain speech, such as "Grandmother died yesterday" (denotative). Or the same thing may be said in a more colorful way, "Grandmother kicked the bucket yesterday" (connotative). An important point to be noted is that even though we may use a figure of speech to refer to Grandmother's death, we are using that figure to refer to an event that literally happened. Some interpreters are mistaken to think that just because a figure of speech may be used to describe an event (i.e., Jonah's experience in the belly of the great fish in Jonah 2), that the event was not literal and did not happen in history. Such is not the case. A "Golden Rule of Interpretation" has been developed to help us discern whether or not a figure of speech was intended by an author.

When the plain sense of Scripture makes common

sense, seek no other sense; therefore, take every word at its primary, ordinary, usual, literal meaning unless the facts of the immediate context, studied in the light of related passages and axiomatic and fundamental truths, indicate clearly otherwise.

The principle of consistent, literal interpretation of the entire Bible logically leads one to the pretribulation position. This means that the prophetic portions of the Bible are interpreted like any other subject matter in Scripture. The prophetic sections of the Bible use the same conventions of language found throughout the Bible.

PREMILLENNIALISM

THE NEXT BIBLICAL principle foundational to pretribulationism is premillennialism. Premillennialism teaches that the second advent will occur before Christ's thousand-year reign upon earth from Jerusalem (Revelation 19:11-20:6). It is contrasted with the postmillennial teaching that Christ will return after He has reigned spiritually from His throne in heaven for a long period of time during the current age, through the church, and the similar amillennial view that also advocates a present, but pessimistic, spiritual reign of Christ. Biblical premillennialism is a necessary foundation for the pretrib position since it is impossible for either the postmillennial or amillennial view of Scripture to support a pretrib understanding of the rapture.

Futurism

THE THIRD CONTRIBUTING principle is futurism. As if understanding the different millennial positions is not complicated enough, diversification is compounded when we consider the four possible views which relate to the timing of when an interpreter sees prophecy being fulfilled in history. The four views are simple in the sense that they reflect the only four possibilities in relation to time - past, present, future, and timeless. The preterist (past) believes that most, if not all, prophecy has already been fulfilled, usually in relation to the destruction of Jerusalem in A.D. 70. The historicist (present) sees much of the current Church Age as equal to the tribulation period. Thus, prophecy has been and will be fulfilled during the current Church Age. Futurists (future) believe that virtually all prophetic events will not occur in the current Church Age, but will happen in the future tribulation, second coming, or millennium. The Idealist (timeless) does not believe either that the Bible indicates the timing of events or that we can know before they happen. Therefore, idealists think that prophetic passages mainly teach great ideas or truths about God to be applied regardless of timing.

Pretribulationism can only be built upon the futurist understanding of prophetic events. Such a conclusion is the result of the application of a consistent literal inter-

Distinction Between Israel and the Church

The final principle related to the pretrib position is the Biblical truth that God's single program for history includes two groups, Israel and the church. This view has been systematized into what is known as dispensationalism. While the basis of salvation (God's grace) is always the same for Jew and Gentile, God's prophetic program has two distinct aspects. Presently, God's plan for Israel is on hold until He completes His current purpose with the church and raptures His bride to heaven. Only pretribulationism provides a purpose for the rapture. That purpose is to remove the church via the rapture, so God can complete His unfinished business with Israel during the seven-year tribulation period. Therefore, if one does not distinguish passages which God intends for Israel from those intended for the church, then the result is an improper confusion of the two programs.

It should not be surprising that God's single plan for history has a multidimensional aspect (Ephesians 3:10) that we know as Israel and the church. If human novelists can weave multiple plots throughout their stories, then how much more can the Great Planner of the universe and history do the same kind of thing?

Those comingling God's plan for Israel and the church destroy an important basis for the pretrib rapture. The

Bible clearly teaches that the church and Israel have in many ways different programs within the single plan of God even though both are saved on the same basis.

Specific Pretribulational Arguments

THE FACT of the rapture was first revealed by Christ to His disciples in John 14:1-3. It is most clearly presented in 1 Thessalonians 4:13-18, which encourages living Christians that, at the rapture, they will be reunited with those who have died in Christ before them. In verse 17 the English phrase "caught up" (NASB) translates the Greek word *harpazo*, which means "to seize upon with force" or "to snatch up." This is the Greek word from which the English word "harpoon" is derived. The Latin translators of the Bible used the word *rapere*, the root of the English term "rapture." A debate swirls around when this takes place relative to the tribulation. At the rapture, living believers will be "caught up" in the air, translated into the clouds in a moment of time.

An interesting tie between the revelation of the rapture by our Lord in John 14:1-3 and Paul's expansion in 1 Thessalonians 4:13-18 has been observed by commentator J. B. Smith. Smith has observed a "thought-for-thought" parallel between the two passages:

Let us now compare two passages of Scripture which, by the words employed, clearly show that they refer to the same event. Let not your heart be troubled; believe in God, believe also in Me. In My Father's house are many dwelling places; if it were not so, I would have told you; for I go to prepare a place for you. And if I go and prepare a place for you, I will come again, and receive you to Myself; that where I am, there you may be also (John 14:1-3).

But we do not want you to be uninformed, brethren, about those who are asleep, that you may not grieve, as do the rest who have no hope. For if we believe that Jesus died and rose again, even so God will bring with Him those who have fallen asleep in Jesus. For this we say to you by the word of the Lord, that we who are alive, and remain until the coming of the Lord, shall not precede those who have fallen asleep. For the Lord Himself will descend from heaven with a shout, with the voice of the archangel, and with the trumpet of God; and the dead in Christ shall rise first. Then we who are alive and remain shall be caught up together with them in the clouds to meet the Lord in the air, and thus we shall always be with the Lord. Therefore comfort one another with these words (1 Thessalonians 4:13-18).

Observe:

- The words or phrases are almost an exact parallel.
- They follow one another in both passages in exactly the same order.
- Only the righteous are dealt with in each case.
- There is not a single irregularity in the progression of words from first to last.

- Either column takes the believer from the troubles of earth to the glories of heaven.
- It is but consistent to interpret each passage as dealing with the same event - the rapture of the church.

SUCH A COMPARISON BODES WELL for the pretribulation rapture of the church, as we shall see below.

Operating consistently upon the foundation of these four Biblical foundations, we will survey six specific Biblical arguments for pretribulationism. These are not all the reasons for a pretrib rapture but are simply a summary of some of the basic arguments.

CONTRASTS **Between the First and Second Coming**

THE RAPTURE IS CHARACTERIZED in the New Testament as a "translation or resurrection coming" (1 Corinthians 15:51-52; 1 Thessalonians 4:15-17) in which the Lord comes for His church, taking her to His Father's house (John 14:3). On the other hand, Christ's second advent with His saints (the church - Revelation 19) descends from heaven and arrives on earth to stay and set up His Messianic kingdom (Zechariah 14:4-5; Matthew 24:27-31). The differences between these two events are harmonized naturally by the pretrib position, while other views are not able to comfortably account for such differences.

Paul speaks of the rapture as a "mystery" (1 Corinthians 15:51-54), that is, a truth not revealed until it was disclosed by the Apostles (Colossians 1:26). Thus the rapture is said to be a newly revealed mystery, making it a separate event. The second coming, on the other hand, was predicted in the Old Testament (Daniel 12:1-3; Zechariah 12:10; 14:4).

The New Testament teaches about the rapture of the church and yet also speaks of the second coming of Christ. These two events are different in a number of ways. Note the following contrasts between the translation at the rapture and Christ's second coming to establish the kingdom.

RAPTURE/TRANSLATION

1. Translation of all believers;
2. Translated saints go to heaven;
3. Earth not judged;
4. Imminent, any moment, no preceding signs;
5. Not in the Old Testament;
6. Believers only;
7. Before the Day of Wrath;
8. No reference to Satan;
9. Christ comes for His own;
10. He comes in the air;
11. He claims His bride;
12. Only His own see Him;
13. Tribulation begins;

. . .

Second Coming/Establishment of the Kingdom

1. No translation at all;
2. Translated saints return to earth;
3. Earth judged & righteousness established;
4. Follows definite predicted signs, including tribulation;
5. Predicted often in Old Testament;
6. Affects all men;
7. Concluding the day of wrath;
8. Satan bound;
9. Christ comes with His own;
10. He comes to the earth;
11. He comes with His bride;
12. Every eye shall see Him;
13. Millennial Kingdom begins.

Dr. John Walvoord concludes that these "contrasts should make it evident that the translation of the church is an event quite different in character and time from the return of the Lord to establish His kingdom and confirms the conclusion that the translation takes place before the tribulation."

Both events mention clouds symbolizing a heavenly role in both, but other differences demonstrate that these are two distinct events. At the rapture, the Lord comes for His saints (1 Thessalonians 4:16); at the second coming the Lord comes with His saints (1 Thessalonians 3:13). At the rapture, the Lord comes only for believers, but His return to the earth will impact all people. The rapture is a translation/resurrection event; the second coming is not.

At the rapture, the Lord takes believers from earth to heaven "to the Father's house" (John 14:3); at the second coming believers return from heaven to the earth (Matthew 24:30).

The best harmonization of these two different events supports a pretribulation rapture (which is sign less and could happen at any moment), while the many events taking place during the tribulation are best understood as signs leading up to the second coming.

A Time Interval Needed Between the Two Advents

An interval or gap of time is needed between the rapture and the second coming in order to facilitate many events predicted in the Bible in a timely manner. Numerous items in the New Testament can be harmonized by a pretrib time gap of at least seven years, while other views, especially post-tribulationists, are forced to postulate scenarios that would not realistically allow for a normal passage of time. The following events are best temporally harmonized with an interval of time as put forth by pretribulationism.

Second Corinthians 5:10 teaches that all believers of this age must appear before the judgment seat of Christ in heaven. This event, often known as the "bema judgment" from the Greek word *bema*, is an event never mentioned in the detailed accounts connected with the second coming of Christ to the earth. Since such an evaluation would require some passage of time, the pretrib gap of seven years nicely accounts for such a requirement.

Since Revelation 19:7-10 pictures the church as a bride who has been made ready for marriage (illustrated as "fine linen," which represents "the righteous acts of the saints") to her Groom (Christ); and the bride has already been clothed in preparation for her return at the second coming, accompanying Christ to the earth (Revelation 19:11-18), it follows that the church would already have to be complete and in heaven (because of the pretrib rapture) in order to have been prepared in the way that Revelation 19 describes. This requires an interval of time which pretribulationism handles well.

The 24 elders of Revelation 4:1-5:14 are best understood as representatives of the church. Dr. Charles Ryrie explains:

> In the New Testament, elders as the highest officials in the church do represent the whole church (cf. Acts 15:6; 20:28), and in the Old Testament, 24 elders were appointed by King David to represent the entire Levitical priesthood (1 Chronicles 24). When those twenty-four elders met together in the temple precincts in Jerusalem, the entire priestly house was represented. Thus it seems more likely that the elders represent redeemed human beings .... the church is included and is thus in heaven before the tribulation begins.

If they refer to the church, then this would necessitate the rapture and reward of the church before the tribulation and would require a chronological gap for them to perform their heavenly duties during the seven-year tribulation.

Believers who come to faith in Christ during the tribulation are not translated at Christ's second advent but carry on ordinary occupations such as farming and building houses, and they will bear children (Isaiah 65:20-25). This would be impossible if all saints were translated at the second coming to the earth, as post-tribulationists teach. Because pre-tribulationists have at least a seven-year interval between the removal of the church at the rapture and the return of Christ to the earth, this is not a problem because millions of people will be saved during the interval and thus be available to populate the millennium in their natural bodies in order to fulfill Scripture.

It would be impossible for the judgment of the Gentiles to take place after the second coming if the rapture and second coming are not separated by a gap of time. How would both saved and unsaved, still in their natural bodies, be separated in judgment, if all living believers are translated at the second coming? This would be impossible if the translation takes place at the second coming, but it is solved through a pretribulation gap.

Dr. John F. Walvoord points out that if "the translation took place in connection with the second coming to the earth, there would be no need of separating the sheep from the goats at a subsequent judgment, but the separation would have taken place in the very act of the translation of the believers before Christ actually sets up His throne on earth (Matthew 25:31)." Once again, such a "problem" is solved by taking a pretrib position with its gap of at least seven years.

A time interval is needed so that God's program for the church, a time when Jew and Gentile are united in one body (cf. Ephesians 2-3), will not become comingled in any way with His unfinished and future plan for Israel during the tribulation. Dr. Renald Showers notes that "All other views of the rapture have the church going through at least part of the 70th week, meaning that all other views mix God's 70-weeks program for Israel and Jerusalem together with His program for the church. A gap is needed in order for these two aspects of God's program to be harmonized in a nonconflicting manner."

The pretribulation rapture of the church fulfills a Biblical need to not only see a distinction between the translation of Church Age saints at the rapture, before the second coming, but it also handles without difficulty the necessity of a time-gap which harmonizes a number of future Biblical events. This requirement of a seven-year gap of time adds another plank to the likelihood that pretribulationism best reflects the Biblical viewpoint.

THE IMMINENT COMING of Christ

THE NEW TESTAMENT speaks of our Lord's return as imminent, meaning that it could happen at any moment. Other events may occur before an imminent event, but nothing else must take place before it happens. Immanency passages instruct believer to look, watch, and wait for His coming (1 Corinthians 1:7; Philippians 3:20; 1 Thessalonians 1:10; Titus 2:13; Hebrews 9:28; 1 Peter

1:13; Jude 21). If either the appearance of the antichrist, the abomination of desolation, or the unfolding of the tribulation must occur before the rapture, then a command to watch for Christ's coming would not be relevant. Only pretribulationism teaches a truly imminent rapture since it is the only view not requiring anything to happen before the rapture. As required by the above-mentioned passages, the New Testament indicates that the believer's hope is to look, watch, and wait for a person and that is Jesus. Only pretribulationism enables a believer to look for Christ and yet at the same time give full meaning to second coming passages and the signs that lead up to our Lord's return to the earth. Immanency is a strong argument for the pretrib rapture and provides the believer with a true "blessed hope."

The Nature of the Tribulation

The Bible teaches that the tribulation (i.e., the seven-year, 70th week of Daniel) is a time of preparation for Israel's restoration and regeneration (Deuteronomy 4:29-30; Jeremiah 30:4-11; Ezekiel 20:22-44; 22:13-22). Revelation 3:10 notes that the tribulation will not be for the church but for "those who dwell upon the earth" (Revelation 3:10; 6:10; 8:13; 11:10 [twice]; 13:8, 12, 14 [twice]; 17:2, 8), as a time upon them for their rejection of Christ is His salvation. While the church will experience tribulation in general during this present age (John 16:33), she is never mentioned as participating in Israel's time of trouble, which includes the great tribulation, the day of the Lord, and the wrath of God. pretribulationism gives the best answer to the Biblical explanation of the fact that the church is never mentioned in passages that speak about tribulation events, while Israel is mentioned consistently throughout these passages.

The Nature of the Church

Only pretribulationism is able to give full Biblical import to the New Testament teaching that the church differs significantly from Israel. The church is said to be a mystery (Ephesians 3:1-13) by which Jews and Gentiles are now united into one body in Christ (Ephesians 2:11-22). This explains why the church's translation to heaven is never mentioned in any Old Testament passage that deals with the second coming after the tribulation, and why the church is promised deliverance from the time of God's wrath during the tribulation (1 Thessalonians 1:9-10; 5:9; Revelation 3:10). The church alone has the promise that all believers will be taken to the Father's house in heaven (John 14:1-3) at the translation, and not to the earth as other views would demand.

The Work of the Holy Spirit

Second Thessalonians 2:1-12 discusses a man of

lawlessness being held back until a later time. Interpreting the Restrainer of evil (2:6) as the indwelling ministry of the Holy Spirit at work through the body of Christ during the current age supports the pretribulational interpretation. Since "the lawless one" (the beast or Antichrist) cannot be revealed until the Restrainer (the Holy Spirit) is taken away (2:7-8), the tribulation cannot occur until the church is removed.

Practical Implications

LIKE ALL ASPECTS of Biblical doctrine, teaching on the rapture has a practical dimension. Dr. Renald Showers has summarized some of the practical implications of the pretrib rapture:

> The fact that the glorified, holy Son of God could step through the door of heaven at any moment is intended by God to be the most pressing, incessant motivation for holy living and aggressive ministry (including missions, evangelism and Bible teaching) and the greatest cure for lethargy and apathy. It should make a major difference in every Christian's values, actions, priorities and goals.

As John writes, "Everyone who has this hope fixed on Him purifies himself, just as He is pure" (1 John 3:3). Our rapture hope is said to urge a watchfulness for Christ Himself (1 Corinthians 15:58); to encourage faithfulness in church leaders (2 Timothy 4:1-5); to encourage patient waiting (1 Thessalonians 1:10); to result in expectation and looking (Philippians. 3:20; Titus 2:13; Hebrews 9:28); to promote godly moderation (Philippians 4:5); to excite "heavenly mindedness" (Colossians 3:1-4); to bring forth successful labor (1 Thessalonians 2:19-20); to experience comfort (1 Thessalonians 4:18); to urge steadfastness (2 Thessalonians 2:1-2; 1 Timothy 6:14; 1 Peter 5:4); to infuse diligence and activity (2 Timothy 4:1-8); to promote mortification of the flesh (Colossians 3:4-5; Titus 2:12-13); to require soberness (1 Thessalonians 5:6; 1 Peter 1:13); to contribute to an abiding with Christ (1 John 2:28; 3:2); to support patience under trial (James 5:7-8); and to enforce obedience (2 Timothy 4:1).

The pretribulation rapture is not just wishful "pie-in-the- sky in the by-and-by" thinking. Rather, it is vitally connected to Christian living in the "nasty here-and-now." No wonder the early church coined a unique greeting of "Maranatha!" which reflected the primacy of the Blessed Hope as a very real presence in their everyday lives. Maranatha literally means "our Lord come!" (1 Corinthians 16:22) The life of the church today could only be improved if "Maranatha" were to return as a sincere greeting on the lips of an expectant people.

13

PROPHECY - FULFILLMENT, NOT FEAR

BY ANGIE PETERS

Revelation, ten-horned beasts, Old Testament books whose pages remain stuck together along the edges from nonuse. Israel, the number 666, Armageddon, the rapture, the millennium.

These words and images, combined with my lack of knowledge about them, painted for me such an alarming and hazy portrait of Biblical prophecy that my habit as a born-again Christian since age nine was to tune out any discussion about the subject.

"It's all Greek to me," I would reason. "That's better left to scholars and theologians. Besides, with all the sad and tragic events going on in the world, I don't want to dwell on the doom and gloom of the end-times."

But one day several years ago, I landed right in the middle of a project editing, of all things, books about Biblical prophecy for a writer whose eyesight was quickly failing. This is one of those books and the writer, of course, was William "Terry" James.

Excited to be a part of the writing scene again - and of Christian publishing, at that - I determined to make sense of the ominous subject as I went along. Surely something was there that I could understand, maybe even something I could use in my personal Christian walk. So, I started combing the material I was editing for "usable" tidbits of information. I picked Terry's brain, asking him to tell me in plain English what "all that apocalyptic jargon" meant. If he told me and I still didn't get it, "explain that again," I would say. I set out to find out what the New World Order, humanism, the mark of the beast, apostasy, and geopolitics has to do with me, a wife and mother of three who worries about discipline strategies, not international peacekeeping strategies.

What I Learned Surprised Me:

I. Prophecy: It's Not the End of the World

Prophecy isn't just about the end of the world system as we know it. It's much more personal than that: It has everything to do with me and my family, today. Maybe that's why we're promised a specific blessing for reading Revelation:

"Blessed is he that readeth, and they that hear the words of this prophecy" (Revelation 1:3).

Unfortunately, many Christians — especially "busy" moms like me - neglect the study of prophecy for much the same reasons that I did for so many years. But if we will learn even a little bit about the subject, then we'll be blessed with the understanding that every detail of our lives — right down to the fact that we can reach across the globe from our home computers via the Internet and that our children are taught about evolution, not creation, in their public-school classrooms - directly relates to God's prophetic Word.

We'll know that evolutionism, the effort to explain all things without God, is a part of the widespread and increasing deception described in 2 Timothy 3:13. We'll know why e-mail, faxes, overnight mail, and other instant forms of communication are compelling us to "run to and fro" to manage both our business lives and our family lives at a breakneck speed Daniel hinted at in chapter 12, verse 4 of his book. We'll never fail to be sickened, but we might not be as surprised when we read of parents murdering their own children (the "unnatural affection" described in 2 Timothy 3:3).

We'll recognize the Internet, one of the most staggering technological advances of our lifetime, as a "knowledge-increasing" tool (Daniel 12:4) that's uniting the world into a cozy "global village" in which the stage is being built for a world leader called antichrist to one day play out his role as predicted in Revelation 13. We'll recognize that the earthquakes, hurricanes, and other natural disasters shaking the foundations from under families like ours worldwide are some of the signals Christ Himself said would be happening as our time on His planet marches on. The lens of my growing understanding of Biblical prophecy and the Revelation have brought my blurry world view into such clear focus that I now wonder how I missed seeing and making sense of all of these signals before.

II. Prophecy: The Word of the Ultimate Promise Keeper

From the birth of Christ — foretold beginning in Genesis 3:15 and fulfilled in the Gospels — to the rebirth of Israel as a nation - foretold in Isaiah 66:7-9 and fulfilled May 14, 1948 - countless prophecies have been fulfilled to date. How incredible, that words penned thousands of years ago outline with detailed events that have already happened and/or are beginning to happen now.

Seeing how the Revelation breathes life into the prophecies sketched out for us in the Old Testament builds our faith, pushes our focus forward and draws our hearts heavenward, giving us all the more reason to "smile at the future" as did the woman of Proverbs 31.

And what better way to reassure our confused kids when headlines about global warming, mass murders, and natural disasters prompt scary "it's-the-end-of-the-world" rumors to echo across the playground, than by saying, "Look! Here the Bible says a baby boy named Jesus would be born to a virgin, and here's where it happened! So, when God's Word promises us that we will be taken out of this world to be with Him before things get too bad, we know we can believe it because He keeps His promises!"

III. Signs of the Times

Terry James and many other prophecy scholars agree that we are living in the most exciting time of all ages. From fighting in the Middle East (an example of the "wars and rumors of wars" referred to in Matthew 24:6) to dizzying technological breakthroughs, each day's news presents God's prophetic Word at work. A solid knowledge of prophecy, combined with a basic overview of what's going on in the world, can help us interpret with a spiritual eye these events as they unfold, and it helps us keep our perspective and our faith when our society seems to be spiraling out of control.

IV. Revelations About the Revelation

Propose a session on the book of Revelation to many Bible study groups and droplets of nervous perspiration immediately start forming on foreheads around the room. Because of a "bad rap" stemming from the book's frightening imagery and extensive system of symbolism, many believe Revelation too difficult to understand. But I've learned to look at it this way: Revelation is not called "The Book of Mystery!" The word itself means, in our language, "a dramatic disclosure of something not previously known or realized," and the Greek word for "revelation" means "apocalypse" or "unveiling." So, if the book presents a symbol or a code, we know that God has placed the key to cracking that code right there in the Bible for us to use. A lot of times, I've found that all it takes is a glance to the bottom of the page at my Bible's notes to help me decipher a mysterious passage.

Another reason the book may seem intimidating:

Couched within its 404 verses are 800 allusions to the Old Testament, that part of the Bible many of us don't study very often except to teach our little ones about Adam and Eve, Moses, Noah, and Daniel. But, as the late Dr. J. Vernon McGee says in his *Commentary on Revelation*, "...we need to know sixty-five other books before we get to this place." He likens Revelation to an airport terminal, into which the "airlines" carrying cargo of key Biblical themes and subjects which originated at other places in Scripture reach their destination. So, if Revelation's treatment of certain subjects leaves me scratching my head, tracing those subjects through their mentions in previous chapters often fills in the pieces of the puzzle I have missed.

Further, many people don't want to tackle the Bible's 66th book because of its gloomy and apocalyptic subject matter. The daily paper is depressing enough; who wants to read about things becoming even worse? But while Revelation does, in fact, describe the end of the world system as we know it, its main focus, as the focal point of the whole Bible, is Jesus Christ. In other words, it's all about Jesus.

What? You mean the star of the Revelation drama isn't Satan, antichrist, or the beast? Absolutely not!

"We can't talk about Biblical prophecy without having Jesus Christ at the center of our thoughts," says Terry. "The Scripture says that, '...the testimony of Jesus is the spirit of prophecy'. By learning the prophetic Word, we're learning the fully revealed truth God has given us about His Son, Jesus Christ."

Now, that's a topic I'm very interested in! Of course, I

want to learn as much as I can about my Lord and Savior Who, even as I am dusting and polishing and vacuuming my modest, four- bedroom home on this earth, is preparing a mansion for me in heaven. If I study most of the rest of the Bible, but skip the Revelation, I'll rejoice in His birth, I'll learn from His teachings, I'll repent because of His sacrifice on the cross, and I'll be sure that I'll spend the rest of eternity with Him because of my absolute belief in His death, burial and resurrection. But I'll miss the end of His story: His glory as it contrasts with the humiliation He suffered on our behalf while He walked on this earth. As a child - and even as an adult - I have always had a craving to see more when a story or movie has had a happy ending. For example, when Cinderella marries the prince and they "live happily ever after," the story ends right there, but I want it to go on. I want to enjoy the wedding celebration with the happy couple. I want to watch the heroine throw away her dirty rags and see her smile as she wriggles into a new rustly silk taffeta dress each morning. I want to see her gain the respect in her kingdom that she deserves after having suffered the humiliation of poverty and servitude. The Revelation gives me that kind of luxury - of peeking into the future to relish some of the most delicious details about Christ's "happily ever after" with His bride, the church.

V. When Are We Gonna Get There?

Any parent who's taken a car trip with a kid of any age knows that refrain. "Pretty soon," is my stock answer to that one. I say that because I know that if I say it is going to be 14 more hours, the kids might come unglued on me at the prospect of spending umpteen more minutes with each other's elbows poking into each other's ears and at having to use the restroom at five more McDonald's. On the other hand, if I say we're almost there, the easily excitable crew will begin unbuckling their seatbelts before we exit the freeway and arguing about who will get to hug Grandma first before the car doors are even open.

"When will the end of the world come?" We would all like to know just which square to circle in red on our calendars to mark the day we meet our Lord to live with Him forever. In fact, the disciples themselves approached Jesus with that very question: "Tell us, when will this happen, and what will be the sign of your coming and of the end of the age?" (Matthew 24:3, NIV). In the passages of Scripture that follow the disciples' question, Christ gives the specifics about the end-time scenario, but He does not give a date. He simply states that when we see the things He's describing start to happen, we will know that the end is near. Then Christ says, "No one knows about that day or hour, not even the angels in heaven, nor the Son, but only the Father" (Matthew 24:36, NIV).

VI. Why Doesn't He Give Us a Date?

"I can't tell you why God does not want us to know," says Terry. "But we shouldn't worry about it because His love letter to all mankind, His Word, tells us that if we just trust in Him, we will be with Him forever in eternity."

I can't speak for anyone else, but I think He doesn't give me the appointment card because He knows all too well how I am. Like with my kids, too much information can be dangerous. I would be likely to drop that appointment card into the jumble of contents in my purse and forget about it until it was much closer to time for my heavenly date. Then I would frantically dig through the empty gum wrappers at the bottom of the bag to find out exactly when I needed to be ready, meanwhile having lost all the intervening days simply carrying out the routine of my life rather than carrying out the routine of my life as if I would see my Lord any minute.

"We must live in the expectation of His any-moment coming for us while working to carry out the commission He has given us, which is to go into the world, and as we go, to sow the seeds of the Gospel," as Terry says.

I know I'm still a long way from grasping some of the more difficult issues in prophecy, but I have at least made some sense out of some of the words and phrases related to the subject that used to intimidate me. I'm no longer afraid to open my Bible to the book of Revelation, or to think about the sequence of events that will lead up to the last days of this earth as I know it.

I have learned that God hasn't given me a spirit of fear, "but of power, and of love, and of a sound mind" (2 Timothy 1:7, KJV). With that spirit of love, and with my sound mind, I can take God's prophetic teachings to heart. In exchange, I receive an enriched understanding of Scripture, a broadened view of the world, and a renewed focus on my journey through life as a Christian woman. I have the comfort of knowing that the end of the world isn't bad - at least, not for me and my brothers and sisters in Christ. For all of us, the last book of the Bible is truly the "happily ever after" to Genesis' "once upon a time"! And most importantly of all, I have the privilege of glimpsing - even if it is "through a glass, darkly" - yet another breathtaking dimension of my precious Lord, the Author and Finisher of my salvation Who will be holding my hand even beyond the end of the age.

PART III
PROBING YOUR PLANET'S PROPHETIC FUTURE

14

BELIEVERS BOW BEFORE THE BEMA

BY JACK VAN IMPE

THE JUDGMENT SEAT OF CHRIST

THE BIBLE MENTIONS at least five different judgments. The first in our chronological listing is:

1. The judgment of the believer's sin

Nearly 2,000 years ago, Christ came down from heaven's glory to shed His precious blood for a world of ungodly sinners. He did not die for His own sin, for He knew no sin, but He became sin for us (see 2 Corinthians 5:21). Through this substitutionary death - dying for you and me - all who receive this Christ can have the past, present, and future stains of sin immediately forgiven, forgotten, obliterated, and liquidated, because the "blood of Jesus Christ [God's Son] cleanseth us from ALL sin" (1 John 1: 7, emphasis mine).

As soon as the washing of regeneration (Titus 3:5)

takes place, God cries, "their sins and their iniquities will I remember no more" (Hebrews 8:12). The result of being so completely washed in the blood is "there is therefore now no condemnation to them which are in Christ Jesus" (Romans 8: 1). This is true because Christ was already judged in the sinner's place. Oh, what love, what compassion. Is it any wonder that Paul asks in Hebrews 2:3, "How shall we escape, if we neglect so great salvation?"

2. The judgment of the believer's service

This investigative probe into a believer's lifetime of works will form the basis of our study in this chapter. We will discuss this bema seat judgment in the next few pages.

3. The judgment of Israel

During the tribulation hour, an enemy comes against Israel from the North (see Ezekiel 38 and 39). Then the armies of the world also converge on the Middle East (see Zechariah 14:2), and this period of bloody devastation becomes the time of Jacob's trouble (Jeremiah 30:7).

4. The judgment of the nations

Matthew 25 pictures the return of Christ to this earth. The text correlates to and is synonymous with Revelation 19:11-16 when Christ returns to earth as King of kings and Lord of lords. Before He establishes His millennial kingdom upon earth for 1,000 years (see Revelation 20:4), He purges the earth of its rebels (see Matthew 25:31-46). The righteous are then allowed to enter God's earthly kingdom utopia for 1,000 years, and eventually heaven, eternally. We observe this transition in 1 Corinthians 15:24-25, which states, "Then cometh the end [millennium], when he shall have delivered up the kingdom to God, even the Father; when he shall have put down all rule and all authority and power. For he must reign, till he hath put all enemies under his feet."

5. The final judgment of the wicked (commonly called "The Great Judgment Day")

Revelation 20:11-15 pictures this solemn universal trial. John says:

And I saw a great white throne, and him that sat on it, from whose face the earth and the heaven fled away; and there was found no place for them. And I saw the dead, small and great, stand before God; and the books were opened: and another book was opened, which is the book of life: and the dead were judged out of those things which were written in the books, according to their works. And the sea gave up the dead which were in it; and death and hell delivered up the dead which were in them: and they were judged every man according to their works. And death and hell were cast into the lake of fire. This is the second death. And whosoever was not found written in the book of life was cast into the lake of fire.

Friends, the hour is coming when every unsaved, unregenerate sinner must meet a holy God for a detailed review of his life upon planet earth. When God's books are opened, every offender's tongue will be silenced. There will be no hope then, but there is now! Why? Because Christ died for our sin (see 1 Corinthians 15:3). This means that the guiltiest of mortals can immediately be absolved by trusting in the merits of the shed blood of Jesus. Don't procrastinate - do it today! Then you, too, will know the blessedness of John 3:18, which declares,

"He that believeth on [Christ] is not condemned because the believing are passed from death unto life" (John 5:24).

So far, we have established that there are five distinct judgments. Men who do not rightly divide the word of truth (see 2 Timothy 2:15) often link the various texts concerning judgment into one confused hodgepodge. We will not be guilty of this practice as we study the bema seat investigation.

The Test

Romans 14:15 states, "We shall all stand before the judgment seat of Christ." And 2 Corinthians 5:10 adds: "For we must all appear before the judgment seat of Christ; that everyone may receive the things done in his body, according to that he hath done, whether it be good or bad."

Millions of God's children across the globe think that they can live nominal Christian lives and still be fully rewarded. They think that they can play "fast and loose" with the world without suffering loss. This is but wishful thinking! The day is coming when every blood-bought believer must stand before a holy God for a scrutinizing investigation. This becomes abundantly clear when one traces the English term "judgment seat" to its Greek origin, which translates to the term "bema seat." When Paul used this terminology in the first century, every educated mind immediately knew the severity of the warning because their thinking took them to the runner's track in Athens, Greece.

It, like today's sports stadiums, contained thousands of seats. However, one seat differed from the rest in that it was uplifted and elevated. The judge of the contest sat there, where no obstructions could mar his view of the race's participants. He could see every movement clearly.

Doesn't this help you picture "the God of Holiness" elevated upon His throne, watching the Christian's race of life? He sees where we go, hears what we say, and watches our every move. Yes, "for the eyes of the Lord run to and fro throughout the whole earth" (2 Corinthians 16:9). God cries, "Mine eyes are upon all their ways" (Jeremiah 16:17), and because of it "all things are naked and opened unto the eyes of him with whom we have to do" (Hebrews 4:13).

God is keeping records for the day when "we must all appear before the judgment seat of Christ; that everyone may receive the things done in his body, according to that he hath done, whether it be good or bad" (2 Corinthians 5:10). Therefore, it behooves each one of us to place Christ first in our daily walk and talk. We cannot live for the flesh and self and hear Christ say in that day, "Well done, thou good and faithful servant." We must fight and win battles. We must trade scars for crowns and earn our rewards.

"Paul who [bore] in [his] body the marks [scars] of the Lord Jesus" (Galatians 6:17) was "[pressing] toward the mark for the prize of the high calling of God in Christ Jesus" (Philippians 3:14). Salvation was his as a gift, but only his works of hardship, suffering, and perhaps death could bring him the prize or crown to lay at Jesus' feet (see Revelation 4: 10, 11). We, too, must know the fellowship of his sufferings to receive the prize of the high calling of God in Christ Jesus (see Philippians 3:10,14).

But there is more. We are just beginning to explore the depths of this judgment. As we delve further into this subject, we discover that God also will investigate the motives behind our works. In other words, we will be asked, "Why did you do what you did when you did it?" "Why were you a pastor, an evangelist, a missionary?" "Why did you hold the office of deacon, elder, or Sunday school teacher?" "Why did you sing or perform solos?" "What was your motive in being a counselor, an usher, a bus driver?" "What purpose was there in desiring to be a full-time Christian worker? Was it for power, prestige, or pride? Was it to be noticed, to be lauded, and applauded?"

We as Christians must examine our hearts in light of Christ's words in Matthew 6:1-6:

> Take heed that ye do not your alms before men, to be seen of them; otherwise ye have no reward of your Father which is in heaven. Therefore when thou doest thine alms, do not sound a trumpet before thee, as the hypocrites do in the synagogues and in the streets, that they may have glory of men. Verily I say unto you, They have their reward. But when thou doest alms, let not thy left hand know what thy right hand doeth: That thine alms may be in secret: and thy Father which seeth in secret himself shall reward thee openly.
>
> And when thou prayest, thou shalt not be as the

hypocrites are for they love to pray standing in the synagogues and in the corners of the streets, that they may be seen of men. Verily I say unto you, They have their reward. But thou, when thou prayest, enter into thy closet, and when thou hast shut thy door pray to thy Father which is in secret; and thy Father which seeth in secret shall reward thee openly.

Christ continues in verses 16-19:

"Moreover when ye fast, be not, as the hypocrites, of a sad countenance: for they disfigure their faces, that they may appear unto men to fast. Verily I say unto you, They have their reward. But thou, when thou fastest, anoint thine head, and wash thy face; That thou appear not unto men to fast, but unto thy Father which is in secret: and thy Father which seeth in secret, shall reward thee openly."

There is no doubt as to the meaning of Christ's startling words. He declares that there are two places to be rewarded - here upon earth as one seeks the praise of men, or later in heaven when the Father who sees the works performed in secret rewards those whose acts were motivated simply by love for Him.

First Corinthians 4:5 states:

Therefore judge nothing before the time, until the Lord come, who both will bring to light the hidden things of darkness, and will make manifest the counsels [or motives] of the hearts.

This teaching is also propounded in 1 Corinthians 3:11-15:

> For other foundation can no man lay than that is laid, which is Jesus Christ. Now if any man build upon this foundation gold, silver, precious stones, wood, hay, stubble; Every man's work shall be made manifest: for the day shall declare it, because it shall be revealed by fire; and the fire shall try every man's work of what sort it is. If any man's work abide which he hath built thereupon, he shall receive a reward. If any man's work shall be burned, he shall suffer loss: but he himself shall be saved; yet so as by fire.

Again, there is no doubt about the explicit teaching within this portion of Scripture. It states, "The fire shall try every man's work of what SORT it is" (emphasis mine). Now notice some interesting observations concerning this judgment.

1. **The judgment is only for the people of God.**

It is only for those who have built upon the foundation of the Lord Jesus Christ.

1. **All of God's people present some form of "works" to Christ at the bema seat.**

The fire then tests every man's work. Every man? Every man!

1. **Though all "work" to some degree, a difference in the quantity and quality of those works is observed.**

Some works are precious and good (the gold, the silver, and the precious stones), while others (the wood, the hay, and the stubble) are bad.

1. **The works are tested by purging fires.**

The good works withstand the fire while the wood, hay, and stubble are reduced to a mass of incinerated rubble. We Christians must ask whether what we are presently doing in the service of God will abide the fires of Christ's bema seat. Will our works endure the tests? Will our rewards be precious or rubble?

1. **The disintegrated ashes bring sorrow and loss.**

Yes, "[They] shall suffer loss: but [they themselves] shall be saved; yet so as by fire" (1 Corinthians 3:15). Notice that the lukewarm, the indifferent, and the careless will be present. They will not miss heaven because of their faults! Instead, they will be saved as by fire - by the skin of their teeth! They will make it to heaven only to sorrow over their waywardness for a millennium, as we will presently see. Their loss is not of salvation, but of rewards. They suffer loss (rewards), but they themselves are saved as by fire. It is obvious, then, that the wayward lose out with God. The loss is not of eternal life but of rewards. Eternal life is freely bestowed upon all who believe as a gift apart from works (see Romans 6:23) and cannot be forfeited; but crowns can be earned and lost, accumulated and liquidated.

1. **Quality works - consisting of gold, silver, and precious stones - performed for the glory of God to win the souls of men, when tested and found genuine, will earn crowns for the faithful for all eternity.**

These crowns will then be placed at the feet of Christ as an eternal memorial of love for a lifetime of service. The scene is portrayed in Revelation 4:10-11. The 24 elders pictured in the text represent all of God's people in both testaments - the 12 patriarchs of Israel and the 12 apostles of Christendom. These 24 stalwarts of both eras have their names written upon the gates and foundations of the future Holy City in Revelation 21:12-14. So there is no doubt as to who they are. They represent all the faithful, blood-bought people of God through the ages. The thrilling scene is described as follows:

> The four and twenty elders fall down before him that sat on the throne, and worship him that liveth forever and ever, and cast their crowns before the throne saying, Thou art worthy, Oh Lord, to receive glory and honour and power for thou hast created all things, and for thy pleasure they are and were created (Revelation 4:10-11).

Christians who long to lay a crown at the feet of the

Savior on the Coronation Day - those who do not wish to be off in the background ashamed (see 1 John 2-28), having experienced a humiliating entrance into the presence of God (see 2 Peter 1:11), can confess their failure (a confession longingly desired by our Heavenly Father [see 1 John 1:9]) to experience rededication and redirection. That prayer of confession offers a new start to a journey that will end with the words "Well done, thou good and faithful servant," from the lips of Jesus.

The Victor's Triumph and the Backslider's Tears

As we've just discussed, someday, perhaps soon, every Christian must meet God for an investigative judgment of his entire life. This moment will be a time of jubilant victory for some. Jesus said, "He that receiveth a prophet in the name of a prophet shall receive a prophet's reward; and he that receiveth a righteous man in the name of a righteous man shall receive a righteous man's reward" (Matthew 10:41). Paul adds, "If any man's work abide which he hath built thereupon, he shall receive a reward" (1 Corinthians 3:14).

On the other hand, this will be a time of weeping for others. Paul, dealing with this hour of judgment, states in 2 Corinthians 5:11, "Knowing therefore the terror of the Lord, we persuade men." Terror? Yes, terror! How often Christians hilariously shout, "Praise the Lord, Jesus is coming soon!" Though this will undoubtedly be the most joyous event of the ages for some, it will be a time of intense and immense sorrow for others.

First John 2:28 declares, "And now, little children, abide in him; that, when he shall appear we may have confidence, and not be ASHAMED before him at his coming" (emphasis mine). Notice carefully that when Christ returns, all believers - the confident and the ashamed - are summoned into His presence. The confident appear before the tribunal with "good works," whereas the ashamed have naught but "bad works" (see 2 Corinthians 5:10).

This is exceedingly important to understand because multitudes today think that one sin can keep a child of God out of heaven. The text plainly states that the "ashamed" meet Christ at His appearing. At the sound of the trumpet, when the dead in Christ rise first and living believers join the dead to meet Christ in the clouds (see 1 Thessalonians 4:16), the "ashamed" also enter heaven. However, the abundant entrance is reserved for those who earned it upon earth (see 2 Peter 1:11).

If English means anything - and it does - this text proves that the wayward go home to meet Christ though ashamed. Since one can only bear shame for error and wrongdoing, then it is dogmatically clear that the wrongdoers meet Christ at His appearing or return. Granted, they are embarrassed and lose all of their rewards, but they are nevertheless present at the roll call of the ages, though saved as by fire (1 Corinthians 3:15), by the "skin of their teeth." What produces their embarrassment and humiliation as believers?

. . .

Neglected Opportunities

MULTITUDES OF GOD'S people could do so much more for Christ if they would, but the flesh stands in the way. When they do serve, it is often with selfish motives. Their cry is often, "What will I get out of this?" "What is in it for me?" The result? Modern Christianity has become big business. Religious performers today charge exorbitant rates, some receiving as much as $1,000 to $2,500 for a performance. What a judgment of terror must await these mercenary "gospel entertainers!" Though saved by fire, their "wood, hay, and stubble" works will surely dissolve into ashes.

Then there are those who have little or no time for spiritual exercises. They seldom read God's Holy Word, attend God's house, or give their tithes - and they never win souls. This is sin! James 4:17 states, "Therefore to him that knoweth to do good, and doeth it not, to him it is sin."

These sins of omission - failing to do God's will - also produce remorse in that day. But those who obey God will not be sorry. The faithful will be rewarded a hundredfold at the bema seat. Scholars calculate this to be a 10,000 percent yield. No wonder Paul said in 2 Corinthians 9:6, "He which soweth sparingly [meagerly] shall reap also sparingly; and he which soweth bountifully [abundantly] shall reap also bountifully." One cannot out give God at 10,000 percent interest. Galatians 6:7, often quoted to the unsaved, but directed to Christians concerning giving, states, "Be not deceived; God is not mocked [or fooled]: for whatsoever a man soweth, that shall he also reap."

Our heavenly mansion will only be as beautiful as we build it now. Jesus said in John 14:2, "In my Father's house are many mansions." The literal rendering should state, "In my Father's house are numerous and differing kinds of dwelling places." Not all mansions will be identical. The building blocks for our eternal homes are being sent ahead from earth. Jesus said, "Lay not up for yourselves treasures upon earth, where moth and rust doth corrupt, and where thieves break through and steal: But lay up for yourselves treasure in heaven" (Matthew 6:19,20). If our earthly treasure is piled up in stocks and bonds and banks, we have had our reward. On the other hand, if the treasure is sent ahead, it awaits us with added and fantastic dividends. We Christians have a choice: We can have it here for 70 years, die and leave it for the ungodly to spend; or we may send it ahead for eternal blessing.

May I share a most heart-moving experience with you?

When Rexella and I were in Hershey, Pennsylvania, a man sitting in a wheelchair asked if he might speak to us. As we reached the area where he sat, he began to weep, saying, "I am an invalid, as you can see. I have multiple sclerosis and osteoarthritis. The pain is more than I can humanly bear. In fact, my pain-destroying medication costs me $100.00 per month. Nevertheless, I have made a decision after much prayer. I want to give you the $100.00 and omit this month's medicine. I know my pain will be unbearable, but it is the least I can do for Christ who suffered so much for me. Take it and use it for His glory."

Rexella and I, both in tears, replied, "We cannot accept this money for your medicine."

He again wept audibly, saying, "Would you deprive me of a blessing? Take it for the glory of God and the salvation of souls."

How many thousands who have a superabundance of material wealth, stocks, bonds, bank accounts and possessions - do nothing but tip God occasionally? We must not think that it won't make a difference at the time of rewards, that it will be the same for all. "Be not deceived; God is not mocked: for whatsoever a man soweth that shall he also reap" (Galatians 6:7). We are all going home soon - either confident or ashamed. Will it be a time of victory or anguish, triumph or tears? It is not too late to make a new start.

Neglected Holiness

THEN, too, there will be tears over neglected holiness. No doubt about it: God demands that His people live holy lives: "For God hath not called us unto uncleanness, but unto holiness" (1 Thessalonians 4:7). "Who hath saved us, and called us with an holy calling" (2 Timothy 1:9). "Follow peace with all men, and HOLINESS" (Hebrews 12:14, emphasis mine). "Be ye holy; for I am holy" (1 Peter 1: 16).

This means that we are not to fashion ourselves

according to the former lusts (1 Peter 1:14), that we are to abstain from fleshly lusts (1 Peter 2:11), and that we are to put on Christ and not make any provision for the flesh, to fulfill the lusts thereof (Romans 13:14). How different from the lowly standards held by many carnal church members who constantly play "musical chairs" with the pagans and God-haters of this world. These indifferent backsliders run with the world - they visit its clubs, casinos, and theaters, all under the guise of being curious. They, like Lot who desired Sodom, want to spend time in Las Vegas and get away from it all.

But the getting and vulgarity matters not as the flesh is on a spree. Are they saved? God alone really knows! One thing is certain: If they are Christ's, their double standards will be investigated. "For we must all appear before the judgment seat of Christ; that everyone may receive the things done in his body, according to that he hath done, whether it be GOOD or BAD" (2 Corinthians 5:10, emphasis mine). Oh, what weeping, what wailing, what travail, what heartache, and heartbreak as they meet Jesus face to face! Their entrance into God's presence will not be abundant (2 Peter 1: 11).

They Will Be Tremendously Ashamed

(1 John 2:28). The terror of the Lord will be meted out in judgment (see 2 Corinthians 5:11) and they then will suffer the loss of all rewards (see 1 Corinthians 3:15). No

wonder the lukewarm are weeping. They blew it. They suffered the loss of all things except salvation.

This loss extends beyond the loss of rewards for a meaningless life. It includes losing, through foolish living, rewards previously earned during years of spiritual service. God has a system of addition and subtraction on His books. Therefore, one's accumulation of "good works" can be wiped out swiftly through disobedient living. Here is proof: "Look to yourselves, that we lose not those things which we have wrought [or earned], but that we receive a full reward" (2 John 8). God says, "Be careful how you live, where you go, how you serve, if you want a full reward." Again, "Hold that fast which thou hast, that no man take thy crown" (Revelation 3:11).

In simpler terminology, God says, "Hang on to your earned crown and do not let anyone entice you, mislead you, drag you down, or destroy the good works already accumulated or you will suffer loss."

Paul, led by the Holy Spirit, also declares in 1 Corinthians 9:27, "But I keep under my body, and bring it into subjection: lest that by any means, when I have preached to others, I myself should be a castaway [a reject for rewards]". He could not mean the loss of salvation by the term "castaway" because we have already seen that the "ashamed" are present at heaven's roll call though they are saved by fire. Instead, Paul is saying, "Look, I am a red-blooded man with desires similar to others. However, I will not allow my flesh to control me. Instead, I constantly battle and batter my fleshly appetites into subjection. Yes, I keep my bodily appetites under control lest I lose everything I have ever earned."

Now if this is true for Paul, it is equally true for all. In fact, Paul's service record is unparalleled in the history of Christendom. Perhaps no one suffered as he did except the Lord himself. Listen to the list of "good works" Paul accumulated in 2 Corinthians 11:23-27. He states:

> In labours more abundant, in stripes above measure, in prisons more frequent, in deaths oft. Of the Jews five times received forty stripes save one. Thrice was I beaten with rods, once was I stoned, thrice I suffered shipwreck, a night and a day I have been in the deep; In journeyings often, in perils of waters, in perils of robbers, in perils by mine own countrymen, in perils by the heathen, in perils in the city, in perils in the wilderness, in perils in the sea, in perils among false brethren; In weariness and painfulness, in watchings often, in hunger and thirst, in fastings often, in cold and nakedness.

Wow! What a servant of God; Paul was beaten, battered, stoned, crushed, robbed, persecuted, hated, and starved. Surely this portfolio of works would bring Paul heaven's greatest "Oscar." It would if he remained faithful. Remember, he said as quoted earlier, "If I did not keep my body under and bring it into subjection, I myself would be a castaway, disapproved and rejected of heaven's 'Emmy Awards.' Therefore, I fight the good fight of faith - fight the world, the flesh, and the devil - so that my Savior will say to me at that day, 'Well done, thou good and faithful servant.'"

. . .

Tears in Heaven

MILLIONS ARE GOING HOME ashamed and embarrassed. The result will be intermittent weeping for 1,007 years. This is proven by studying the chronological outline of the Book of Revelation. Let's look at it.

Revelation 1:19 states, "Write these things which thou hast seen, and the things which are, and the things which shall be hereafter." One immediately notices the three tenses of the English language - past, present, and future:

CHAPTER 1 IS PAST TENSE:
"Write the things which thou hast seen."
Chapters 2 and 3 are present tense:
"Write the things which are."
Chapters 4 through 22 are future tense:
"Write the things which shall be after these things."

We are presently awaiting the homegoing of the believers. This occurs in Revelation 4:1 with the words, "Come up hither." The seven years of tribulation follow in Chapters six through 18. Christ returns to earth as King of kings and Lord of lords (Chapter 19:11-16). He rules the earth for 1,000 years (Chapter 20:4-6) and judges the world after the thousand years (Chapter 20:11-15). Then, finally and forever, God wipes all tears away from their eyes (see Revelation 21:4). Chronologically, this is after the tribulation, after the millennium. In other words, from the rapture call in Revelation 4:1 onward, there is intermittent and spasmodic crying for the next 1,007 years.

Two Simultaneous Judgments

IN DWELLING FURTHER on the teaching of "tears" in God's presence, we discover that the weeping takes place simultaneously with the tribulation hour. Two judgments are occurring at the time. One is in heaven, the other upon earth. One is a judgment of believers regarding service, the other a judgment of Israel. One is called the bema seat judgment, the other, the tribulation hour. Both prove to be heartbreaking for the participants.

Let's look at the tribulation period for a few moments. This is the time of Jacob's trouble (see Jeremiah 30:7), and Jacob represents Israel. Satan, the old devil, hates Israel. She was used of God as a channel for producing His only begotten Son on earth. Revelation 12:5 states, "And she [Israel] brought forth a man child." Because of Israel's connection with Christ's birth, the nation has always been Satan's prime target of hatred. He has relentlessly persecuted her throughout the annals of history and will increase his persecution during the tribulation hour. His attack will be most vicious when he realizes that the end of his power struggle for world supremacy over Jehovah God is about to cease.

Therefore, Revelation 12:13 states, "And when the dragon saw that he was cast unto the earth, he persecuted the woman which brought forth the man child." This will be the world's bloodiest hour. Seven seals, seven trumpets, and seven vials are judgments that will be unleashed upon planet earth. These will produce murder, starvation, war militarism, earthquakes, hail, fire, oceanic disruptions, cosmic catastrophes, pestilence, inflation, sores, infections, pain, pollution, darkness, and finally, ARMAGEDDON! The hour will be so dreary and hopeless that earth's inhabitants will cry to the mountains and rocks to fall on them (see Revelation 6:16). earth's most agonizing hour will make men desire death over life. Simultaneously, the people of God are being examined at Christ's judgment seat. This, too, will be an unpleasant situation because the Holy Spirit speaks about the terror of the Lord in connection with the investigation of believers' works (2 Corinthians 5:11). I have no doubt that some believers will be so ashamed, so embarrassed, so humiliated, and so frightened to face the fireworks (see 1 John 2:28) that they will want to exchange heaven for earth, the judgment seat exposure for the tribulation woes. They would rather cry for the mountains to fall on them than to meet Christ with wasted lives. Small wonder the songwriter said, "Must I go in empty-handed, my Redeemer thus to meet?"

What sadness, yea, what vehement crying shall then ensue as rewards are lost forever.

At Last, the Treasure!

To this point we have repeatedly mentioned rewards.

We have discussed the victor's triumph and the backslider's tears. We have observed that some will rejoice while others will remorsefully weep. But what are the crowns and why are they presented?

The Watcher's Crown

This meritorious award is given to all who longingly watch for Christ's return. Paul declares in 2 Timothy 4:8, "Henceforth there is laid up for me a crown of righteousness, which the Lord, the righteous judge, shall give me at that day; and not to me only, but unto all them also that love his appearing." Imagine, God gives a special crown to believers who fix their eyes and hearts heavenward in watchfulness of Christ's return.

This is reasonable when one realizes that "expectancy" and "purity" are closely related. One cannot longingly look for Christ's return and practice abominable sins. The two never coexist in a rational mind. That is why 1 John 3:2,3 states, "Beloved, now are we the sons of God, and it doth not yet appear what we shall be: but we know that, when he shall appear, we shall be like him; for we shall see him as he is. And every man that hath this hope [of His appearing] in him purifieth himself, even as he is pure."

Adulterers, fornicators, homosexuals, drunkards, drug addicts, extortioners, swindlers, liars, and those living for the things of this world are not anxiously awaiting Christ's return. Neither are carnal believers who neglect the Bible, prayer, God's house, soul-winning, and personal holiness. No, those who look daily and expectantly for Christ's return are not among those of this world who sit in bars, theaters, rock concerts, gambling casinos, and other pagan dens. They do not want to be found there when Jesus comes. Their desire - that "blessed hope, and the glorious appearing of the great God and our Savior Jesus Christ" (Titus 2:13) - makes them consistently live for His return. They want to be commended, congratulated, and crowned in their fight to the finish. They do not want a confrontation producing consternation and castigation at that day. They long to hear Jesus say, "Well done, thou good and faithful servant."

Because the Savior's appearing is closely aligned with holiness of life, it is to be expected that the carnal rebel and refuse the teaching of prophecy. They cry, "Do not preach prophecy! It is sensational and speculative nonsense anyway. Instead, tell us about 'Parbar westward, four at the causeway, and two at Parbar' (1 Chronicles 26:18). This does not hit us where we live!"

One should expect this from the indifferent, the lethargic, the worldly, and the backslidden. They definitely do not want to hear about a time when they must meet Christ with wasted lives because His appearing means the disintegration of their selfish, substandard works. They know that they are going to be among the "ashamed" (see 1 John 2:28), and that they shall be "saved as by fire" (1 Corinthians 3:15). They hate to think of meeting Jesus empty-handed and being "rejects" at the judgment seat. Small wonder they dislike this Bible doctrine, but, like it or not, it will happen!

May I, therefore, plead with preachers, "Preach the

message of Christ's return. Present the signs. Tell the people the moment is near. Beg them to keep their eyes fixed on heaven so that you and they will receive the watcher's crown." Only those who "look," receive!

The Runner's Crown

We find the background for this award in 1 Corinthians 9:24-27. Paul says:

> Know ye not that they which run in a race run all, but one receiveth the prize? So run, that ye may obtain. And every man that striveth for the mastery is temperate in all things. Now they do it to obtain a corruptible crown; but we are incorruptible. I therefore so run, not as uncertainly; so fight I not as one that beateth the air. But I keep under my body and bring it into subjection: lest that by any means, when I have preached to others, I myself should be a castaway.

Consider this tremendous portion of Scripture expository. The writer says in verse 24 that though there are numerous runners - and he undoubtedly has the athletic field of Athens, Greece in mind - only one becomes the winner. The analogy follows that although tens of thousands of believers have run and are running in the race of Christian service, competing for "good works," only a minority will receive the runner's crown. Hence, the admonition, "Run that you may obtain."

Next, we observe the rules of the race. The Greek athletes were temperate in all things, subjecting their bodies to the most stringent health rules. They trained, exercised, and abstained from anything that would render them unfit for the big day. Verse 25: "And every man that striveth for the mastery [victory] is temperate [under self-control] in ALL things" (emphasis mine).

We must examine whether our habits are under control in our lives. There are those who say, "I don't think a little cigarette can keep me out of heaven." I agree. In fact, I think it might get a smoker there sooner! However, it, along with any other uncontrolled bodily habits, will get us there ashamed. It will help reduce our runner's crown into incinerated rubble (see 1 Corinthians 3:15). This crown is only for victors, for winners who have battered the cravings of the body into submission.

This explains Paul's words in verses 26,27: "I therefore so run, not as uncertainly; so fight I, not as one that beateth the air" (emphasis mine). Paul was saying, "I keep under my body, and bring it into subjection: lest that by any means, when I have preached to others, I myself should be a castaway [a reject for heaven's rewards, God's 'Oscars']."

As cited numerous times in this chapter, the term "castaway" has nothing to do with salvation. This is evident because the "ashamed," saved-by-fire crowd goes home at the rapture to weep. The Greek word from which we get the English term "castaway" means "to be disapproved" for crowns. Therefore, I again plead with the lukewarm to enthrone Christ in the heart. Get your first love rekindled. Serve Him with all your might.

Throw off every encumbrance of the flesh, including tobacco. Yes, "let us lay aside every weight and the sin which doth so easily beset us [trip us] and let us run with patience the race that is set before us" (Hebrews 12:1). The result? An incorruptible crown (see 1 Corinthians 9:25).

Paul concludes with a final scene of the race by saying, "The Greek runners subjected their appetites to the strictest regimentation imaginable simply to win the race and receive a corruptible crown [a wreath of laurel leaves that would decay and die in a few days]." Then, by way of analogy, he again says, "If God's people batter their fleshly wants into submission, they shall receive an incorruptible crown that endures for eternity." It will be worth it all when we see Jesus.

Adoniram Judson and his sweet wife, Ann, were missionaries in India and Burma. During their tour of service, Adoniram was arrested as an enemy agent when his homeland, England, and the nation in which he served became disenchanted with one another. Immediately, Judson was imprisoned. The tiny cell in which he was incarcerated was so crowded that the prisoners had to take turns sleeping. There was not enough room for all of them to lie down. The hot sun beating upon the dingy cell caused unbearable suffering through heat prostration. The stench also became obnoxious as the men were never allowed to bathe.

One day the government officials decided to punish the prisoners and Judson was hoisted into the air by his thumbs. Pain filled his body as he remained suspended in midair for hours at a time. His precious helpmeet, Ann, came by the cell daily, looked inside, and wept. However, this soldier of the cross always encouraged her man by saying, "Hang on, Adoniram. God will give us the victory." As the days and weeks passed, faithful Ann no longer made the visits and Adoniram's loneliness increased. No one had informed him that she was dying. All he had now was a memory of his sweetheart saying, "Hang on, Adoniram. God will give us the victory."

Months later, upon his release, Adoniram immediately began to search for Ann. As he approached the area where he formerly lived, he saw a child so dirty that he failed to recognize the little one as his own. He then dashed into the tent and saw the form of one so small and weak from malnutrition that she appeared to be a skeleton. Her beautiful flowing hair had also fallen out and she was bald.

As Adoniram called, she failed to respond. It seemed as though she were already dead. He took her in his arms and wept. The hot tears dropping on her angelic face revived Ann and she said, "Hang on, Adoniram; God will give us the victory."

Adoniram lost his sweetheart, but not his faith and courage. He continued under dire circumstances to preach and to build churches, and by the time this man of God was buried, scores of churches had come into existence through his labors. Adoniram and Ann ran the race faithfully unto the end and experienced the "abundant entrance" we have been discussing.

The Shepherd's Crown

. . .

This award mentioned in 1 Peter 5:1-4 undoubtedly is reserved for faithful ministers. In the text, the Apostle Peter says:

> The elders which are among you I exhort, who am also an elder, and a witness of the sufferings of Christ, and also a partaker of the glory that shall be revealed: Feed the flock of God which is among you, taking the oversight thereof, not by constraint, but willingly; not for filthy lucre, but of a ready mind; Neither as being lords over God's heritage, but being ensamples to the flock. And when the chief Shepherd shall appear, ye shall receive a crown of glory that fadeth not away.

Peter, in writing to the elders or spiritual shepherds, exhorts his fellow ministers to "feed the flock." God so loves His precious people that He wants the pastors to meet the nutritional needs of His children spiritually. Hence, the shepherds are to feast on the Word of God daily in order to meet the needs of the hungry. This takes discipline and perseverance. It means that the golf game, the tennis match, and other recreational amusements must take second place. It means that the obedient preacher cannot wait until the last minute and prepare a "Saturday Night Special" for the Lord's Day.

The ministers are to lead exemplary lives. They are not to be power-crazy dictators. They must lead in love and rule the church as God's appointed directors, but with compassion. As rulers they are not to be bored-dominated "puppets" - an insult to God and His Word. That's right! First Timothy 3:4,5 states a minister should rule "well his own house, having his children in subjection with all gravity; (For if a man know not how to rule his own house, how shall he take care of [or rule] the church of God?)"

This God-appointed leader, the pastor, must be obeyed. Hebrews 13:17 instructs us to "Obey them that have the rule over you and submit yourselves: for they watch for your souls, as they that must give account, that they may do it with joy, and not with grief for that is unprofitable for you."

Imagine! God's shepherds are to be obeyed. This is specifically true as they teach doctrine and ethics. Those who ignore these commandments will suffer great embarrassment at the bema seat. They will weep as their spiritual guardians, and their pastors, report their disobedience, stubbornness, and carnality.

This truth may be hard to accept. But again, Hebrews 13:17 states, "They watch for your souls, as they that MUST give an account, that they may do it with joy, and not with grief: for that is unprofitable for you" (emphasis mine).

Think of it! The shepherd's testimony produces joy and grief, victory and heartache, triumph and tears, as the reports are presented. This does not mean that the shepherd is free from investigation. He, too, must obey the Word he preaches, and live according to the God-demanded requirements mentioned in 1 Timothy 3:2-7, which says:

> A bishop [or preacher] then must be blameless, the husband of one wife, vigilant, sober, of good behaviour, given to hospitality, apt to teach, Not given to wine, no striker, not greedy of filthy lucre; but patient, not a brawler, not covetous; One that ruleth well his own house, having his children in subjection with all gravity; (For if a man know not how to rule his own house, how shall he take care of the church of God?) Not a novice, lest being lifted up with pride [becoming arrogant] he fall into the condemnation of the devil [who also fell through pride; see Isaiah 14:12-14], Moreover he must have a good report of them which are without [the unsaved world]; lest he fall into reproach and the snare of the devil.

Shepherds who make these God-ordained standards their goal receive an exclusive crown at that day, for 1 Peter 5:4 declares, "When the chief Shepherd shall appear ye shall receive a crown of glory that fadeth not away."

The Soul Winner's Crown

Heaven's fourth crown is awarded to soul winners. Daniel 12:3 declares, "And they that be wise shall shine as the brightness of the firmament; and they that turn many to righteousness as the stars for ever and ever."

Stand outside on a clear night, fix your eyes upon heaven and study God's breathtaking creation. Stars, billions of miles away, twinkle as plainly as the flickering candle on the dining room table. No wonder Christians joyfully sing, "O God, how great Thou art."

However, an even more majestic scene is portrayed for the future as children of God who have won souls are coronated with star-studded crowns. Hallelujah! Yes, "they that turn many to righteousness as the stars for ever and ever."

Is it any wonder that Proverbs 11:30 states, "He that winneth souls is wise." The inference here is: "He who does not win souls is foolish." Why? He casts aside eternal rewards as though they were bubble gum wrappers. Wise men have more sense than this. They do not trample on God's commands. Instead, they longingly obey Matthew 28.19: "Go ye therefore, and teach all nations;" Mark 16.15: "Go ye into all the world, and preach the gospel to every creature;" Luke 14.21: "Go out into the highways and hedges, and compel them to come in;" Acts 1:8: "Ye shall be witnesses unto me both in Jerusalem, and in all Judaea, and in Samaria, and unto the uttermost part of the earth."

They love God and will not allow business or pleasure to stand in the way of the highest calling in the world - the winning of souls for eternity. They heed the warning of Jesus about the bushel of business and the bed of relaxation and pleasure as hindrances to the candle's flame (see Mark 4:21). Their love for Christ and for the souls of men make them press forward for the prize of the high calling of God in Christ Jesus (Philippians 3:14). They want to present their troubles of grace to Jesus, not the husks of a barren life. They want a soul winner's crown; and a crown they receive as they, with Paul, triumphantly present their converts in that day saying, "For what is our hope, or joy, or crown of rejoicing? Are not even ye [converts] in the presence of our Lord Jesus Christ at his coming?" (1 Thessalonians 2:19).

At this great roll call, will you be able to make a presentation to the Savior? Will you have any spiritual children? Will you receive a crown that shines like the brightness of the firmament? Don't procrastinate; become a soul winner today! Then and only then will you be coronated with heaven's glittering "Oscar."

THE SUFFERER'S Crown

THE FIFTH AND final crown is presented to those who have suffered for the sake of Christ and the gospel. James 1:12 states, "Blessed is the man that endureth temptation [testing and trials] for when he is tried, he shall receive the CROWN OF LIFE, which the Lord hath promised to them that love him" (emphasis mine). Some will receive this glorious reward for having experienced the taunts and jeers of sinners.

Jesus said, "Blessed are they which are persecuted for righteousness' sake: for theirs is the kingdom of heaven. Blessed are ye, when men shall revile you, and persecute you, and shall say all manner of evil against you falsely for my sake. Rejoice, and be exceeding glad: for great is your reward in heaven" (Matthew 5:10-12). The reward will also be presented to those who have borne illness and infirmity with a smile, believing that "all things work together for good to them that love God" (Romans 8:28).

Some believers constantly praise the Lord in the midst of adversity while others continuously grumble in the midst of prosperity. Some Christians gripe so much that they will probably even complain about heaven's streets of gold, saying, "The glitter affects my eyes!" God help us!

How different from the saint who lost five sons in the service. Her minister, in a state of frustration, went to the godly little lady's home to share the sad news. When he arrived, she greeted him with the words, "I already know. The Lord spoke to me during my prayer time. Which one is it?" The pastor replied, 'All five." She said, "Praise the Lord! Praise the Lord! The last time my boys were home I led all five of them to the Savior. Had they died prior to that furlough I would never have seen them again. Now they are already on heaven's shore awaiting Mom's homecoming. Isn't God good?" Oh, what a reward this suffering saint shall receive at the great Coronation Day!

The crown is also given to those who are faithful unto the end. Revelation 2:10 declares, "Be thou faithful unto death, and I will give thee a crown of life." Again, I want to emphasize that this is not a reward for salvation, but for service, and is presented to those who have remained faithful throughout life. It is the same crown mentioned previously in James 1:12 presented to all who have endured trial and testing out of love for the Lord Jesus.

Time

. . .

CHILD OF GOD, the time is at hand for the distribution of heaven's awards. Where do you stand at this moment? What rewards would you receive were Jesus to come today? He is coming soon and immediately upon His arrival; the judgment of the believer's service record begins. That's right. The investigation begins at the appearing of Christ. Luke 14:14 states, "Thou shalt be recompensed [rewarded when?] at the resurrection of the just." First Peter 5:4 adds, "And when the chief Shepherd shall appear, ye shall receive a crown of glory that fadeth not away." First John 2:28 also verifies the time by stating, "And now, little children abide in him, that, when he SHALL APPEAR, we may have confidence, and not be ashamed before him AT HIS COMING" (emphasis mine).

THE THRILL

THEN, if we are rewarded, we shall present our crowns with millions of others from all ages. Let me illustrate:

Eight men wrote the New Testament. Seven were murdered. Matthew was slain with a halberd. Mark was dragged through the streets of Alexandria by a team of wild horses until he was dead. Luke was hanged in an olive tree. John survived the painful ordeal of being thrown into a cauldron of boiling oil but was disfigured for life and banned to the isle of Patmos. One day he undoubtedly saw his seared face reflected in a stream of water and wept. God said unto him, "Son, cheer up. I will allow you to write 1 John 3:2, which promises new bodies to all of My children." It says, "When he shall appear, we shall be like him, for we shall see him as he is." What joy must have filled the suffering servant's soul as he realized a better day was coming in which he would be changed to be like Jesus.

Paul was beheaded. Jude and Peter were crucified, and James was battered to death with a fuller's (blacksmith's) club.

Now Get the Future Picture

THE GREAT HOUR HAS ARRIVED, and all God's children are present. The investigation begins. What will each of us say as we stand with such an array of heroes - believers who gave all, who proved their first love for Christ during an entire lifetime- even unto death!

Christ's return may be tomorrow, next week, next month, or next year. We know not the day or the hour when Jesus shall break through the blue to call us home. However, we do know that it is near, even at the door. Therefore, my closing question is: Are you ready? Could you bear the investigative judgment were it to take place tomorrow? Would you be ashamed, embarrassed, red-faced, and brokenhearted? Would tears of sorrow intermittently flow from your eyes for the millennial age? Is your present disobedience worth such heartache?

Would you not rather serve God with all your heart and hear Him say, "Well done, thou good and faithful servant?" It is not too late to make a change, to reverse your lifestyles and put Christ first.

I ask you to obey 1 John 1:9 now. It says, "If we confess our sins, he is faithful and just to forgive us our sins, and to cleanse us from all unrighteousness." Do it, then live for Him.

It Will Be Worth It All When We See Jesus!

15

BABYLON — REBUILDING A DEBACLE

BY DAVE BREESE

A MAGNIFICENT CITY STOOD ON THE PLAIN OF SHINAR. Surrounded by a great wall, it was protected by motes and watchtowers 300 feet high. It was thought impenetrable by conquering armies and was the object of the confidence of everyone. The ancient historian, Herodotus, estimated that the city in the great plain was square in its plan and measured 120 furlongs each way, 480 furlongs in all. Each side was therefore about 14 miles long, making a circuit of nearly 56 miles, and an area of nearly 190 square miles. These figures may be open to question. The space involved is so great that traces of the wall are extremely hard to define. Around the city, Herodotus says, "There was a deep and broad mote full of water and then came a wall 50 royal cubits thick and 200 cubits high pierced by about 100 gateways with brazen gates in lintels."

Reckoning the cubit at 181 inches, this means that Babylon's walls were no less than 311 feet high and considering that the royal cubit was about 21 inches, their thickness would be something like 87 feet. Despite that Babylon has served as a quarry for the neighboring builders for two millennia, it is surprising that such extensive masses of brickwork would have disappeared "without leaving at least a few recognizable traces.

No doubt, ancient Babylon was magnificent almost beyond description. It was great in every way - in size, in wealth, in golden talents, in all of the things that would understandably make it the most famous city of its day. Certainly, travelers came from great distances and from every direction to see this, the most remarkable building in the entire world.

All who saw Babylon gave great credit to the gods Semiramis and Nitocris, who in the minds of the people, had masterminded the plans and the construction of this unspeakably beautiful structure.

Even the world of scholarship concedes that Babylon, its city and its tower, were splendid. The object of everyone's confidence, it was indeed the capital of the world.

This being the case, think ahead concerning the testimony of Babylon and let us see how its wealth and prestige influenced all mankind, both in those days and in these final days. The book of the Revelation brings us to what we may well call the final chapters of everything. Regarding the destiny of Babylon, it reveals:

> And after these things I saw another angel come down from heaven, having great power; and the earth was lightened with his glory. And he cried mightily with a strong voice, saying, Babylon the great is fallen, is fallen,

> and is become the habitation of devils, and the hold of every foul spirit, and a cage of every unclean and hateful bird. For all nations have drunk of the wine of the wrath of her fornication, and the kings of the earth have committed fornication with her, and the merchants of the earth are waxed rich through the abundance of her delicacies. And I heard another voice from heaven, saying, Come out of her, my people, that ye be not partakers of her sins, and that ye receive not of her plagues. For her sins have reached unto heaven, and God hath remembered her iniquities (Revelation 18:1-5).

It's almost as if the Lord is speaking of a different city, a different nation from the Babylon we find in Daniel's prophecy. But it is indeed Daniel's Babylon which, despite its distinct material advantages, ends up in the condition presented in the book of the Revelation. In all of literature, surely nothing more morosely describes the finality of sin than the Revelation analysis. After detailing the immense wealth of Babylon, the Revelation passages give a moving account of the physical and moral bankruptcy that the great city's fortune produced. The remarkable contrast is plainly presented in the Word of God for all to read.

It can almost be said that a summary of the life of the world is given to us in the Word of God. Many observers of the last days are saying that the earth's religious and commercial systems are now before us. The judgment that will come upon our pitiful world is given to us in the Word of God. About all of those who have not believed the Gospel of Jesus Christ, the Scripture says, "And the woman was arrayed in purple and scarlet color and decked with gold and precious stones and pearls having a golden cup in her hand full of abominations and the filthiness of her fornication." So, the iniquities of our world - presented in the form of a voluptuous woman - will be brought to devastating and final judgment. How interesting that the destruction of illicit religion will not be brought to pass by the religious world. The titans of last-days commerce will move in to destroy "the whore," making her desolate and naked, eating her flesh and burning her with fire. One of the interesting conclusions to this judgment is the statement that, "...God has avenged you on her" (Revelation 18:20). Out of this experience, an announcement of finality is made by the Lord. "Thus with violence shall that great city Babylon be thrown down and shall be found no more at all" (Revelation 18:21).

As we see the consummation of history and God's final judgment upon the world, we consider the seriousness of the facts before us. God sends these judgments based upon the reality of the sins produced by the world and incorporated into its own way of thinking. His judgment is not ordinary or fickle! The fact is that "the judgment of God is according to truth against them which commit such things" (Romans 2:2).

Judgment and death are the results of man's own foolhardy behavior; God is righteous in all things, including judgment. Revenge, especially in our time, is a most foolish action. "Vengeance is mine, I will repay" (Deuteronomy 32:35). He commands, "Let all bitterness, wrath, anger, clamor, and evil speaking be put away from you, with all malice. And be ye kind one to another, tenderhearted, forgiving one another, even as God for Christ's sake hath forgiven you" (Ephesians 4:32).

Through the attitude of revenge, many have made a covenant with death. They contend God is bent on avenging the wrongs they have suffered. These hapless individuals may well have every right to take offense at the murder, pillage, rape, and thievery that has come upon them and their families. With such ungoverned anger, these thoughts might fester into repine intentions. The blood of Christ alone can neutralize these deadly attitudes.

We need, therefore, to remind ourselves that there are but two consequences to our actions. Consequence number one is to suffer the results of sin. "All have sinned and come short of the glory of God" (Romans 3:23). The Word continues with the reminder that "...the wage of sin is death" (Romans 6:23). Under the justice of God, the soul that sins will die. Many millions in today's world are now under that condemnation. The Scripture says, "He that believeth on him is not condemned: but he that believeth not is condemned already, because he hath not believed in the name of the only Son of God" (John 3:18). The second consequence of our actions is eternal life, which comes only by faith in Jesus Christ. Each individual must understand that no person in all the world has the righteousness sufficient to bring him safely to heaven and to know the joys of eternal life. From where does this personal righteousness come? Instantly, the Scripture responds, "ABRAHAM BELIEVED GOD, AND IT WAS COUNTED UNTO HIM FOR RIGHTEOUSNESS" (Romans 4:1). The greatest of all gifts which God has given to man is that of imputed righteousness, righteousness without works. Jesus Christ alone finished the work of salvation on the cross. It is that faith and that alone which saves.

Most of us believe by this time that the ultimate truth in all of history is available to us from this remarkable book, the Bible. The way we know history, philosophy, and the doings of men down through the ages is from the informative pages of the Word of God. We've also appreciated the fact that the Bible gives us not merely the wide, general track of history, but also the details. From these, it is possible for the thinking inquirer to learn well the story in which each of us is involved. Here we have the remarkable scenario of the interaction between sin and righteousness, between beautiful good and great evil. In the Scriptures, we can know where history is going and what will be the final outcome of the ever true and ever imperative reports which we have from the Word of God.

A special study of the prophetic Word can help us to understand what has taken place in history and what is in fact occurring now. Furthermore, that study is especially interesting when we look into the accounts that give us the coming to pass of all things. An examination of Bible prophecy focusing on the great prophetic voices of the Old Testament is informing and inspiring indeed.

When looking into the pages of the prophetic Word, we find one scenario that could almost be called "the tale of two cities." The two cities are Babylon and Jerusalem. Babylon is the story of human efficiency producing great evil. Jerusalem is the fascinating account of faith in the midst of evil. In fact, one could almost assert that the account of faith in the midst of evil is almost indicative of the nature of sin and righteousness and the result of these two things making history what it is. In this study, we will particularly emphasize the nature of evil, the doings of Babylon. This is a particularly timely subject now that Babylon is being rebuilt.

Of Nimrod, the father of Babylon, the Bible says, "And Cush begat Nimrod: he began to be a mighty one in the earth. He was a mighty hunter before the Lord: wherefore it is said, Even as Nimrod the mighty hunter before the Lord. And the beginning of his kingdom was Babel..." (Genesis 10:8-10). Under the powerful help of Jehovah, the piece-by-piece history of Babylon is interesting indeed.

It is frightening to note how soon Babylon became the quintessence of evil in the world. Again and again, Babylon asserted its purposes in history. The religion of Babylon became materialism. To note the life of Babylon down through history can be instructive. Babylon was first of all a concept. Babylon said to itself, "Go to, let us build us a city and a tower, whose top may reach unto heaven; and let us make us a name, lest we be scattered abroad upon the face of the whole earth" (Genesis 11:4). The Lord described this by saying, "Behold, the people is one, and they have all one language; and this they begin to do: and now nothing will be restrained from them, which they have imagined to do" (Genesis 11:6). The text shows that the concept of Babylon then was embodied in the expression, "Let us build us a city and a tower" (Genesis 11:4). By making this announcement, Babylon showed that it believed in and wanted to build a society without God and a city without the Lord.

The expression of Babylon's philosophy should not come as a surprise to anyone who reads the Scriptures and then examines even the trends of our time. History has seen the story of Babylon being rebuilt again and again, causing the world to persist in the notion that human effort and ingenuity are superior to the teaching of the Bible. Babylon became the symbol of false ideology, false purposes and false prophecies. These purposes produce the near-destruction of Babylon.

These purposes and doctrines can also be shown to be a major, subversive influence in our troubled time. The Word of God warns us about the destructive effect of false doctrine, false teachers and Godless ambition. In fact, again and again, the Scripture warns us that these things will characterize the world as we move to the end of the age. The Scripture says, "But there were false prophets also among the people, even as there shall be false teachers among you, who privily shall bring in damnable heresies, even denying the Lord that bought them, and bring upon themselves swift destruction" (2 Peter 2:1).

What will be the result of this form of spiritual subversion? "And many shall follow their pernicious ways; by reason of whom the way of truth shall be evil spoken of. And through covetousness shall they with feigned words make merchandise of you: whose judgment now of a long time lingereth not, and their damnation slumbereth not" (2 Peter 2:2-3).

The moving words that comprise the balance of this

chapter should never be forgotten. Here we have the effect of the combination of materialism and wickedness:

> And through covetousness shall they with feigned words make merchandise of you: whose judgment now of a long time lingereth not, and their damnation slumbereth not. For if God spared not the angels that sinned, but cast them down to hell, and delivered them into chains of darkness, to be reserved unto judgment; And spared not the old world, but saved Noah the eighth person, a preacher of righteousness, bringing in the flood upon the world of the ungodly; And turning the cities of Sodom and Gomorrah into ashes condemned them with an overthrow, making them an ensample unto those that after should live ungodly (2 Peter 2:3-6).

The founders of Babylon may have altered their course had they had available to them the Word of God. He is reserving the unjust unto "the day of judgment to be punished: But chiefly them that walk after the flesh in the lust of uncleanness and despise government. Presumptuous are they, self willed, they are not afraid to speak evil of dignitaries" (2 Peter 2).

Wicked men are well-described in the Word of God:

> But these, as natural brute beasts, made to be taken and destroyed, speak evil of the things that they understand not; and shall utterly perish in their own corruption; And shall receive the reward of unrighteousness, they that count it pleasure to riot in the day time. Spots they are and blemishes, sporting themselves with their own

deceivings while they feast with you; Having eyes full of adultery, and that cannot cease from sin; beguiling unstable souls: a heart they have exercised with covetous practices; cursed children (2 Peter 2:12-14).

Old Testament characters are noted as illustrating this time of last-days judgment. "Following the way of Balaam the son of Bosor, who loved the wages of unrighteousness" (2 Peter 2:15).

These moving words from the Apostle Peter are delineate of last-days judgment which should be studiously considered by the devious-minded people of our time.

But alas, the promoters of today's humanistic organizations are continuing in their attempt to literally and spiritually rebuild Babylon, which has now been turned into a philosophy offering to people as utopian fulfillment. The system called Babylon is being stimulated by the activities of this day as people trade the true for the false and make the tower and the politics of Babylon a part of the promise of the future.

Babylon was a wicked city which became an intolerable spiritual force in the day of its physical existence. As an ideology for our time, it appears to be perfectly fulfilled in our leaders and indeed our people.

One of the very first dangers of the early church was the easy, permissive fashion in which it allowed false doctrine to move in and then take over the churches and religious institutions of those days.

This early subvertibility caused the apostle Paul to send heavy admonitions to the church of the apostles.

This became clear when he wrote the church at Galatia, saying:

> I marvel that ye are so soon removed from him that called you into the grace of Christ unto another gospel: Which is not another; but there be some that trouble you and would pervert the gospel of Christ. But though we, or an angel from heaven, preach any other gospel unto you than that which we have preached unto you, let him be accursed. As we said before, so say I now again, if any man preaches any other gospel unto you than that ye have received, let him be accursed (Galatians 1:6-9).

Under great concern, the apostle Paul wrote to his friends at Galatia, reprimanding them for their early turn from the truth of Christ into a gospel of human works. These people became Christians by being called, "into the grace of Christ" (v.6.) The apostle Paul was very aware that another Gospel did not simply bring interesting variety to Christianity, but it was a deadly poison. So crucial was it that people stay true to the Gospel that a person who departed from that Gospel was to be accursed. Paul also warned those who knew the truth of the Gospel but did not confront people with that truth were not the servants of Christ.

Do we have this concern today? Indeed, we do! There are millions of Christians in today's world. Quite obviously, however, many of these people content themselves with "religiosity" rather than faith in the Gospel. Obviously then, one must stay true to the revealed faith of Christ, no matter what the attractive alternative might be.

This concern is also strongly stated where Paul said, "Oh foolish Galatians, who hath bewitched you, that you should not obey the truth before whose eyes Jesus Christ hath been evidently set forth, crucified among you?" (Galatians 3:1).

It is interesting to note that as the Lord Jesus preached, His warnings about the great tribulation came very close to the time in which He reminded His listeners that false prophets shall deceive many. He implied that this would be especially true at the beginning of the tribulation:

"And many false prophets shall rise and shall deceive many. And because iniquity shall abound, the love of many shall wax cold" (Matthew 24:11-12). Soon the Lord is found warning His listeners when He says, "For then shall the great tribulation, such as was not since the beginning of the world to this time, no, nor ever shall be" (Matthew 24:21).

Here is another one of the many occasions in which the Word warns about the appearance of false prophets. They will bring dangerous spiritual subversion into the church and be responsible for the naive Christians to be deceived "and many false prophets shall arise and shall deceive many" (Matthew 24:11). Because of the proximity of the warning about deception and the announcement of the great tribulation, we do well to be very thoughtful. Is it possible that Christ is specifically condemning false prophets because they preach an erroneous prophetic message? They do not warn people about the nearness of the return of the Lord and, therefore, Christians are deceived into believing the wrong things about the truth of the Word of God in the last days. This being the case, we believers of our time must see ourselves as particularly warned. He has told the people that the future will bring awful destruction of spiritual Babylon rather than a new utopia that "positive thinking" will bring to pass. Concerning the great tribulation, it is almost as if this were a particular time in which God has said to the unsaved, "All right, have it your way." Those of the world have certainly bragged about their capability to run the world and now they are given that chance by the Lord. Is the result a human utopia? This prospect has been announced for the future by many liberal religionists who continue to believe that the world is getting better and better. They are blind to the obvious deterioration of morals, the false doctrine of pseudo-religionists, the foolish and dangerous results of government without God. Quite obviously, the product of this preaching is tribulation, not utopia.

The coming to pass of the great tribulation is prompted by man's last indignant rebellion against the God of heaven, but the tribulation proves the inadequacy of mere human systems to run the world and give true eternal hope to people. Humanism has put its best foot forward and is now totally incapable of handling the affairs of a defeated and demoralized world.

One lesson is clear: We must not make the efforts of our lifetime focus on producing human good out of the inadequate, the evil things of earth. God has made man to be a creature of eternity and not a poor victim of this world's false thinking. Our hearts go out to the myriads of people who believe in the "great pretenders" and who totally ignore the message of Christ and the redemption He offers. It is astonishing how the world can, in cavalier fashion, turn its back on the blessings of faith in Jesus Christ and the spiritual reality which He brings to pass. Refusing this, religious and commercial Babylon of our day flirts with the message of the Gospel and the reality of eternal hope.

We do well to ask, "Why is there such false faith in our time, why such a turning from God?" There are many reasons, of course, but one contributing factor is quite obvious that the world of technology has replaced faith in the lives of many people. A superficial analysis of computer power makes it possible for us to witness the impact of these infernal machines. Man, with a device or two, can theoretically speak to anyone on the face of the earth.

No doubt that knowledge is being increased in our times by many times. This is a part of the treacherous promise made to Adam by Satan himself: If he took the forbidden fruit, his knowledge would be increased, and he would be "like God." It must have taken a particular form of deadly insanity for him to believe this, but there he did.

From then until now, and especially now, superficially intelligent man continues to promise the world to the student, the businessman, the religious leader - if only they will take the time to master the computer. This technology, along with its related cybernetics, has indeed opened the door of knowledge to many millions. If the computer brings truth and understanding, why do concerned parents already face the criminal danger of their children watching pornography and licentious activity on their television screens? Originally touted to be the answer to everything, the computer screen and the television set have become the promoters of many forms of anti-God treachery.

Remembering this, we note with interest that Daniel's sign of the end-time was to be a book, the Word of God. Instead of abiding by this, man turned from his true destiny and committed the terrible sin of disobedience to the Lord. This short activity again proves that the high purposing on the part of men is far inferior to simply surrendering to the will of God. Man would rather construct Babylon than bow the knee to the God Who stands behind it all. History certainly has a testimony about this. We look back at the pages of the Old Testament and find the story of Babylon in the Genesis record. That story is a dynamic one and was quick to change. Nimrod's Babylon was quite an illustration of this. The city was developed into a magnificent institution and became the envy of the nations of the world. However, it did not find itself filled with awestricken people ready to enroll themselves in the purposes of this amazing city. There was no dream about Nimrod's Babylon becoming the intelligence center of all things and the place from which God was served by all of the nations of the world. No, indeed! Nimrod's Babylon fell into ruins in a very short time. The story of Belshazzar's Babylon is quite similar – the most beautiful kingdom of the world. That amazing early city was the object of global envy and global assault. The day soon came when alien vessels moved under the Watergate beneath the castle and the enemy came in. That night Belshazzar died as well as a great crowd of his followers. Babylon, with its great potential, became a wicked and godless nation. The doom of which the book of the Revelation speaks was initiated in those days of Nebuchadnezzar's Babylon.

Described for us in the book of Revelation is the brief but overwhelming story of the two Babylons. Religious Babylon was first. It is called in Scripture "the mother of harlots and abominations of the earth." It is more than surprising that a great religious center and message should be destroyed, all in one brief hour. Religious Babylon is represented by a drunken woman; there could not be a more degrading comparison. "And upon her forehead was a name written, MYSTERY, BABYLON THE GREAT, THE MOTHER OF HARLOTS AND ABOMINATIONS OF THE EARTH. And I saw the woman drunken with the blood of the saints, and with the blood of the martyrs of Jesus: and when I saw her, I wondered with great admiration" (Revelation 17:5).

Commercial Babylon soon follows. The Word of God brings us an actual description of the commercial products that are deposited with religious Babylon. Nevertheless, the Scripture says, "For her sins have reached unto heaven, and God hath remembered her iniquities" (Revelation 18:5).

The day finally comes when the world of commerce, money, and possessions comes to its doom, "And the merchants of the earth shall weep and mourn over her; for no man buyeth their merchandise anymore" (Revelation 18:11). The epitaph for Babylon might well be, "And the fruits that thy soul lusted after are departed from thee, and all things which were dainty and goodly are departed from thee, and thou shalt find them no more at all" (Revelation 18:14).

Here we certainly have the consummation of human history, the end of everything associated with this world. Babylon, that greatest of all human cities, is fallen. There remains no music, no dainties of food, no illicit love, nothing. Is not God speaking to the people of earth? Is He not telling us that our vaunted accomplishments, apart from Jesus Christ, amount to nothing whatsoever?

The people of Babylon thought that they had built an adequate foundation grounded in commerce, food, music, flattery, and wealth untold. At this point, they should have been able to read, "For other foundation can no man lay than that is laid, which is Jesus Christ" (1 Corinthians 3:11). In fact, is this not in effect what the Scripture says to every individual person? The message is clear, "Now if any man build upon this foundation gold, silver, precious stones, wood, hay, stubble; Every man's work shall be made manifest: for the day shall declare it, because it shall be revealed by fire; and the fire shall try every man's work of what sort it is" (1 Corinthians 3:13).

16

FOREWARNING THE FUTURE FUHRER

BY DAYMOND R. DUCK

FUHRER MEANS "LEADER" AND IT IS ONE OF THE BETTER-known titles of Adolf Hitler, the infamous dictator of Nazi Germany. Only a few of the world's young people know much about the fuhrer, but the mere mention of his title quickly conjures up bad memories in the minds of our planet's senior citizens. It is permanently tied to the evil leader who gave us the Third Reich, the Gestapo, the Storm Troopers, the Hitler Youth, the Society of German Maidens and other despicable groups. It spurs images of World War II: the arming of 70 million troops worldwide, the death of about 17 million troops, the death of about 20 million Soviet citizens, the death of about 10 million Chinese citizens, and so many more from other nations; no one really knows how many perished. Fuhrer or "leader" also reminds people of the swastika, goose-stepping German troops, concentration camps, death camps, the ovens of Auschwitz, the bombing of England, the ruins of Europe, bitter winters in Russia, famine, fire, pestilence and large national debts. It reminds people of the depraved man who touched off the world's darkest hour. But the wicked fuhrer of WW II was just a forewarning of the final fuhrer, and the disaster the first fuhrer caused will pale in comparison to what the Bible says the final fuhrer will bring in.

Something often overlooked is Hitler's fascination with the dark forces of the spirit world. He exposed himself to drugs and witchcraft as a young man. It has been written that he sold his soul to Satan, surrounded himself with people who made blood oaths to the Serpent, and often credited demons with influencing his decisions. He even gave credit to demonic forces for helping him with his plan to unite Europe and with his desire to bring in a "New World Order."

Although some people do not like to acknowledge the existence of unseen evil spirits, conservative Christians have no trouble believing that the fuhrer's mass slaughter of millions of Jews, Jehovah's Witnesses, priests, preachers and others, his systematic torching of synagogues, and his less frequent burning of churches was an order from hell. It is not even hard to believe that his New World Order originated in hell. He wanted a world government, something God has always opposed because He plans to establish one for His own Son to rule over.

World War II came to an end and so did Hitler's earthly life (he killed himself). But Hitler's concept of a united Europe, his vision of a New World Order, and the Satanic influence was still around. They spread like a virus that cannot be cured and soon the whole world was infected. Concerning a united Europe, powerful individuals on that continent were soon prompted to organize committees, groups and nations. It wasn't long until they began to merge into what students of Bible prophecy call the Revived Roman Empire. Their merger-mania was motivated by a desire to recover the power and control that shifted to the United States and the former Soviet Union.

Concerning the New World Order, other men of stature were persuaded to create the United Nations. This group started out small, but it grew like a giant octopus with tentacles reaching into every corner of the earth. It is now being transformed into a powerful one-world government that wants to control even the tiniest aspects of every individual's life. And concerning the Satanic influence, religious luminaries were moved to promote cooperation among the churches, people of other religions and cults who called upon guides of darkness from the gloomy pits of hell. This unseemly cooperation produced an unholy alliance called the World Council of Churches. It also produced a vile compromising of basic Christian beliefs, and even worse, the acceptance of many false doctrines.

Some conservative Christians believe the World Council of Churches has lost its Christian identity. Many believe it is responsible for a weakening of the true church and more than a few believe it will ultimately help bring in a demonic one- world religion. The birth of these three groups - the Revived Roman Empire, the one-world government, and the one-world religion - is the beginning of three institutions which Bible prophecies say will exist when the final fuhrer comes on the scene. They will form the backbone of a government more evil than the one started by the odious Adolf Hitler himself.

This is very significant, but all Bible prophecy experts know that it would be meaningless without the appearance of a fourth party. This happened on May 14, 1948, when the nation of Israel came back into existence. The great prophet Daniel told us that the individual we are calling the final fuhrer will rise to power over the Revived Roman Empire and sign a covenant with many nations and leaders of the earth to protect Israel for seven years (Daniel 9:27). We also know that every jot and tittle of Bible prophecy must be fulfilled. And it is a most amazing thing that after hundreds of decades the Revived Roman Empire, the one-world government, the one-world religion and the nation of Israel have all arrived on the scene at the same time. This is nothing less than a forewarning of terrible things to come when viewed through the microscope of Bible predictions. It means that the stage is now set for the tribulation period, the four horsemen of the apocalypse, the mark of the beast, the Battle of Armageddon and all of those dreaded things, and for true Christians, it also means that the rapture of the church is very close, even at the door.

THE ANTICHRIST

THE BIBLE CALLS the last world leader many things, but final fuhrer is not one of them. Just a few of his titles are: the king of fierce countenance, the prince that shall come, that man of sin, the son of perdition, the lawless one, the vile person, and the beast. These titles are very descriptive, but these multiple titles for referring to the final fuhrer are also more than a little bit confusing. Christians want everyone to know they are referring to the same individual, so they use a collective title. They call the final fuhrer the antichrist.

The word "antichrist" appears five times in the writings of John, but it does not appear even once in any other book of the Bible (1 John 2:18, 22; 4:3; 2 John 7). Most scholars agree that John's usage of the word implies two different meanings: 1) against the Christ, and 2) instead of the Christ. Both meanings fit the final fuhrer. The antichrist will be against the Christ; that is, he will be an enemy of the Christ, and he will try to replace the Christ; that is, he will be a false Christ.

Daniel revealed the final fuhrer's opposition to the Christ when he said the antichrist will "stand up against the Prince of princes" (Daniel 8:25). And Paul revealed the evil one's effort to replace the Christ when he said the antichrist will sit in the Temple as God "shewing himself that he is God" (2 Thessalonians 2:3, 4). Many people have opposed Christ, but other than Satan, there has never been a more sinister or worthy opponent on the face of planet earth. Many false Christs have arisen, and some have been noteworthy imposters, but there has never been a greater or more evil deceiver than this one.

What We Do Not Know **About the Antichrist**

. . .

Four things we do not know about the antichrist are the subject of much speculation. The first is his nationality. It is not hard to find writers who teach that the antichrist will be a Syrian. The Bible does not say he will come from that ancient nation, but some conclude this through reasoning that usually goes like this: "Antiochus Epiphanes was a type of the antichrist and he was a Syrian. Therefore, the antichrist will be a Syrian." The problem with this kind of reasoning is that it overlooks those individuals of other nationalities who were also a type of the antichrist. Nebuchadnezzar was a type of the antichrist and he was a Chaldean. So why not say the antichrist will be a Chaldean? Adolf Hitler was a type of the antichrist and he was a German. So why not say the antichrist will be a German? The same can be said for Pharaoh, an Egyptian. We could go on and on, but the point is that this kind of reasoning does not settle the issue.

The second thing we do not know about the antichrist is whether he will be a Jew or a Gentile. Some say he will be a Jew because the Bible says, "neither shall he regard the God of his fathers" (Daniel 11:37 KJV). Others say he will be a Gentile because this verse has been incorrectly translated and it should read, "He will show no regard for the gods of his fathers" (Daniel 11:37 NIV). If the correct translation is "God," he will come from a monotheistic religion (probably Jewish); if the correct translation is "gods," he will come from a polytheistic religion (probably Gentile).

Then there are those who reason that "The antichrist will be Jewish because the Jews will accept him as their

Messiah and they would never accept a Gentile." Or "The antichrist will be Jewish because he will be a counterfeit of Christ and He was a Jew." The Reverend Jerry Falwell, whose theology is almost always very sound, got in trouble on this one. He believes the antichrist will be a Jew, and he may be right, but the fact is, whether the antichrist will be a Jew, or a Gentile is not revealed in the Bible. And those who think he will be are definitely in the minority. Incidentally, one of the complaints against the Reverend Falwell has been that he is anti-Semitic for thinking like this. On the contrary, Falwell has long been one of Israel's strongest supporters and has done much to help the Jewish people.

The third thing we do not know about the antichrist is his name. We know "his number is Six hundred threescore and six," but that is different from his name (Revelation 13:18). Several elaborate systems have been developed in an effort to reveal the name of the antichrist, but they have all been wrong. Some names these systems have come up with are Adolf Hitler, Benito Mussolini, Henry Kissinger, Ronald Reagan, William 'Bill' Clinton, and several of the Popes. These should be seen for what they are - just wild guesses. Furthermore, trying to identify antichrist is just a waste of time because he will not be revealed until after the rapture (2 Thessalonians 2:1-12). Dr. Ed Hindson concisely stated it when he said:

> Only after the rapture of the church will the identity of the antichrist be revealed. In other words, you don't want to know who he is. If you ever do figure out who he is, you have been left behind!

This is absolutely true. Nothing is more futile than trying to identify the antichrist before the rapture. Doing so would be an effort to prove the Bible wrong. That has never happened, and it is not going to happen now. All anyone does by trying to identify the antichrist before the church is taken out is embarrass himself and bring criticism upon Christians.

In connection with this, let me hasten to add that 666 is the antichrist's number. It is not my driver's license number, my credit card number, my Social Security number or any other number associated with me. Also, it is not any of your numbers. It will not be several billion different numbers for the several billion different individuals on earth. It is his number, one specific number that identifies one specific individual.

The fourth thing we do not know about the antichrist is whether or not he is already alive as a person. It seems reasonable that he will have to be a full-grown man when he appears. And if the rapture is as close as most prophetic authorities think, it makes sense to assume that he is not only alive, but already grown. The thing to remember is nobody knows, and all a person can do is speculate.

What the Antichrist Will Be Like When He Appears

We can better understand what the antichrist will be like when he appears by observing a few things about the first and second coming of Jesus. The official first coming of Jesus, commonly called His triumphal entry into Jerusalem, occurred while Jesus was riding upon a donkey, a symbol of peace (Luke 19:28-38). The official second coming of Jesus, commonly called the Revelation, will take place at the end of the tribulation period when Jesus returns in righteousness to judge and make war riding upon a white horse, a symbol of conquest. (Revelation 19:11-21). The first time, Jesus came peacefully as the Lamb of God and the second time He will come conquering as the KING OF KINGS AND LORD OF LORDS (John 1:36; Revelation 19:11-16).

This has relevance to what the antichrist will be like as he carries out his bloody career. During his rise to power, he will present himself as a man of peace. So, we might expect the prophets to depict him riding upon a donkey, a symbol of peace, but that is wrong. John said, "And I saw, and behold a white horse: and he that sat on him had a bow; and a crown was given unto him: and he went forth conquering, and to conquer" (Revelation 6:2).

The antichrist will ride across the pages of history on a white horse, a symbol of conquest. His sweet-sounding words of peace will not match his terrible acts of war. This fictitious Christ will present himself as a lamb, but he will really be a wolf in sheep's clothing. When asked about the sign of His coming and the end of the age, Jesus answered, "Take heed that no man deceive you. For many shall come in my name, saying, I am Christ; and shall deceive many" (Matthew 24:4, 5). The list of people who have done this is long, but the ultimate false Christ will be the antichrist. Multitudes will think they have met the Messiah, but he will really be the man of sin.

The bow was a weapon of war and a symbol of military power in John's day. The antichrist will appear with a bow in his hand, but he will have no arrows. This is like carrying a gun without bullets. The antichrist will have weapons of war, but he will act like he is unarmed. Daniel said, "by peace shall [he] destroy many" (Daniel 8:25).

A crown is worn by people who earn or inherit the right to wear one, but the antichrist will not earn or inherit the right to wear his crown. It will be a gift from the wicked power brokers of the world. What a terrible mistake! The world's gullible politicians will empower a leader without doing the all-important background check. Some will think they are crowning a godly man, but they will be elevating a fake with a very dark side. The Bible says this fake will "ascend out of the bottomless pit" (Revelation 17:8). That is the gruesome subterranean abode where God is holding the very worst of Satan's demonic spirits. It makes one wonder what kind of background this man will have. Considering his origin, it must be filled with terrible atrocities.

What the World Will Be Like When the Antichrist Appears

WHEN ADDRESSING THIS, the Apostle Paul used the phrase "perilous times" (2 Timothy 3:1). "Perilous times" includes war, and one of the signs of the last days that Jesus talked about is "wars and rumors of wars" (Matthew 24:6). While the antichrist is negotiating peace and consolidating his power, God will release a second horse and rider. John said, "there went out another horse that was red: and power was given to him that sat thereon to take peace from the earth, and that they should kill one another: and there was given unto him a great sword" (Revelation 6:4). The second rider will bring war to the earth. God will allow him to do this to show the world that the antichrist is not the true Prince of Peace, Jesus.

"Perilous times" also includes "economic disaster." While the antichrist is boasting about having solutions to the world's problems, God will release a third horse and rider. John said, "I beheld, and lo a black horse; and he that sat on him had a pair of balances in his hand. And I heard a voice in the midst of the four beasts say, A measure of wheat for a penny, and three measures of barley for a penny; and see thou hurt not the oil and the wine" (Revelation 6:5, 6).

The third rider will bring economic collapse to the world. God will allow him to do this to show the world that the antichrist is not the true Bread of Life, Jesus. Food will be so valuable it will have to be weighed on scales before it is sold. Money will be so worthless that what a man earns in one day will purchase barely enough for one person to survive on. It definitely seems that America, and perhaps the entire world, has forgotten that a good economy is a blessing of God and not a benefit of having the right kind of politician in office. This moral confusion will be disastrous in the days to come.

"Perilous times" also includes starvation and sickness, and two more signs of the last days Jesus talked about are "famine" and "pestilence" (Matthew 24:7). God will release a fourth horse and rider that will fulfill this. John said, "I looked, and behold a pale horse: and his name that sat on him was Death, and Hell followed with him. And power was given unto them over the fourth part of the earth, to kill with sword, and with hunger, and with death, and with the beasts of the earth" (Revelation 6:8). God will allow this horse and rider to come on the scene to show the world that the antichrist is not the Great Physician, Jesus. One-fourth of the world's population will die as war and economic disaster spreads like wildfire triggering hunger and disease on every continent.

Most conservative Christians believe the "perilous times" have arrived. China, North Korea, India and Pakistan are developing and selling several different kinds of missiles. Pakistan is even placing nuclear warheads on some that country is selling. China has stolen some of America's top secrets and what they could not steal has been sold to them with the approval of President Clinton. Many experts believe Chinese nuclear missiles will be powerful enough to strike the heart of America in just three to four years. They are talking about portable intercontinental missiles that America probably will not be able to find and destroy. Asia is struggling with massive economic problems that appear unsolvable to many. Russia is crumbling in every sense of the word. Its government seems totally paralyzed and President Yeltsin resigned on the final day of 1999, after attempts to impeach him had failed. It is unlikely that now President Putin, appointed by outgoing President Yeltsin, will fare any better.

The United States is in a moral crisis that worsens

with each passing day. We can't look to the White House for guidance because the man living there has been impeached and found in contempt of court for treading his own immoral path. Judge Susan Weber Wright ruled that not finding him in contempt of court would be a threat to the rule of law.

Russia, China, Iraq and Yugoslavia have formed an alliance to weaken America. With every passing day they seem to be succeeding. Terrorism reigns all over the Middle East. The entire region is an armed camp. World food supplies are low, natural disasters are ever-increasing, and drug-resistant diseases are spreading all over the globe.

In short, the world is in a terrible mess. Serious problems are waxing worse and worse, and we can honestly say that large portions of the earth are like a powder keg just waiting to explode. These problems are so great some are calling for a one-world government to deal with them. According to the Bible, they will get it. But with God's help, a brain-dead crash- dummy could solve more problems than the popular antichrist ever will.

The World's Political Structure When the Antichrist Appears

Those watching for the appearance of the antichrist could better spend their time watching the world's political developments. Daniel had several visions of the "times of the Gentiles" and he saw a great disturbance in

PIERCING THE FUTURE

the Middle East as the tribulation period arrives (Daniel 7). Three groups of nations will exercise power (possibly England and her allies, Russia and her allies, and an African coalition of nations). Then a fourth group will rise to power and crush all the others. This fourth group will be a terrifying world kingdom. When explaining this fourth kingdom to Daniel, an angel said, "The fourth beast shall be the fourth kingdom upon earth, which shall be diverse from all kingdoms, and shall devour the whole earth, and shall tread it down, and break it in pieces. And the ten horns out of this kingdom are ten kings that shall arise: and another shall rise after them; and he shall be diverse from the first, and he shall subdue three kings" (Daniel 7:23, 24).

Notice the sequence of events involving this fourth kingdom. First, it will appear as a world government crushing and trampling down all the other governments. It will set aside the sovereignty of individual nations and assume authority over the whole earth. Second, the world government will be divided into ten regions with each region having its own leader or king. These ten regions correspond to the ten toes on the famous statue Nebuchadnezzar dreamed about (Daniel 2). They are also mentioned by the Apostle John in the Book of Revelation (17:12). Third, the antichrist will begin his rise to power after the ten kings have appeared and he will soon become strong enough to take over one of them. His next step will be to quickly seize control of two more regions. Following that, the leaders of the other seven regions will turn their power over to him (Revelation 17:12-14). When they do that, the antichrist will have absolute control over the entire world. But the point is that the world government will appear and be divided into ten regions before the antichrist shows up. So, it would be better for Christians to be watching for a world government than to be watching for the antichrist. And even after the world government appears, it would be smarter for Christians to be watching for its division into ten groups than to be watching for the antichrist. World government will be the first big step - and the tenfold division of world government will be the second big step - in the escalating cycle of conflict and depravity that will ultimately result in the man of sin taking control.

We see this shaping up in the world today. In fact, it may only be a heartbeat away because the world community is already trying to restructure the United Nations into a world government. They are even using this embryonic world government to trample upon the cherished sovereignty of independent nations such as Iraq, Israel, Haiti and Yugoslavia. Furthermore, several high-powered groups have already called on world leaders to divide the planet into ten regions and empower the United Nations to rule over them. One of those ten regions is Europe. This is the exact pattern that will exist when the antichrist rises to power. He will rise to power after a world government has been established and divided into ten regions with one of them being in Europe (Daniel 9:26).

This is the kingdom Satan offered to Jesus (Luke 4:5-7). The world does not belong to Satan, but the power and splendor of the world are his and he can give that to anyone he chooses. Jesus refused it, but Satan still wants to be worshipped and he will find a willing world leader in the antichrist. As soon as the church is raptured, everything will fall in place.

More Information About the Sequence of Events

THE BIBLE DOES NOT REVEAL the day or hour the antichrist will show up, but it does provide several clues.

First, the good news about when the antichrist will appear is that it cannot happen until God allows it and He will not allow it until the church is raptured. Paul said, "Let no man deceive you by any means: for that day [the Day of the Lord or the tribulation period] shall not come, except there comes a falling away first, and that man of sin be revealed, the son of perdition ... And now ye know what withholdeth that he might be revealed in his time. For the mystery of iniquity doth already work: only he who now letteth will let, until he be taken out of the way" (2 Thessalonians 2:3, 6, 7). The antichrist cannot appear until the One holding him back is removed. There is wide agreement that the One holding him back is the Holy Spirit. He will stop restraining the antichrist and leave the earth when the church is raptured.

Second, the antichrist will rise to power before the tribulation period begins. The Book of Revelation is a very sequence- oriented book. Most authorities agree that the rapture occurs in the Book of Revelation when John is caught up into heaven (Revelation 4:1, 2). Following that, the antichrist comes on the scene as the rider on a white horse (Revelation 6:2). Then the tribulation period or the day of wrath begins (Revelation 6:17). This sequence is necessary because the antichrist must be a recognized world leader possessing the authority to make agreements before the tribulation period can begin.

Third, as a world leader, the antichrist will sign one particular agreement that will mark the beginning of the tribulation period. According to Daniel, "he [the antichrist] shall confirm the covenant with many for one week" (Daniel 9:27). "One week" is a Bible term meaning one week of years or seven years. It is the worthless signature of the antichrist on a covenant with many to protect Israel for seven years that begins the tribulation period.

Fourth, the covenant to protect Israel will be voided three and one-half years later and that will mark the midpoint of the tribulation period. Daniel divided the tribulation period into two equal segments of three and one-half years each when he said, "in the midst of the week he shall cause the sacrifice and the oblation to cease" (Daniel 9:27). At the middle of the tribulation period, the antichrist will set aside the seven-year covenant to protect Israel and stop the sacrifices and offerings at the Temple.

Fifth, his world government will be ended by the second coming of Jesus. This is the great stone that struck the feet on the famous statue Nebuchadnezzar dreamed about (Daniel 2:34, 35, 44, 45). Jesus will seize the antichrist and throw him into the lake of fire (Revelation 19:20). No one will help him (Daniel 11:45). Never before has a world leader fallen like this. Never again will anyone praise the New World Order. It will be a dead issue from that day forward. That highly touted political concept will be just as dead as the first Fuhrer was when he killed himself.

The False Prophet

NO ONE WILL HELP the antichrist when Jesus takes him captive, but he will have a lot of help when he rises to power. His most famous ally will be a very powerful leader in the religious community. The Bible does not identify this one by name, but it calls him two things: "the beast coming up out of the earth" and "the false prophet" (Revelation 13:11; 19:20). This religious beast will present himself as a lamb, which means he will try to impersonate Jesus, the Lamb of God. And he will speak like a dragon, which means most of what he says will be Satanic (Revelation 13:11). We can only speculate about what he will say, but it seems likely that he will be an expert in political correctness. He will probably put a great deal of emphasis on diversity and inclusiveness. He will probably stress gender equality, same- sex marriages, tolerance, population control and things like that. Some Scriptures indicate that he will stress children's rights in such a way as to turn children against their parents.

This powerful religious leader will appear to be a great miracle worker and multitudes will be deceived when he causes fire to fall from heaven (Revelation 13:13). Many more will be deceived when he places an image of the antichrist in the Temple and seemingly makes it appear to come to fife (Revelation 13:15). How he will do this is a big question, but both Jesus and the prophet Daniel foretold it and there can be no doubt that it will get the world's attention (Matthew 24:15; Daniel 9:27).

Once he has done these things, he will demand that all the world direct worship that God alone deserves toward the antichrist and his image. To back up his demand, he will institute a system to force the compliance of every individual on earth. The Apostle John said he will cause "all, both small and great, free and bond, to receive a mark in their right hand or in their foreheads: And that no man might buy or sell, save he that had the mark, or the name of the beast, or the number of his name" (Revelation 13:16, 17). This mark, which is usually called the "mark of the beast," will place everyone in peril. Complying will ignite the wrath of God and result in a person being cast into the lake of fire (Revelation 14:9-11). Not complying will ignite the wrath of the antichrist and result in a person being beheaded (Revelation 20:4). Everyone will have to decide whether or not to take the mark. Cooperation will open the door for a person to obtain food, water, medicine, housing, electricity, clothing and more. But not cooperating will prevent a person from obtaining the necessities of life. It doesn't require much imagination to realize just how bad this will be. There will be widespread famine; and multitudes of Christians and Jews will be hated, arrested, persecuted and killed (Matthew 24:7-9).

This mark of the beast is why so many prophecy experts talk about the coming "cashless society." They know that a system will be needed to track all buying and selling. They also know that computers can do that if every transaction is scanned. So, they believe money will be replaced by a computerized scanning system that will make the infamous mark of the beast both practical and plausible. Fingerprint scanners, voice print scanners, eye scanners, computerized smart cards and implanted computer chips are already a reality that is only step away from what the Bible predicted almost 2,000 years ago.

And something else is looming on the horizon. The United Nations now wants everyone on earth numbered, and it is even pressuring all nations to do just that. Funds were requested in the 1998 United States Budget for this very purpose. What happened was the insertion of a clause in the budget agreement that prohibits expenditures on this for 12 months. Prophecy experts know that once every citizen on earth is numbered and entered into a computer, it will be easy for the false prophet to order them to take the "mark" and track whether or not they obey. A complete list of who has been marked and who hasn't will be as easy as pushing a button.

How Could This Happen?

ALL OF THESE things will be the bitter fruit of spiritual darkness, corruption and adultery. The Holy Spirit will be gone when the church is removed in the rapture. Once His restraining influence is taken away, God will send strong delusion upon the earth to punish those who are refusing to love the truth and be saved (2 Thessalonians 2:10, 11). Those left behind will witness the rise of the antichrist, but they will not recognize him for what he is.

He will be empowered by Satan (2 Thessalonians 2:9). He will claim to be God (2 Thessalonians 2:4). He will become very strong and kill those who become true believers (Daniel 8:24). He will be helped by "seducing spirits and doctrines of devils" (1 Timothy 4:1). He will seemingly work miracles. Jesus said, "there shall arise false Christs, and false prophets, and shall shew great signs and wonders; insomuch that, if it were possible, they shall deceive the very elect" (Matthew 24:24). This will be all the antichrist needs to blind a spiritually sidetracked world and lead it astray. Dr. Ed Hindson has said:

> The lure of false doctrine is that it presents itself as the truth. It appears as a corrective measure to established doctrine. It is propagated by those who are certain they have discovered some new revelation of truth or a better interpretation of old, established truth. Either way, they are convinced they are right and everyone else is wrong.

And Dr. Dave Breese has said:

> The essential battle of our time is not between Communism and civilization, it is not between the Protestant atheists and the Catholic atheists in Ireland, it is not between the free world and the barbarians - it is between earth and heaven. It takes the form of a civil war. It is a battle between revolutionary, radical man and the government of God.

What Will Happen to Those Who Take the Mark

Being left behind when the rapture occurs will be no blessing. Besides being cast into the lake of fire (Revelation 14:9-10), here is just a partial list of the terrible things those who take the mark of the beast will face if they are lucky enough to live very long:

1. Violent wars (Revelation 6:3, 4; 9:15-18).
2. Economic collapse, hunger and starvation (Revelation 6:5, 6).
3. Famine, pestilence and wild animals (Revelation 6:7, 8).
4. Earthquakes, extreme darkness and perhaps nuclear bombs and missiles (Revelation 6:12).
5. Hail and fire that burns one-third of the trees and grass on earth (Revelation 8:7).
6. One-third of the sea turning to blood (Revelation 8:8, 9).
7. One-third of the fresh water being polluted (Revelation 8:10, 11).
8. One-third of the sun, moon and stars being darkened (Revelation 8:12).
9. Demon-possessed locusts with the sting of scorpions (Revelation 9:3-5).
10. Painful sores (Revelation 16:2).
11. Worldwide pollution of the seas (Revelation 16:2).
12. Worldwide pollution of fresh water (Revelation 16:4).

13. Scorching fire from the sun (Revelation 16:8).
14. Total darkness with extreme agony on earth (Revelation 16:10).

JOINING the world religious system will not help. Even that will be destroyed. God will place it in the hearts of the antichrist and his ten puppet kings to do this at the tribulation period midpoint (Revelation 17:16,17). They will act with great vengeance, leaving nothing of the false church.

What Will Happen to Those Who Refuse to Take the Mark

PEOPLE WILL PAY DEARLY for refusing the mark of the beast and accepting Jesus after the rapture. Here is a partial list of things revealed in the Scriptures:

1. God's people will be oppressed, and their religion will be slandered (Daniel 7:25; Revelation 13:16, 17).
2. God's people will be betrayed, hated and killed (Matthew 24:9, 10; Revelation 20:4).
3. Many will grow weak and fall away (Matthew 24:12).

But all the news is not bad. Accepting Christ after the rapture and refusing the mark of the beast will mean that people will possess the kingdom of God (Daniel 7:18, 27). They will serve in His temple (Revelation 7:14-17). The dead will be raised, and they will live and reign with Jesus here on earth for 1,000 years (Revelation 20:4).

His Anti-Christian Activity

The Bible provides a long list of clues about the religion of the antichrist. To say that he will oppose the Judeo-Christian ethic is simply too mild. It would be more accurate to say he will go on a rampage against the world's newly-converted Christians and brutally kill all he can (Daniel 7:19-25; Revelation 6:9-11; 12:17; 13:7). This can be attributed to the demonic influence in his life (2 Thessalonians 2:9). He will defy God, oppose God, resist God, try to replace God, and claim to be God (2 Thessalonians 2:4). He will be a blasphemer of the highest sort (Daniel 7:25; Revelation 13:5). He will try to change the Christian calendar (Daniel 7:25), promote witchcraft (Daniel 8:25), demand that the world worship him (Revelation 13:15), and promote a one-world harlot religion (Revelation 17:1-18). This will probably be the politically correct social values now being promoted by the United Nations.

His Dealings With Israel

. . .

WHEN HE FIRST rises to power, the antichrist will be well received by the Jews. Some commentators even believe they will accept him as their long-awaited Messiah. This is because Jesus said, "I am come in my Father's name, and ye receive me not: if another shall come in his own name, him ye will receive" (John 5:43). They rejected the true Christ and it appears as if they will accept the antichrist. Signing the seven-year covenant to protect Israel will make him even more popular. That covenant will probably grant the Jews the right to rebuild their much-desired Temple, reinstitute the animal sacrifices, and resume the offerings (Daniel 9:27).

But his love affair with Israel will not last very long. God will quickly seal 144,000 Jewish evangelists to preach the gospel to the world (Revelation 7:1-8). He will also call two witnesses and empower them to the same thing in Jerusalem (Revelation 11:3-13). Many Jews will turn away from the antichrist and accept Jesus as their Messiah. This will stir his wrath. He will begin to persecute the Jews. After three and one-half years he will break his covenant to protect them, defile the Temple he let them rebuild, stop the animal sacrifices, and stop the offerings (Daniel 9:27; 11:31; 12:11).

Many of the Jews will flee into the wilderness (Matthew 24:15, 16). Most scholars believe they will go to the ancient rock city called Petra. The antichrist will send his armies to destroy them and it will take nothing short of divine intervention to preserve them (Revelation 12:13-16). God's help will make the antichrist furious. He will quickly kill two-thirds of those Jews who do not escape (Zechariah 13:8). He will attack Jerusalem, capture the Holy City, rob and kill many of its citizens, make slaves out of others, and his troops will rape the Jewish women (Zechariah 14:1, 2; Daniel 7:25; 12:7). The Bible calls this "the time of Jacob's trouble" (Jeremiah 30:7). According to Thomas Ice and Timothy Demy:

> One of the major reasons for the tribulation is to prepare Israel for her conversion. Thus, both Israel as a nation and a people will experience the manifestations of evil during this era. In fact, many of the events of the tribulation revolve around Israel. Geographically and spiritually, Israel is at center stage during the tribulation.

Do not overlook this. It often seems like most of those who write about the antichrist, end-of-the-age events, etc. are riding the hobbyhorse of bad news, but they do not intend to do that. And a lot of good things will result from these terrible events. The conversion of Israel is one of the really big ones.

WHAT ABOUT THE UNITED STATES?

ALMOST TWO THOUSAND YEARS AGO, the Apostle John was talking about world kingdoms when he said, "Five are fallen, and one is, and the other is not yet come" (Revelation 17:10). The "five are fallen" kingdoms were Egypt, Assyria, Babylon, Medo- Persia and Greece. The "one is" refers to the sixth, the Roman Empire that was in existence when John received the Revelation. The seventh, or one "not yet come," is the future kingdom of antichrist. That one will be a global dictatorship (Revelation 13:7). National sovereignty will be a relic of the past. The United States will cease to be an independent nation. American troops will have only a fraction of the power of a world military. World court rulings will supersede those of the United States Supreme Court. The American economy will be controlled by the global economy. Dr. Ed Hindson says:

> All through the 20th century, we have allowed godless secularism to replace the Judeo-Christian values of our society. God has been deliberately and systematically removed from prominence in our culture and in our intellectual lives. We have made Him irrelevant to our culture. Tragically, we have also made our culture irrelevant to God. In so doing, we have abandoned our spiritual heritage. The Christian consensus that once dominated Western culture is now shattered. The world is already mired in the quicksand of secularism, relativism, and mysticism. It is a wonder we have survived as long as we have.

This is hard for many people to accept. We have an earnest desire to believe that America has a special place in God's heart. It once did, but that was because God had a special place in America's heart. We can no longer say that. As a nation we have kicked God out of our schools. As a nation we have told Him not to interfere in our decisions regarding abortion, homosexuality, and things like that. As a nation we have said character doesn't matter.

Some of our most faithful church members have decided that God should set aside His commandments about adultery and lying because the economy is good, and the stock market keeps going higher and higher. America's most secret weapons, and along with them America's treasured security, have been sold to some of the most wicked people on earth, but most voters are asleep, and few could care less. A Fuhrer worse than Adolf Hitler ever dreamed of being is waiting in the wings. He wants to take over the world, including our beloved United States, and the church, like the five foolish virgins, is in a deep sleep. "What about the United States," we ask? The Bible doesn't say. America desperately needs a revival, but her economy is so good most don't want it. Therefore, it is the opinion of this writer that something must change in a hurry, or we can kiss our cherished country goodbye forever.

Closing Remarks

SKEPTICS QUICKLY POINT out that Jesus said, "of that day and hour knoweth no man, no, not the angels of heaven, but my Father only" (Matthew 24:36). They willingly overlook the fact that He gave us many signs and inferred that we can tell when they "begin to come to pass" (Luke 21:28). Also, that He said, "when ye shall see all these things, know that it is near, even at the doors" (Matthew 24:33). Conservative Christians believe they see all these things coming on the scene now. This means the rapture will soon take place and multitudes of lost people are in real danger. The lukewarm, and all those who have heard the Word and refused to believe it, will be deceived and lost forever (Revelation 3:14-22; 2 Thessalonians 2:9-12). If there ever was a time when true revival was needed, this is it. Those who are not Christian should prepare and the only way to do that is to accept Christ.

17
FORECASTING EARTH'S FURIOUS FINISH

BY PHIL ARMS

Terror! Terror unimaginable and unprecedented in scope and impact will soon convulse the inhabitants of planet earth. The horror of these coming events will be so chilling that, according to the prophets, many of those who simply witness them will die of sudden heart failure.

Students of history are familiar with the frightening and powerfully destructive potential of both mankind and nature. Nature's "groaning" has often fiercely assaulted earth's inhabitants through hurricanes, volcanoes, earthquakes and dozens of other natural phenomena. Atrocities, perpetrated by man upon man, have also left their bloody and terrifying tracks through history as reminders of the savagery that the depraved heart of man is capable of, unless he is redeemed by the transforming power of God.

In my travels I have visited numerous places that stand as vivid reminders of such cruelty.

In Israel one can walk through the Yad Vashem

Memorial built to remind the world of the barbaric acts that Hitler's Third Reich committed against the Jewish people during World War II. The repulsive deeds of the demented, demonized Nazi regime against innocent men, women and children were so diabolic that they physically nauseate and emotionally traumatize many who visit the sight. This murderous rampage of sadistic, vicious hatred, resulting in the death of six million Jews, is referred to as the "Holocaust."

The London Dungeon at London's Museum of Medieval History graphically chronicles the bestial means of torture and punishment during the Middle and Dark Ages.

Likewise, in the city of York, England, is the infamous York Dungeon, where visitors are stunned to learn about the coldblooded means employed by the executioners and torturers of that day.

And yet, the heinousness of all history's inhumane acts by men upon other men are but a small microcosmic view of the villainous horror that much of mankind will soon experience. When such cruelties are combined with the impersonal destruction of nature gone mad, it is little wonder this period is called "the tribulation."

However, I, along with millions of other Christians, cling to the glorious promise of deliverance repeatedly assured to believers throughout the Scriptures. This Blessed Hope, the imminent return of Jesus Christ to remove His bride from the earth before this seven-year period, gives great peace to the child of God. Certain that others have more than adequately dealt with this wonderful moment called the rapture, I will focus our attention on those days that follow.

Jesus, in describing these days and their increasing crescendo of terror, says. "For then shall be great tribulation, such as was not since the beginning of the world to this time, no, nor ever shall be. And except those days should be shortened; there shall no flesh be saved..." (Matthew 24:21-22a).

Daniel, the most revealing of God's prophets, writes of this final seven-year period.[1] He prophesies with great precision that the beginning of this horrible finale will be marked by the signing of a peace treaty between Israel and one the Bible calls the antichrist. This "man of sin," through a process of rapid- fire political maneuvers, supernaturally becomes a despotic dictator while pretending to be a benevolent ambassador of peace. He rises to power at the helm of a revived Roman Empire, a confederacy of European nations. Ultimately, this Wicked One will wage his final battle against all things holy and be "destroyed by the brightness" of the coming Messiah.[2]

During this horrendous seven-year period, according to the prophets, all creation will be seized with the agonizing contractions of excruciating birth pangs. Nature, corrupted by the Edenic fall, through this divine reclamation will be restored to an equatorial paradise.

In this tribulation period, God not only judges the world's unrighteousness, but simultaneously redeems His chosen, Israel.

The covenant-keeping God fulfills His promises to Israel and establishes their millennial kingdom with their true Messiah upon the throne.

Though the Old Testament prophets pointed to it and the Lord Jesus preached about it, the most comprehensive and chronologically specific overview of this remarkable seven years is found in the Book of Revelation.

Enough volumes have been written describing, analyzing and speculating on the 21 judgments recorded in the last book of the Bible to easily fill several large libraries.

And with each passing day come new technologies that create another menagerie of Orwellian possibilities for the already complex Book of Revelation. With no desire to add yet another echo to the substantial number of voices, many of which are superb analyses, I have chosen to look at John's prophecy from the perspective of the unfolding drama that will be the reality shared by billions of people.

Let us focus upon one young man caught in the swirling waters of this raging flood of judgment.

Our character is fictional. The events in which he is trapped are not.

(Daniel 9 & 2 Thessalonians 2:8)

MILLIONS WERE MISSING

NOT EVEN THE always-sensationalistic media had been able to come up with a final number. The sudden, unexplained disappearance of millions of people from all over the world had triggered a rapid-fire sequence of shocking crises that looked as though they would never end.

David sat on an old wooden crate in the squalor of what had been his Uncle Trevor's study. The middle-class neighborhood with its once-manicured lawns, lovely tree-lined streets and well-kept homes now reminded David of pictures he had seen of European villages just after World War II. Those once quaint little country hamlets had been the scene of intense battles between American GIs and a retreating German Army. The Nazis had been determined to leave nothing of value to the liberators; hence the picturesque villages were left as smoldering heaps of ruin.

The only room left intact in this once-lovely home was the study in which David now sat. Every house in the small town had first been looted, then either burned or dismantled piece by piece by the roving, desperate mobs. It was now too dangerous to stay in these once-populated areas. Survivors had fled to the most remote places they could find. Only in the dark of night would some dare venture back, and then only to scavenge.

All food had long since disappeared. Those who after sunset sneaked back into the area were looting anything that could be used to barter, to burn for fuel or to build a better, makeshift shelter for their ragged families, if they had any family left. David didn't.

But today he had decided to return to the area before sundown. He was too exhausted, too hungry and too tired of struggling to survive to care any more about the violent gangs that now controlled the area. He had recently heard of their cruelty and that they had even turned to cannibalizing those foolish enough to be caught here.

David, numb from hunger and emotionally depleted from his nonstop battle to survive the unending series of crises that had destroyed his once-comfortable, secure world, was ready to give up his struggle. His will to go on was gone.

He had not had a hot bath or shaved in over three years. His clothes were mere rags clinging to his emaciated frame. His hair was beyond shoulder length. Shoes were a long-forgotten luxury. Fear was every living being's constant companion. The world had gone mad. David had had enough.

But before it was all over, he had determined to search the remains of his uncle's study one last time. He had to know for sure if Uncle Trevor had been right.

"If only he were here," David mumbled to himself as he shuffled through piles of trash and debris. Kicking over his uncle's half-burned, upended desk, he frantically scoured through the rubble in a last desperate search for books, notes, a diary - anything to help him remember.

Frustrated after an hour of futile prospecting for even the slightest clue, David breathlessly plopped down in the midst of the debris-covered floor. He propped his elbows on his folded legs, thrust his face into his hands and sobbed, "Oh, why didn't I listen? Why, why, why?"

David had been a senior at the university and was to graduate in the spring with his degree in business. Every time there had been any sort of family get together, ol' Uncle T. was ever present, spouting his religious "bunk." Everyone tolerated the kind, old fella. When they would tire of listening to his talk about the "doomsday prophecies" of the end-times, they would simply excuse themselves. Uncle Trevor must have understood the family's reluctance to sit and listen. He would always smile and nod as they walked away. Then he would wait until he could corner another "victim," as David and his cousins called those who got trapped by Uncle T.

But then one day in this study, Uncle T had questioned David about his relationship with God. David had been in an especially melancholy mood and had decided to be nice and listen to his uncle, or at least act like he was listening.

Pleased and a bit surprised that David was willing to give an ear, Uncle T had pulled out his well-marked and extremely worn Bible. Once again, step-by-step, he had gone through the "last days" series of events described by the prophets. But of special interest to David on that day had been the events his uncle told him of that were written in the Book of Revelation.

Just when Uncle T had David on the edge of his seat, the phone had rung. It was the hospital. Dr. Trevor Watkins was needed in the emergency room STAT. As they hurried their separate ways that afternoon, they had promised each other that they would meet again here in the study the following Saturday morning.

Now smiling to himself, David remembered being surprised that he had actually looked forward to it. He had been very moved by what his uncle had spoken of and now David had questions, more questions and some serious concerns.

But the next Saturday had never come for Uncle T nor for a lot of others whom David knew shared Dr. Trevor Watkins' beliefs.

Sitting in the rubble of the ramshackle study, his head in his hands, David was now ready to give up. "If only I could have found something," David softly mumbled through his despair, "at least I'd know for sure."

Finally, he decided to go. Where? He had no idea. Perhaps, he thought, he would return to his little lean-to well-concealed in the hills surrounding the town. As he began to get up, a brisk gust of wind stirred the stacks of papers on the floor. As the gale whipped trash in every direction, he caught a glimpse of something that had been buried beneath the blowing papers. "A book!" David gasped. Looking closer, he saw it wasn't just any book, but Uncle Trevor's personal well-marked Bible. David fell to his knees, grasped it, clutched it to his breast, and with tears pouring down his face, said, "Thank you, oh God, thank you, thank you."

The candle flickered. It was almost spent. Made from the old wax drippings of other candles long since burned out, it lit only a small corner of the lean-to that David called home. David worked hard to position the pages so they would catch what little light the sputtering candle stingily gave up. With his face close to the open Bible, David had read for hours in the Book of Revelation. His uncle's scribbled comments, notes and references to corresponding passages in the margins answered almost all the questions David had.

Now, in stunned, contemplative silence, having finished reading the final book of the Bible, David sat staring at the flame as it struggled to stay alive.

"It's all there," David sighed. "All of it. Just like a newspaper story. Only written thousands of years before it happened." Glancing back down at its pages, he reread Revelation 6:2, "And I saw, and behold a white horse: and he that sat on him had a bow; and a crown was given unto him: and he went forth conquering and to conquer."

David's mind flashed back. Television had still been on then. It was just after the "great disappearance." Many had blamed it on some "alien force" that was purging Mother Earth. "Sounds so ridiculous now," David thought, "but most people fell for it. What fools. How could we have been such fools?"

Lying on his old cot, he laid his head back, closed his eyes and let his mind drift back, back to the beginning of the madness. In a semiconscious, dream-like state, the images began to return. David remembered every detail with uncanny clarity.

It was January, some years earlier

Superbowl Sunday. America was preoccupied with "the game." Around the world, normality marked the day. For David and his friends, it meant beer, girls, food, a party and a big screen TV.

Over three dozen guys and gals gathered in the campus frat house. It was already noisy. The stereo blared in competition with the pregame show. That, added to the cacophony of a dozen different conversations scattered throughout the large room, set a real party atmosphere. Laughter. Debates about the best quarterback.

"Who wants another beer?"

"Has anyone seen my car keys?"

"Have you heard who's pregnant?"

Finally, someone yelled, "Quiet! Everyone pipe down! It's time for kickoff."

The loud roar lessened to a low rumble as all the guys maneuvered for a good spot around the tube, and the girls, well, most of them, grouped up in the back to continue their conversations, only quieter now.

A minute later a collective "Awwh," rose from those around the television. "What's wrong with the TV?"

"This can't be happening!"

"Somebody check the power."

"It's not the power, we've got lights."

"It's the TV."

"No, it's a brand-new set."

"Somebody kick it."

"You break it, you buy it!"

As a couple of guys attempted to adjust the set, others reminisced about the World Series game in 1987. Millions of fans had been sitting in front of their televisions to watch that game being played at San Francisco's Candlestick Park when right at game time, screens went blank. An earthquake measuring 6.7 on the Richter scale had shaken the city and the coliseum, knocking off network television.

As the self-appointed repairmen in the frat house were just about to give up their efforts, the picture returned. A disheveled news anchor scrambled to get his notes together. The room grew silent as everyone gathered around the set.

Clearly shaken, the anchor was not prepared for this moment.

"Ladies and gentlemen, we apologize for interrupting the Superbowl, but at this moment confusion reigns on the field and..."

The reporter stopped, put his right index finger to his ear, and strained to listen to someone talking over his earpiece.

"Ladies and gentlemen," he continued, "please excuse me but we are having some major technical difficulties."

Then, speaking to someone off-camera in a frustrated, demanding tone, he said, "Just give me the copy now! It's all we've got." Turning back to the camera with paper in hand, the reporter apologized again and stammered, "Folks, as you can see, we are just as confused as you may be about what's going on. We've got Bill Terry at the stadium and I think we've a connection. Hello, Bill, are you there? Can you hear me?"

"Hello," came the voice of the on-scene reporter as the picture blinked off and on.

"Yes, I'm here and I wish I could tell you more than that. It seems that just as the kick-off was about to take place, a sudden disturbance rolled through the stadium," stammered the reporter.

"Can you tell us the cause? Has there been an explosion or anything like that?" interrupted the anchor.

"Uh, not that we're aware of, Randall, but things are chaotic here. I mean the strangest thing I've ever seen happened, but there's gotta be some explanation. It seems ... uh ... it happened in a split second. Football players from both teams simply, suddenly vanished."

The confused anchor interrupted, "Can you explain that? Do you mean they got kidnapped, or what?"

"Well," continued the shaken reporter, "I ... uh, we're not sure. I've asked a cameraman to get a shot for you, a shot of the field so you can see. There. Do you see that?" The screen showed a close-up of an empty uniform, pads, shoes, and helmet. They looked as though they had simply been dropped in a pile. "That's it, Randall? That's all that's left of at least nineteen, that's the count, nineteen so far, nineteen players. Now I'm getting reports that the same thing has happened to hundreds of fans." Terry, speaking to someone off-camera said, "Tell camera fourteen to pan the crowd." Then addressing the anchor, the reporter said, "Randall, uh, I know this sounds nuts, but these people have just vanished!"

Viewers saw a quick, distant crowd shot of thousands of stunned fans in the stadium.

"Aw, come on, Terry," the anchor interrupted with nervous laughter. "Surely you jest. People don't just disappear."

"Look," said the on-scene reporter, before stopping to answer off-screen directors, "If it's ready now. It is?" Turning again to face the camera, Terry said, "Randall, excuse me, but I've just been told that we've a piece of footage that captures the exact moment of this disappearance. This is the replay ... Let's ... Can we go with it now? Yes? OK. Randall? Here is the shot of the teams lining up for the kick-off."

The screen showed the teams lined up on the field for kick-off. "Now watch. Just as the head referee blows the whistle, now look," the excited reporter trying to describe what viewers were seeing said, "As the kicker runs toward the ball ... boom. He's gone. Did ya' see that? Just gone! And as we freeze-frame ... look! There're how many? Maybe a dozen more empty uniforms suddenly lying on the field. From one frame to the next they're gone! Wham. Just like that! It couldn't have taken more than fractions of a second."

With this the anchor interrupted again, saying, "Uh, Terry, uh, this is a bit too much. I'm sure all of this has a perfectly logical explanation. We're being told by the boss to go to break. So folks, we'll be right back."

THE STUDENTS SAT **in stunned silence.**

A SINGLE RAY of sun penetrated the brush roof of David's small lean-to and lit on his forehead. The heat woke David from a deep sleep. It took only seconds for him to reorient himself to that which had so occupied him the night before. He had returned very late and spent most of the night reading the retrieved Bible. Then he had struggled to reconstruct the events that seemed to have started this nightmare that he was now living. He had finally fallen asleep.

As he rubbed his eyes and started to stretch, he became aware of the still-open Bible lying across his outstretched legs.

As the familiar hunger pangs stirred deep within his stomach, he decided to forego his routine search for breakfast this morning. Breakfast, as did every other meal, meant foraging around in the woods for bugs, ants, beetles or an edible root or plant. Survivors had been reduced to eating things that in better times they would have never even dreamed of putting in their mouths.

Focusing again on the open Bible, he began comparing the events he had been living through with those foretold in the Scriptures. The similarities were undeniable.

He recalled how short-lived the world's preoccupation with the "sudden disappearance" of all those people had been. Before anyone could come up with a satisfactory explanation, war had broken out in the Middle East. It was speculated that Russia wanted to take advantage of the world's confusion after "the disappearance." So, she had gathered her allies and invaded the little country of Israel. David didn't know much about the geopolitical realities of the Middle East or anywhere else for that matter. He did, however, remember how often Uncle Trevor used to talk about just such an invasion.

Uncle T's words were deeply etched in his memory. "Thousands of years ago, Ezekiel foretold with uncanny precision even the types of nuclear weapons to be used, of the location of the great battle, and about how God would supernaturally move to save the little nation of Israel."

They had laughed at him behind his back. David, shaking his head, mused out loud, "But no one's laughing now."

His eyes were drawn back to Revelation 6:2. David was deeply grateful that Uncle T had scribbled a considerable number of related Bible references and short explanations of each verse.

David squinted and was able to make out the words

jotted in the margins. "Antichrist, Daniel 9 ... makes a peace treaty ... short-lived ... AC to dictate over New Roman Empire ... Euro nations ... see." Here the edge of the page had been burned, obscuring Uncle T's remaining thought.

But David understood. He had watched with the world as 24-hour television covered the bloody battles that had raged on the "mountains of Israel." "That's all anyone did," David quietly reflected. "We just watched. All of Israel's allies, America and the other NATO countries had refused to get involved." David recalled the excuses of his country's leaders who had claimed to be overwhelmed with "our own struggle to survive." A week after that infamous Superbowl Sunday, America's economy had crashed, followed by massive civil unrest. Martial law had been declared but when communication systems were lost a short time later, anarchy ruled most American cities. The whole country had turned upside down. Society had convulsed. The rest of the world had been in much worse shape than America. Chaos had gripped the globe.

The TV talking heads went on and on with their prognoses and editorializing. "Israel will soon be no more ... Russia will be restored as a world power. The oil supply from the Middle East to the West will be stopped."

Network anchors commented how, with a quick victory in the Middle East, Russia's allies, the Arab nations, would finally have what they had always wanted: millions of dead Jews, the end of Israel, the occupation of Palestine, Jerusalem, and for Islam, The Temple Mount.

David strained to recall the events, the names and the

reports. Shaking his head, he thought with remorse, "Why didn't I pay attention or write it down?" He was becoming convinced that everything that had been happening since that Superbowl Sunday had been foretold in the pages of the very Book in his hands. "What was it Uncle T used to say?" David mumbled. "Something like, 'The Word of God is more current than tomorrow's newspapers!'" Suddenly David bolted up from his prone position on the cot.

"Newspapers," David laughed. "Newspapers. Yeah! I got newspapers."

David had just remembered all those gigantic stacks of old newspapers he had found months before. After reading and rereading them for something to do, until he had them almost memorized, he had decided to use them as insulation in his lean-to walls. He was ecstatic that he had kept them.

He furiously dug into the thickened walls of his little hut until he retrieved every single page of old newspaper he had so carefully inserted months ago. Thumbing rapidly through hundreds of pages of newsprint, he eventually came upon all the articles he had hoped to find.

"Yes, here's another one," David excitedly mumbled, as he eyed the bold headlines. "Israel Saved ... Secret Weapon Destroys Invaders."

The article read, "Against overwhelming odds, in a last-minute gasp for its national life, tiny Israel surprised the world with a defense-strike capability that even most Israelis did not know existed."

He found a multitude of other related articles and headlines. "Israelis Dance In the Streets," "'God Saved Us,' says Israeli Prime Minister," and "Miracles in Israel ...

Enemy Routed." The article beneath said, "Not since ancient days in Biblical times has this little nation seen such a powerful demonstration of miraculous intervention. Old rabbis dancing in the streets of Jerusalem, Haifa and Tel Aviv are quick to give their God, Jehovah, all the credit for their unexpected and sudden military victory. However, analysts are now speculating that the salvation of Israel more likely came from new high- tech secret weapons rather than the 'Old Man Upstairs.'"

David also found related stories of the war's devastation that had made Israel a wasteland. He read of the new despair of all Israelis over their new vulnerability in a world that, for the most part, still detested these whom Uncle T had always called "the chosen of God."

For hours, David dug through the pile of crumbling old newspapers. Finally, his tired eyes fell on an especially large headline and accompanying picture, giving him first a sense of exhilaration and then one of sheer terror, "New European Prime Minister Extends Olive Branch." Under the headline was a picture of the United States of Europe's newly elected Prime Minister, Sir Richard Montebaum. He stood with the heads of state of ten recently united European nations, all shaking hands with the Prime Minister of Israel. The hair on the back of David's neck stood on end as he began to read the article.

"Sir Richard seems to have no end to diplomatic miracles in his new portfolio as Prime Minister of the United States of Europe.

Just as most nations were still reeling from the massive problems following D-Day (disappearance day - when millions vanished), Sir Richard took office. Since then he has demonstrated an almost supernatural ability to resolve every conflict that has tested him. He is the first in history to bring a promise of lasting peace to the Middle East. For the first time, all parties are pleased with his new treaty's terms, especially Israel, who finally has guaranteed borders and a security to be insured by the word and influence of Sir Richard.

According to the Prime Minister of France, Francois Petrouli, 'Sir Richard has the charisma of Galahad, the oratory skills of Churchill, the love for peace of Ghandi, the intellect of Thomas Jefferson and the political appeal of Kennedy.' Petrouli added, 'To date the new United States of Europe's Prime Minister has solved every problem facing the new Euro-coalition, the Middle East and for that matter, the world, seemingly without effort.'

The latest benefactors of Sir Richard's heartfelt longing for world peace and prosperity are the bleeding but victorious people of Israel. After decades of nonstop warfare and following their greatest military victory since the crossing of the Red Sea, it appears, at last, peace, in the person of Sir Richard, the new Prince of Peace, has come to the Holy Land."

Finishing the article, David cynically mused, "So, Sir Richard is the serpent. It's little wonder Mr. Peacenik couldn't keep it all together. Uncle T had always referred to Satan as 'the Destroyer.' Well, that's what this guy's been doing lately." As the reality sank in, David involuntarily shivered. He had read the ninth chapter of Daniel repeatedly. All the facts from Scripture, the well-marked references of Uncle T and the supernatural rise to power settled the matter. Sir Richard, he now understood, was evil incarnate.

The months of malnutrition, of exposure to the rainy winter conditions and the complete absence of any medical attention had destroyed David's immune system. Unable to ward off the many infectious assaults upon his body, his physical condition had deteriorated to such a state that he was having great difficulty breathing.

Pulling himself to his feet, David became faint. He hadn't eaten anything at all for over 24 hours and it had been months since he had had any real nourishment other than bugs, berries and the one dead bird he had found. What little had been left after the ants had finished it had made David sick for days. He knew that unless something changed soon, he wouldn't live much longer. His only reason for staying alive now was to solve this horrifying mystery that had become his life - or to at least make some sense of it.

After a long stretch, David crossed his legs, sat down in the midst of the stacks of newspapers, and reached again for the Bible. He read Revelation 6:4, "And there went out another horse that was red; and power was given to him that sat on it to take peace from the earth..."

David needed no help in interpreting this verse. He had witnessed its fulfillment. "Sir Richard's peace program was short-lived indeed," sneered David as he recalled the devastating nuclear exchanges that had broken out around the world only months after the signing of the peace treaty in the Middle East.

He also remembered that only a month after "the disappearing," America had elected a President with isolationist leanings. "We thought," said David as though he were addressing a group of his friends, "America could escape a nuclear holocaust, and for a while we did. But then one by one, our major cities over a two-week period were annihilated by hydrogen bombs."

No one could believe how quickly, almost overnight, their great nation, the United States of America, had been so easily and completely destroyed. David bowed his head and softly wept. The memories were too real. He had seen what men were capable of doing to each other, not only with long-range, impersonal, intercontinental ballistic missiles, but with their bare hands.

Yes, the "red horse" whose rider took peace from the earth removed it not only from amongst the nations but from among friends and even families. David had witnessed the savagery of women and even children slaughtering each other for no other reasons than sheer hatred or to secure a crust of bread. Humanity had been reduced to an animalistic state, no, lower than that, to the level of the demonic.

David's tears dripped onto the pages of the Bible. Distraught, yet determined to continue, he opened his eyes and read the next verse about another "rider on a black horse" who would curse the earth with famine.

David had always thought that Uncle T had been referring to Third World countries when he talked about this passage.

David had watched as this prophecy had sprung to life before his eyes. He tried so often to shut out the hellish vision of the emaciated bodies, the stench of death and the wanton cries of children pleading for a piece of bread.

He wanted to forget the cruelty and the depravity. He hated the memories of watching people he had known all his life turn into snarling, vicious animals fighting in the streets over a carcass of something - or was it a someone? David had been repulsed, turning his head, not wanting to know.

But these memories were seared into his soul. Memories not of faraway places, but of the streets of his own hometown. The flashbacks of these horrid weeks of hell caused a wave of nausea to overcome him. Gasping, with his hand held over his mouth, he stumbled out of his lean-to.

After the nausea had subsided, David slept for three hours. Upon awakening, he reached again for the old Bible. David had felt worse in his life, he told himself, but he couldn't remember when.

Pulling himself into sitting position, he peered through the worn tarp that hung over the entrance to his tent-like shelter. The sun, as he suspected, was about to sink below the tree line. He knew he must work quickly or else he would be forced to burn the last of his candle.

The roving violent gangs could easily spot campfires in the dark of night, so survivors would not dare risk starting one after sunset, regardless of how cold it got.

Straining to focus his eyes on the well-marked passages of Revelation, David softly said, "I've got to know where and how it's all going to end." He wondered if these pages would reveal any hope for him. He had long feared that the only way out of this nightmare was death. As the storm of God's judgment hammered his world, he felt his time was running out.

He looked down on Revelation 6:8 and read of the rider upon the pale horse. "And power was given unto him ... to kill with the sword, and with hunger and with death and with the beasts of the earth."

Closing his eyes, he could recall the terrifying images that had filled the news reports night after miserable night.

"Such unimaginable massive hemorrhaging of humanity," he thought as he remembered the suicides of so many of his friends, and the reports of men killing their entire families, then themselves. He shuddered at the memories of how various large groups of neighbors had made death pacts and then helped each other die. It was massive insanity. Fearing the pale horse would soon gallop into their own lives, so many, no longer able to bear the horror, the terror, the deprivation, simply chose to end it all. David had never understood suicidal tendencies before, but he did now. So often he had wanted to die rather than face another day of this living death, but something had kept him alive.

And then there were those who had lived just outside the cities where death rained from the sky with nuclear, biological and chemical agents of annihilation. Not close enough to be killed in the initial blasts, they were simply left to die a little at a time. Diseases spread through rotting corpses left unburied, the starvation of millions and the murderous grab by survivors for any remaining food, water and shelter left in their wake a world gasping for a breath, to live just a little longer.

Those who did live, with few exceptions, wished they hadn't.

David also contemplated the ferocity of all those animals, domestic and wild, that had lost any fear of humans. Mad with hunger, the animal kingdom had begun to assault people with a new savagery. But almost all animals had now become extinct, with the exception of various insects, many of which were also assaulting humankind with a seeming vengeance.

Shaking his head in an attempt to clear his mind, he read again in Revelation 6:9, "I saw under the altar the souls of them that were slain for the word of God and (their) testimony."

David tried to remember why these particular verses had always excited his uncle.

Scanning the margin of the Bible, he noticed the inked-in passages and remarks. Squinting his eyes and holding the Bible sideways to better read his uncle's scribbled notes, David was finally able to make out the faded words, "Mercy for those who seek Him, even in the midst of tribulation." The words arrested his attention. He read the phrase over and over again.

Closing his eyes, he could easily see the family dining over a New Year's Day feast their last time together. At the first lull in conversation, sweet ol' Uncle T had started sharing how some would experience the grace of God even during the seven-year tribulation.

"Now I remember," David spoke to himself with increasing excitement, "God will even now work in some hearts."

His eyes brimming with tears of hope, David fumbled through the pages reading each of the Scriptures that Uncle Trevor had etched in next to this verse. With every reference he read, his hope soared still higher. "Is it possible, oh God," David half-prayed, "that you care?" Finding the right book and chapter to the last reference his uncle had written in the margin, David hurried his finger down the page to find the exact verse.

Tears now burst over the rims of his eyes as he read out loud, "Acts 16:31, 'Believe on the Lord Jesus Christ and thou shalt be saved.'" The words pierced David's heart with visible conviction. This is the exact verse that he and Uncle T had been discussing that day the hospital had called his uncle to the emergency room.

Trembling, he read the verse over and over.

The same sense of crushing need that had overwhelmed him the day his uncle had run to the hospital again swept over him. Could he still believe? Would God still hear him?

Falling on his face, David sobbed. "Oh God, I've been so wrong, so dirty, so long. How could you ever forgive me?"

A rebellious heart, once cold and bitter against God, melted into sweet submission as the prayers of a faithful, godly uncle were answered.

In the crucible of an angry, raging furnace of judgment, another soul found the Savior.

David spent the night on his face, broken at the feet of his new Lord. David knew this was the beginning not only of a new day, but of a new life. He couldn't believe how clean he felt.

He now knew that he was among those of whom he had read, those who came to know Christ during this time of "great judgment." He also remembered that Uncle

T had always taught that the majority of those who would turn to Christ during this period would pay with their heads. Smiling at such a thought, David remarked to himself, "What a privilege. It'd be such a paltry sum to pay for all He's done for me." If he was to be among those so honored to be martyred for Christ or among the very few to witness the second coming of his Lord before the angel of death touched them, he would be happy. His heart was finally at peace.

Having returned to the lean-to, David read further in Revelation. Under the subtitle of "the sixth seal," he read verses 12 through 16:

> I beheld .... a great earthquake .... sun became black ... and the moon became as blood .... and men hid trembling in the caves ... and said to the mountains .... fall on us .... hide us from the face of Him .... on the throne.

David stopped and thought back. Television, radio, and newspaper had long since been gone. Then the only communication anyone in his hometown had with the outside world had been a single ham radio operated and owned by David's brother-in-law. David and a few others had gathered day and night to listen to reports from others scattered around the hemisphere. The broadcasts were ominous. News came of the total collapse of most national governments. The few exceptions were in the Far and Middle East, and the remaining European coalition. Reports told of the total disruptions of entire civilizations and of gargantuan, devastating earthquakes. Entire cities were swallowed by the earth and radical continental shifts reshaped the earth's topography.

David lived in the Midwestern part of North America, in what used to be called Ohio. This rural area was far away from metropolitan areas that had been so completely decimated.

Some survivors like David still wandered the hills scratching out an animalistic existence and, of course, there were the violent squatters who controlled the demolished town. But clearly, this tiny little corner of the globe had suffered far less than most of the world.

On rare occasions, from a distance, David would see someone from the other side of these walls as they foraged for something to eat, but there were no friendships. There was no trust, loyalty or, seemingly, love left in the world. Daily life for everyone was one of hiding from every other living soul or of killing before one was killed.

David had heard that most of North America was a vast wasteland wrought by war, internal chaos and natural disasters unprecedented in scope.

The fact was, civilization as David had known it no longer existed within thousands of miles of this place or possibly anywhere on earth. If the last few pieces of information he had heard were to be believed, then societies in parts of Europe, Asia and some remote areas of Africa still functioned. However, judging from what he had discovered in the Scriptures, the world as it probably now existed was not a world that David would care to live in.

Long ago he had decided to live out what there was left of his life here, in this wilderness.

PIERCING THE FUTURE

Sometimes he could approach river travelers, who sometimes passed along the news that they had heard.

The scenes they described were of cataclysmic convulsions of nature that had caused the death of literally billions of people. He had been told that less than thirty percent of the earth's population still existed and that many who had perished did so "while cursing the Almighty God" whom they blamed for this "universal convulsing of all nature."

It was said that the survivors, even the once most powerful leaders of the world, the wealthy and the influential, now lived in caves, holes in the ground and in dens like animals.

"No wonder," David had thought when hearing such tales, "the towns and cities lie in radioactive and chemically laced poisonous heaps of ruin, contaminated with the smell of death and disease." One traveler had despairingly remarked, "The whole earth is crawling with human maggots like one giant rotting corpse."

He had wanted to close his ears to these horrid stories, to dismiss them as foolish rantings. But, even from this, perhaps the safest place left on the globe, David could see and hear as the earth increasingly groaned. The heavens seemed to be collapsing like a giant circus tent that had just had all of its poles jerked from beneath it.

Reading the Apostle's description in Revelation 6, there remained no doubt in David's mind that this moment in time was the "future" John had so clearly seen on the Isle of Patmos almost 2,000 years earlier. It read like a script of the hellish drama that was now being played out on the stage of the universe.

With great effort, David walked to the highest point overlooking the river and sat down in the shade of the few tall trees still alive. "This may be," David sighed, "the only spot left on earth not yet totally destroyed by the fury of the last several years." Closing his eyes, David strained to think. "How long has all this been going on?" He had stopped trying to keep up with the days, months, and years a long time ago. The struggle for survival had been all-consuming. With a sigh, David looked up into the clear sky, smiled and prayed, "Heavenly Father, how I thank you for taking away all the fear and darkness. But now, in this world of nightmares, what is it, Father, that you'd have me do? I feel so alone. Please, Father, speak to my heart."

Wearily looking back to the Bible on his lap, David randomly flipped it open. His heart leaped with joy as his eyes fell on Psalm 139. He read the verses that Uncle Trevor had heavily underlined. "Whither shall I go from Thy Spirit? Or whither shall I flee from Thy presence? If I ascend up into heaven, Thou art there; if I make my bed in hell, behold Thou art there. Even there shall Thy hand lead me and Thy right hand shall hold me. If I say, surely the darkness shall cover me; even the night shall be light about me. Yea, the darkness hideth not from Thee, but the night shineth as the day; the darkness and the light are both alike to Thee. How precious are Thy thoughts unto me, O God! How great is the sum of them."

Tears fell from tired eyes onto the pages of the Bible. And then he slept.

A sudden gust of wind woke David with a start. Instinctively looking around for any danger, David realized he must have fallen asleep. Gathering his thoughts, he decided to finish the passages describing what John the Apostle had prophesied for those, like David, who would be alive during this time called the tribulation.

He opened to Chapter 8 of Revelation and read through to the end of the 9th chapter.

His mind rolled through each horrible description of six different judgments that the Apostle called "trumpets."

"This must be, it's got to be what the leader of that last group of river people was describing," David thought. "If so, then the end can't be much further."

Laying his head back against the tree, David thought back to his meeting with the funny, little guy. The shabbily clad, gray-bearded, skinny little old man had told him, "Son, down river, beyond the eastern falls where the old state of Tennessee used to lie, on a line as far north and as far south as one can travel, there ain't nothing! No hills, no mountains, no cities, no towns, and certainly no people."

Hearing the man's report that there no longer existed an eastern seaboard to North America, David had smiled.

"Laugh if you will, boy," grumbled the gravelly-voiced old traveler, "but everything from the western-most state line of Tennessee to the East Coast is now under the Atlantic Ocean." David remembered politely nodding but inwardly wondering if this leader of the two or three families with him, like so many others, had lost his mind.

"Furthermore, at least so I's told nigh on a year ago," rambled this elder, "same thing and worse has happened on the West side of this once-vast continent."

The old man had scratched his beard as though he was

trying to remember what he'd been told. "It seems the next generation, if there be one, will be able to buy pretty nice beachfront property up around Denver, Colorado. The Rockies be the only thing that stopped the 2,000-foot-high tidal wave that struck the entire Pacific Rim."

David was dubious but shaken when he had heard that. He couldn't help but ask, "Why? What could have caused..."

The old leader interrupted, "You sure don't know much, do ya', boy? Ain't ya' heard?"

"If you'll join up with us, you can hear it from those who seen it, and some who've heard firsthand 'bout things - that is if the hostiles don't get us. That's why folks roam about with me. I knows where's they ain't. Have ye heard, son, word is, a batch of em's gone to eatin' folk."

David, ignoring the old news of cannibals, had pushed the old fella for more details. "Then you gotta know more, more about what's happened?"

The old man had spit, cocked one eye, and said, "Boy, ya' look old enough to know, ain't nothing fer free. What ye got to trade for such information?"

David understood the language of barter. Money was worthless. Reaching into the leather pouch hanging on his trousers David had pulled out a closed fist. The old man's beady eyes had peered suspiciously down a crooked nose at the fist David held out.

For a long few seconds David had watched the wrinkled face until the old eyes looked back into his own. "Well, boy," the elder had snapped, "you gonna tell me whatcha' holdin' in yer hand or make me guess?" David had been forced to smile.

He had turned his fist over and in a teasing manner slowly opened his hand as the old man's eyes returned to see the secret treasure.

"Whoa, them's good uns!" the old man exclaimed as reached to touch the merchandise. But David had moved quickly to remake a fist hiding away the booty that had so excited the elder. "Uh-uh," David smiled. "First, you brief me, then the whole batch is yours. What do you say?"

"Let's sit," said the elder, closing the deal.

Several hours later, David and the old man had stood and stretched. All questions answered and satisfied that he had made a good deal, David had been ready to hand over his pouch's contents.

"Wait a minute," said the elder as he had run 25 yards back to his ragged old tent, returning quickly with a beat-up pan. The winded elder's eyes had danced with anticipation as he said, "Now, jest dump that there pouch into this here cookin' pot. And I want all of 'em, don't ya' hold out on me, boy."

The old man brimmed with excitement as David had emptied out his entire pouch full of the fattest, juiciest earthworms either of them had ever seen. It had taken David eight hours to dig this batch. Such delicacies were rare and were the closest thing to a grand banquet anyone would dare dream of. David knew that the half-pound of worms would've lasted him three days. He knew the old man had no intention of rationing these beauties. Even as David had turned to wave good-bye, he had seen that the old man was already too preoccupied with his treasure to notice David's exit.

Glancing back over his shoulder one last time, David

had seen the excited old man with his head cocked all the way back, his mouth gaped open and his hand holding the spaghetti-like, wiggly bunch of night crawlers over his waiting lips. As his stomach had growled in envy, David disappeared into the brush.

Now from his perch high above the river, David recounted the news that he had traded his fresh worms to get. Comparing the old man's information and with that gathered over months from various eyewitnesses with the prophecies of the Apostle John left no doubt in David's mind.

The old man's words had rolled like a script beneath David's closed eyes. After they had struck a bargain on the worm pouch, the old man pulled David away from earshot of those in his group. Checking over his shoulder to be sure no one in his small entourage could hear him, the elder had said, "Look son, I only act the part of an ol' codger. Those I guide think I'm an ol' river cap'n." David had indeed heard the sudden marked change in the diction and vocabulary of the man.

"I discovered a long time ago, it's best to cover one's tracks when moving around what's left of this country. A lot of those still alive don't care much for those of us who used to run the nation's business. They blame all this on us."

David had sat without answering. The older man took it as a cue to continue. "Anyway, I am, or I used to be, Senator Norm Hathaway from the great state of Kentucky. I was flying my private plane back to Washington, D.C., when the bottom fell out of the world. To make a long story short, after flying around, then running out of fuel, I crash-landed in what was Virginia. Injured, I spent months crawling about in those hills. Guess everyone thought I had disappeared with that flying saucer bunch. Six months later I was found by some other survivors, chiseled out a new identity, name and ... uh ... I guess you'd call it, 'lifestyle.' The senator had then laughed and said with a bit of irony, "Ha! Didn't we all? I mean, change lifestyles. Nothing was the same anymore."

Then the senator had begun to tell his story. At one point he said he had gotten to a government installation prepared years ago as safety bunkers for congressmen and their families in case of a national emergency. He was, he said, able to penetrate security perimeters, get in, identify himself and gain access to the secret communications area. "There is where most of my info comes from, so what I'm telling about what's going on in the world isn't hearsay. I know it's true."

David had listened in rapt attention as the senator told him the unbelievable events that had been unfolding in the world. "At last, toward the end of my life in the compound things began to fall apart. The 800 or so people inside, well, we ran out of food, then water. Folks started going mad, insane ... that's when I decided to take my chances on the outside." David had listened to the senator, knowing it was the final confirmation he needed of all his suspicions.

Continuing, Senator Hathaway had said, "So after two or three years this new superman, Mr. Wonderful over in Europe, began to get weird. We had people, I mean our government had people across the pond. For a good while they stayed in contact with us by using satellite phones, and high-tech systems most people don't even know exist. Pretty sophisticated stuff, the best tax dollars could buy. But anyway, Mr. - I mean Sir Richard - began to act like a new Hitler. He also invoked new laws, opened concentration camps for dissenters, called 'em rehabilitation centers. He alone decided who ate, who didn't, who lived, who died. He controls the military, the government. - No, he is the government. He's even got a system for economic exchange, purchasing, and selling all based on his own little numbers scheme.

"Then some got upset, but hey, the world's self-destructing, right? This guy gave people a rallying point. They started looking to him like he's a god or something, ya' know? But slowly privacy vanished, personal rights disappeared. Hey, the SS and Hitler's Gestapo boys are like little old ladies compared to this crowd. After a while, we all thanked our lucky stars we were stuck here."

David had been so intrigued he did not want to interrupt the man who kept talking, "But, then the Ruskies, still ticked about being blown to pieces in Israel years before, came back strong. They still had all their nukes and much of their air power though their navy was gone. America? Ha! What America? Lots of folks said God finally judged America. No, what took us out was, well, nobody really knows what hit us.

"It seemed like we'd escaped the limited nuclear exchanges in Europe and the Middle East. Then some rinky-dinky terrorist group hit DC and Red China at the same time. The Chi- comms thought we hit them, we thought they'd hit us. Before you knew it, both of us became little more than smoldering ash heaps. Everyone thought, at least those left alive, that everything was over then. Fact is, it was just beginning. Right when we thought it couldn't get any worse, it got worse and all hell broke loose. NASA might have seen it coming, but NASA had long since gone up in smoke.

"I'm sure you saw. The whole world did - the light shows, I mean. What a sight in the skies! Fires are still raging across the globe. We'll never know how many are dead or dying. The question is, how has anyone survived? Last estimates before I left the compound were that less than two billion souls, two billion out of six billion, were still alive. Those still living turned to Mr. Answers, still running the show in Europe, but he already had his hands full. No one knows where the creatures came from. It seemed they covered the earth with torment. Imagine! Ungodly stinging, demonic, uh ... things - some called 'em aliens - an army of 'em - terrorizing the world - mean, it's like Stephen King comes alive or Hitchcock's birds gone high tech crazy, attacking everything and everyone. They had to be the Russians' or the Chicomms' or uh, maybe even our own secret weapons gone awry.

"Oh, yeah, on top of all this crazy stuff, as if it's not enough, Sir Richard decides he's not happy just ruling the known world. He wants to be the Pope, too.

"Hey, you would pledge allegiance to his church of the Humane or lose your head. Ha! But you know something, kid? There's one group out there that thumbed their noses at Sir Richard the Pope. Yeah, they had their own God. Ticks Sir Richard off big time, it does. These Christians decided martyrdom is better than life in Sir

Richard's great new world. The more he kills of 'em, Sir Richard, I mean, the more of 'em there are.

"I'll tell ya' one thing, Davey boy, the guy, Sir Richard, he don't quit. Hey, did ya' hear what he did next? Ha! He did the Pope thing one better. He ups and decides being Pope isn't enough, so he goes over to Jerusalem, Israel, walks into the new Temple they built, and claims to be God. Yeah, God! He tells everyone to bow down and worship him. Now that's a good one. Why didn't I ever think of that when I considered running for President back in, uh, em ... aw ... it doesn't matter. GOD! Imagine that."

David had felt compelled to ask the senator if that had been the last he had heard.

In response, the senator has looked down as though studying his feet, sighed and said, "Well, guess it makes no difference if you know. But two days ago, I met an old colleague of mine. He'd gone to a different compound than I had. It seems they lasted longer. Ultimately, he, too, had left, but not before he found out the latest from Europe and the Middle East.

"The word is Red China's amassed a standing army of 200 million men who have been slaughtering their way across Asia. Only a week ago they were moving into some strategic positions south of Lebanon. Seems our eastern brothers have their own ideas about who should be runnin' things. It's fixing to turn into one bloody mess over there." The senator sighed and paused.

David had been stunned at what he was hearing. He had spent the last many weeks studying this very scenario.

Knowing what was coming next, David had asked anyway, "What will happen then?"

"Well," the senator continued with a sigh of resignation, "Sir Wonderful has brought the armies of Europe to meet 'em and," the senator, picking up a twig and drawing a map in the dirt, continued, "to make it real interesting, another group of nations from the southern hemisphere, African and Moslem, with some oil-rich Arab states like Iraq and Iran, have marched into place to make sure they get their piece of the pie."

Again, David had known but decided to ask anyway, "And the pie is...?"

"It seems everyone sees the need to control these ancient trade routes from the richest mineral fields in the world. It's no surprise, every world leader in history understood the strategic necessity of controlling this valley smack dab in the middle of Israel. Alexander the Great, the Romans, Napoleon, the Ottomans, the Turks, even Hitler. The most valuable piece of real estate on the face of this planet is this land bridge between North Africa and Eurasia." The senator had paused, looked down at his map in the dirt and stabbed his twig hard into the ground, saying, "Right here in this valley are gathered the greatest armies of destruction in the history of warfare."

David had said, "Armageddon."

The senator had replied, "Yep, the Valley of Megiddo. Obviously, Davey, all the wars fought in this valley through history, and as you probably know there's been a lot of 'em, have been dress rehearsals for this main show."

David had thought out loud, "Then the end, I mean the war, is probably just about to get underway, huh?"

The senator, leaning back against a tree, had replied, "That's right. And when it's done, Sir Richard, in his new role as master of the universe, or God, won't have much left to be God over."

It had been several days since David had talked with Senator Hathaway. Since then, it seemed to David a lifetime had passed. He couldn't help but wonder if the last great battle prophesied in the Word of God had started yet. David knew now what the Scriptures taught about the second coming of Christ. He had read it a thousand times over the last few weeks.

Still leaning against the large old tree, David recalled the words his Uncle T had spoken so often. "And the Lord Jesus will return at that moment when, after seven years of horrid judgments, He intervenes in man's and Satan's mad rush to destroy all flesh."

"Hasn't it been long enough? Maybe I've just been hoping against hope. Maybe this is hell. Maybe I was too late in reaching out to Him. I was so foolish," David spoke out loud to himself.

Before he could finish his thought, he was suddenly convulsed with a hacking cough. He was forced onto the ground upon his hands and knees unable to control the coughing that brought searing pain to his lungs. Looking on the ground beneath him he saw that he was coughing up a steady flow of blood.

Finally, able to stop the hacking, David slumped back into a sitting position against the tree.

Now each breath was taken with great effort as he gasped in the air. He felt as though his lungs were already full of some kind of fluid that resisted his excruciatingly painful efforts to breathe.

"Oh, Lord," looking upward David spoke between gasps, "I have no strength left. I cannot go on. Please, God, help me. I just can't go on any ..." Unable to complete his sentence without any air in his lungs, David groaned as his eyes closed involuntarily.

David felt himself dying. In a semiconscious effort, he resigned himself to the moment as a new swirling sensation engulfed him. "Yes," David mumbled. "Welcome death. Welcome release. Thank God, it's over."

Suddenly, David felt a tremendous shaking. With his eyes still closed, unable to rouse himself to full consciousness, David angrily spoke, "No, no, no! Don't stop me. Leave me alone. Let me die!"

But the trembling of the world around him increased. Slightly opening his eyes, he became conscious of the fact that the increased shaking was a powerful earthquake.

Before he had time to formulate another thought, he saw a dazzlingly brilliant point appear in the eastern sky.

Its brilliance was more intense than the sun's, but for some reason it was not uncomfortable to look into it. Immediately, David was fully conscious, as a feeling of intense joy and ecstatic wonder washed over him.

Then David could hardly believe his eyes. As the brilliance began to fill the sky, he saw an innumerable host of riders upon horses.

David sat transfixed with his back to the giant old pine and his eyes fixed in shock to the scene unfolding before him.

Out of the great hoard of horsemen a rider came

straight toward David. As he came closer, David was able to recognize the features of the one on the horse.

"Oh, my," David breathed with his eyes fixed on the horseman, "Uncle Trevor?" As he said the name, the beautiful horse upon which his smiling uncle sat reared up on its back legs. David was suddenly warmed with a peace he had never experienced. His uncle, looking like a gallant knight, smiled broadly at David and waved his arm as if to say, "Come on, let's go, son."

And then he heard the shouting and the cheering like nothing he'd ever heard before. The voices of tens of thousands of thousands filled the skies punctuated by the most beautiful music and singing of praises to the Lamb of God.

And then, as if on cue from above the vast throngs of victorious horsemen, there came another Rider on a magnificent white stallion. At the sight of Him an even louder declaration of exuberant praise rolled through the masses, "Glory to the Lamb of God," followed by an increasing crescendo of ecstatic cheering.

As the Rider came closer, David saw His eyes were more beautiful than the most fiery diamonds.

His head was crowned, breath-taking in beauty. The dazzling robe upon Him was dripping with what looked like blood, though David somehow knew it was not the rider's blood. And then he saw what was written upon the robe, "King of kings and Lord of lords."

As David sat immobilized with an ecstatic joy over what he was seeing, the white stallion descended until it and its rider hovered only a few feet above him.

At that moment, David buried his face in his hands

and felt as though the shame of his wicked life was lying open for all creation to see. He was crushed by the guilt of his own evil heart and wanted to run from the presence of this One whose wondrous holiness now penetrated his soul. David felt he should be condemned to a million deaths and was unworthy to even lie at the feet of this King of kings. "Let me die, let me die!" David wanted to yell.

But then, all the resounding praise that had filled the universe suddenly went silent. David, still afraid to look up into the face of all that is holy, just, righteous, and pure, felt a hand touch his shoulder. He froze. He dared not look back into those piercing eyes.

Again, he felt the touch communicating the Master's desire for David to look up. Slowly, with great trepidation, he began to lift his head out of his hands.

As his eyes met those of the One before him, David was embraced by the tender, loving, and forgiving gaze of the King of kings.

"My Lord, my God, my Savior," wept David.

The Master then reached out to David with His hand extended and opened.

David's eyes fell upon the outstretched hand. There in the palm of His hand that crafted all that is and all that ever shall he, was a deep scar. David reached out his own shaking hand and touched the nail-scarred palm.

Looking with wonder back into the sweet eyes of the Lord Jesus Christ, David heard Him say, "For you. Now, come, good and faithful servant."

David did.

18

PEERING INTO THE MILLENNIUM

BY TIM LAHAYE

THE AGES-LONG CONFLICT BETWEEN GOD AND SATAN FOR the souls of men is rapidly coming to an end. For at least 6,000 years, ever since he deceived Mother Eve about God keeping His word, Satan has tried to deceive all mankind, challenging, "Has God said ... you won't surely die!" In so doing he has compelled the majority of people on earth to disbelieve God and to do their "own thing."

But his time of deception is rapidly coming to an end. If we are truly in "the last days" or the "end of this age," as many prophecy scholars believe, we may only be a decade or less away from the most glorious period this world has seen since the Garden of Eden. First, Christ must come and rapture His church and take all "the dead in Christ" and "those who are alive and remain" (millions of believers since Pentecost to the rapture) to His Father's house, as He promised in John 14:1-3. Then the world will go through the greatest seven years of tribulation in history, "since the beginning of the world until this time, no, nor ever shall be" (Matthew 24:21). At the end of that seven years, Jesus Christ will come back to this earth in power and great glory in what the Apostle Paul called "the glorious appearing." Then He will set up His earthly kingdom, which, as we shall see, will last 1,000 years.

The blessings God will rain on this earth during that kingdom of Christ are beyond human comprehension. Can you even imagine a time so blessed of God that the best word I can think of to define it is "utopia"? It will literally be a bit of heaven on earth. As we shall see, it will be a time of righteousness, for Christ will reign over the whole earth. It will be a time of unprecedented material blessing; the prophets tell us that the reapers will follow the sowers. Almost everyone has heard that there will be no more war, through the use (and often misuse) of the prophetic message that in that day they will "beat their swords into plowshares." And, as we shall see, Satan, the master deceiver of the souls of men, will be bound in the bottomless pit for the entire 1,000 years. I intend to show you in this chapter that the population will be so enormous during that period that the majority will become Christians, causing the ultimate victory of Christ over Satan. In other words, more people will be going to heaven than hell, based upon the number of Christians from all the ages of history added to the number involved in the great soul harvest during the tribulation period.

But in my enthusiasm, I am getting ahead of my story. Suffice it to say here, we Christians are not on the losing side! Jesus' death for our sins and His resurrection, according to Scripture, will admit more people into the eternal heaven God has prepared for those who love Him than will miss His "so great salvation." For many future soul harvests are described in Scripture, including "the multitude that no man can number" during the tribulation described in Revelation 7:9-15. The fact of the long conflict of the ages over the souls of men ends in a thrilling story of victory for Jesus Christ and is guaranteed by the Word of God.

If the story of this incredible utopian kingdom age God has planned for mankind were better known by this world, I believe millions more would want to learn about salvation. Particularly if we were to compare God's incredibly great plans for His children with any other religious teaching or philosophical concept in the world. Nothing else even comes close! How could reincarnation, soul sleep, purgatory, "the happy hunting grounds" or any other man-made doctrine of life in the afterlife compare with the wonderful plan God details in the Bible for our future?

Unfortunately, this incredible plan is one of the best-kept secrets in the world. That must be part of the deception of Satan, to keep people from being inspired by the prophetic plan of God for their future. But whether known or unknown, it is going to come to pass, for it is guaranteed by the Word of the Lord; for the same prophet of God (Daniel) who interpreted that most important description of world empires from 606 B.C. to the end-times has guaranteed the return of Jesus the Messiah to this earth to set up His kingdom. Why have there only been four world empires since the days of Nebuchadnezzar and his Babylonians (Medo-Persia, Greece and Rome)? Because God, through His prophet Daniel, said that is all there would be! Genghis Khan tried to conquer the world and failed, as did Napoleon, Kaiser Wilhelm, Adolf Hitler, Josef Stalin, Mao Tse-Tung, and others. They never succeeded - and won't until "the man of sin" comes on the scene and becomes king over ten kings, after which Christ, the stone cut out of the mountain without hands, will grind the kingdoms of the world to powder and His kingdom will fill the whole earth. Read this prophecy very carefully:

> And in the days of these kings shall the God of heaven set up a kingdom, which shall never be destroyed; and the kingdom shall not be left to other people; but it shall break in pieces and consume all these kingdoms, and it shall stand forever. For as much as you saw that the stone was cut out of the mountain without hands, and that it broke in pieces the iron, the bronze, the clay, the silver, and the gold, the great God has made known to the king what will come to pass after this. The dream is certain, and its interpretation is sure. Then King Nebuchadnezzar fell on his face, prostrate before Daniel, and commanded that they should present an offering and incense to him. The king answered Daniel, and said, "Truly your God is the God of gods, the Lord of kings, and a revealer of secrets, since you' could reveal this secret" (Daniel 2:44-47).

Keep in mind that while on this earth, Jesus Christ referred to Daniel several times as a prophet. There is no question he was God's man for his age. The future kingdom of Christ will happen just as Daniel said. For proof, the four empires he foretold are facts of history, as is the fact that there has never been a fifth! Just as these four empires were literally fulfilled, so will the coming kingdom of Messiah, and Revelation tells us that it will last "one thousand years." I agree with Clarence Larkin when he wrote:

> It is to be regretted however, that the word "millennium" ever supplanted the Biblical word "kingdom." For we are not dependent on the twentieth chapter of Revelation for our understanding of the kingdom age. It is mentioned and described so many times by the Hebrew prophets that the Bible would not make sense unless there is a literal kingdom. In fact, if there is no kingdom, God's word cannot be trusted, and many of the promises of God to both Israel and the Gentile nations would go unfulfilled. That is impossible. God means what He says and says what He means. And as the angel said of Jesus after the resurrection, "He is not here He is risen AS HE SAID!" The kingdom is guaranteed if for no other reason than that Jesus promised He would return and set it up and permit His twelve disciples to rule on thrones and as we shall see, so will His "saints." [1]

My friend, Dr. Arnold G. Fruchtenbaum, a careful prophecy scholar, has defined the basis for the belief in the Messianic kingdom in his excellent book, *The Footsteps of Messiah*. Even though this is a long quote which I am using by permission, it is worth reading carefully.

Premillennialists have often been criticized for basing their belief in a millennium entirely on one passage of

Scripture, Revelation 20. Because it is found in a book well noted for its high use of symbols, they say it is foolish to take the 'one thousand years' literally. But that is hardly a valid criticism.

To begin with, while it is true that Revelation uses many symbols, it has already been shown that the meaning of all those symbols is explained either by Revelation itself or elsewhere in the Scripture. Furthermore, never are years used in a symbolic way in this book. If they are symbolic, the symbolism is nowhere explained. The mention of 1,260 days, 42 months, and 3 ½ years are all literal and not symbolic. Hence, there is no need to take the 1,000 years as anything but literal years. The desire to spiritualize the text always places the burden of proof on the interpreter. Without objective proof it will result in a subjective interpretation.

It is of course true that the figure of one thousand years is only found in Revelation 20. But it is recorded six different times in this one text and if repetition tries to do anything, it certainly endeavors to make a point.

But while it is true that the millennium (that is, 1,000 years) is found only in Revelation 20, the belief in the messianic age does not rest on this passage alone. In fact, it hardly rests on it at all. The basis for the belief in the messianic age is the numerous prophecies of the Old Testament that speak of the coming of the Messiah who will reign on David's throne and rule over a peaceful kingdom. There is a great amount of material in the Old Testament on the messianic age. The belief in a messianic age rests on the basis of a literal interpretation of this massive material.

The only real contribution that Revelation makes to the knowledge of the kingdom is to disclose just how long the messianic kingdom will last, namely 1,000 years, for which the term millennium is used. This is the one key truth concerning the kingdom that was not revealed in the Old Testament.

It is in light of this that it is possible to understand why so much of the book is spent on the great tribulation and so little on the millennium. While much of the material in Revelation 4-19 is found scattered in the pages of the Old Testament, it is impossible to place these events in chronological sequence using only the Old Testament. The Revelation provides the framework by which this can be done. A great portion of the Revelation was used to accomplish this goal.

On the other hand, all of the various features and facets of the messianic age have already been revealed in the Old Testament. They portray the general characteristics of life in the kingdom, which do not raise the problem of an order of sequence. Hence, there was no reason to spend a great deal of time on the messianic age in Revelation. Most of what was needed to be revealed was already known from the Old Testament.

However, there were two things about the messianic age which were not revealed in the Old Testament. The first was the length of the messianic age. While the Old Testament prophets foresaw a long period of time of a peaceful messianic reign, they did not reveal just how long this would last. To answer this question, the Revelation states that it will be exactly 1,000 years.

A second thing that was unknown from the Old Testament prophets was the circumstance by which the kingdom would come to an end and how this would lead into the Eternal Order. This is also revealed by the Revelation.

These two items are all that Revelation 20 added to the knowledge of the messianic age. The belief in a messianic kingdom does not rest on this passage but is based on the numerous prophecies of the Old Testament prophets.

Another basis for the belief in a coming kingdom rests on the four unconditional, unfulfilled covenants God made with Israel. These covenants are unconditional and so rely solely on God for their fulfillment and not on Israel. They are also unfulfilled and since God is One who keeps His promises, they must be fulfilled in the future. They can only be fulfilled within the framework of a messianic age or a millennial kingdom.

The first of these is the Abrahamic Covenant that promised an eternal seed developing into a nation that will possess the promised land with some definite borders. While that nation, the Jews, continues to exist, never in Jewish history have they possessed all of the promised land. For this promise to be fulfilled, there must be a future kingdom. Besides, the possession of the land was not merely a promise to Abraham's seed, but to Abraham personally when God said, "To thee will I give it and to thy seed forever." For God to fulfill His promise to Abraham (as well as to Isaac and Jacob), there must be a future kingdom.

The second covenant is the Palestinian Covenant that spoke of a worldwide regathering of the Jews and repossession of the land following their dispersion. While the dispersion has already occurred and is in effect today, the regathering and repossession of the land still awaits fulfillment in the future. This too requires a future kingdom.

The Davidic Covenant is the third covenant which promised four eternal things: an eternal house (dynasty), an eternal throne, an eternal kingdom, and one eternal person. The dynasty became eternal because it culminated in a Person who is Himself eternal: Jesus the Messiah. For that reason, the throne and kingdom will be eternal as well. But Jesus has never yet sat on the throne of David ruling over a kingdom of Israel. The reestablishment of the Davidic throne and Christ's rule over the kingdom still awaits a future fulfillment. It requires a future kingdom.

The last of these covenants is the New Covenant that spoke of the national regeneration and salvation of Israel encompassing each individual Jewish member of that nation. This, too, awaits its final fulfillment and requires a future kingdom.

It is the extensive prophetic writings as well as all of these covenants that provide the basis for the belief in a future messianic kingdom, and not merely one chapter of a highly symbolic book.[2]

Our Lord made it clear there is to be a kingdom on this earth in His Olivet Discourse. He even foretold how it would begin:

> When the Son of Man comes in His glory, and all the holy angels with Him, then He will sit on the throne of His glory. All the nations will be gathered before Him,

and He will separate them one from another, as a shepherd divides his sheep from the goats. And He will set the sheep on His right hand, but the goats on the left. Then the King will say to those on His right hand, 'Come, you blessed of My Father, inherit the kingdom prepared for you from the foundation of the world: for I was hungry and you gave Me food; I was thirsty and you gave Me drink; I was a stranger and you took Me in; I was naked and you clothed Me; I was sick and you visited Me; I was in prison and you came to Me.' Then the righteous will answer Him, saying, 'Lord, when did we see You hungry and feed You, or thirsty and give You drink, When did we see You a stranger and take You in, or naked and clothe You? Or when did we see You sick, or in prison, and come to You?' And the King will answer and say to them, 'Assuredly, I say to you, inasmuch as you did it to one of the least of these My brethren, you did it to Me' (Matthew 25:31-40).

It seems that when Christ returns with His church at the end of the seven-year tribulation, He calls all the nations of the earth before Him and separates those on the left hand, "the goats" from those on the right, "the sheep." The "sheep" He calls "righteous." These people demonstrate by their treatment of the Children of Israel during the terrible tribulation days of antichrist persecution that they have a true heart for God. Much like the family of Corrie Ten Boom who defied Hitler and protected the Jews, some in their nations will be pro-Semitic and help the persecuted Jews. For this they are allowed to enter the kingdom which "He has prepared" for them. There will, of course, be many Jews who will go into that kingdom in their natural bodies, but all will be redeemed. These, like their benefactors, the Gentiles who protected them, will have children and start the incredible population of the millennial kingdom.

Clarence Larkin points out that the kingdom age will be a "theocracy." Any kings of nations - and there will be some - serve at the pleasure of the King of kings, Jesus Christ. Larkin quotes Luke 1:30-33 in this connection.

And the angel said unto Mary, thou shalt bring forth a son and shalt call His name Jesus. He shall be great and shall be called the "Son of the Highest," and the Lord God shall give unto Him the Throne of His Father David; and He shall reign over the House of Jacob FOREVER, and of His kingdom There Shall Be NO END (Luke 1:30-33).

> Seven of God's "shalls" are in this passage. Four of them have been fulfilled - for Mary did bring forth a "son," He was called "Jesus," He was "great," and was called the "Son of the Highest" - the other three must and will be fullfilled.
>
> Daniel the prophet describes the event.
>
> I saw in the night visions, and, behold, one like the 'Son of man' came with the clouds of heaven, and came to the 'Ancient of Days' (God), and they brought Him near before Him. And there was given Him dominion, and glory and a KINGDOM that all people, nations, and languages, should serve Him; His dominion is an everlasting dominion, which shall not pass away, and His KINGDOM that which shall not be destroyed (Daniel 7:13,14).3

Can you even imagine a government of righteousness? It will be led by the Righteous King Jesus and all in authority will uphold His laws. Think of it: no pornography, no drugs, no abortion, no murders, no gambling - the list goes on. In fact, the TV networks, or whatever we will have in their place, will only carry programs that glorify God and please the King. Children will not be shocked out of their moral sensibilities and the prurient interests of today will not exist. What a climate for people to be "saved." Yes, unsaved people will be born in that day who will have to call on the name of the Lord. But Satan will not be on earth to deceive them. The entire world, under the righteous reign of King Jesus, will be conducive to mankind calling on the Lord. It will be a day of justice.

It is hard for us to imagine a just judicial system. We are used to seeing a jury hang up on one stubborn juror who refuses to find a murderer guilty even though he was identified by two accomplices. In that day, all injustices of the court system will be a thing of the past as our Lord Jesus will be the just judge. For the first time in human history, government will be a friend of people instead of the greatest destroyer of people.

Jesus, the King of kings, will actually be a benevolent dictator. The world has dreamed of having just such a person to head up their world government and bring "social justice" to the world. That won't happen until the Lord Jesus Christ comes as King to set up His benevolent kingdom, for only He combines loving compassion and true justice.

. . .

Other Basic Characteristics of the Kingdom

For the benefit of those who would like to know more details of the divine characteristics of the millennium to come, I will quote extensively from two who have studied the Scriptures of that period carefully, Dr. Arnold G. Fruchtenbaum and Clarence Larkin.

1. The Seat of Government and Physical Changes to the Earth

The seat of Government will be at Jerusalem. Jerusalem is to be trodden down of the Gentiles, until the 'times of the Gentiles be fulfilled' (Luke 21:24). Then it will be rebuilt. The prophet Ezekiel gives us a detailed description of the restored land and city in Ezekiel 48:1-35. The 'royal grant' of land that God gave to Abraham and his descendants extended from the 'river of Egypt' unto the 'great river,' the River Euphrates (Genesis 15:18). Ezekiel fixes the Northern boundary at Hamath, about 100 miles north of Damascus (Ezekiel 48:1), and the southern boundary at Kadesh, about 100 miles south of Jerusalem (Ezekiel 48:28). This "royal grant" was not conditional and was never revoked. It is eight times as large as that formerly occupied by the twelve tribes. This "royal grant" is to be divided among the restored twelve tribes in parallel horizontal sections, beginning at Hamath on the north with a section for Dan, next come Asher, then Naphtali, Manassah, Ephraim, Reuben, Judah. In the center of this section the city (Jerusalem) is located. This helps us to map out the whole of the "Holy Oblation," as the "new city" is to be located on the site of the old. The "new city," however, is to be much larger than the old. It is to be nine miles square, and with its suburbs, ½ a mile on a side, 10 miles square. It will have a wall around it with three gates on each side like the New Jerusalem (Ezekiel 48:15-18, 30-35), these gates being named after the 12 sons of Jacob.

The "temple," or "sanctuary," will not be rebuilt in the "new city," but in the "midst" or middle of the "Holy Oblation" (Ezekiel 48:10, 20, 21). This will locate it at or near Shiloh, where the tabernacle rested after the Children of Israel conquered the land, and where it remained until the Temple of Solomon was finished. A "highway" shall lead from the "sanctuary" to the "new city" (Isaiah 35:8). It will be a magnificent boulevard, twelve miles long, lined with beautiful shade trees.

The "new temple" or "sanctuary" will occupy a space of 500 reeds on a side, or nearly a mile square (Ezekiel 42:15-20). The old temple was not a mile in circuit. The prophet Zechariah tells us (Zechariah 14:8), that in "that day" (the millennial day) "living waters shall go out from Jerusalem;" half of them toward the former sea (Red Sea) and half of them toward the hinder sea (Mediterranean): in summer and in winter shall it be."

But those "living waters" will not have their "source" in Jerusalem. The life-giving spring from which they flow will be located under the "sanctuary." Ezekiel tells us how he saw in a vision the "new temple" or "sanctuary," where he saw the waters come forth from under the threshold of the door, and flow past the "Altar of Burnt Offering" on the south side eastward until the stream was deep enough to swim in.

"Then said he unto me, these waters ... go down into the desert (by way of Jerusalem) and go into the sea (Dead Sea), which being brought forth into the sea, the waters (of the Dead Sea) shall be healed (lose their saltness).

"...And everything shall live whither the river cometh. And it shall come to pass that the fishers shall stand upon it (Dead Sea), from Eneglaim (on the east shore); there shall be a place to spread forth nets; their fish shall be according to their kinds, as the fish of the Great Sea (Mediterranean) exceeding many ... And by the river upon the banks thereof, on this side and on that side, shall grow all trees for meat, whose leaf shall not fade, neither shall the fruit thereof be consumed: it shall bring forth new fruit according to its months, because the waters they issued out of the 'sanctuary;' and the 'fruit' thereof shall be for meat and the 'leaf thereof for medicine" (Ezekiel 47:8-12). Compare Revelation 22:1, 2.

The size of the "new city," the location of the "new sanctuary" and the elevation of the Dead Sea, which is now 1,200 feet below the level of the Mediterranean Sea, call for great physical changes in the land surface of Palestine. How are these changes to come about?

When Christ comes back it will be to the Mount of Olives from whence He went up (Acts 1:9-12). The prophet Zechariah describes what will then happen:

"His (Christ's) feet shall stand in that day (the day of His return) upon the Mount of Olives, which is before Jerusalem on the east, and the Mount of Olives shall cleave in the midst thereof toward the east and toward the west, and there shall be a very great valley; and half of the mountain shall remove toward the north and half of it toward the south...

"All the land shall be turned as a plain from Geba to Rimmon south of Jerusalem; and it shall be LIFTED UP AND INHABITED" (Zechariah 14:4, 10, 11). These great changes will probably be brought about by earthquakes or volcanic action.

"For, behold, the Lord cometh forth out of His place, and will come down, and tread upon the high places of the earth. And the mountains shall be molten under Him, and the valleys shall be cleft, as wax before the fire, and as the waters that are poured down a steep place" (Micah 1:3,4).

These great physical changes will level the land surface of Palestine, and make room for the "new city," and raise the Dead Sea, so its waters can flow into both the Red and Mediterranean Seas. Ezekiel tells us that the name of Jerusalem in that day shall be "Jehovah- Shammah," the Lord Is There (Ezekiel 48:35) [4]

2. The Restored Messianic Temple of the Millennium

As we have seen, the temple or sanctuary will be located in the center of the "Holy Oblation." A full description of the temple and its courts is given in Ezekiel 40 - 44:31. No such building as Ezekiel so minutely describes has ever yet been built, and so the prophecy cannot refer to either Zerubbabel's or Herod's Temple, and as there is to be no temple in the New Jerusalem, it must be a description of the temple that is to be on the earth during the millennium. That it does not belong to the new earth is also clear, for the land in which it is located is bounded by the sea, and the waters that flow from it, flow "into the sea," but in the new earth there is "no more sea" (Revelation 21:1). This is still further confirmed by the Prophet's mention of the "desert," the "River Jordan," the Mediterranean Sea," and other localities that will not be found on the new earth after its renovation by fire.

The "Aaronic Priesthood" will be reestablished, and the sons of Zadok shall officiate and offer sacrifices (Ezekiel 44:15-31). The new temple, however, will lack many things that were the features of the old temple. There will be no "Ark of the Covenant," no "pot of Manna," no "Aaron's rod" to bud, no "Tables of the Law," no "Cherubim," no "Mercy Seat," no "Golden Candlestick," no "Shew Bread," no "Altar of Incense," no "Veil," no unapproachable "Holy of Holies" where the High Priest alone might enter, nor is there any "High Priest" to offer atonement for sin, or to make intercession for the people, unless a rather obscure passage in Zechariah 6:12,13 means that Christ (The Branch, Jeremiah 23:5, 6) shall be a "King-Priest," and perform the duties of High Priest conjointly with His Kingly office.

While the Levites as a class shall perform temple service, they shall be barred from priestly duties for their past sins (Ezekiel 44:10-14). There shall be a daily "morning" sacrifice, but no evening sacrifice (Ezekiel 46:13-15). The offerings will be the "Burnt," the "Meal," the "Drink," the "Sin," the "Peace" (Ezekiel 45:17), and the "Trespass" offering (Ezekiel 42:13). Two feasts are to be observed, "The Passover," but no Passover Lamb will be offered as

Jesus fulfilled that Type (Ezekiel 45:21-24), and the "Feast of Tabernacles" (Zechariah 14:16-19). This feast is to be observed by all the nations under penalty of "drought" or "plague."

The "Feast of Pentecost" will be done away with on account of its fulfillment. The "Day of Pentecost," recorded in Acts 2:1-4, was only a partial fulfillment of the prophecy of Joel 2:28-32. No such wonders in the heavens and the earth as "blood," and "fire" and "pillars of smoke" the "sun turned to darkness," and the "moon into blood," occurred at Pentecost. But all those things will happen before "the great and terrible day of the Lord."

The conversion of the Jewish nation will be sealed with a great outpouring of the Holy Spirit. Whether this shall be universal, or only upon Israel is not clear. The original prophecy in Joel was given to Israel and its partial fulfillment at Pentecost seems to have been limited to them. The knowledge of the Lord, however, will be worldwide, and "it shall come to pass that ten men of all languages and nations shall take hold of the skirt of him that is a Jew, saying, 'We will go with you; for we have heard that God is with you'" (Zechariah 8:22,23). There will be one "universal religion" in that day (Malachi 1:11). The "Shekinah Glory" that departed from the temple at the time of the Babylonian captivity (Ezekiel 10:18-20; 11:22,23), will again take up its residence in the "new temple" (Ezekiel 43:1-5).[5]

One of the questions often asked by critics of a premillennial kingdom is: What is the reason for the temple since the sacrifice of Jesus was "'once for all?'" While it is true there will never again be a need to offer sacrifices for sin since Jesus finished that on the cross, we find that the sacrificial system in the temple is a memorial to what He has done. Remember that sacrifice has always been the way God covered the sin of man, from Adam to the millennium. During that utopian period, Christians and the people living in their natural bodies will need to be reminded of our Lord's sacrifice for them and for God's merciful plan that has always been available - even to those like Cain who rejected God's plan of salvation.

During the millennium, the temple sacrifice will have the same role as does the communion table to the church today. We do not partake of the bread and cup to be saved, but to "remember Him" and what He did. It is a classic memorial. We are saved and baptized only once, but we should take communion regularly to remind us of our "so great salvation" and Him who made it possible. So the temple will be for the Jews in the kingdom age.

3. A Kingdom of Righteousness

Lord, who may abide in Your tabernacle?
Who may dwell in Your holy hill?
He who walks uprightly, and works righteousness,
And speaks the truth in his heart;
He who does not backbite with his tongue,
Nor does evil to his neighbor,
Nor does he take up a reproach against his friend;
In whose eyes a vile person is despised;
But he honors those who fear the Lord;
He who swears to his own hurt and does not change;

He who does not put out his money at usury,
Nor does he take a bribe against the innocent.
He who does these things shall never be moved

(Psalm 15:1-5)

This passage describes the righteousness that will characterize a citizen in the kingdom. Although not every individual in the kingdom will necessarily be characterized with this kind of righteousness, for reasons to be discussed later, most will be.

The earth is the Lord's, and all its fullness,

> *The world and those who dwell therein.*
> *For He has founded it upon the seas,*
> *And established it upon the waters.*
> *Who may ascend into the hill of the Lord?*
> *Or who may stand in His holy place?*
> *He who has clean hands and a pure heart,*
> *Who has not lifted up his soul to an idol,*
> *Nor sworn deceitfully.*
> *He shall receive blessing from the Lord,*
> *And righteousness from the God of his salvation.*
> *This is Jacob, the generation of those who seek Him,*
> *Who seek Your face. Selah*

(Psalm 24:1-6)

This passage describes the establishment of the kingdom and the righteousness that will characterize a man who will be rightly related to God at that time. [6]

4. A Kingdom of Peace and Prosperity

Now it shall come to pass in the latter days,
That the mountain of the Lord's house Shall be established on the top of the mountains,
And shall be exalted above the hills;
And all nations shall flow to it.
Many people shall come and say,
"Come, and let us go up to the mountain of the Lord, to the house of the God of Jacob;
He will teach us His ways,
And we shall walk in His paths."
For out of Zion shall go forth the law,
And the word of the Lord from Jerusalem.
He shall judge between the nations,
And rebuke many people;
They shall beat their swords into plowshares,
And their spears into pruning hooks;
Nation shall not lift up sword against nation,
Neither shall they learn war anymore

— (Isaiah 2:2-4)

In this passage Isaiah describes one of the major characteristics of the Messianic kingdom, that of universal peace. While differences between nations will arise, such differences will no longer be settled by military conflicts but only by the Word of the Lord from Jerusalem. Even the art of warfare will be forgotten.[7]

5. Satan Will Be Bound!

Then I saw an angel coming down from heaven, having the key to the bottomless pit and a great chain in his hand. He laid hold of the dragon, that serpent of old, who is the Devil and Satan, and bound him for a thousand years; and he cast him into the bottomless pit, and shut him up, and set a seal on him, so that he should deceive the nations no more till the thousand years were finished. But after these things he must be released for a little while (Revelation 20:1-3).

The wolf also shall dwell with the lamb, the leopard shall lie down with the young goat, the calf and the young lion and the fatling together; and a little child shall lead them. The cow and the bear shall graze; their young ones shall lie down together; and the lion shall eat straw like the ox. The nursing child shall play by the cobra's hole, and the weaned child shall put his hand in the viper's den. They shall not hurt nor destroy in all My holy mountain, for the earth shall be full of the knowledge of the Lord as the water cover the sea (Isaiah 11:6-9).

The universal peace described in the earlier passage will extend even to the animal kingdom. All animals will return to the Edenic state and become vegetarians (verses 6-7). The oldest of enemies, man and snake, will live compatibly in that day (verse 8), for the knowledge of God will permeate throughout the entire world, affecting man and animal alike (verse 9).[8]

6. Curse Shall Be Removed

The only animal that escapes the lifting of the curse is

the serpent; it will still crawl on its belly and "eat dust." Women will no longer be afraid of the serpent, but they will still bear the mark of having been used of Satan to deceive the whole world.

7. An Age of Longevity

For behold, I create new heavens and a new earth; and the former shall not be remembered or come to mind. But be glad and rejoice forever in what I create; For behold, I create Jerusalem as a rejoicing, and her people a joy. I will rejoice in Jerusalem, and joy in My people; the voice of weeping shall no longer be heard in her, nor the voice of crying. No more shall an infant from there live but a few days, nor an old man who has not fulfilled his days; for the child shall die one hundred years old, but the sinner being one hundred years old shall be accursed. They shall build houses and inhabit them; they shall plant vineyards and eat their fruit. They shall not build and another inhabit; they shall not plant and another eat; for as the days of a tree, so shall be the days of My people, and My elect shall long enjoy the work of their hand. They shall not labor in vain, nor bring forth children for trouble; for they shall be the descendants of the blessed of the Lord, and their offspring with them. It shall come to pass that before they call, I will answer; and while they are still speaking, I will hear. The wolf and the lamb shall feed together, the lion shall eat straw like the ox, and dust shall be the serpent's food. They shall not hurt nor destroy in all My holy mountain, says the Lord (Isaiah 65:17-25).

This passage begins with the announcement of the creation of new heavens and a new earth (verse 17). These new heavens and new earth are not to be confused with those of Revelation 21-22. The latter describes the new heavens and new earth of the eternal order, while the Isaiah passage describes those of the Messianic age, which will be a renovation of the present heavens and earth. Those of the Revelation are not a renovation but a brand-new order. Hence, for the millennium, there will be a total renovation of the heavens and the earth. The term "create" shows that this renovation will be a miraculous one possible by God alone. The result of this renovation will be a continuation of many things of the old order and the institution of a number of new things. We can see a good example of the old and the new in what the Scriptures say about the land of Israel. Israel also will undergo the renovation process. The Mediterranean Sea and the Dead Sea of the old order will remain, but the exceeding high mountain (the highest in the world) in the center of the country, for example, will be brand new. Following this announcement of new heavens and a new earth, there is a description of the millennial Jerusalem (verses 18-19).

Verse 20 is especially significant, for it discusses life and death in the kingdom. This verse teaches several things. First, it points out that there will no longer be any infant mortality in the millennium; everyone born in the kingdom will reach a certain age. Secondly, it specifies that the age at which one may die is 100 years. So, with infant mortality removed, everyone born in the millennium will live at least until his 100th year of life. Because lives in the millennium will be so long, those who do die at the age of 100 years will be considered as having died young. Third, this verse limits the people dying at the age of 100 years to those who are sinners, namely, unbelievers, because only they would be considered accursed. So then, death in the kingdom will be for unbelievers only.

Comparing this passage with what is stated about salvation in other passages, the entire concept of life and death in the kingdom can be summarized as follows: When the kingdom begins, all-natural men, both Jews and Gentiles, will be believers. The Jews in their entirety will be saved just prior to the second coming of Christ. All unbelieving Gentiles (goats) will be killed during the 75-day interval between the tribulation and the millennium, and only believing Gentiles (sheep) will be able to enter the kingdom.

However, in the process of time, both Jews and Gentiles will be born in the kingdom. These newly born, natural people will continue to inherit the sin nature from their natural parents and will also be in need of regeneration. Although Satan is confined, thus reducing temptation, the sin nature is quite capable of rebelling against God apart from Satanic activity. In time, unsaved people who are in need of regeneration will live in the kingdom.

As in the past, the means of salvation will be by grace through faith and the content of faith will be the death of Christ for sin and His subsequent resurrection Those born in the kingdom will have up until their 100th year to receive Christ. If they do not, they will die in their 100th year. In other words, the unbeliever will not be able to live past his first century of life. However, those who do receive Christ will live throughout the millennium and never die. Thus, death in the millennium will be for unbelievers only. This is why the Bible does not speak of a resurrection of millennial saints, and why the resurrection of the tribulation saints is said to complete the first resurrection (Revelation 20:4-6).

It is also clear from the new covenant of Jeremiah 31:31-34 that no Jewish unbelievers will be in the kingdom; all Jews born during the kingdom will accept the Messiah by their 100th year. Unbelief will be among the Gentiles only; therefore, death will exist only among the Gentiles.

Verses 21-24 continue to describe life in the kingdom as a time of personal peace and prosperity. It will be a time of building and planting. He who builds and plants is guaranteed the enjoyment of the labors of his hands, for many of the effects of the curse will be removed (verses 21-22a). Life will be characterized by longevity (verse 22b), absence of calamity and turmoil (verse 23), and instantaneous response from God (verse 24). As in Isaiah 11:6-9, members of the animal kingdom will be at peace with each other and with man (verse 25).

THE ENORMOUS POPULATION of The Millennium

SEVERAL OLD TESTAMENT Scriptures prophesy that there will be an enormous population during the kingdom age. Fertility will be normal and there is little indication that birth control will stifle population growth (as it does today), consequently family sizes will grow during those 1,000 years. Women will not have to fear birth pains in childbirth, for the curse will have been lifted from the earth. God's lofty view of family and children will once again hold forth and children will again be considered "an heritage of the Lord."

An examination of Ezekiel 36:10-11, 33:37-38, Jeremiah 33:10-11, and particularly 33:22 reveals this enormous population, "As the host of heaven cannot be numbered, nor the sand of the sea measured, so will I multiply the descendants of David My servant and the Levites who minister to Me." In Zechariah 8:4-5, we see that "the streets will be full of boys and girls," proving that the population of Israel will increase dramatically. To my knowledge, no prophecies specify that the same will happen to the Gentile nations, but I would think the same would happen there. It naturally follows that when the ideal conditions of the millennial kingdom of Christ exists, population will increase and the mass murder of the unborn in the name of "abortion" will be outlawed - as it should be today! The prince of the power of the air (Satan), the archenemy of God and man, the devil himself will be chained in the bottomless pit. Once he is removed, the culture of the day will promote marriage, virtue, family, and children, and family life will flourish. Add to that the principle of "peace on earth" guaranteed for 1,000 years and the result would of course be a population increase. History reveals there have been 15,000 wars. Governments have massacred millions. Our century alone has seen communism, other repressive forms of government, and those who fought against their spread to control the whole earth, kill in excess of 180 billion people! That makes the 20th century the most barbaric in the history of man. Just imagine how many children all the men killed in battle would have fathered, and through their children, grandchildren, and millions more, it is easy to see that this century's wars have eliminated upwards of billions of people. Conceivably, the population of the millennium, without a single war to kill innocent people, could result in a population more than twice that of the world today, or even more.

One other factor: Since Isaiah 65 indicates that a child will die being 100 years old, people in their third to seventh centuries or later may still bear children, further contributing to this exponential growth in population. Dr. Henry Morris suggests that the population could be as many as 20 billion. I am inclined to think it will be at least the aggregate population of the world, which, based on today's figures, is estimated at 12 billion people. I think we can safely assume it will be somewhere between 12 and 20 billion, or more.

Further evidence that the millennial population will be enormous is seen in the brief final rebellion at the end of the millennium described in Revelation 20:7-10. Satan is loosed from his prison to "deceive the nations" and prepare the population for eternity by calling together all the Christ rejecters living on the earth at that time. It says that the number of them is "as the sands of the sea," in other words, billions. But keep in mind that is a youth movement! Only those under 100 years of age will respond! In order for the youth of the land who won't have received Christ in such a righteous and blessed age to number in the billions, an astronomical number of adults will have to be available to produce them. The population of the millennial kingdom will doubtless be enormous by present-world standards.

The Massive Millennial Soul Harvest

NOW WE COME to what I consider the most exciting message of this whole chapter. Many times more people will be converted during the millennial kingdom than will be lost! Because the millennial population will undoubtedly exceed the total world population during the whole of human history, and since the majority living at that time will be Christians, it follows that more people will be in heaven than in hell. Consequently, God will achieve His grand purpose - salvation - for the majority of mankind (2 Peter 3:9).

Estimating the number of souls saved during the millennial kingdom is as speculative as estimating the population during that period, even though the figures are obviously related to each other. However, we can draw some comparisons between America and the conditions of the kingdom age of Christ that may prove helpful. A Gallup poll on religion in America indicates that 41 percent of the population have had a "born-again experience with Jesus Christ." We can only hope that this figure is true, considering all the opportunities to sin that are so readily available today and that Satan is still doing his deceptive work of fooling people about God. The church is not perfect, but obviously we are still doing a fairly good job of getting the Gospel out to our families and to the nation in general in the face of such social, governmental, and media- inspired cultural corruption.

The millennium, as we have seen, will be drastically different. Satan will be bound for 1,000 years and will not be able to tempt mankind, while Jesus will be here in person running a "kingdom of righteousness." Only Christians will have children after their 100th birthday, further escalating the Christian population at a time when "everyone shall know" the truth of God. I would assume then that if 41 percent could be saved in our country today, then two or more times as many would accept the Savior during the millennium. That means that at least 80 to 90 percent of the enormous population of the millennium could be saved people! That could result in 12 to 20 or more billion people gaining eternal life through the sacrifice of God's Son on Calvary's cross and His subsequent resurrection just during the millennium.

Don't miss the point of all this: When all the Scriptures addressing the millennium are taken into account, and if my reasoning is accurate - and I believe it is - then my conclusion should be right: "There will be more people in heaven than in hell." Oh, I haven't forgotten about the "broad way that leads to destruction" and the "many that go there," which Jesus mentioned. He obviously had the period of "time" in mind from Adam until He comes again to reign and set up his righteous kingdom. All during that period of human history when Satan has had access to the minds of men to do his deceiving work, only a minority have believed. However, a case can be made for the fact that during most of human history, half the population has died before the age of accountability when the mortality rate was above 50 percent. These, I believe, are covered by the blood of Christ. When

Christ comes and establishes His kingdom of righteousness, Satan will be bound in the bottomless pit. Then only the flesh and man's free will can cause him to reject God's marvelous plan of salvation. So when we add the minority of believers of all human history to the mortality rate, and add that total to the enormous number of people who will receive Christ during the millennial kingdom, we end up with more people in heaven than in hell.

Don't miss the significance of this fact. It literally means that Satan loses! God and Jesus Christ win the battle of the ages against Satan and all his forces for the souls of men! No wonder the capital city of heaven is 1,500 miles high, 1,500 hundred miles wide, and 1,500 miles deep. That's large enough to provide ample space for more than 20 billion people! And that's only the capital!

It's a Matter of Choice

THE ONE COMMON denominator in all ages, from Adam to the millennium, is that all men have a choice to make about God: whether or not to accept His so great salvation. Those who choose Him will enter the heaven God has prepared for His followers who have chosen to turn their lives over to Him. Those who do not choose Him will die in their sins, be judged, and then sent to the eternal lake of fire.

It is no exaggeration, then, to say that the choice you make about receiving Jesus Christ is without doubt the most important decision you will ever make on this earth. So I would ask you, have you personally invited Jesus the Christ into your life as your Lord and Savior? If you haven't, then I want to invite you to do so right where you are. I would urge you to pray the following prayer...

Dear God, Thank you for sending your Son Jesus to die on the cross for my sins.

I confess I am a sinner, and I ask your forgiveness.

Today I want to invite Jesus into my life as Lord and Savior. I give my life and future to You.

In Jesus' name I pray,

Amen.

Jesus said: "Most assuredly, I say to you, unless one is born again, he cannot see the kingdom of God" (John 3:3).

Jesus also said: "Most assuredly, I say to you, unless one is born of water and the Spirit, he cannot enter the kingdom of God. That which is born of the flesh is flesh, and that which is born of the Spirit is spirit. Do not marvel that I said to you, 'You must be born again'" (John 3:5-7).

Jesus said: "For God so loved the world that He gave His only begotten Son, that whoever believes in Him should not perish but have everlasting life. For God did not send His Son into the world to condemn the world, but that the world through Him might be saved. He who believes in Him is not condemned; but he who does not believe is condemned already, because he has not believed in the name of the only begotten Son of God" (John 3:16-18).

Don't miss this so great offer of eternal salvation. Invite the Savior into your heart today!

19

WORLD WITHOUT END

BY JOHN WALVOORD

INTRODUCTION

The prophet Isaiah, speaking of Israel's future restoration, states, "But Israel shall be saved in the Lord with an everlasting salvation; ye shall not be ashamed nor confounded world without end" (Isaiah 45:17, KJV). Variations in wording are found in other versions. The NIV in regard to Israel declares, "You will never be put to shame or disgraced to ages everlasting." The NRSV renders it, "But Israel shall be saved by the Lord with an everlasting salvation." All of these translations state simply and yet profoundly that the fulfillment of prophecy and the human race continue forever. The perspective of the entire Bible is that human life once begun never ends but is perpetuated even after death and continues after resurrection. For the saved the destiny is clear. They will go to heaven in what Scripture calls the New Jerusalem (Revelation 21:22). The destiny of the wicked is everlasting punishment, as stated in Revelation

20:15, "If anyone's name was not found written in the Book of Life, he was thrown into the lake of fire." Its torment goes on forever and ever, according to Revelation 20:10.

The Panorama of History and Prophecy Fulfilled

The glorious future that is ahead for Christians is set in the context of the entire Scriptures with its panorama of history and prophecy fulfilled. The Bible begins in Genesis 1:1 with an eternal God who created the physical world. As Scriptures unfold with the details and man is created, the first prophecy of Scripture is recorded. This prophecy told Adam and Eve not to eat of the tree of the knowledge of good and evil; to do so would cost their death (Genesis 2:16-17). This prophecy was sadly fulfilled when they ate the fruit and immediately became sinners, with their bodies taking on mortality and ultimate death. In this context, however, the anticipation of the coming of the Messiah, His crucifixion and sacrifice for sin is first recorded in Genesis 3:15. Both these Scriptures, which are the foundation of human history and prophecy, have already literally been fulfilled.

The Old Testament provides an amazing account of how history and prophecy combine to fulfill the purposes of God. The early history of man is tragic, with Adam and Eve being driven out of the garden. Abel was the first to be murdered. The world eventually became so wicked that God had to destroy with a flood the entire human race except for Noah and his family. The detailed prophecies concerning the ark were literally fulfilled.

The judgment of the world in the time of Noah did not deter man from wickedness, and in Genesis 11 their recorded rebellion is symbolized in the Tower of Babel where God had to condemn the people to various languages.

In Genesis 12, beginning with Abraham, a new chapter is written that is extensive in its application to human history and prophecy. Abram, as he was first called, was promised that he would become a great man, the father of a great people. He would be specially protected by God and ultimately would be the channel of a Redeemer who would bless all the peoples of the earth. This prophecy was fulfilled, of course, in Christ Jesus and His death on the cross. These promises have also literally been fulfilled. Along with these promises, God stated that the Holy Land would be Israel's permanent possession, even though they would not possess it in certain periods of history (12:7).

It is significant that while the first 11 chapters of Genesis covers thousands of years from creation to the time of Abraham, the next 39 chapters are devoted entirely to Abraham, Isaac, Jacob and the 12 sons of Jacob, indicating God's special interest in Abraham and his descendants. Of course, this topic relates to the Jewish nation and the Messiah as Savior. The Old Testament fulfills many prophecies about Israel, the Jews' departure into Egypt and the Jews' prophesied return (15:13-14). With Moses came the Mosaic Law with its many regulations, but Israel's failure led to the Assyrian captivity (2 Kings 15:29;

17:5-6, 23) which involved the Israelites being carried off and installed in the land of Assyria. Moses' warning in Deuteronomy 28 that if Israel did not keep the Law, the nation would be driven out of the land, was sadly fulfilled. Later, when Babylon conquered Judah, the remaining tribes were carried off to Babylon. Here again, the accuracy of prophecy is demonstrated, for Jeremiah 29:10 predicted that after 70 years they would be able to go back, and of course the Book of Ezra records that return. The prophecy in Deuteronomy 28 that they would be scattered all over the world, however, was not fulfilled until the New Testament and following the rejection of Christ when Israel was scattered all over the world after AD 70.

The New Testament brings another amazing chapter in the revelation of God, however, summarized as follows: "For the law was given through Moses; grace and truth came through Jesus Christ" (John 1:17). While the Old Testament presents the doctrine of grace in salvation, the dispensation of grace as a rule of life began at Pentecost, which is recorded in the New Testament. In the present age, not only is the way of salvation by grace, but the way of life is determined by grace as well. God is free to bless people who do not deserve it because Christ died for them.

Unfortunately, however, even the present age is witnessing apostasy and turning from the truth as was anticipated in 2 Peter 2. The unsaved will merit the judgment of Christ at His second coming.

As a token of the grace of God, He promised that a rapture of the saved will take place prior to the end-time trouble of discipline and judgment during the period leading up to the second coming of Christ.

The pattern of future fulfillment of prophecy is clearly written in Scripture beginning with the rapture of the church, the time of trouble following, and then the second coming of Christ.

Three important periods will immediately follow rapture: First of all, a period of preparation will take place for the second coming. This period will feature the emergence of the antichrist and the revival of the Roman Empire, according to Daniel 7:7, 24.

A period of peace before the time of trouble is pictured next in Daniel 9:27. A seven-year covenant will be imposed upon Israel by the antichrist during which the first half (three-and- a-half years) will experience a measure of peace. This will end with the antichrist's takeover as world ruler as predicted in Daniel 7:23. He will clearly align with Satan and execute those who do not recognize him as god during this period of persecution. Thus, the time between the rapture and the second coming is divided into these three periods: preparation, peace, and persecution.

The second coming will not only bring judgment on the unsaved but will introduce the millennial kingdom, described graphically in both the Old and New Testaments, and especially in Revelation 20. At the end of the millennium, Satan, who will have been bound during the thousand years, will be loosed once again to gain converts. Led by Satan, they will turn against Christ's rule and will be judged by fire from heaven. Immediately after, the earth and heaven now in existence will flee away and be destroyed. The judgment of the great white throne in space will introduce the eternal state with a new heaven and new earth and new Jerusalem. The concept of a world without end is revealed in the glorious revelation of what is ahead for the saints in the city of God, the new Jerusalem, which is the home of the saints of all ages throughout eternity future. The great panorama of history and prophecy fulfilled serves as a remarkable and thrilling background for all of God's purposes and grace which will extend throughout eternity.

The New Jerusalem, the New Heaven and the New Earth

PRACTICALLY ALL THE facts about the world to come following the millennial kingdom are found in the last two chapters of the Book of Revelation, chapters 21 and 22. Remarkably in many respects, a subject so important and so extensive and infinite in its duration has only two chapters in which to reveal its details. At first thought it would seem that a special book of the Bible would be required to cover this wonderful subject. In contrast, the details of the life of Christ are revealed in four Gospels. Also, the Book of Revelation devotes 14 chapters to describing the period between the rapture and the second coming, a period of slightly more than seven years.

An underlying reason exists, however, for amplifying the description of events that led up to the second coming and the millennial kingdom. It should not be overlooked in the study of prophecy that its main purpose is to alert us of things to come in order that we take the necessary actions to qualify for God's salvation, mercy, and grace. Even in Revelation 22 we are given an exhortation to salvation and preparation for the end-times, but the details of the world to come in themselves do not need to be fully known in advance and, as a matter of fact, will have to be experienced to be appreciated. The world to come is so foreign to our present experiences, it is difficult at best to understand fully the grand picture that the Bible paints. However, the prophecies presented in Revelation 21-22 contain many important facts.

As previously mentioned, Revelation 20:7-15 fully describes the world to come for the unsaved. First of all, Satan, who will be bound during the thousand years, and will be released at the end of the thousand-year reign of Christ, will secure a following to gather around the city of Jerusalem, the capital city, to take it by force. How inconceivably foolish is the concept that the devil and his power is sufficient to overcome Christ. The Bible disposes of the matter in a few words, "But fire came down from heaven and devoured them" (Revelation 20:9).

These rebels who apparently will be born in the millennial kingdom will reject the deity and saviorhood of Christ in spite of all the evidence. They will show their true colors in following Satan and will receive the righteous judgment of God. Satan will also come to his final hour of doom. Scripture states, "The devil who deceived them, was thrown into the lake of burning sulfur, where the beast and the false prophet had been thrown. They will be tormented day and night for ever and ever"

(20:10). It is significant that the beast and the false prophet who are cast into the lake of fire before the thousand-year kingdom will still be there, tormented with the prospect of future torment day and night forever.

Revelation 20:11-15 writes the great finale for those who refuse to receive Christ and choose to follow Satan in spite of all the evidence supporting the claims of Christ. John wrote that he "saw a great white throne and him who is seated on it. Earth and sky fled from his presence, and there was no place for them." In this summary way, the physical universe as we know it, which was created from nothing by the command of God, will be commanded back to the place of nonexistence. This apparently includes not only the earth and the sun, but the whole expanse of space with its millions of stars and planets as well. The great white throne will apparently be suspended in space. The final drama will be witnessed by the unsaved dead standing before the throne. Having been in Hades, the temporary place of the dead throughout Scripture, they will be taken out of Hades to face their final judgment. We are told that the books will be opened - the record of their deeds along with other books - including the Book of Life, and they will be judged by what the book records of their works. The sad conclusion is that, "the sea gave up the dead which were in it, and death and Hades gave up the dead that were in them, and each person was judged according to what he had done. Then death and Hades were thrown into the lake of fire. The lake of fire is the second death. If anyone's name was not found written in the Book of Life, he was thrown into the lake of fire" (20:13-15). What a tragic picture! These are souls for whom Christ died when He died for the sins of the whole world, but they will have rejected God's one and only way of salvation, faith in Jesus Christ, and chosen to follow Satan instead of the Spirit of God.

This judgment, however, will pave the way for the world to come for the saints as presented in Revelation 21-22. After the present earth is destroyed and a new heaven and new earth is created, John wrote, "I saw a new heaven and a new earth, for the first heaven and the first earth had passed away" (21:1). It is apparent that the whole physical world will be much different than it is today. Very little information is given about the new earth except that it seems to be round like our present earth but perhaps larger or smaller, and lacking almost all of its present characteristics. A major difference is that there will be no more sea or ocean. None of the landmarks of our present earth will exist.

Attention, however, is directed to the new Jerusalem, the one feature described in detail in the new heaven and the new earth. John recorded, "I saw the holy city, the new Jerusalem, coming down out of heaven from God, prepared as a bride beautifully dressed for her husband" (21:2). Because the city is declared to be a bride here and also in Revelation 21:9 where it is described as "the wife of the lamb," some have tried to contend that the city is not a real city. However, the subsequent description of the city which unfolds makes it clear that it is a place of residence, which would not be true of a bride. Why, then, is the city called "a bride?"

Apparently, it is described this way because of its beauty. A bride is beautifully dressed for her husband, according to the Scriptures, and the city is dressed for the occasion. The fact that the city is a dwelling is stated in Revelation 21:3 and the city is described as occupied by human beings and also by God Himself. A summary of its dramatic change over the present earth is given in verses 3-4, "And I heard a loud voice from the throne saying, 'Now the dwelling of God is with man and He will live with them. They will be His people and God Himself will be with them and be their God. He will wipe every tear from their eyes. There will be no more death or mourning or crying or pain, for the old order of things has passed away.'" The world to come will not be a place of sorrow but a place of rejoicing and marvelous grace of God. Some have tried to imagine from the fact that God will wipe away every tear that there will be crying in heaven, particularly in remorse over the deeds of the flesh on earth. However, there will be no tears in heaven any more than there will be death or crying or pain. Scripture states, "For the old order of things has passed away" (21:4).

The city as a whole is described as something entirely new and different than any in the previous earth.

Believers who are overcomers, an expression which applies to all believers, will inherit this city, but others who are unsaved and guilty of immorality will be cast into the fiery lake of burning sulfur, described as the second death (21:8).

General facts concerning the New Jerusalem precede a detailed description beginning in Revelation 21:9. John, taken by an angel to a high mountain, saw the holy city, the new Jerusalem, coming down out of heaven from

God. This simple statement has given way too much speculation. The passage previously had indicated that the new heaven and the new earth will be created at this time, but here the new Jerusalem is said to descend from God out of heaven, implying its prior existence. If it existed prior to the eternal state, then it may have existed during the millennial kingdom, but there is no description of it in the millennial kingdom. Accordingly, it would have to be a satellite not resting on the earth but suspended in space throughout the millennial kingdom. If so, why was it created earlier?

The Scriptures do not satisfy our curiosity here. But it is a distinct possibility that the New Jerusalem will be the home of the saints who are resurrected or translated. Significant passages like Isaiah 65:17-25, which describes the millennial situation, omit any mention of resurrected individuals. The passage describes normal life in the millennium. The longevity of the human race is extended until a person's death at the age of 100, when he is considered still a youth (Isaiah 65:20). The residents are described as having normal lives, with houses they will have to build and dwell in. They will plant vineyards and eat the fruit. The tranquil nature of the millennial kingdom is described in verse 25, "'The wolf and the lamb will feed together, and the lion will eat straw like the ox, but dust will be the serpent's food. They will neither harm nor destroy on all my holy mountain,' says the Lord." Significant in this description of life in the millennium is that we have a picture of a person in his natural body who will enter the millennial kingdom after the tribulation. He will live on earth in a normal way.

But omitted is any mention of a person with a resurrection body living in the house next door. The natural question is, where are the millions of saints who were resurrected or translated who came with Christ from heaven?

A possible answer is that if the new Jerusalem exists during the millennial kingdom, it would be possible for the saints who have been resurrected or translated and the angels to live in the new Jerusalem as a satellite city over the earth and then commute to earth to carry on the functions which the Bible describes them as doing, that is, participating in earthly government and serving the Lord in the millennial situation and then returning to their homes in the new Jerusalem when their earthly duties have concluded. Because so little Scripture addresses this, it becomes a matter of conjecture and cannot be assumed as doctrine. But it is a possibility based on the facts that we do know.

The New Jerusalem Described

REVELATION 21:11 portrays the new Jerusalem as a gigantic jewel, "It shone with the glory of God, and its brilliance was like that of a very precious jewel, like a jasper, clear as crystal." The reference to a jasper as well as to other jewels in this section have often raised some questioning as to its exact character. A jasper is not known today as being as clear as crystal, and what is described compares much more to a diamond. The city, however, is brilliant with light and light goes all through it like it would on a beautiful jewel.

Prominent in the description is the number 12. There are 12 gates, three on each side of the city described as having a square base. On each of the gates is inscribed the name of one of the twelve tribes of Israel (21:12-13). The fact that the names of Israel's tribes are on the gates indicate that Israel will be in the New Jerusalem. The city also has 12 foundations (21:14). The foundations are described as made of 12 kinds of jewels (21:19-20) and inscribed with the names of the 12 apostles, which makes it clear that the church will be there. Each jewel is described as beautiful and in various colors. There are 12 pearls (21:21) and 12 kinds of fruits (Revelation 22:2). The city is described in size as being 12 thousand stadia on each side, approximately 1,500 miles. The walls of the city consist of 12 times 12 cubits (21:17). Some manuscripts indicate 144 cubits "thick." It is more probable that its height is referred to here.

The 12 jewels of the city begin with the jasper previously mentioned, which may be more like a diamond than a modern jasper. The second foundation is that of a sapphire, blue in color. The third is a chalcedony, possibly referring to a jewel found in Turkey and believed to have various stripes of color. The fourth jewel, an emerald, is dark green in color. Sardonyx, the fifth jewel, is believed to be a red and white stone. A sixth jewel is the carnelian, also called the sardius, which is reddish in color. In Revelation 4:3 the one sitting on the throne is described as like a jasper, a carnelian, and an emerald. The seventh stone, described as a chrysolite, is gold-colored and apparently different from the modern stone of that name which is green. The eighth, a beryl, is held to be a dark green stone. The topaz, listed as the ninth jewel, is yellow-green. The tenth stone, a chrysoprase, is also of greenish tint. The jacinth, the eleventh, is violet, and the twelfth and final jewel, an amethyst, is purple. Imagine all these jewels together, realizing that the glory of God shines through them. It must be an unbelievably brilliant ray of colors reflecting the glory of God.

The new Jerusalem is declared to be the temple of God and therefore there is no other temple in the city, with God sitting on the throne in this city. The glory of God is such that there will be no need for a sun or moon, for these will no longer exist. The light of the glory of God will shine through all these materials of the new Jerusalem which apparently are translucent. While no unclean person can enter the city, its gates will not be shut, as there is no night in the new Jerusalem. Through the gates will come the glory and honor of the nations, referring to all the saved, according to Revelation 21:26. The city will be inhabited only by those whose names are in the Lamb's Book of Life (21:27).'

A major feature of the city is "the river of the water of life" (22:1) which will flow from the throne of God.

The question has been raised as to whether the city is a cube or a pyramid. Judging by the description of the River of Life flowing from the throne of God, it would seem that it might be a pyramid, with the throne of God on top and the water coming down the pyramid. The description is somewhat difficult to understand because the water is said to come down the great street of the city, and yet in the next statement, the tree of life is said to be on each side of the river (22:2). Either there is more than one tree of life or its branches span the river's two banks.

Another problem for expositors is the fact that the Tree of Life bears leaves which are declared to be "for the healing of the nations" (22:2). The question as to why healing will be necessary in heaven has been raised. Some expositors speculate that the millennial kingdom is the situation being described here. The explanation seems to be, however, that the word translated "healing" is also the word for "health." It may somehow be that the leaves of the tree will support health for those in heaven, though it is inconceivable that anybody will be sick. It is specifically said that the curse on the human body will no longer exist (22:3).

The question has often been raised as to what the saints will do in heaven. Scriptures are very simplistic in answering this. They state that the servants of God will worship and will serve Him (22:3). God will be visible to them and His name will be on their foreheads (22:4). The fact that God will provide the light of the city is stated again in Revelation 22:5.

Much of the remainder of the chapter is a plea to qualify for the blessings of God in the world to come. He states, "I am coming soon! Blessed is he who keeps the words of the prophecy in this book" (22:7). John was instructed, "'Do not seal up the words of the prophecy of this book, because the time is near.'" Those who are holy will continue to be holy; those who are vile will continue to be vile, according to Revelation 22:11.

The coming of Christ brings His reward to the saints.

The unsaved are said to be outside the city and are not permitted to enter. And as a matter of fact, they will be in the lake of fire. An urgent invitation to accept the salvation of God is given, "The Spirit and the bride say, 'Come!' And let him who hears say, 'Come!' Whoever is thirsty, let him come; and whoever wishes, let him take the free gift of the water of life" (22:17).

A final word of warning is addressed to those who would add to or subtract from this book. In view of the fact that so many people have criticized, treated nonliterally, and neglected the Book of Revelation, this warning should he heeded today. The Book of Revelation, with all of its tremendous revelation, ends with the statement," 'Yes, I am coming soon.' Amen. Come, Lord Jesus. The grace of the Lord Jesus be with God's people. Amen" (22:20-21).

Words are inadequate to describe the wonders of the world to come described so graphically in these two chapters. The revelation, however, is sufficient for us to realize that the best is yet to come, and it increases our longing for the rapture of the church and the beginning of all the end-time events that will wind up history and lead the Christian into the eternal state.

Though it is difficult for anyone to understand completely all the aspects of the world to come, it is obvious that God intends us to know something about the future, and while all questions have not been answered, certainly enough has been given to give us the clear picture of how wonderfully glorious our future will be. The very fact that half the prophecies of Scripture have already been fulfilled literally gives a solid basis for believing that the prophecies that are yet unfulfilled will have their fulfillment in due time as the work of God unfolds. It also supports the concept of literal fulfillment in prophecy where these are not idle pictures but a graphic description of that which someday will be even more real than what we can possibly comprehend today.

How true is Christ's statement that He came to make our life more abundant (John 10:10), and that is true for today as well as in the life to come. How glorious it will be that day when the shout will come out of the blue and the church will be on its way to heaven and the tremendous events that will lead up to the world to come will begin.

CONCLUSION

BY WILLIAM T. JAMES

The Blessed Hope/Your Eternal Destiny

Fear gripped mankind in a choke-hold of doomsday predictions during the mid-20th century. The atomic, then the hydrogen bomb, combined with irreconcilable differences between the communist world and the democracies to bring about an entirely new industry. Bomb shelters became fashionable while the sense of threat grew to near-panic dimension.

In retrospect, it seems laughable that the American public was convinced by the promoters of the bomb-shelter mentality that a small concrete-encased hole just under the earth in their backyards could somehow protect them from a multimegaton nuclear explosion. Such weapons consume enormous amounts of matter, vaporizing in some test cases vast portions of entire islands.

Perhaps people today understand the ludicrous nature of trying to hide from nuclear weapons of mass destruc-

CONCLUSION

tion. Whether this is true or not, attitudes now seem to be that since it hasn't happened, it won't happen. Nature on the rampage through tornadoes, earthquakes, etc., seems to gather far more fear-engendered attention than does the nuclear threat.

Yet the words of some of the twentieth century's most-notable geopolitical observers echo in our time with almost biblical resonance.

Dr. Harold C. Urey, who worked on the atomic bomb, said, "I'm a frightened man. All the scientists I know are frightened. Frightened for their lives. And they're frightened for your life." Dr. John R. Mott, after having surveyed the world situation following World War II, stated, "[this is] the most dangerous era the world has ever known When I think of human tragedy as I saw it and felt it, of the Christian ideals sacrificed as they have been, the thought comes to me that God is preparing the way for some immense direct action."

Winston Churchill said, "Time may be short." Henry Luce, editor of *Time, Life,* and *Fortune* magazines, stated shortly before his death regarding his view of the world's deteriorating condition and his own father's often-espoused view that there will be no premillennial return of Christ, "I wonder if there wasn't something to [the position that says Christ will return to reign for a thousand years] after all."

Dr. Charles Beard, the famous American historian, said, "All over the world, the thinkers and searchers who scan the horizon for the future are attempting to assess the values of civilization and speculating about its destiny." Dr. William Yogt, in *The Road to Civilization,* said,

CONCLUSION

"The handwriting on the wall of five continents now tells us that the day of judgment is at hand." Dr. Raymond B. Fosdick, past-president of the Rockefeller Foundation, said, "To many ears comes the sound of the tramp of doom. Time is short." H.G. Wells declared just prior to his death, "This world is at the end of its tether. The end of everything we call life is close at hand."

General Douglas MacArthur said following World War II, "We have had our last chance." Former president Dwight Eisenhower stated, "Without a moral regeneration throughout the world, there is no hope for us as we are going to disappear one day in the dust of an atomic explosion." Former Columbia University president Dr. Nicholas Murray Butler said, "The end cannot be far distant."

Dr. J. Vernon McGee, who presented these quotations in his commentary on the Book of Revelation, added, "For a long time now men in high places have looked into the future and have said that there is a great crisis coming. I wonder what they would say if they lived in our day!"

Indeed, those quoted would most likely be astonished to learn of developments that have transpired since their time on earth. Dr. McGee, who himself went to be with His Lord in 1988, would no doubt be deeply fascinated by developments, but I think he would not be astonished. Moreover, anyone with a true understanding of God's prophetic Word who suddenly returned to the earthly scene after such an absence would *expect* such changes for the worse.

The Anesthetizing Factor

CONCLUSION

Earth's inhabitants today - particularly those of the Western World who have access to instantaneous news coverage - should feel the noose of doom tightening. Yet busy lives of Christians and non-Christians alike buffer our generation from the reality that times are even more dangerous than when the men just quoted observed the circumstances of their day.

While there is much anxiety in world society today, most of it is of the inwardly turned variety. People have their noses pressed up against the windows of their own psychological exigencies. The business of personal advancement or equilibrium maintenance is top priority. That is, the state of world affairs is most often left for the politicians, sociologists, clergymen, etc., to handle. Ours is a generation of upwardly mobile, entertainment-hungry pleasure seekers who, when they do think about the future, explore their fears of that future with nervous laughter while considering horoscopes, psychic readings, and futurist mumbo-jumbo psychobabble presented them through the pop psychologists of our time. Unfortunately, the gobbledy- gook that desensitizes people so that they cannot discern between false prophecy and God's prophecy infects and affects the church today.

Yet, in the still moments of our lives, there come the nagging questions. When the hustle and bustle has given way to body-aching, mind-fatigued time of winding down, the thoughts gnaw. What is the source of the thread that bedevils? What is the possibly fearsome thing that lurks in the unknown just ahead?

Despite best efforts to allay apprehensions about that impending something-or-the-other that can't quite be defined, the uncertainty kills optimism in the black void of introspection. There the trepidation gestates until life's hectic schedules force the fear-besieged again into their frantic rat race.

New World Orderliness

In spite of nuclear saber rattling by Communist China and somber undercurrents of threatened chemical and bacteriological terrorism and war-making by Iraq, Libya, Iran, North Korea and numerous clandestine organizations throughout the world, there seems to be little attention paid by the public at- large to such troubling signals. After all, the world survived the Cold War and all of its potential for nuclear Armageddon's.

All of the dire predictions of Churchill, Eisenhower, MacArthur, and the others never came to pass. Surely today's leaders have learned from past debacles how to steer this generation through the international turmoil of our time. Certainly, the glowing rhetoric from today's world leaders about a coming revised international order indicates that the great minds of globalism believe everything is well under control, despite developing nuclear powers such as India and Pakistan who glare angrily across borders constructed of ancient hatreds and blood feuds.

Humanistic hope springs eternal in the breasts of the one-world elitists that man ultimately is his own savior. Well-meaning as such grandiose speechmaking is, it is needful to search for substance behind the grand eloquent words.

CONCLUSION

Since John F. Kennedy proclaimed, "Man holds in his mortal hands the power to abolish all forms of human poverty and all forms of human life" (John F. Kennedy, presidential inaugural address, January 20, 1961), great strides have been made. The problem is the strides have been toward the capability of abolishing all forms of human life rather than toward abolishing all forms of human poverty. Mr. Kennedy's subsequent words, perhaps misconstrued by many of his successors in world leadership, seem to be central to the internationalist government's imperative today. Mr. Kennedy stated that concerning human government, people of earth and his upcoming administration were, "asking His help and His blessing but knowing that here on earth, Gods work must truly be our own" (JFK inaugural address, January 20,1961)

Of course, that God's name is invoked at all in such matters as global governing in present-day geopolitical atmospherics is a nonissue. Men of great power in our time have assumed the mantle of "little gods" and have - they foolishly presume - relegated the one true God to folklore status. Their words flow smoothly and crescendo into the stratosphere of high-mindedness as Paul predicted in 2 Timothy 3. "New World Orderliness," they proclaim, holds in its leadership's mortal though god-like hands the power to abolish all forms of human suffering and to create utopia for all forms of human life.

Humanistic Hope

Almost forgotten are the forewarnings of doom. Eisen-

CONCLUSION

hower, Churchill, MacArthur and others who forecast nuclear apocalypse if morality-based common sense fails to insert itself into human affairs seems now to be considered an anachronism by today's governing or would-be governing elite.

"The Cold War is over," they proclaim. The Soviet Union and the United States, they say, no longer point their nuclear-tipped ICBM's at each other. Nuclear stockpiles are being downsized with the thought toward eliminating the super weapons of mass destruction altogether.

For some reason beyond any sense of rationality, the globalists espouse these falsities despite the fact that Russia continues to build even more-sophisticated weapons and delivery systems and China is reported to have nearly 20 highly advanced ICBM's targeted on American cities. Perhaps this is what Walter Cronkite, the former CBS anchorman, meant when he said recently that today's world is without true leadership (reported on *Point of View*, September 29, 1999). They seem to be willingly ignorant of the facts.

The New World Order puts forward the humanistic hope that, as John Lennon sang in the song "Imagine," "all will be as one." This is the same song, or one very similar to the song Nimrod was likely singing as he ordered the construction of the Tower of Babel (read Genesis 11).

Even American administrations have gotten in on the act of one-world-building, prompting one prominent American to say: "If the administration has a vision of a New World Order, it is time to share it with Europeans and Americans, because a New World Order is precisely what is emerging on the continent of Europe today."

CONCLUSION

Jean Kirkpatrick's concerns were no doubt spawned by declarations made by U.S. President George Bush on a number of occasions.

Bush said in a TV address on October 1, 1990, "The United Nations can help bring about a new day, a New World Order and a long era of peace." He stated on October 26, 1990, "When we succeed, we will have invigorated a UN that contributes as its founders dreamed. We have established principles for acceptable international conduct and the means to enforce them." Bush said on January 1, 1991, "There is no room for lawless aggression in the Persian Gulf for this New World Order we are trying to create." And in his State of the Union address, January 29, 1991, President Bush said, "What is at stake is more than one small country; it is a big idea: a New World Order, where diverse nations are drawn together in security, freedom, and the rule of law."

The hope for mankind, according to the humanists, is a matter of bringing all people together as one. National sovereignty will be the first major casualty of the rearranging global order, according to UNESCO Publication 356. "As long as the child breathes the poisoned air of nationalism, education and world-mindedness can produce only precarious results. As we have pointed out, it is frequently the family that infects the child with extreme nationalism. The school should therefore use the means described earlier to combat family attitudes that favor jingoisms [those who favor warlike aggressive foreign policy] ... We shall presently recognize in nationalism the major obstacle to world-mindedness."

The UNESCO report assertion that parents are most

CONCLUSION

often the source of extreme nationalism in their children cuts directly to the heart of the globalist agenda. The elitist's theme is to separate parents from children and substitute the state as the molder and shaper of young minds. This is, of course, an anti-God, anti-Christ concept. "Scripture that says "bring up a child in the way and he will not depart from it" is God's instruction to mankind with regard to raising children.

Goals 2000, championed by the Clinton Administration and the international community elite in general, sits regally at the heart of this anti-Christ postulate. America's First Lady, Hillary Clinton, is credited to have authored *It Takes a Village,* which in effect proclaims that it is up to the state to control matters of education - education which must emanate from the globalist perspective.

Strobe Talbott, a key Clinton administration policy shaper, put forward what he considers the hope for mankind. That hope differs little from President George Bush's vision.

Talbott said, in expressing his vision, that in the next century, America will not exist in its current form. He stated, "All states will recognize a single, global authority." Talbott wrote in *Time Magazine* shortly before joining the Clinton administration, "Here is one optimists' reason for believing unity will prevail ... Within the next hundred years nationhood as we know it will be obsolete. All states will recognize a single global authority." Talbott continued, "all countries are basically social arrangements, accommodations to changing circumstances. No matter how permanent, even sacred they may seem at any one time, in fact, they are all artificial and temporary."

No matter what the globalist elite claim, they seem intent on using the same methods that Hitler, Stalin and Mao Tse Tung used in consolidating and solidifying their regimes. They seem to want to take control of the youth and turn them against parents. The one-world architects plan to employ the very methods and means the ultranationalists used in the construction of their dictatorships all the while they decry national sovereignty for the sake of unifying the human race under the cliched banner of "the brotherhood of man."

Humanism will not long tolerate freedom in any form. Darwin's survival of the fittest - and the elite are the fittest, they arrogantly believe - rules as the operative imperative in the one-world agenda. Liberty of thought and action must be made to conform to that agenda. We can look to Hitler, Stalin and Mao Tse Tung, as well as other tyrants throughout history, to understand what happens to those who do not conform.

The Blessed Hope

The hopelessness of humanism contrasts sharply with the hope that is in Jesus Christ. The Lord said, "If the Son, therefore, shall make you free, ye shall be free indeed" (John 8:36).

Darkening skies of the apocalyptic storm scheduled to crash upon a judgment-bound world surround planet earth today. Although that last seven-year period of God's judgment upon incorrigibly rebellious mankind has not yet arrived, certainly the lightning strikes and ominous thunder rumblings of wrath seem not far distant.

CONCLUSION

Wars and rumors of wars fill our daily headlines. False teachers dominate the Christian scene in terms of media dollars to spend in television, radio and other media. Ethnic strife is at the heart of bloodshed around the globe, including on the streets and in the communities of America. Unprecedented great storms that wreak devastation are undeniably on the increase. Earthquakes of major magnitudes such as those in Turkey, Taiwan and Mexico make Christ's Olivet forewarning come to life on our TV screens with alarming frequency. Surely, we are witnessing "the beginning of sorrows" (Matthew 24:8).

But the Christian can take heart. Jesus said, "when ye shall see all these things, know that [my coming] is near, even at the doors" (John 24:33).

Jesus no doubt spoke of all the prophetic signs for the end of the age when He said, "when ye see all these things". Those *things* He spoke of included not only the general signs for the tribulation period, but *all* signs given in God's Word.

Specific signals include the nation Israel, the revived Roman Empire, the Magog invasion force, increase in knowledge, apostasy, a generation filled with wickedness as violent as the generation alive just before the flood of Noah's day.

All of these signals for the end of the age have been dealt with in detail throughout this book. When analyzing the world today in light of prophetic Scripture, there seems little doubt that we are very near the moment when Christ shouts from heaven, "Come up hither" (Revelation 4:1), for Jesus said, "when these things begin to come to pass, then look up, and lift up your heads, for your redemption draweth nigh" (Luke 21:28).

This should for Christians be a tremendous time of anticipating Christ's suddenly calling them home. No prophecy is left to be fulfilled; the rapture is imminent. Jesus Christ, the Blessed Hope of Titus 2:13, must at this very moment be standing before the portals of heaven ready to open the door and call God's children home. One can almost sense Christ the bridegroom readying to meet His bride, the church, in the air and take her home to His Father's house where He has prepared a place for every born-again believer (read John 14:1-6).

Jesus will call and, in a moment, millions of living believers will vanish from the planet and will join with the dead in Christ to meet Him in the air (read 1 Thessalonians 4:13-18 and 1 Corinthians 15:51-55).

While believers accompany Christ into heaven, earth-dwellers will participate in the astonishing New World Order rearrangements the humanist-elitists have so long sought to institute.

Israel will sign a seven-year covenant of peace with a great leader who will have emerged from the revived Roman Empire. The nation Israel will no doubt be coerced into giving in to demands that provide her antagonists in the region advantages the antagonists cannot resist. In return, Israel will be promised peace and safety guaranteed by the leader and his powerful military forces.

Almost astonishingly, that pseudopeace seems to be far along in the making. The Middle East peace negotiations have been in the headlines off and on for years with the Oslo accords, the Wye River agreement, etc.

CONCLUSION

Now, however, prophecy seems to be leaping from the screens and off the front pages with the European Union more and more taking an aggressive role in shaping the process. *CNN Online* on March 26, 1999 stated in a report, "The EU supports Palestinian statehood. Israel given a one-year deadline." The report further stated, "The European Union on Friday issued its strongest support yet for Palestinian statehood, which drew angry criticism from Israel and praise from Palestinians. The statement issued by EU leaders at a summit in Berlin gave Israel a one-year deadline for fulfilling the unqualified Palestinian right to independence." The CNN report went on to say that the EU suggested in the statement that it would be ready to recognize a Palestinian state unilaterally by saying, "Palestinian self-determination is not subject to any veto."

So, it appears the European Union has begun flexing its collective muscles and exerting powerful influence not only in the Yugoslav and Balkan conflicts but in the more prophetically relevant peace process involving Israel as well. Soon the *prince that shall come* (the prophesied world dictator) will make his appearance, but not before the church makes its exit from planet earth, according to 2 Thessalonians 2.

The most horrific and bloody period of human history will develop from the peace agreement Israel makes with antichrist. That last seven years is outlined in frightening detail in Revelation chapters 6-18.

Although many feel that the language in this portion of God's Word is merely symbolic, keep in mind that the words are symbolic of real, literal events even more terrifying than the symbolism that describes them.

More than half of all people on earth at that time will die and many others will prefer death to the living hell in which they find themselves. For Christians, the foreknowledge of those awesome and tragic times ahead makes Titus 2:13 and 1 Thessalonians 5 welcomed Scriptures for study indeed!

Your Eternal Destiny

Piercing the future to gain insight into what lies ahead for mankind individually and collectively continues to be the intense focus of the world's politicians, sociologists, philosophers, et al. No human being or group of human beings has nor has ever had the ability to accurately project things to come. God only is omniscient. Thankfully, He provides many answers to the questions burning in the hearts and minds of His creation called man. The problem, of course, is that the great majority of that creation rejects His truth. Fallen man prefers false prophets and their false prophecies, false teachers and their false teachings. Lucifer's great deceptions and delusions are thus firmly entrenched within all cultures and societies of planet earth.

Here is God's truth. God loves you so much He sent His Son, who willingly came from the majestic throne of God to die on the cross on a rocky, skull-shaped, windswept hill called Golgotha just outside Jerusalem. Christ's shed blood is the only remission (cure) for the deadly soul disease called sin. You cannot rationalize God's method

CONCLUSION

for saving lost mankind. He is God. He created you and all that is. He alone has the right and the righteousness to determine such eternal matters.

Christ came as a baby born to a Jewish mother through a miracle conception performed by God himself. As fully human and fully God, Jesus Christ felt your temptations, pains, frustrations and heartbreaks while He walked the earth. He died a perfect, sinless man through cruel crucifixion, taking upon Himself your sins past, present and future. He resurrected the third day following His death, victorious over sin, death, and the grave. He was and is the Lamb slain from the foundation of the world (a part of God's eternal plan) who provided the one sin sacrifice necessary to satisfy God the Father and His righteousness.

Christ's once and for all atonement for sin that separates fallen man from God is freely offered. It is a *grace gift* from the heart of Almighty God, whose love for you is unfathomable to all but those who accept it. No one can come to the Father unless He calls him. Thankfully, God calls all men, women and children unto Himself. God is "not willing that any should perish, but that all should come to repentance" (2 Peter 3:9).

God's grace gift of salvation through Jesus Christ is freely offered. God will not force it upon you. You must accept it just as it is - just as you are, a lost sinner who is headed for eternal damnation in hell if you refuse the only redemption plan ever offered.

Refusal of God's salvation through Jesus Christ means eternal condemnation, separated forever from God. For, "He that believeth on him is not condemned; but he that believeth not is condemned already" (John 3:18) One who rejects Jesus Christ as the only Way to salvation will go through the time of God's great wrath if alive when the tribulation begins. The lost person who dies prior to that time or during that time awakes instantly in torment and will suffer the penalty of sin for eternity (read Luke 16:19-31).

These dire, depressing truths are not the opinions of this writer. Like it or not, they are warnings from the Word of God. To fail to relay this all-important message would be to do great disservice both to the heavenly Father and to the reader. While it is true that God is perfect Love, His perfect Love includes absolute righteousness. God's righteousness demands that sin - which is the only thing He hates - be dealt with justly. His love gift - His only begotten Son, Jesus Christ - is the only Way to deal with sin justly and banish it forever.

The Beautiful Side of Eternity

A glorious future beyond all imagination awaits the believer. For "eye hath not seen, nor ear heard, neither have entered into the heart of man, the things that God has prepared for them that love him" (1 Corinthians 2:9).

While the rebellious go through the seven-year tribulation period on earth, which includes Gods pouring His wrath out upon Christ-rejecting people, those who have been saved begin an eternal way of life magnificent beyond comprehension. Most glorious of all, the redeemed will be joint heirs with Christ. In other words, God the Father not only redeems, but imputes Christ's

CONCLUSION

righteousness to the redeemed. This means that all of heaven's everlasting glory, beauty and riches belong to the saints in exactly the same way they belong to God's beloved Son.

Most every prophetic indicator, as described throughout this volume, points to the probability that this generation is the generation Jesus spoke of when He said, "This generation shall not pass away, till all be fulfilled" (Luke 21:32). This *is* that generation, and you are a part of it. The urgency of doing something about your eternal destiny is obvious. Accept Christ today, for "now is the day of salvation" (2 Corinthians 6:2).

Christ could shout from heaven literally at any second: *"Come up hither!"* (Revelation 4:1).

EVEN SO, COME, LORD JESUS!

ENDNOTES

Chapter 5: What About America?

1. Taken from William D. Watkins, The New Absolutes (Minneapolis: Bethany House, 1996), pp. 207-208.

2. Ibid. p. 227.

3. Taken from American Government and Economics In Christian Perspective (Pensacola: Pensacola Christian College, 1984), p. 43.

4. John F. Walvoord, The Nations, Israel and the Church in Prophecy (Grand Rapids: Zondervan, 1988), p. 172.

5. Ibid. p. 173.

6. Midnight Call (September 1999), p. 20.

7. Noah W. Hatchings and Lariy Spargimino, Where Leads The Road To Kosovo? (Oklahoma City: Hearthstone, 1999), p. 18.

8. Peter Jones, Spirit Wars: Pagan Revival In Christian America (Mukilteo, WA: WinePress, 1997), p. 15.

9. George Stephanopoulos, All Too Human: A Political Education (Boston: Little, Brown and Co., 1999), p. 5.

10. Ibid. p. 162.

11. Dennis Cuddy, Secret Records Revealed: The Men, The Money & The Methods Behind The New World Order (Oklahoma City: Hearthstone, 1999), p. 183.

12. Noah W. Hatchings, Daniel The Prophet (Oklahoma City: Hearthstone, 1998), p. 62.

13. Louis S. Bauman, Russian Events In The Light Of Bible Prophecy (London: Revell, 1942), pp. 149-150.

14. Ibid. pp. 150-151.

15. S.C. Gwynne, "I Saluted A Witch," Time (July 5, 1999), p. 59.

16. Richard Lee and Ed Hindson, Angels Of Deceit: The Masterminds Behind Religious Deceptions (Eugene, OR: Harvest House, 1993), p. 153.

17. John B. Taylor, Ezekiel: An Introduction And Commentary. In Tyndale Old Testament Commentaries, Vol. 20, D. J. Wiseman, ed. (Downers Grove, IL: Intervarsity, 1969), pp. 238-239.

18. David Allen Lewis, Prophecy 2000 (Green Forest, AR: New Leaf, 1990), pp. 105-106.

19. Ibid. p. 106.

20. Victor Mordecai, Christian Revival For Israel's Survival (Taylors,

SC: privately published, 1999), p. 8.

21. Ibid. ix.

22. Vladimir Seikharov, with Umberto Tosi, High Treason (New York: G. E Putnam's Sons, 1980), pp. 96-97.

23. Taken from Watkins, New Absolutes, p. 146.

24. Ibid. p. 148. 408

25. B.K. Eakman, Cloning Of The American Mind: Eradicating Morality Through Education (Lafayette, LA: Huntington House, 1998), pp. 473-474.

26. Ibid. p. 421.

27. Ibid. p. 423.

28. Ibid. p. 196.

29. Ibid. p. 416.

30. Malachi Martin, The Keys Of This Blood: The Struggle For World Dominion Between Pope John Paul II, Mikhail Gorbachev, and the Capitalist West (New York: Simon and Shuster, 1990), p. 16.

31. Cuddy's entire book. Secret Records Revealed is devoted to this.

32. Dan Quayle, Worth Fighting For (Nashville: Word, 1999), p. 33.

33. "Apocalypse? Yep, But Not Yet, Poll Finds." The Daily Oklahoman (Dec. 30, 1998), p. 6.

34. Ann Blackman, "Cradles of Contention," Time (Aug. 9,1999), p. 46

35. "News Roundup," The Daily Oklahoman (8/9/99).

36. Taken from Don McAlvany, Storm Warning: The Coming Persecution Of Christians And Traditionalists In America (Oklahoma City: Hearthstone, 1999), p. 132.

37. Joan Veon, The United Nations Global Straitjacket (Oklahoma City: Hearthstone, 1999), p. 299.

38. Taken from McAlvany, Storm Warning, p. 123.

Chapter 9: Your Future Living Conditions

. . .

1. "WEB OF DEATH," iVeiasiaee^, April 7, 1997, p.26. "The Meirker We've Been Waiting For," Time, April 7,1997, p. 28. "Who They Were," People, April 14, 1997, p.40.

2. "Christ and Comets," Newsweek, April 7, 1997, p. 40. "The Return of the Great Comet," Newsweek, March 24, 1997, p.56.

3. "Far From Home," Newsweek, April 7, 1997, p.37. "Who They Were," People, April 14, 1997, p.40-56. The People article says Joyce Scalla was working for a TV station at the time she joined the cult. This is wrong; she had previously worked for the station, but at the time she left to join "Heavens Gate," she was working for my department in Tulsa Public Schools.

4. Time, April 7, 1997, p.31.

5. Richard Abanes, End-Time Visions, (Nashville, TN: Broadman & Holman Publishers, 1998).

6. Ibid., p.255.

7. The term "the last days" is often seen in prophecy as the entire church age between the two advents of Christ, (see Thomas Ice and Timothy Demy, Prophecy Watch; [Eugene, OR, Harvest House Publishers, 1998, p.9,10.] But there is a scriptural concept "last of the last days," based on the context of the passage in view. Referring to 2 Peter 3:3, Biederwolf says "The times referred to are those immediately preceding the Second Coming of Christ, and, says Salmon, immediately introducing the age described [w.7-10] as the 'age to come.'" William E. Biederwolf, The Second Coming Commentary, (Grand Rapids, MI, Baker Book House, 1985), p.528-29.

8. Thomas Ice, "Has Bible Prophecy Already Been Fulfilled? Part II," Pre-Trib Perspectives, June 1999, a monthly publication of the Pre-Trib Research Center, Arlington, TX.

9. Abanes, Visions, p.300.

10. Ibid, pp.256-7.

11. "The End of the World as We Know It? Target: Jerusalem," Time, January 18, 1999, p.67.

12. Arno Froese, "European Union on the Brink," Foreshadows of Wrath and Redemption, William T. James, ed. (Eugene, OR: Harvest House Publishers, 1999) p.195-9.

13. See a listing of 14n of the major signs of the end time in "The Promise Watch Page," a monthly publication of The Spiritual Armour Project, Phillip Goodman, ed., April, 1999.

14. Reginald Dale, "The Search for a Common Foreign Policy," Europe, July-August, 1999, p.28.

15. Revelation 17:12,17; The 10 kings of New Rome together control a union of nations, i.e., a "kingdom," not "kingdoms."

16. Phillip Goodman, The Assyrian Connection, (Lafayette, LA: Prescott Press, 1993) pp.138-45.

17. Revelation 17:12.

18. Daniel 7:24.

19. Revelation 17:12, 17.

20. Daniel 7:8; Compared to the ten kings, at the start of his rise the antichrist is "a little one."

21. Daniel 9:27.

22. Daniel 7:20; The antichrist, in his rise to power, becomes "larger in appearance" than the ten kings.

23. Daniel 7:24.

24. Revelation 6:2-4.

25. Ezekiel 38-39; Daniel 11:40-42.

26. Revelation 13:3-4.

27. Revelation 17:16-17.

28. Revelation 13:4.

29. Rev. 13:6-7; 20:4; Revelation 12 shows the sequence of the persecution of Christians during the tribulation period-first the "Woman,:" Israel, and then "the rest of her offspring [gentiles eveuigelized by the 144,000]," v.l7.

30. Revelation 13:8.

CHAPTER 10: Your Future and Religions

1. Elliot Miller, A Crash Course on the New Age Movement (Grand Rapids, MI: Baker Book House, 1989), p. 15.

2. Ibid., p. 16.

3. For a general survey of New Age ideas, see the "spiritual Counterfeits Project" study hy Karen Hoyt, The New Age Rage (Old Tappan, NJ: Revell, 1987), pp. 21-32.

4. See the insightful study of transpersonal psychology by William Kilpatric, The Emperor's New Clothes: The Naked Truth About the New Psychology (Westchester, IL: Crossway Books, 1985). See also Garth Wood, The Myth of Neurosis (New York: Harper & Row, 1986); and Jay Adams, the Biblical View of Self-Esteem, Self-Love, and Self-Image (Eugene, OR: Harvest House, 1986).

5. See Dave Hunt and T.A. McMahon, The Seduction

of Christianity (Eugene, OR: Harvest House, 1985), pp. 77-84.

6. See Teilhard de Chardin, The Future of Man (New York: Harper & Row, 1964); Man's Place in Nature (London, Collins, 1966); The Vision of the Past (New York: Harper & Row, 1966). For an analysis of his teaching, see N.M. Wildiers, An Introduction to Teilhard de Chardin (New York: Harper & Row, 1968); and G.D.Jones, Teilhard de Chardin: An Analysis and Assessment (Grand Rapids: Eerdmans, 1969).

7. Teilhard de Chardin, Hymn of the Universe (New York: Harper & Row, 1961). He argued that the convergence of all material and psychic forces will eventually combine in an implosion of energy forces.

8. Fritjof Capra, The Turning Point (Toronto: Bantam Books, 1982), p. 22.

9. Ibid., p. 302.

10. Miller, p. 65.

11. Donald Keys, Earth at Omega: Passage to Planetization (Boston: Branden Press, 1982), p. iv.

12. John White, "Channeling: A Short History of a Long Tradition,"Holistic Life (summer 1985), p. 20.

13. Margot Adler, Drawing Down the Moon (Boston: Beacon Press, 1979), p. V.

14. Hunt and McMahon, Seduction of Christianity, pp. 120-136.

15. Morton Kelsey, The Christian and the Supernatural (Minneapolis: Augsburg, 1976), pp. 113-123.

16. Douglas Groothuis, Unmasking the New Age (Downers Grove, IL: InterVarsity Press, 1986), pp. 113-123.

17. Shirley MacLaine, Out on a Limb (New York: Bantam Books, 1984), p. 236.

18. Ron Rhodes, The Counterfeit Christ of the New Age Movement (Grand Rapids, MI: Baker Book House, 1990), pp. 15-18.

19. Ihid., p. 19.

20. Elliot Miller, A Crash Course on the New Age Movement (Grand Rapids, MI: Baker Book House, 1989), p. 24.

21. Ihid., pp. 21-22.

22. Marilyn Ferguson, The Aquarian Conspiracy (Los Angeles: J.E Teu-cher, 1980). Her claim that there are "legions of conspirators" at every level of government, society, and education is probably overstated but accurately reflects the hopes emd dreams of New Age "evangelists."

23. Reproduced and quoted by Constance Cumhey, The Hidden Dangers of the Rainbow (Shreveport, LA: Huntington House, 1983), pp. 13-15.

24. Ihid

Chapter 15: Forewarning the Future Fuhrer

— Grant R. Jeffrey, Prince of Darkness, pp.83- 84.

— Hindson, Ed, Is The Antichrist Alive And Well, p. 22.

— Ed Hindson, Is the Antichrist Alive and Well, p. 47.

— Breese, Dave, The Coming Invasion From Heaven, pamphlet.

— Ice, Thomas & Demy, Timothy, Prophecy Watch, pp. 174-175.

— Ed Hindson, Final Signs, p. 102.

CHAPTER 17: Peering Into the Millennium

1. Clarence Larkin, Dispensational Truth, (Philadelphia: Clarence Larkin Publishing, 1918), p.92.

2. Arnold Fruchtenhaum, The Footsteps of the Messiah, Ariel Ministries Press, 1995. p.267-269.

3. Larkin, p.92.

4. Larkin, p.93-94.

5. Larkin, p.94.

6. Fruchtenhaum, p.270.

7. Ihid, p.271.

8. Ihid.

A LOOK AT: ARE YOU RAPTURE READY?

SIGNS, PROPHECIES, WARNINGS, AND SUSPICIONS THAT THE ENDTIME IS NOW

A book based on the popular web site, RaptureReady.com, draws on biblical prophecy along with current world issues and events to share revelations about the coming Rapture, how it will affect each person's life, and how to prepare for the future.

AVAILABLE NOW ON AMAZON.

ABOUT TERRY JAMES

Terry James is author, general editor, and co-author of numerous books on Bible prophecy, hundreds of thousands of which have been sold worldwide. James is a frequent lecturer on the study of end time phenomena, and interviews often with national and international media on topics involving world issues and events as they might relate to Bible prophecy.

He has appeared in major documentaries and media forums, in all media formats, in America, Europe, and Asia. He appeared in the History Channel series, The Nostradamus Effect.

Terry James has been blind since 1993 due to a degenerative retinal disease (retinitis pigmentosa). He uses the Jobs Accessible Word System (JAWS) –which is voice synthesis—to write and conduct business over the Internet.

His former profession was in public relations, advertising, marketing, and publicity and promotion. He served in both corporate and government positions for 25 years, before becoming a full-time writer.

James also served in the United States Air Force from October 1966 through October 1970.) He served at Randolph AFB, Texas, in the T-38 section, a mission dedicated to training pilots in high-performance jet fighter-trainers.

Terry James and his wife, Margaret, live near Little Rock, Arkansas.

www.ingramcontent.com/pod-product-compliance
Lightning Source LLC
Chambersburg PA
CBHW031322230426
43670CB00006B/208